Modern European History

A Garland Series of Outstanding Dissertations

General Editor
William H. McNeill
University of Chicago

Associate Editors

Eastern Europe
Charles Jelavich
Indiana University

Great Britain
Peter Stansky
Stanford University

France
David H. Pinkney
University of Washington

Russia
Barbara Jelavich
Indiana University

Germany
Enno E. Kraehe
University of Virginia

MODERN EUROPEAN HISTORY

"Trading Peasants" and Urbanization in Eighteenth-Century Russia

The Central Industrial Region

Daniel Morrison

Garland Publishing, Inc.
New York and London 1987

Library of Congress Cataloging-in-Publication Data

Morrison, Daniel, 1945–
  "Trading peasants" and urbanization in eighteenth-century Russia.

  (Modern European history)
  Thesis (Ph. D.)—Columbia University, 1981.
  Bibliography: p.
  1. Rural-urban migration—Russian S.F.S.R.—History—18th century.   2. Urbanization—Russian S.F.S.R.—History—18th century.   3. Cities and towns—Russian S.F.S.R.—History—18th century.
  I. Title.   II. Central Industrial Region.   III. Series.
HB2068.S65M67   1987   307.2   87-7425
ISBN 0-8240-8059-9 (alk. paper)

All volumes in this series are printed on acid-free, 250-year-life paper.

Printed in the United States of America

"TRADING PEASANTS" AND URBANIZATION IN EIGHTEENTH-CENTURY RUSSIA:

THE CENTRAL INDUSTRIAL REGION

Daniel Morrison

ABSTRACT

"Trading Peasants" and Urbanization in Eighteenth-Century Russia:

The Central Industrial Region

Daniel Morrison

Rural-urban migration and its contribution to the development of
the urban sector in eighteenth-century Russia have received no substantial treatment in previous literature, because of conceptual obstacles and the difficulty of assembling an adequate concentration of
source material. This study, based on research concerned primarily
with the Central Industrial Region and making use of a wide variety of
archival and published sources, overcomes the latter problem by focus-
ing on a category of immigrants which is comparatively well documented
in official records, those who enlisted formally in the urban burgher
classes (the posad population). The principal contributions of this
dissertation are: (1) clarification of the legal provisions governing
such enlistment, which have not been adequately explored or even correctly summarized in earlier literature; (2) the introduction for the
first time of a large amount of data on this enlistment; and (3) the
use of these data, of individual case records and of other materials
to illuminate the processes by which peasants were absorbed into the
urban population in eighteenth-century Russia.

Among the major findings emerging from this study are the following:
Substantial but previously overlooked legal changes in the last quarter
of the century made enlistment in the posad easier and more desirable.
Contrary to the prevailing impression that only a few very wealthy

villagers were able to gain entry to the _posad_, enlistment rose precipitously during this period and also underwent a marked shift in regional distribution, probably reflecting changing patterns of rural-urban migration. Moreover, the peasants recruited into the _posad_ were primarily individuals of modest economic attainments rather than possessors of great wealth and included a surprisingly large number of freed serfs, who managed to extricate themselves from bondage in a variety of ways. Kinship and other personal ties between peasant and urban families were widespread and played a role in encouraging and facilitating migration. Because of these ties and for other reasons, individual _posad_ members regularly assisted peasant immigrants in breaching the barriers to urban settlement and involvement in the urban economy, ignoring differences in hereditary status and legal rights.

CONTENTS

LIST OF TABLES

CHAPTER I: "TRADING PEASANTS" AND THE PROBLEM OF URBANIZATION IN
EIGHTEENTH-CENTURY RUSSIA

Rural-urban migration and its contribution to the development of
the urban sector in eighteenth-century Russia is a subject which remains little explored in the historical literature. Neglect of this
issue has resulted in part from the discrepancy between official
classification of population groups and actual patterns of residence
and economic activity, and from the ensuing confusion over what constituted the urban population during the specified period. Until
recently most historians of the Russian urban sector have accepted the
official population categories as an adequate framework for discussion
of the country's social history and have therefore focused their attention on the tax-bearing urban commune or posad, the hereditary estate
of urban "citizens" which was subject to special tax and service obligations and in return was awarded exclusive rights in urban trade and
industry.[1] On the other hand, peasants who settled in towns and remained there on a more or less permanent basis, despite continuing
legal ties to rural communities and serfowners, have seldom been identified as part of the urban population in the relevant literature, any
more than they were so regarded by contemporary officialdom. In the
official viewpoint, widely adopted by historians, these peasants were
only "temporarily" absent from their villages and not an integral part

---

[1] In the eighteenth century, up to 1775, the term kupechestvo
(merchantry) was more or less synonymous with posad. After 1775 urban
taxpayers were divided into the kupechestvo (merchants) and meshchanstvo
(townsmen). In the historical literature the term gorodskie sosloviia
(urban classes) is often used to designate all of these categories.

of the urban sector. Thus virtually ruled out of existence by defini-
tion, rural-urban migration has been easy to overlook as a factor in
the development of Russian towns.

Preoccupation with the posad and indifference to the role of
other groups in the urban population has been particularly characteristic of the still-influential pre-revolutionary Russian historiography
and of most Western work on the urban history of early modern Russia.[2]
Soviet scholars predictably have rejected this "legalistic" approach
but have failed to evolve a coherent alternative to it and in practice
have often fallen back on more or less the same conceptions as their
much-castigated predecessors. For example, in Soviet as well as
"bourgeois" literature figures indicating the number of posad members
are often cited, with or without qualification, as representing the
size of the town population.[3] Although Soviet historiography has frequently called attention to the widespread participation of peasant

[2]The principal pre-revolutionary works on the urban history of
eighteenth-century Russia are I. I. Ditiatin, Ustroistvo i upravelenie
gorodov Rossii v XVIII stoletii, 2 vols. (Vol. 1: St. Petersburg,
1875; Vol. 2: Iaroslavl', 1877) and A. A. Kizevetter, Posadskaia
obshchina v Rossii XVIII stoletiia (Moscow, 1903). Western works
sharing the propensity to deal with the urban sector on the basis of
research pertaining to the posad alone include J. Michael Hittle, The
Service City: State and Townsmen in Russia, 1600-1800 (Cambridge,
Mass., 1979); Bernd Knabe, "Die Struktur der russischen Posadgemeinden
und der Katalog der Beschwerden und Forderungen der Kaufmannschaft
(1762-1767)," Forschungen zur osteuropäischen Geschichte, Band 22 (1975);
Samuel H. Baron, "The Town in 'Feudal' Russia," Slavic Review, Vol. 28,
No. 1 (March 1969), pp. 116-22. A notable exception to this tendency is
the recent work of Gilbert Rozman, Urban Networks in Russia, 1750-1800,
and Premodern Periodization (Princeton, 1976), and "Comparative
Approaches to Urbanization: Russia, 1750-1800," in Michael F. Hamm, ed.
The City in Russian History (Lexington, Ky., 1976), pp. 69-85.

[3]For example, see Sovetskaia istoricheskaia entsiklopediia, Vol. 13
(Moscow, 1971), p. 543; Ocherki istorii SSSR, period feodalizma:
Rossiia vo vtoroi polovine XVIII v. (Moscow, 1956), p. 151; Iu. R.
Klokman, Sotsial'no-ekonomicheskaia istoriia russkogo goroda, vtoraia
polovina XVIII v. (Moscow, 1967), pp. 31, 207-08, 311, 316-17; V. N.

migrants in the urban economy, it has remained surprisingly ambivalent about the extent to which these interlopers can be viewed as part of the urban population, and this confusion has blurred the issue of rural-urban migration in Soviet works as well as those of pre-revolutionary

Bernadskii, "Ocherki po istorii klassovoi bor'by i obshchestvenno-politicheskoi mysli Rossii v tretei chetverti XVIII v.," Uchenye zapiski Leningradskogo gosudarstvennogo pedagogicheskogo instituta im. A. I. Gertsena, Vol. 229 (1962), p. 69; G. L. Vartanov, Kupechestvo gorodov Moskovskoi gubernii vo vtoroi polovine XVIII v. (kandidat dissertation, Leningrad, Gosudarstvennyi pedagogicheskii institut im. A. I. Gertsena, 1966), p. 52; P. I. Liashchenko, History of the National Economy of Russia to the 1917 Revolution, trans. L. M. Herman (New York, 1949), p. 273.

Occasionally a higher figure has been cited, crediting the towns with about 7.5 percent of the total national population, in place of the 3 to 4 percent commonly given. This estimate derives from the work of the contemporary statistician Heinrich Storch, who used data from the government census (revision) of 1782 in an effort to determine the number of persons actually residing in towns, without regard to their legal status. In addition to the posad population, Storch's estimate includes members of such tax-free categories as nobles, officials, clergy, military personnel, state and court artisans and a variety of specialized categories of state servitors. It also includes serf laborers in manufactories, house serfs ascribed to urban households and inhabitants of peasant settlements within or adjacent to the towns. More recently, V. M. Kabuzan in the Soviet Union and Gilbert Rozman in the United States have prepared new estimates of the eighteenth-century urban population on this inclusive basis and have credited the towns with 8 to 10 percent of the total population during the reign of Catherine II. Even these expanded estimates, however, do not take into account peasant immigrants residing in towns with passports, since these immigrants were recorded by the census as inhabitants of their native villages, not of the towns. On the Storch estimate, see H. Storch, Statistische Übersicht der Statthalterschaften des russischen Reichs (Riga, 1795), p. 123; A. G. Rashin, Formirovanie promyshlennogo pro-letariata v Rossii (Moscow, 1940), pp. 82-83; F. Ia. Polianskii, Gorodskoe remeslo i manufaktura v Rossii XVIII v. (Moscow, 1960), pp. 30, 35; Jerome Blum, Lord and Peasant in Russia (New York, 1964), p. 280. On Rozman's work, see Rozman, "Comparative Approaches," pp. 74-79, as well as the more detailed exposition in his Urban Networks, especially Ch. 5. On the still unpublished work of Kabuzan, see Rozman, "Comparative Approaches," pp. 74-76; V. K. Iatsunskii, "Nekotorye voprosy metodiki izucheniia istorii feodal'nogo goroda v Rossii," in Goroda feodal'noi Rossii (Moscow, 1966), p. 87; R. N. Pullat, "Istoricheskaia demografiia v SSSR (znachenie, mesto, itogi i perspektivy razvitiia)," in Problemy istoricheskoi demografii SSSR (Tallinn, 1977), p. 13.

and Western authors.[4] Moreover, Soviet students of Russia's urban

history have been concerned primarily with the role of towns in the

"genesis of capitalism" and have therefore concentrated on investiga-

tion of the urban economy, while the demographic aspects of urban de-

velopment have drawn comparatively little attention.

These conceptual obstacles, along with the practical difficulty

of assembling an adequate concentration of source material, account

for the fact that the published literature contains no substantial

treatment of rural-urban migration in eighteenth-century Russia. The

information hitherto available has been a by-product of work on related

topics, such as studies of individual towns, urban trade and industry,

---

[4] P. G. Ryndziunskii, for example, appears to limit genuine membership in the urban population to inhabitants possessing "the full legal
rights of urban citizenship" (polnopravnoe grazhdanstvo), while depict-
ing those remaining in a condition of "feudal-serf dependence" as only
potentially urban or "urbanizing" elements. Iu. R. Klokman, along with
Ryndziunskii the most prominent Soviet authority on the eighteenth-
century urban sector, occupies an ambiguous and inconsistent position
on this issue but implicitly supports Ryndziunskii's views in many instances. Characteristically, references to peasant immigration into
the urban population (vykhod krest'ian v gorod) in the works of these
authors deal with formal absorption of peasants into the posad or
illegal flight from the village, while authorized "temporary" migration
is not mentioned in this context. Some recent Soviet scholars, such
as M. Ia. Volkov and A. S. Cherkasova, have called for a broader conception of the urban population, based primarily on demographic and
economic criteria, but the concrete application of such a model to study
of this period is in most respects yet to be realized. The apparent
suppression of Kabuzan's work on the size of the urban population would
seem to reflect strong resistance to this sort of conception in influen-
tial Soviet academic circles. See Ryndziunskii, Gorodskoe grazhdanstvo
doreformennoi Rossii (Moscow, 1958), pp. 12-14, 52-61; Ryndziunskii,
"Soslovno-podatnaia reforma 1775 g. i gorodskoe naselenie," in Obshchestvo
i gosudarstvo feodal'noi Rossii (Moscow, 1975), pp. 92-95; Ryndziunskii,
"Osnovnye faktory gorodoobrazovaniia v Rossii vtoroi poloviny XVIII v.,"
in Russkii gorod (Moscow, 1976), pp. 105-27; Klokman, Sotsial'no-ekonomicheskaia istoriia, pp. 93-100, 123, 207-313, 316-17; Klokman, "Gorod v
zakonodatel'stve russkogo absoliutizma vo vtoroi polovine XVII i XVIII
vv.," in Absoliutizm v Rossii (Moscow, 1964), pp. 344-51; Volkov, "Puti
formirovaniia gorodskikh poselenii Rossii v XVIII v.," in 250 let Permi:
Materialy nauchnoi konferentsii "Proshloe, nastoiashchee i budushchee
Permi" (15-17 noiabria 1972 g.) (Perm', 1973), pp. 14-20; Cherkasova,
"Nekotorye voprosy istoriografii russkogo goroda XVIII stoletiia," Uchenye
zapiski Permskogo gosudarstvennogo universiteta im. A. M. Gor'kogo, vol.
227 (1970), pp. 50-61.

the industrial labor force and the peasant economy.[5] In this literature,
peasant migration to towns emerges as one facet of a broader phenomenon
in the social and economic history of early modern Russia: the widespread and steadily growing diversification of the peasant economy
into non-agricultural activities. The heavy involvement of peasants
in occupations usually considered intrinsically urban has been recognized as one of the most important and characteristic features of
Russian economic life in the era before modern industrialization, but
the relationship of these activities to the question of urban development has not been clearly demarcated. To be sure, the participation of
peasants in commercial and industrial occupations took on a variety of
forms, not all of which involved resettlement in towns or even a temporary appearance on the urban scene. In what was no doubt the great
majority of cases, such activities were pursued as a supplement to
agriculture, on a seasonal basis or as part of the diversified economy

---

[5]Examples of such contributions include Istoriia Moskvy, Vol. 2
(Moscow, 1953); Ocherki istorii Leningrada, Vol. 1 (Leningrad, 1955);
B. B. Kafengauz, "Khlebnyi rynok v 30-40-kh gg. XVIII v.," Materialy
po istorii zemledeliia SSSR, Vol. 1 (Moscow, 1952), pp. 459-510; G. L.
Vartanov, "Kupechestvo i torguiushchee krest'ianstvo tsentral'noi
chasti Evropeiskoi Rossii vo vtoroi polovine XVIII v.," Uchenye zapiski
Leningradskogo gosudarstvennogo pedagogicheskogo instituta im. A. I.
Gertsena, Vol. 229 (1962), pp. 161-96; E. I. Zaozerskaia, Rabochaia
sila i klassovaia bor'ba na tekstil'nykh manufakturakh Rossii v 20-60-
kh gg. XVIII v. (Moscow, 1960); M. N. Artemenkov, "Naemnye rabochie
moskovskikh manufaktur v 40-70-kh gg. XVIII v.," Istoriia SSSR, 1964,
No. 2, pp. 133-43; I. V. Meshalin, Tekstil'naia promyshlennost' krest'ian
Moskovskoi gubernii v XVIII i pervoi polovine XVIII v. (Moscow-Leningrad,
1950); E. I. Indova, "Les activités commerciales de la paysannerie dans
les villages du tsar de la région de Moscou (première moitié du XVIIIe
siècle)," Cahiers du monde russe et soviétique, Vol. 5, No. 2 (Apr.-
June 1964), pp. 206-28; S. I. Volkov, Krest'iane dvortsovykh
vladenii Podmoskov'ia v seredine XVIII v. (Moscow, 1959); L. V. Sretenskii,
"Pomeshchich'ia votchina Iaroslavskoi gubernii vo vtoroi polovine XVIII
v.," Uchenye zapiski Iaroslavskogo gosudarstvennogo pedagogicheskogo
instituta im. K. D. Ushinskogo, Vol. 25/35 (1958), pp. 475-530.

of a large peasant household. As contemporary observers frequently
pointed out, however, it was sometimes the "urban" occupations which
were the chief source of income for the peasants, while agriculture
was reduced to a supplementary role.[6] Growing numbers of peasants,
especially those very successful in their commercial and industrial
pursuits and those from ruined households unable to participate further
in the agricultural economy, abandoned the fields altogether and devoted themselves full time to non-agricultural occupations.

Many peasants turned to village industry in the search for non-
agricultural income. The most common form of rural craft industry in
Central Russia was household textile production, but the production of
leather goods, articles of clothing and footwear, metal goods, wooden
articles and utensils, vehicles and wheels, candles, soap, bast mats
and sacks, rope and a variety of other goods was also widely practiced
in the countryside. Such industries typically played a supplementary
role in the village economy, but there were also highly developed industrial settlements where virtually all the inhabitants were occupied
full time in specialized industrial activities and where large peasant-
owned manufactories were in operation. Such settlements frequently
resembled towns in terms of their size, appearance and economic character
and were compared to towns by many contemporary observers.[7] Other

[6] For example, see I. G. Georgi, "O pobochnykh krest'ianskikh
rabotakh," Trudy Vol'nogo ekonomicheskogo obshchestva (hereafter Trudy
VEO), Vol. 33 (1783), p. 115; K. German, Statisticheskoe opisanie
Iaroslavskoi gubernii (St. Petersburg, 1808), p. 90.

[7] On Ivanovo village and other centers of textile production in
Vladimir guberniia (province), see A. M. Razgon, "Promyshlennye i
torgovye slobody i sela Vladimirskoi gubernii vo vtoroi polovine XVIII
v.," Istoricheskie zapiski, Vol. 32 (1950), pp. 133-72. Pavlovo village,
a well known center of metallurgical industries, and other industrial
villages of Nizhnii Novgorod guberniia are discussed in Chapter V of

villages developed into busy local markets or important transshipment points along major trade routes.[8] Many peasants were occupied in local rural trade, buying up village production for sale to urban merchants or for shipment to towns and trade fairs and supplying the local populace with goods brought in from elsewhere. Peasants also participated extensively in the long-distance transit trade in grain, fish, livestock, flax, hemp, hides, tallow, furs and industrial products, acquiring these goods in the major producing regions or at transshipment centers and delivering them to Moscow, Petersburg and other major markets for sale. In addition, peasants served the transit trade through their role in the provision of transport services. They virtually monopolized the overland transport of goods (izvoz) and also provided most of the massive amount of labor needed by shipping on the Volga and other inland waterways. Some peasants were the owners of cargo vessels and contracted with merchants and with state monopolies for shipment of their goods.

---

this dissertation. Some recent writers have suggested that these "villages" should be defined as towns and their inhabitants as part of the urban population, although this idea has not achieved general acceptance. In this study we will leave aside this question and under the heading of "rural-urban migration" deal only with peasant migration to settlements officially designated as towns. For various views on the "urban" character of industrial villages, see M. Ia. Volkov, "Puti formirovaniia," pp. 14-21; Cherkasova, pp. 52-60; Klokman, Sotsial'no-ekonomicheskaia istoriia, pp. 123, 317; Klokman, Ocherki sotsial'no-ekonomicheskoi istorii gorodov severo-zapada Rossii v seredine XVIII v. (Moscow, 1960), pp. 120-22, 221; Ryndziunskii, "Osnovnye faktory," pp. 105-09; Ia. E. Vodarskii, Naselenie Rossii v kontse XVII-nachale XVIII v. (chislennost', soslovno-klassovoi sostav, razmeshchenie) (Moscow, 1977), pp. 115-26.

[8] Among the latter were Rogachevo, in Dmitrov uezd (district), and Lyskovo (Nizhnii Novgorod, later Makar'ev uezd), both of which were important centers of the long-distance grain trade.

In addition to activities taking place in a rural setting or along the routes between markets, peasants invaded the home territory of the posad population, settling in towns to become temporary or permanent participants in the urban economy. Among these settlers were substantial commercial entrepreneurs who controlled stores and traded on a large scale as well as street peddlers selling their wares from carts, benches and sacks, independent craft producers and owners of small industrial enterprises, apprentices of urban craftsmen and hired laborers working in industry or in enterprises and households of urban merchants. These masses of peasants lurking on the fringes of urban life included large numbers of seasonal migrants, who took advantage of slack periods in the village economy to seek supplementary income elsewhere. Many migrants, however, spent all or most of the year in towns. These long-term settlers, already de facto members of the urban population, sometimes were eventually inducted into it formally through a legal process of enlistment in the posad.

Various factors have been cited, by eighteenth-century observers as well as recent scholars, to account for the remarkably strong inclination of the Russian peasantry to supplement or even replace agriculture with commercial and industrial pursuits. The unfavorable climatic and soil conditions in much of European Russia, particularly the northern and northwestern areas and the central districts north of the Oka River, and the resultant poor return on agriculture in these severe and infertile areas provided the peasantry with a strong inducement to seek other sources of income.[9] Surplus labor power in the peasant household

---

[9] Among the many works which have cited this factor are the following: V. A. Fedorov, Pomeshchich'i krest'iane tsentral'no-promyshlennogo raiona Rossii kontsa XVIII-pervoi poloviny XIX v. (Moscow, 1974), p. 83; K. V.

provided further encouragement in this direction. The short growing
season left the peasants free from agricultural work for a prolonged
period.[10] Even during the growing season agriculture often required
the full-time attention of only part of a large peasant household, while
the remaining members were able to depart from the village to pursue
other occupations, returning only at harvest time and sometimes not
even then.[11]

In the eighteenth century growing population density and the resulting shortages of agricultural land in some provinces further enhanced the surplus of labor and reduced the adequacy of income from
agricultural sources.[12] At the same time, the increasing availability
of grain supplies from the more productive agriculture of the black-soil
territories relieved the infertile areas of the necessity of relying on

Sivkov, "Podmoskovnaia votchina serediny XVIII v.," Moskovskii krai v
ego proshlom, Vol. 1 (Moscow, 1928), p. 88; Sretenskii, "Pomeshchich'ia
votchina," pp. 478-82. Eighteenth-century observers who put forward
this idea included A. N. Radishchev and the authors of various descriptions of individual provinces. See A. N. Radishchev, materialy i
issledovaniia (Moscow-Leningrad, 1936), p. 197; E. Ziablovskii,
Zemleopisanie Rossiiskoi Imperii dlia vsekh sostoianii, Vol. 4 (St.
Petersburg, 1810), pp. 5-9; K. German, Statisticheskoe opisanie
Iaroslavskoi gubernii (St. Petersburg, 1808), p. 3.

10 Fedorov, p. 83; L. F. Zakharova, Pomeshchich'i krest'iane
Nizhegorodskoi gubernii i ikh klassovaia bor'ba vo vtoroi polovine
XVIII v. (dissertation, Gor'kii, Gor'kovskii gosudarstvennyi universitet,
1954), pp. 92-93; Georgi, "O pobochnykh krest'ianskikh rabotakh," pp.
104-05.

11 Sbornik Imperatorskogo russkogo istoricheskogo obshchestva (hereafter Sb. IRIO), Vol. 8 (St. Petersburg, 1871), p. 56 ("Mnenie deputata
ot chernososhnykh krest'ian Olonetskoi gubernii Sevast'iana Vonifat'eva");
Topograficheskoe opisanie Iaroslavskogo namestnichestva, sochinennoe v
Iaroslavle v 1794 g. (Iaroslavl', 1794), pp. 26-27; German, Statisticheskoe
opisanie Iaroslavskoi gubernii, pp. 90-91; E. I. Drakokhrust, "Rassloenie
krepostnogo krest'ianstva v obrochnoi votchine XVIII v.," Istoricheskie
zapiski, Vol. 4 (1938), pp. 113-40; Zakharova, p. 92

12 Fedorov, p. 83; Zakharova, pp. 63-64; German, Statisticheskoe
opisanie Iaroslavskoi gubernii, p. 94.

their own agricultural production and allowed larger numbers of peasants
to become net consumers rather than producers of grain. By the end of
the century, according to one source, the provinces of Moscow and
Vladimir were producing only one-third to one-half of the grain they
consumed annually.[13] The increasing use of money payments in the collection of taxes and dues, the rising level of these payments, and
economic differentiation in the village, which deprived some households
of the ability to participate in the agricultural economy, have also
been cited as contributing factors in the steady expansion of the
peasantry into non-agricultural occupations.[14] Finally, the inadequate
development of the urban sector (within its legally defined limits) and
its inability to provide the necessary services in the production and
exchange of goods throughout a vast empire have been seen as encouraging
and even compelling the intrusion of the peasantry into these normally
urban occupations.[15] In some parts of Russia the network of urban
settlements was spread so thinly that peasants had to take over urban

---

[13]Fedorov, pp. 56-58.

[14]Zakharova, pp. 63-66; Sretenskii, "Pomeshchich'ia votchina," pp.
503-04; A. L. Shapiro, "Krest'ianskie otkhody i krest'ianskii naem v
petrovskoe vremia," Uchenye zapiski Leningradskogo pedagogicheskogo
instituta im. M. N. Pokrovskogo, Vol. 5, No. 1 (1940), p. 37; L. V.
Milov, Issledovaniia ob "Ekonomicheskikh primechaniiakh" k general'nomu
mezhevaniiu (k istorii russkogo krest'ianstva i sel'skogo khoziaistva
vtoroi poloviny XVIII v.) (Moscow, 1965), Ch. 5.

[15]I. M. Kulisher, Ocherk istorii russkoi torgovli (Petrograd, 1923),
pp. 250-51. This view was also expressed by eighteenth-century officials
who opposed the demands of the posad for tighter restrictions on peasant
commerce, such as G. N. Teplov and Count Ernst Münnich. See Sb. IRIO,
Vol. 8, pp. 200-03; S. M. Troitskii, "Obsuzhdenie voprosa o krest'ianskoi
torgovle v Komissii o kommertsii v seredine 60-kh godov XVIII v.," in
Dvorianstvo i krepostnoi stroi Rossii XVI-XVIII vv. (Moscow, 1975), pp.
227-39.

commercial functions in order to assure the marketing of rural production and the provision of goods necessary for local consumption.[16]

The widespread commercial and industrial activity of the Russian
peasantry arose in the face of serious legal obstacles, the most obvious of which was serfdom itself. The eighteenth-century Russian
peasant, bound to a particular lord or estate and watched by a government suspecting him of the intention to break these bonds through
flight, did not have the right to move about freely for economic purposes. However, the growing need of peasants for temporary departure
from the village (otkhod) to earn money for payment of taxes and dues
was appreciated both by lords and by the government, which in the eighteenth century established an elaborate passport system to accommodate
these interests.[17] With permission of the lords or institutions controlling them, peasants could obtain government documents authorizing
departure from the village for periods of up to three years, and with
repeated renewal of these passports the departure could become essentially permanent. The need to secure seigneurial permission, which
could of course be refused, and to have this authorization ratified by
slow-moving and frequently corrupt government institutions of course

---

[16]This point was raised at the hearings of the Legislative Commission
of 1767 by deputies from the state peasantry of the provinces of Nizhnii
Novgorod and Arkhangel'sk and the district of Olonets. Sb. IRIO, Vol. 8,
pp. 96-97, 204, 230.

[17]See B. N. Kazantsev. "Zakonodatel'stvo russkogo tsarizma po
regulirovaniiu krest'ianskogo otkhoda v XVIII-XIX vv.," Voprosy istorii,
1970, No. 6, pp. 20-31.

remained a limitation on the peasant's freedom of movement, but these obstacles did not prevent large numbers of villagers from obtaining passports and circulating throughout the country. It has been esti- mated that in the late eighteenth century 20 to 30 percent of the adult male population in some of the central provinces was normally on _otkhod_.[18]

Another obstacle faced by trading peasants was legislation re- stricting the right to participate in some forms of commercial and in- dustrial activity and reserving these pursuits for the _posad_ population or some other favored group.[19] The most stringent regulations applied to activities in the towns. The government, reguiring heavy tax pay- ments and burdensome services from the urban commune, felt compelled to protect its sources of income by limiting the intrusion of outsiders into the urban economy. The _Ulozhenie_ (Law Code) of 1649 established the principle that "only the Sovereign's /urban/ taxpayers" had the right to operate stores (_lavki_), warehouses (_ambary_) and other commercial facilities and industrial enterprises in the towns.[20] With the excep- tion of a brief period during the reign of Peter I, this prohibition remained in force through the end of the eighteenth century.[21] However,

---

[18]Zakharova, p. 117; M. Tugan-Baranovskii, _Russkaia fabrika v proshlom i nastoiashchem_, Vol. 1 (7th ed., Moscow, 1938), pp. 42-43.

[19]The legislation governing the right to engage in trade has not been well studied and should be the subject of a separate detailed in- vestigation. Many authors have contented themselves with the statement that peasants were "forbidden to engage in trade" or "forbidden to trade in the towns," or have cited a few decrees with only a perfunctory effort to define exactly what activities were prohibited and how the situation changed over time.

[20]_Polnoe sobranie zakonov Rossiiskoi imperii s 1649 g._ (hereafter PSZ), Vol. 1, No. 1, Ch. 19.

[21]In 1711 Peter instituted a policy of "free trade" (_svobodnyi torg_), which allowed persons of all categories to obtain full commercial rights if they paid urban taxes. However, this policy produced undesir- able consequences from the government's point of view and was soon

the Ulozhenie and subsequent decrees did allow peasants to bring "all
kinds of goods" from the countryside for sale in the gostinnyi dvor
or "from their carts and boats" in designated marketplaces.[22] Peasants
were thus barred from possessing commercial and industrial enterprises
within the towns, but they retained the right (as did non-resident
merchants and other outsiders) to deliver shipments of goods to the urban
market for wholesale purchase by local merchants. They could also sell
foodstuffs and small shipments of other goods directly to the urban
consumer.[23] Nor did the Ulozhenie place restrictions on commercial
activity in the countryside. Rural markets, however, were regulated by
the internal customs system, which required that trade be conducted only
in "authorized" places, those where provision had been made for the
collection of tariffs. Rural markets were established by government
charters, usually at the request of the owner of the settlement in
question. These charters specified the days on which trade could take
place and often the kinds of goods which could be sold.[24]

---

abandoned. (See below, Chapter II.) Both before and after this unsuccessful experiment, the 1649 prohibition was restated repeatedly.
See PSZ, Vol. 3, No. 1723 (1699); Vol. 4, No. 1775 (1700); Vol. 7, No.
4312 (1722-3); Vol. 8, No. 6043 (1732); Vol. 11, No. 8757 (1743); Vol.
12, No. 9201 (1745); Vol. 13, No. 10042 (1752); Vol. 20, No. 14595
(1777).

[22]Gostinnyi dvor: the central bazaar of Russian towns and the headquarters for wholesaling of shipments delivered by non-resident merchants,
who did not have the right to engage in retail trade in the urban market.

[23]See PSZ, Vol. 2, No. 1027 (1683); Vol. 3, Nos. 1641 (1698), 1646
(1698); Vol. 4, No. 1972 (1704); Vol. 7, No. 4634 (1725); Vol. 12, No.
9201 (1745); Vol. 14, No. 10191 (1754); M. Ia. Volkov, "Otmena vnutrennikh
tamozhen v Rossii," Istoriia SSSR, 1957, No. 2, p. 88.

[24]See M. Ia. Volkov, "Otmena vnutrennikh tamozhen," pp. 79-85.

At the end of Peter I's reign and under his successors, government pressure on trading peasants was intensified. Enforcement of the
existing restrictions was stepped up and a series of new prohibitions
was issued.[25] Peasants were forbidden to trade in export commodities
in the port cities and to deal in imported goods.[26] Peasant participation in the farming of state monopolies and in contracts for the delivery of goods to state institutions, permitted under Peter, was
prohibited in 1731.[27] In 1745 the government issued a decree limiting
trade in rural areas. Trade was permitted only in "large" (znatnyi)
settlements located on main roads and not near a town, and only in
certain types of goods.[28] During the reigns of Anna and Elizabeth
(1730-1762), in an effort to strengthen the position of large government-
chartered manufactories, it was made illegal to engage in "unauthorized"

---

[25]On increasing enforcement of existing restrictions, see the examples cited in Ibid., pp. 82, 85; M. Ia. Volkov, "Materialy pervoi
revizii kak istochnik po istorii torgovli i promyshlennosti Rossii
pervoi chetverti XVIII v.," Problemy istochnikovedeniia, Vol. 11 (1963),
pp. 300-05; Klokman, Ocherki, pp. 159-60, 187-88; Materialy po istorii
krest'ianskoi promyshlennosti (hereafter MPIKP), Vol. 1 (Moscow-Leningrad,
1935), pp. 68-69, 73-74.

[26]PSZ, Vol. 7, No. 4312 (1722-3); Vol. 8, No. 5987 (1732); Vol. 14,
No. 10486, Ch. 2, Art. 1 (1755); Vol. 15, No. 10862 (1758).

[27]PSZ, Vol. 8, No. 5789 (Art. 20, 22); A. L. Shapiro, "Krest'ianskaia
torgovlia i krest'ianskie podriady v petrovskoe vremia," Istoricheskie
zapiski, Vol. 27 (1948), pp. 209-18, 239.

[28]PSZ, Vol. 12, No. 9201. The list of permitted goods included a
variety of textiles, articles of clothing, metal tools, wooden vessels
and utensils, pottery, horse gear and other goods normally produced or
used by the peasantry. The restrictions did not apply to the sale of
grain and other foodstuffs. The Customs Charter of 1755 (PSZ, Vol. 14,
No. 10486, Ch. 10, Art. 4) repeated the above provisions and specified
that trade could not take place in settlements located closer than five
versty to a town. (1 versta = 1.06 km.) The relationship between these
provisions and the previously issued charters authorizing markets in
individual villages is not entirely clear.

production of many kinds of goods, and large numbers of peasant craftsmen working in both towns and villages were thus placed outside the law.[29] In the second half of the eighteenth century, however, the trend toward intensified repression of peasant commerce was reversed. The abolition of internal tariffs in 1753 represented a significant relaxation of controls on trade, since the locations where trade could take place had earlier been limited in order to assure the collection of tariffs and since goods had been subject to repeated checking to see if the duties had been paid. Beginning in 1758, the government gradually withdrew from the struggle against "unauthorized" industrial production and ended the monopolistic privileges awarded to factory owners.[31] Restrictions on trade in the port cities were cancelled in 1760.[32] The government of Catherine II again allowed peasants to participate in farming the state liquor monopoly and took a favorable attitude toward the development of rural markets.[33] As regards the participation of peasants in commerce within the towns, however, the prescriptions of Catherine's

---

[29]MPIKP, Vol. 1, pp. 12-16, 22-46, 60-129, 168-71, 229-42, 369-75; Vol. 2 (Moscow-Leningrad, 1950), pp. 66-107.

[30]At the time of the Legislative Commission of 1767 many urban communes called for restoration of such controls, in the form of documents issued by the local urban authorities, to facilitate the suppression of illicit trade. For example, see Sb. IRIO, Vol. 93 (St. Petersburg, 1894), pp. 398-400 (Romanov), 465 (Kashin), 517-18 (Nerekhta); Vol. 107 (St. Petersburg, 1900), p. 43 (Sol' Bol'shaia). According to a scholar who has investigated the customs reform, one of the main objectives of its principal author, P. I. Shuvalov, was to reduce obstacles to small-scale trade by peasants. (M. Ia. Volkov, "Otmena vnutrennikh tamozhen," pp. 89-94.)

[31]MPIKP, Vol. 1, pp. 257-58, 373-75.

[32]E. I. Indova, A. A. Preobrazhenskii, Iu. A. Tikhonov, "Klassovaia bor'ba krest'ianstva i stanovlenie burzhuaznykh otnoshenii v Rossii (vtoraia polovina XVII-XVIII v.)," Voprosy istorii, 1964, No. 12, p. 41.

[33]PSZ, Vol. 19, No. 14123 (1774); Vol. 22, No. 16187 (Charter of the Nobility, 1785), Ch. A, Art. 29.

legislation differed little from those of the 1649 Law Code.[34]

In any case, efforts to restrict the involvement of peasants in "urban" economic activities were remarkably ineffective. The Russian state of the eighteenth century did not have the administrative resources to police the economy effectively, nor did it have the will to crush completely the commercial and industrial activities of the peasantry. To do so would have been to strike an extremely serious blow against the national economy, against the lords and government institutions which collected dues from trading peasants, and against the government's own tax base. Individual peasant entrepreneurs might suffer harassment, confiscation and punishment, and more restrictive policies might slow the expansion of peasant activities, but at no time did these restrictions prevent trading peasants from playing a major role in the economy and competing effectively with the posad population. The protests of the urban communes to the Legislative Commission of 1767, coming at the close of a period of relatively intense repression of peasant commerce, are ample proof of this contention.

"Trading peasants" were adept at circumventing legal obstacles to their activities and in doing so received assistance from several quarters. In their complaints to the Legislative Commission and other government institutions, the urban communes correctly identified the backing of lords as an important asset to the illegal commerce of peasants.[35] The lords were a useful source of credit for the enterprises of their trusted serfs. They also allowed peasants to use urban

---

[34] PSZ, Vol. 20, No. 14595 (1777); Vol. 22, No. 16188 (Urban Charter, 1785), Art. 11, 24.

[35] See Sb. IRIO, Vol. 8, pp. 225-26 (Vologda); Vol. 93, pp. 183 (Borovsk), 201 (Serpukhov), 251 (Vereia), 339-40 (Iaroslavl'), 376-77 (Ruza), 398-400 (Romanov), 463-64 (Kashin); Vol. 107, pp. 102-03 (Kaluga); Vol. 134 (St. Petersburg, 1911), pp. 24-25 (Arzamas), etc.

property they owned for commercial purposes and to pose as their agents
in conducting commercial transactions. Fear of conflict with powerful
nobles often deterred the urban authorities from even attempting to enforce the prohibitions against commercial activity by peasants.[36]
However, the testimony of the urban communes reveals that many individual posad members also abetted the activities of trading peasants and
connived in their evasion of the law.[37] Urban merchants did not hesitate
to enter into profitable dealings with trading peasants and provided
peasants with training in commercial and industrial skills through
apprenticeship and employment. Moreover, in direct contravention of the
law many peasants were able to buy or rent stores from urban merchants
and pose as their employees or otherwise "trade under their names" in
conducting business. The complaisance of these merchants was attributed
by one town to the fact that they were bound to their peasant collaborators through family relationships, friendship, debt or some other ties.[38]
Despite their demands for greater and more effective restriction of
peasant commercial activities, some urban communes recognized that
dealings with trading peasants were to some extent inescapable and for

[36]The institutions governing crown estates sometimes played a
similar protective role, particularly in the case of the estates belonging to the imperial court. On the intervention of the court estate
administration in favor of court peasants involved in trade, see PSZ,
Vol. 11, No. 8608; Indova, "Les activités commerciales," pp. 209-10;
Indova et al., "Klassovaia bor'ba," p. 38. See also below, Chapters II,
IV.

[37]See Sb. IRIO, Vol. 8, p. 291 (Orenburg); Vol. 93, pp. 164-66
(Kostroma), 339 (Iaroslavl'), 376-77 (Ruza), 398-400 (Romanov), 434
(Zaraisk), 517 (Nerekhta); Vol. 107, pp. 16-19 (Suzdal'), 42-43 (Sol'
Bol'shaia), 118-19 (Meshchovsk), 149-50 (Pereslavl'-Zalesskii), etc.

[38]Ibid., Vol. 93, pp. 420-21 (Viazniki). Other evidence, to be presented elsewhere in this dissertation, amply supports the claims of the
urban communes regarding the assistance trading peasants received from
nobles and individual posad members.

this reason urged that peasants be allowed to sign promissory notes, which had been prohibited by a decree of 1761.[39]

Rural-urban migration in eighteenth-century Russia was thus part of a broader movement of the peasant population into non-agricultural pursuits, a movement which encompassed the proliferation of rural trade and industry and involvement in itinerant commercial activities as well as seasonal and long-term migration to towns. Under the prevailing conditions of enserfment and rigid legal stratification of the population, such migration was possible through the government's passport system, which authorized absences from the village that were temporary in theory but could become permanent in fact. Since it did not usually relieve the settler of his original legal status as a serf or crown peasant, this migration has been easy to overlook as a factor in Russia's urban development and has been given little sustained attention in this context. Consequently, much remains to be learned about the specific features of the peasant influx and its impact on the towns. In the absence of systematic investigation of the subject, the information provided by the literature is necessarily fragmentary and superficial. It conveys the impression that peasant immigrants played a major role in the population and economy of many eighteenth-century Russian towns, successfully circumventing legal obstacles to their activities. To define this role precisely and show how it varied with time and place, however, requires much additional research. Nor have the prevailing geographical patterns of migration, the forces drawing peasants into the urban environment and the processes by which immigrants were

---

[39]Sb. IRIO, Vol. 107, pp. 57-58 (Bezhetsk), 130-31 (Kineshma), 177-78 (Gorokhovets); Vol. 134, pp. 9 (Nizhnii Novgorod), 38 (Balakhna).

assimilated into the recipient community been more than dimly illuminated in the existing literature.

Thorough investigation of these questions would do much to advance our knowledge of the urban sector in eighteenth-century Russia and the processes affecting its development. In the non-Soviet literature pre-occupation with the posad population and its role in the state order has produced a tendency to minimize Russia's urban development and to assign the interests and initiatives of the state an all-encompassing role in shaping that development. This view portrays the urban popula-tion as unusually small and incapable of substantial growth, the urban economy as weak, backward and dependent on state support, and urban life as dominated by the burdens of state service.[40] The presence of a large contingent of peasant immigrants, who did not share in service obliga-tions or benefit from state support for their economic activities and whose infiltration into the urban population was neither intended nor controlled by the state, obviously undermines this traditional and still widely accepted view, and it seems clear that the question of urban development cannot be adequately assessed without taking this immigra-tion into account.

---

[40]Characteristic of this attitude is Ditiatin's statement that "the history of.../Russian7 towns is nothing but the history of the regulation and transformation of the...urban population by the supreme power," as well as P. N. Miliukov's contention that Russian towns were "not a natural product of the country's economic development" but rather an artificial creation of the state. See Ditiatin, Ustroistvo, Vol. 1, p. 109; Miliukov, Ocherki po istorii russkoi kul'tury, Vol. 1 (St. Petersburg, 1909), p. 241. See also A. A. Kizevetter, "Posadskaia obshchina v Rossii XVIII stoletiia," in Kizevetter, Istoricheskie ocherki (Moscow, 1912), pp. 242-63. For similar Western views, see Baron, "The Town in 'Feudal' Russia," pp. 118-21; Hittle, The Service City, pp. 11-15, 104-11, 239-42; David H. Miller, City and State in Muscovite Society: Iaroslavl', 1649-1699 (Ph.D. dissertation, Princeton University, 1974), pp. 359, 367.

In repudiating the "legalistic" approach and recognizing peasant immigrants as an important if unofficial segment of the urban population, however, it would be unwise to ignore the possible impact of differences in legal status, origin and background within that population on the interactions of its members and its behavior as an economic and social unit. The fact that many urban residents remained legally attached to peasant communes and even serfowners may have had important effects on the economic, social and political development of the urban sector, and such consequences need to be carefully investigated. To what extent, for example, did these circumstances constrain the economic activities of peasant immigrants and limit their potential contribution to the urban economy? To what extent did these cleavages impede the assertiveness of urban social strata in defense of their interests? In what ways were economic collaboration, social interaction and marital behavior affected by the legal and other differences between peasant immigrants and the remainder of the urban population? In addition to illuminating the structure of urban social relations, study of rural-urban migration, through its search for the causes which gave rise to the exodus of peasants to towns, can be expected to provide useful insights into the social and economic history of the peasant village. One central question bearing on the evolution of both urban and rural Russia is the relation between migration to towns and the development of commercial and industrial activity in the countryside, the factors which determined the choice of one or another of these divergent paths in the search for non-agricultural income.

Besides the conceptual obstacles outlined previously, the researcher seeking to investigate rural-urban migration in eighteenth-century Russia confronts the serious practical difficulty of assembling an adequate concentration of source material. One solution to this problem is to focus on a category of immigrants which is documented by comparatively extensive and accessible materials, those who enlisted in the officially recognized urban classes (the posad population). Provisions for such enlistment were introduced by the government of Peter I in an effort to absorb peasants entrenched in urban commerce and industry into the posad, thus expanding the number of urban taxpayers and protecting the economic privileges intended to make possible the fulfilment of urban tax and service obligations. Since the transfer of individuals from one official population category to another as authorized by this legislation was a laborious administrative process which was discussed and recorded by government institutions at various levels and is also reflected in census materials, peasants who registered in the urban classes are much more systematically documented than are other immigrants. Although the registrants comprised only a small portion of the total peasant influx, they numbered in the tens of thousands and thus provide a sample of urban immigration well worth investigating.

Moreover, we can assume many similarities between registered and unregistered immigrants, with the former representing in general those settlers who were most advanced in their assimilation and most success-ful in overcoming the obstacles to a change of legal status. Enlistment in the posad was frequently preceded by years or even decades of actual urban residence, during which the future registrant belonged to the ill-documented pool of immigrants subsisting in the urban population without official recognition, and records dealing with such registrants often contain evidence on what occurred during this preparatory period of migration, settlement and assimilation. Study of enlistment in the posad can thus be informative about the larger influx from the country-side, and particularly about geographical patterns of migration, economic and occupational characteristics of the migrants, the influences drawing them into the urban environment, the interaction of the newcomers with other elements of the urban population and the factors encouraging or impeding their assimilation.

Like the larger problem of rural-urban migration, peasant enlist-ment in the urban classes has not been seriously investigated in the existing literature, which offers only what one scholar has termed "extremely sparse and fragmentary data" on the subject.[41] Lack of ade-quate evidence has led to the incorrect assumption that legal and pro-cedural obstacles kept the level of enlistment very low throughout the century and that in general only very wealthy peasants could hope to circumvent these obstacles and penetrate the ranks of the posad popula-tion.[42] Nor have the legal provisions governing this enlistment been

---

[41]Vartanov, "Kupechestvo i torguiushchee krest'ianstvo," p. 192. In addition to the data cited by Vartanov (Ibid., pp. 186-95), some data can be found in the following: Kizevetter, Posadskaia obshchina, pp. 43-48; Ryndziunskii, "Osnovnye faktory," p. 113; S. I. Volkov, Krest'iane dvortsovykh vladenii, pp. 63-66; E. I. Indova, "Rol' dvortsovoi derevni pervoi poloviny XVIII v. v formirovanii russkogo kupechestva," Istoricheskie zapiski, Vol. 68 (1961), pp. 189-210; V. N. Iakovtsevskii, Kupecheskii kapital v feodal'no krepostnicheskoi Rossii (Moscow, 1953), p. 50; Istoriia Moskvy, Vol. 2, pp. 317-19; George E. Munro, The Development of St. Petersburg as an Urban Center during the Reign of Catherine II (1762-1796) (Ph.D. dissertation, University of North Carolina, 1973), p. 303. A recent German monograph reprints the data of Kizevetter and Vartanov but mistakenly attributes the latter's contribution to V. N. Bernadskii (Knabe, "Die Struktur der russischen Posadgemeinden," pp. 300-63).

[42]Klokman, Sotsial'no-ekonomicheskaia istoriia, pp. 93-94; Ryndziunskii, Gorodskoe grazhdanstvo, pp. 52-61; Ryndziunskii, "Soslovno-podatnaia reforma," pp. 92-95; Ryndziunskii, "Osnovnye faktory," pp. 112-13; Vartanov, "Kupechestvo i torguiushchee krest'ianstvo," pp. 188-89; Istoriia Moskvy, Vol. 2, pp. 318-19.

adequately explored or even correctly summarized. In general, those who have dealt with the question have confined their attention to a few decrees or documents and have carelessly assumed that the requirements and procedures reflected therein were in force over a much longer period than that covered by the evidence.[43] As a result of such mis-understandings, the data offered in the literature have sometimes been accompanied by faulty interpretation, and the incorrect perception of government policy as unchanging and rigidly unfavorable to enlistment has reinforced the tendency to underestimate the magnitude of the peasant influx into the posad population.[44] The failure to discern even the broad outlines of this influx has naturally precluded any useful extrapolations regarding the larger currents of peasant immigration.

This study represents a preliminary exploration of the subject, intended not to offer definitive answers to the questions noted previously but to provide the basic information needed to evaluate the significance of enlistment in the posad and to show how evidence relating to this phenomenon, in conjunction with other evidence, can be used to illuminate the above issues. Much of the dissertation is devoted to making avail-able for the first time a substantial amount of quantitative data on

_____

[43]Vartanov, "Kupechestvo i torguiushchee krest'ianstvo," pp. 188-89; Klokman, "Gorod v zakonodatel'stve," pp. 344-51; Ryndziunskii, Gorodskoe grazhdanstvo, pp. 52-61, as well as the discussion of this issue in other works of Klokman and Ryndziunskii.

[44]Of the examples cited above (n. 41), Istoriia Moskvy attempts to compare data on peasant registrants from 1764 and 1797 without taking into account that one figure represents a cumulative total and the other the number of registrants added in the preceding two or three years. Vartanov draws similar and equally dubious comparisons and also concludes incorrectly, on the basis of a misinterpreted document, that virtually no seigneurial peasants enlisted in the Moscow posad between 1742 and 1782. Iakovtsevskii identifies the peasant registrants listed in his data only as "trading peasants" and displays no awareness of their actual status.

the numbers, origins, economic status, occupations and other characteristics of peasants who enlisted in the urban classes, on the basis of
which it is possible in some measure to chart the patterns of this
population transfer. Analysis of the results of enlistment is preceded,
however, by a detailed exploration of the relevant legislation (Chapter
II), since a thorough understanding of these provisions is essential to
correct interpretation of the evidence.

This dissertation is based on research concerned primarily with
the area known as the Central Industrial Region, comprising a broad
ring of territory around the city of Moscow.[45] The indicated region is
a suitable place to begin an investigation of rural-urban migration,
since it contained one of the two urban giants of eighteenth-century
Russia as well as many of the country's older and more mature urban
settlements. It was the home of roughly one-third of the total posad
population of all "Great Russian" provinces and was also known for the
diversified economic activities of its peasant population.[46] However, a
brief chapter will be devoted to summarizing the available nationwide
data on enlistment in the urban classes, which will permit us to identify
major changes in the magnitude and distribution of enlistment which
occurred in the course of the century (Chapter III). The importance of

---

[45]In this study, the Central Industrial Region is defined as the
following post-1775 provinces or gubernii: Moscow, Vladimir, Kaluga,
Tver', Iaroslavl', Kostroma and Nizhnii Novgorod gubernii. Throughout
the dissertation reference is made exclusively to the post-1775 provincial units, rather than the very different units created by Peter I and
remaining in existence up to the 1775 reform of territorial administration, unless otherwise indicated.

[46]Areas such as the Ukraine, Belorussia and the Baltic provinces,
where the legal and institutional framework of urban life was much
different, are excluded from consideration here and elsewhere in the
dissertation.

Moscow as a commercial, industrial and population center and as an
attraction for migrating peasants, combined with the availability of
unusually rich and detailed information on the resulting influx, requires that a separate chapter be devoted to analyzing migration to
this one city (Chapter IV). In another chapter (Chapter V), the lesser
towns of Moscow guberniia and the towns of two other Central Industrial
provinces are surveyed in the lesser detail warranted by the available
sources and the level of peasant immigration recorded in them. These
three provinces, as will be demonstrated elsewhere, provide a sampling
of various zones within the region. In investigating peasant migration
to specific towns, we shall supplement the data on enlistment in the
urban classes with other relevant evidence, including information on
the degree and character of economic development in the towns involved,
on the participation of peasants in these urban economies and on the
development of commercial and industrial activities in the surrounding
countryside. The quantitative data are further supplemented by an
investigation of peasant immigration from the standpoint of individual
experience, based on case records and other documents relating to individual peasants who enlisted in the urban classes (Chapter VI). These
materials provide further insight into the processes by which peasants
were absorbed into the urban population in eighteenth-century Russia.

The quantitative data on enlistment in the urban classes presented
in this dissertation derive in one way or another from the census or
"revision" carried out periodically by the government for fiscal purposes.[47]

---

[47]The practices and results of the "revision" census have been explored by V. M. Kabuzan in Narodonaselenie Rossii v XVIII-pervoi polovine
XIX v. (po materialam revizii) (Moscow, 1963), esp. pp. 48-77, 94-104,
117-68.

Since the system of direct taxation during most of the eighteenth century was based on a poll tax assessed on males (regardless of age), population data from official sources are usually given in terms of male "souls," and most of the figures offered in this study are necessarily in those terms as well.[48] The most detailed demographic information is to be found in the depositions (skazki) submitted by individual households and the registers (perepisnye knigi) compiled from these depositions in each community. The voluminous character of these primary census materials has led to their neglect by historians, and even the documents on the Moscow posad, available in published form for nearly a century, have been sparingly used.[49] In this dissertation the Moscow census materials are explored extensively and form the basis of most of the data on enlistment of peasants in the Moscow posad.

During the intervals between revisions (which in the eighteenth century took place roughly every other decade), the government's data on the number of "souls" did not take into account changes due to births and deaths, but at least in the later years of the century changes resulting from the transfer of individuals from one population group to another were incorporated into the tax assessments in periodic updatings. The central fiscal institutions were advised of such changes in reports from the provincial treasuries (kazennye palaty), and these reports are a valuable source of data on peasant registrants and other newcomers to

---

[48]From the Third Revision (1762-5) onwards women were also counted in the census. However, documents reporting census results, particularly those intended for fiscal purposes, frequently ignore females.

[49]The materials from the five revisions conducted in the eighteenth century are in Materialy dlia istorii moskovskogo kupechestva (hereafter MDIMK), Vols. 1-4 (Moscow, 1883-6). Subsequent volumes contain materials from the later revisions.

the posad.[50] Many such reports, dating from the 1790's and relating to Moscow, Iaroslavl' and Nizhnii Novgorod gubernii, have been used in this dissertation.[51] Local urban administrations also prepared reports on changes in the number of taxpayers, and useful information has been drawn from a series of such reports covering the Iaroslavl' posad in the years 1789-1795.[52] Data on enlistment of peasants in the urban classes can sometimes be found in tax registers (okladnye knigi) for various territorial units.[53] Such data may also be reported in various other documents summarizing census results or discussing the formulation of tax assessments and the taxes to be paid by particular groups.[54]

---

[50]The submission of such reports by local chancelleries on a semi-annual basis was ordered by a 1774 decree. (See PSZ, Vol. 20, No. 14326.) This function was subsequently assumed by the provincial treasuries created as a result of the 1775 reform of territorial administration. In the research for this dissertation, however, no such reports dating from earlier than the 1790's were discovered.

[51]The reports are found in collections of fiscal documents relating to individual provinces and preserved in the files of the Senate's Expedition for the Audit of State Accounts (Ekspeditsiia dlia revizii gosudarstvennykh schetov). Tsentral'nyi gosudarstvennyi istoricheskii arkhiv, Leningrad (hereafter TsGIA), f. 558, op. 2, dd. 126, 128, 129 (Moscow guberniia); dd. 148, 149 (Nizhnii Novgorod guberniia); dd. 316, 317, 318 (Iaroslavl' guberniia).

[52]Gosudarstvennyi arkhiv Iaroslavskoi oblasti, Iaroslavl' (GAIaO), f. 501 (Iaroslavskaia gorodskaia duma), op. 1, dd. 13, 15, 18, 28, 31.

[53]The nationwide tax register of 1800 provides information on the number of crown peasants enlisted in the urban classes of each province since the Fifth Revision (1795). TsGIA, f. 571 (Ministerstvo finansov, Departament raznykh podatei i sborov), op. 9, d. 1 ("Okladnaia kniga po vsemu gosudarstvu o chisle dush po piatoi revizii po 1 genvariia 1800 g."). Also used in this dissertation is a series of tax registers for individual districts of Iaroslavl' guberniia, dating from 1783. TsGIA, f. 558, op. 2, dd. 303-314.

[54]Gosudarstvennaia publichnaia biblioteka im. Saltykova-Shchedrina, Leningrad, Rukopisnyi otdel (hereafter GPB RO), Ermitazhnoe sobranie, No. 242 ("Vedomost' o chisle dush po gorodam," 1767); Tsentral'nyi gosudarstvennyi arkhiv drevnikh aktov, Moscow (hereafter TsGADA), f.248 (Senat, 1 departament), kn. 3676, ll. 769-791 ob. ("Vedomost' o chisle dush po nyneshnei revizii..." 1765-7); kn. 4109, ll. 209-25.

The quantitative evidence on enlistment of peasants in the urban classes is supplemented by case records on individual registrants, found mostly in the files of local and provincial institutions of Iaroslavl'.[55] The Moscow census materials also provide valuable information on individual registrants. The principal source on the legislative history of enlistment is of course the Complete Laws of the Russian Empire, which is already familiar to the reader from citations earlier in this introductory chapter.[56] The above archival documents on individual registrants and on the number of "souls" in each tax category provide additional references to relevant decrees and legislative issues.

For information on the economic life of towns and rural districts and the participation of peasants in these local economies, this study relies to a large extent on descriptive surveys, of which a great many were compiled in the second half of the eighteenth century. The materials used most extensively here derive from the official series of "topographical descriptions" (topograficheskie opisaniia) of individual provinces drawn up in the last quarter of the century and associated with the contemporaneous work of the General Land Survey.[57] In addition to describing the topographical and physical characteristics of the territory involved, these surveys offer much valuable information on the development

---

[55]TsGADA, f. 455 (Iaroslavskaia provintsiial'naia kantseliariia); f. 807 (Iaroslavskii gorodovoi magistrat); GAIaO, f. 55 (Iaroslavskii gorodovoi magistrat); f. 100 (Iaroslavskaia kazennaia palata).

[56]Polnoe sobranie zakonov Rossiiskoi imperii s 1649 g. (PSZ), 45 vols. (St. Petersburg, 1839-43).

[57]On the origins and characteristics of the "topographical descriptions," see N. L. Rubinshtein, "Topograficheskie opisaniia namestnichestv i gubernii XVIII v.--pamiatniki geograficheskogo i ekonomicheskogo izucheniia Rossii," Voprosy geografii, Vol. 31 (1953), pp. 39-89.

of trade, industry and agriculture and the occupations of both urban and
rural inhabitants. The manuscripts of these descriptive surveys survive
in various archives, often in several versions, differing in the date of
composition, the amount of detail accorded to particular subjects and
the figures given for the numbers of inhabitants, settlements, structures,
industrial enterprises, commercial facilities and so forth.[58] In addition,
quite a few of these surveys have found their way into print in complete
or abridged form.[59] The "topographical descriptions" were also the most
important source for the "geographical dictionaries" and similar
publications issued around the beginning of the nineteenth century
and were drawn upon by the authors of various "statistical descriptions"
of particular provinces.[60] Another valuable source of information on
local economies and particularly on the commercial and industrial

[58]This dissertation makes use of "topographical descriptions" found
in various fondy of GPB RO and in Tsentral'nyi gosudarstvennyi voenno-
istoricheskii arkhiv, Moscow (TsGVIA), f. Voenno-uchenogo arkhiva (VUA).
(See source list at end of dissertation.) Important holdings of these
manuscripts can also be found in Arkhiv Leningradskogo otdeleniia
Instituta istorii Akademii nauk SSSR (LOII), f. 36.

[59]The following are used in this dissertation: Sostoianie stolichnogo goroda Moskvy, 1785 g. (Moscow, 1879); Topograficheskoe opisanie
Iaroslavskogo namestnichestva, sochinennoe v Iaroslavle v 1794 g.
(Iaroslavl', 1794); "Opisanie gorodov Nizhegorodskogo namestnichestva,"
in Sobranie sochinenii, vybrannykh iz mesiatseslovov, Vol. 6 (St. Petersburg, 1790), pp. 242-58.

[60]The following are used in this dissertation: A. Shchekatov,
Geograficheskii slovar' Rossiiskogo gosudarstva, Vols. 1-7 (Moscow,
1801-9); E. Ziablovskii, Zemleopisanie Rossiiskoi Imperii dlia vsekh
sostoianii, Vols. 3-4 (St. Petersburg, 1810); S. Chernov, Statisticheskoe
opisanie Moskovskoi gubernii 1811 g. (Moscow, 1812); K. German, Statisticheskoe opisanie Iaroslavskoi gubernii (St. Petersburg, 1808). On the
sources used in the works of Ziablovskii and Shchekatov, see Rubinshtein,
"Topograficheskie opisaniia," p. 67; L. V. Milov, "K istorii sozdaniia
'Geograficheskogo slovaria' Afanasiia Shchekatova," Arkheograficheskii
ezhegodnik za 1968 g. (Moscow, 1970), pp. 166-83.

activities of the peasantry is the "economic notes" (ekonomicheskie primechaniia) of the General Land Survey, which provide individual descriptions of each rural settlement in the territory covered.[61] However, because of the voluminous nature of this material and the short time available for archival research, it has been possible to make only limited use of this source.[62] A variety of other published descriptions and travel accounts have also been consulted.[63]

Valuable information on the involvement of peasants in commerce and industry can be found in the complaints about these activities submitted by urban communes to the Legislative Commission of 1767. These documents, consisting of "instructions" (nakazy) of the communes to the deputies representing them and the statements of these deputies during sessions of the commission, were published by the Imperial Russian Historical Society and have already been referred to several times in this introductory chapter.[64] A few years earlier, the urban communes had submitted similar complaints in response to the request of the Commerce Commission for information on the "burdens and needs" of the posad population.[65] The materials collected by the Commerce Commission also

---

[61]See Milov, Issledovaniia ob "Ekonomicheskikh primechaniiakh," Ch. 1-4.

[62]In the research for this dissertation, ekonomicheskie primechaniia for Iaroslavl' and Dmitrov uezdy were examined. GPB RO, Sobranie A. Titova, No. 1716 (Iaroslavl' uezd); TsGIA, f. 1350 (Mezhevoi departament), op. 312, dd. 198-199 (Iaroslavl' uezd); TsGVIA, f. VUA, No. 18859, ch. 1 (Dmitrov uezd).

[63]See source list (Part III).

[64]Sb. IRIO, Vols. 8, 93, 107, 134, etc.

[65]TsGADA, f. 397, dd. 441, 445.

contain important data on the economic stratification and occupational
distribution of the posad population in each town.[66]

The records of local administrative institutions are another source
of information on economic activity. Useful materials were found in the
surviving files of the Iaroslavl' provincial chancellery (provintsial'-
naia kantseliariia) and town magistracy (magistrat), including registries
of cargo vessels arriving at Iaroslavl' with grain and other goods (in
which peasants are sometimes identified as the owners of such vessels),
records of suits for non-payment of promissory notes (in which peasants
were involved both as debtors and as creditors), and petitions from
posad members mentioning various economic activities of peasants in the
town.[67] The extensive excerpts from documents of local and provincial
institutions of Nizhnii Novgorod published by V. I. Snezhnevskii are of
great value as a source of information on commercial and indistrial
activity in the towns and villages of Nizhnii Novgorod guberniia.[68]
Finally, the documents published in the collection Materialy po istorii
krest'ianskoi promyshlennosti, dealing with the involvement of peasants
in various industrial pursuits, are a major source for this dissertation.[69]

---

[66]A digest of this information has recently been published in Knabe,
"Die Struktur der russischen Posadgemeinden," pp. 300-63.

[67]TsGADA, f. 455, op. 1, dd. 409, 730, 836; f. 807, op. 1, dd. 44,
546. The files of the Iaroslavl' magistracy contain many additional
documents dealing with suits for non-payment of promissory notes. These
are not used in this dissertation but will be explored in a separate
article.

[68]V. I. Snezhnevskii, "Opis' delam i dokumentam Nizhegorodskogo
gorodovogo magistrata (1787-1861)," Deistviia Nizhegorodskoi gubernskoi
uchenoi arkhivnoi komissii (hereafter Deistviia NGUAK), Vol. 2, No. 15
(Nizhnii Novgorod, 1895), pp. 3-120; Snezhnevskii, "Opis' zhurnalam
Nizhegorodskogo namestnicheskogo pravleniia za 1781-83 gg.," Deistviia
NGUAK, Vol. 3 (Nizhnii Novgorod, 1898), pp. 89-192; Snezhnevskii,
"Opis' delam Nizhegorodskogo namestnicheskogo pravleniia (za 1790-1799
gg.)," Deistviia NGUAK, Vol. 3, pp. 193-269.

[69]MPIKP, Vols. 1-2 (Moscow-Leningrad, 1935-50).

In addition to the above primary sources, this study draws for back-ground information and factual support on the works of many Russian historians of the pre-revolutionary and Soviet periods dealing with the social and economic history of early modern Russia.

CHAPTER II: LEGISLATION ON ENLISTMENT OF PEASANTS IN THE URBAN CLASSES

The legislative issue of enlistment in the urban classes was an
outgrowth of the state's interest in strengthening the traditional role
of the posad as an "obligated community" (tiaglaia obshchina), responsible to the state for a specified set of taxes and services and relying
on income from commerce authorized and protected by the state. To insure
fulfilment of these obligations, the state took steps to maintain and
if possible expand the membership of the posad and to curtail its competitors. Efforts in this direction on the part of the Muscovite grand
princes are discernible as early as the mid-fifteenth century, and such
measures continued to be applied, albeit somewhat sporadically, during
the succeeding two centuries.[1] These long-standing tendencies culminated
in the Ulozhenie (Law Code) of 1649, which made membership in the posad
hereditary and immutable and established the principle that with a few
specified exceptions "only the Sovereign's /urban/ taxpayers" had the
right to operate commercial and industrial enterprises in the towns.[2]

If the law was to be enforced, outsiders engaged in the restricted
activities had to be either made members of the posad or prevented from

---

[1] S. M. Kashtanov, "The Centralized State and Feudal Immunities in
Russia," Slavonic and East European Review, Vol. 49, No. 115 (April
1971), p. 240; P. P. Smirnov, Posadskie liudi i ikh klassovaia bor'ba
do serediny XVII v., Vol. 1 (Moscow-Leningrad, 1947), pp. 104-59, 343-
454.

[2] Polnoe sobranie zakonov Rossiiskoi imperii s 1649 g. (hereafter
cited as PSZ), Vol. 1, No. 1 (Sobornoe ulozhenie), Ch. 19. According
to the Ulozhenie, several categories of "enlisted" or "salaried" military servitors (strel'tsy, cossacks, dragoons) had the right to trade
without assumption of urban obligations. They were responsible for
customs duties and obrok (quitrent) for the use of trade facilities
(Art. 4, 11). Peasants had the right to bring in "all kinds of goods"
from the countryside and sell them in the gostinnyi dvor or "from carts
and boats" (Art. 17).

pursuing their enterprises. The Ulozhenie, although ordering the confiscation and compulsory incorporation into the posad of large numbers
of trading peasants living in towns or in adjacent seigneurial settlements, did not allow voluntary enlistment in the urban commune. It
sought instead to establish a permanent and immutable boundary between
the urban and rural populations: henceforth, peasants were forbidden
to encroach on the commercial occupations and enterprises assigned to
the town population or to settle in towns, except as hired laborers or
household servants.[3]

However, the government's administrative network was not equal to
the task of preventing unauthorized infiltration of the urban economy,
and the presence of trading peasants continued to be a prominent feature
of town life in the second half of the seventeenth century.[4] Some of
these migrants passed inconspicuously into the town population by reaching
their own accommodation with the posad authorities, agreeing to pay an
obrok (quitrent) or even the entire complex of urban obligations, without resolving the question of future relations with their masters or
provoking the intervention of the state.[5] Such settlers were often

---

[3]Ibid., Ch. 19, Art. 1, 2, 5, 7-9, 14-17.

[4]PSZ, Vol. 1, No. 35; Vol. 2, Nos. 998, 1123, 1138; Akty istoricheskie, sobrannye i izdannye Arkheograficheskoiu komissieiu (hereafter AI),
Vol. 4 (St. Petersburg, 1842), No. 29; Vol. 5 (St. Petersburg, 1842),
Nos. 226, 228; A. G. Man'kov, Razvitie krepostnogo prava v Rossii vo
vtoroi polovine XVII v. (Moscow-Leningrad, 1962), pp. 261-306; L. V.
Zaborovskii, "Bor'ba posadov Vladimira i Suzdalia s belomestsami v XVII
v.," in Goroda feodal'noi Rossii (Moscow, 1966), pp. 239-246; A. M.
Orekhov, "Iz istorii bor'by nizhegorodskogo posada protiv belomestsov,"
in Goroda feodal'noi Rossii, pp. 247-55.

[5]Man'kov, pp. 294, 301, 310, 316.

numbered among the posad population in the subsequent cadastral surveys.
In other cases, the peasant settlers resisted the claims of the posad,
relying on the protection of a powerful lord.

Unauthorized urban settlement could come to the government's
attention in a variety of ways: through petitions from the posad population protesting against the illegal competition of peasant interlopers,
through attempts by lords to recover such peasants, or in the course of
recurrent campaigns against runaway serfs. When this occurred, the
government's usual response was to repeat the confiscatory tactics of
the Ulozhenie, ordering prior migrants permanently bound to the posad
while forbidding any further migration. Such decrees initially were
applied to individual groups of peasants or particular towns, but
between 1685 and 1693 they were extended to many additional localities
and finally made applicable to all towns. Customarily the decrees
specified that peasants who had been included in the posad population
by the most recent cadastral surveys or who had arrived before a certain
date were entitled to permanent posad membership, although such criteria
as long residence in tne town, possession of taxable urban property,
involvement in urban commerce, and marriage into urban families, all of
which acts were prohibited by the Ulozhenie, were sometimes mentioned
as well. Often no distinction was made between runaways and peasants
who had the permission of their lords to leave the village, as long as
the former were not the subject of long-standing complaints by their
masters. Seigneurial rights to both kinds of migrants were abrogated
and all ties between master and serf were severed on the ground that
the lords "had not petitioned for many years" about their missing peasants.
Unwilling either to deprive the urban economy of productive elements

firmly entrenched in it or to relax curbs on population movement, the
government was brought to the paradoxical policy of legalizing retroactively violations of the Ulozhenie while reiterating the same unen-
forceable provisions.[6]

The government of Peter I saw the need for a departure from these
haphazard practices. In one of his earliest attempts at administrative
reform, Peter sought to improve the institutions of urban government,
for the equal benefit of the town population and the state treasury.
A decree of 1699 created the Burmistrskaia palata (Chamber of the Burgo-
master), later renamed the Ratusha (Rathaus), as a central institution
of urban government and placed it at the head of a system of local
urban administrations staffed by members of the town population itself.
The towns were relieved of the notoriously corrupt rule of appointed
local governors (voevody).[7] Contemporaneous legislation sought to provide for the expansion of the posad through the inclusion of suitable
elements from other population categories, especially the peasantry.
On January 1, 1699, the government authorized crown, church and seigneurial peasants who "desire" to live in Moscow for the purpose of
commercial activity to register in the Moscow posad, and later that
year another decree ordered that wealthy trading peasants from the court
domains be drafted into the posad population, "each one wherever suitable."[8] Subsequent legislation markedly narrowed the criteria for

---

[6] PSZ, Vol. 1, No. 307; Vol. 2, Nos. 980, 981, 982, 998, 1147; Vol.
3, No. 1471; AI, Vol. 5, No. 226; Man'kov, pp. 264-99.

[7] PSZ, Vol. 3, No. 1674; Ocherki istorii SSSR, period feodalizma:
Rossiia v pervoi chetverti XVIII v. (Moscow, 1954), pp. 294-95, 319.

[8] PSZ, Vol. 3, Nos. 1666, 1718.

enlistment in the urban commune, however. According to the decree of November 24, 1699, only those peasants who already lived in towns and possessed stores or craft workshops there, or were engaged in itinerant trade (ot"ezzhie torgi), were eligible for inclusion, and the government demanded documentary proof that the applicants met these qualifications. Those who did not "wish" to belong to the posad were again barred from engaging in these enterprises and were ordered to "live under their lords." Peasants who sold goods hauled in from the countryside wholesale, as authorized by the Ulozhenie, were not subject to these provisions. To curb the eagerness of urban communities to induct new taxpayers whether they were qualified or not, the government enacted tight controls over the process of enlistment in the posad. Such enlistment could be effected only by decree of the Ratusha, which acted after reviewing reports on suitable candidates submitted by the local urban authorities.[9]

In considering this early Petrine legislation on the incorporation of trading peasants into the posad, A. L. Shapiro has observed that it contains "many ambiguities," the most blatant of which is that no mention is made of the wishes of landlords or of their future relations with serfs who were admitted to the posad.[10] Responding to Shapiro, A. G. Man'kov has pointed out that this omission should be understood

[9]PSZ, Vol. 3, No. 1723; Vol. 4, Nos. 1775, 1819. Man'kov has established through archival research that the text of the decree of November 24, 1699, is not complete as given in No. 1723 and that the complete text contains the same additional provisions as are found in the subsequent decrees cited (Man'kov, p. 313). These laws also authorized qualified individuals from other population groups to enlist in the posad.

[10]A. L. Shapiro, "Krest'ianskaia torgovlia i krest'ianskie podriady v petrovskoe vremia," Istoricheskie zapiski, Vol. 27 (1948), p. 231.

in the context of the seventeenth-century practice of confiscating urbanized trading peasants without reference to the interests of their erstwhile masters.[11] However, continuation of these confiscatory practices, the severity of which had been mitigated by their extraordinary character, was not compatible with voluntary registration in the posad unless the government contemplated a frontal assault on the interests of serfowners. This fact perhaps explains the government's retreat from the decree of January 1, 1699, which seemed to incorporate the principle of voluntary registration on a widespread basis, to the more restrictive norms of the November 24 decree. The latter measure, unlike comparable seventeenth-century enactments, did not include a cut-off date after which settlement in the town would no longer be sanctioned or an explicit prohibition against further settlement, but it did apply chiefly to peasants who had already become entrenched in the urban economy, in violation of the law, and it thus retained to some extent the character of an exceptional act rectifying a situation not in accord with the prescriptions of the Ulozhenie. The government had not yet devised a suitable compromise between the interests of serfowners and those of the urban commune regarding the fate of trading peasants, and it was on just such a compromise that an ongoing system of voluntary enlistment would have to be based.

Further development in this direction was interrupted by Peter's experiment with "free trade" (svobodnyi torg), which opened full commercial rights to all categories of the population without membership in the posad. The first signs of this change in policy appeared in

---

[11]Man'kov, pp. 315-16.

1709, when peasants who did not "wish" to register in the posad were authorized to participate in urban trade nevertheless if they paid a ten percent tax on the value of their enterprises (equivalent to the desiataia den'ga or "tenth penny" tax paid by posad merchants).[12] In 1711 the government granted "all ranks" the right to trade "everywhere in all commodities" in return for payment of the desiataia den'ga and the established customs duties.[13] In 1714 it was further specified that peasants taking advantage of these provisions were subject to all urban taxes but not to the burdensome communal services of the posad population. Such peasants were also reminded that they remained responsible for "all seigneurial dues..., in equality with their fellow peasants."[14]

The policy of "free trade" was a failure, however, because it did not take into account the connection between the burdensome tax and service obligations imposed on the posad population and protection of its sources of income. This relationship had long been at the root of state policy on the apportionment of commercial rights, but the Petrine government now withdrew the protection while its demands for revenue and services continued to escalate. As in other periods when government defense of its economic prerogatives weakened, the posad began to disintegrate and the number of urban taxpayers contracted sharply. Positions in the urban economy formerly controlled by posad members

---

[12]PSZ, Vol. 4, No. 2220. This decree also renewed the authorization for enlistment in the posad and specified possession of 100 rubles in capital as the criterion of eligibility.

[13]PSZ, Vol. 4, Nos. 2327, 2349, 2433.

[14]PSZ, Vol. 5, No. 2770.

were taken over by outsiders, while many townsmen found membership in
the urban commune no longer sufficiently advantageous to compensate for
its burdens and sought to escape into other population categories, where
they would be free of urban service obligations and could more easily
evade the taxes on trade.[15]

The measures initially adopted by Peter's government to cope with
this situation resembled those employed by his seventeenth-century predecessors. Prohibitions against transfer of urban taxpayers to other
population groups were reiterated.[16] Runaway townsmen were hunted down
and returned to the posad, while commercially active elements not belonging to the urban commune were involuntarily attached to it.[17]
But rather than continuing to rely on such makeshift expedients, the
Petrine government sought to devise a more viable urban policy and in

---

[15]Of 7325 taxpayers registered in Moscow in 1701, only 2834 remained in 1716, and by 1721 another 1100 had disappeared. The causes
of this attrition were heavy conscription and unauthorized transfer to
other population groups, principally the factory labor force and peasant
communities. (E. I. Zaozerskaia, "Moskovskii posad pri Petre I,"
Voprosy istorii, 1947, No. 9, pp. 21-24; Ia. E. Vodarskii, "Chislennost'
i razmeshcheniia posadskogo naseleniia v Rossii vo vtoroi polovine XVII
v.," in Goroda feodal'noi Rossii, p. 278.)

Many aspects of Petrine rule weighed heavily on the urban commune
(as on everyone else), but a number of contemporary observers attributed
its disastrous condition to the unbridled competition and "injury" from
non-posad traders. (See N. P. Pavlov-Sil'vanskii, Proekty reform v
zapiskakh sovremennikov Petra Velikogo /St. Petersburg, 1897/, pp. 124-
26.)

[16]PSZ, Vol. 5, Nos. 2794, 2812.

[17]Of 377 individuals identified as having abandoned the Moscow posad
and joined peasant communities, 253 were recaptured in 1716 and returned
to the posad. Also in 1716, 1776 individuals active in Moscow commerce
were ordered added to the posad. Most were trading peasants of the suburban court villages of Pokrovskoe and Taininskoe and other settlements.
Zaozerskaia, "Moskovskii posad," p. 27; Istoriia Moskvy, Vol. 2 (Moscow,
1953), p. 66.

the closing phase of the reign returned to the direction laid down in 1699-1700. The autonomous network of urban governmental institutions staffed by members of the posad, which had been allowed to lapse after 1708, was resurrected.[18] Now called magistracies (magistraty), these institutions were responsible not to local and provincial governors but to a central urban institution, the Chief Magistracy in Petersburg.[19] The government sought to improve the economic organization of the posad through the introduction of merchant guilds (gil'dii) and craft guilds (tsekhi).[20] The exclusive rights of the posad in urban trade were re-confirmed.[21]

The return to a policy of limiting full commercial rights to members of the posad revived the need for suitable procedures to encourage the absorption of traders and craft producers from other groups into the officially recognized mercantile classes. Early in 1722 the newly created Chief Magistracy addressed itself to the problem, suggesting a confirmation of the relevant decrees of 1699-1700. The

---

[18]In 1708 Peter had divided the empire into eight large gubernii, each headed by a governor who received authority over all aspects of government in his territory. At the uezd level, the voevody, renamed komendanty, were again given authority over urban administration. The Ratusha lost its role as a central institution of urban government and continued to function mainly as a local Moscow institution. (See Ocherki istorii SSSR, period feodalizma: Rossiia v pervoi chetverti XVIII v., pp. 295, 320-23; Iu. R. Klokman, "Gorod v zakonodatel'stve russkogo absoliutizma vo vtoroi polovine XVII--XVIII v.," in Absoliutizm v Rossii (Moscow, 1964), p. 333.

[19]PSZ, Vol. 6, No. 3708.

[20]PSZ, Vol. 5, No. 3318 (Art. 19); Vol. 6, No. 3708 (Ch. 7), No. 3980.

[21]PSZ, Vol. 7, Nos. 4312, 4398; see also M. Ia. Volkov, "Materialy pervoi revizii kak istochnik po istorii torgovli i promyshlennosti Rossii pervoi chetverti XVIII v.," Problemy istochnikovedeniia, Vol. 11 (1963), pp. 301-05.

Senate, with the personal participation of Peter I, responded to this proposal with a "clarification" of the earlier decrees which became known as the "decree of April 13, 1722."[22] According to this enactment, trading peasants were "free" to enlist in the urban classes if they possessed a capital of 500 rubles, or 300 rubles in the case of those engaged in transit trade "toward the port of St. Petersburg." Seigneurial permission was not required for registration in the posad. The registrants were subject to continued taxation as peasants and remained responsible for payment of the "customary" dues to their lords, but they were not to be charged increased dues "according to their wealth." The decree thus created a category of persons who were simultaneously members of both the posad and the peasantry. In subsequent documents these registrants are sometimes referred to as kupechestvuiushchie krest'iane, a term which might be translated roughly as "mercantile peasants."[23]

The decree of April 13, 1722, remained the basic law on enlistment of peasants in the urban classes during the succeeding half-century. It has been stated repeatedly in the literature that in the eighteenth

---

[22]PSZ, Vol. 7, No. 4312. The decree is printed under the date September 27, 1723, identified as the date of publication, but with the notation that the legislation "actually appeared in 1722." In subsequent documents the provisions described are usually referred to as "the decree of April 13, 1722." (For example, see PSZ, Vol. 11, No. 8608; Vol. 12, Nos. 9216, 9372, 9383; Vol. 15, No. 11288.) The archival research of M. Ia. Volkov has confirmed the fact that these proposals were introduced, discussed and acted upon in 1722 (Volkov, "Materialy pervoi revizii," pp. 300-01).

[23]PSZ, Vol. 20, No. 14326; Gosudarstvennaia publichnaia biblioteka im. Saltykova-Shchedrina, Leningrad, Rukopisnyi otdel (hereafter GPB RO), Ermitazhnoe sobranie, No. 242, ll. 1-2; Tsentral'nyi gosudarstvennyi arkhiv drevnikh aktov, Moscow (hereafter TsGADA), f. 248 (1 departament Senata), kn. 3676, ll. 769-791 ob.

century peasants registering in the _posad_ had to pay "double taxation" (_dvoinoi oklad_) until the next census or "revision," after which they were released from peasant status and held responsible only for urban obligations.[24] In reality, such a practice came into existence only in the last two decades of the century. Under the 1722 law, the regis- trants remained in an intermediate status, responsible for obligations as both peasants and townsmen, not until the next revision but perma- nently. The decree committed them "and their posterity" to payment of peasant taxes and seigneurial dues in perpetuity, with no provision for future release from these burdens. In 1745, at the time of the Second Revision, the Senate considered the fate of peasants who had registered previously in the urban classes and determined that under the 1722 law they had to remain attached to the peasantry as before.[25] The permanent character of this dual status is also reflected in several other decrees and in census documents, while in a dozen relevant decrees from the period before the reign of Catherine II not a word can be found on release from peasant status after the next revision.[26] Nor is it

---

[24]Klokman, "Gorod v zakonodatel'stve," pp. 344-51; P. G. Ryndziunskii, "Soslovno-podatnaia reforma 1775 g. i gorodskoe naselenie," in Obshchestvo i gosudarstvo feodal'noi Rossii (Moscow, 1975), pp. 92-95; Istoriia Moskvy, Vol. 2, pp. 318-19; G. L. Vartanov, "Kupechestvo i torguiushchee krest' ianstvo tsentral'noi chasti Evropeiskoi Rossii vo vtoroi polovine XVIII v.," Uchenye zapiski Leningradskogo gosudarstvennogo pedagogicheskogo instituta in A. I. Gertsena, Vol. 229 (1962), p. 184; J. Michael Hittle, The Service City: State and Townsmen in Russia, 1600-1800 (Cambridge, Mass., 1979), pp. 180-81. The same inaccuracies are reiterated in various other works of Klokman and Ryndziunskii.

[25]PSZ, Vol. 12, No. 9216.

[26]See particularly PSZ, Vol. 7, No. 4566; Vol. 15, No. 11426. Census materials show clearly that the peasant registrants were retained in a separate category and continued to be held responsible for peasant obligations in the aftermath of a new revision. See GPB RO, Ermitazhoe sobranie, No. 242, ll. 1-95; TsGADA, f. 248, kn. 3676, ll. 769-791 ob.;

entirely accurate to say that these registrants were subject to double taxation. The 1722 decree stated only that they were to pay the peasant "soul tax" of 80 kopecks. A surcharge of 40 kopecks, payable through the urban communes, was introduced by a decree of 1724, bringing the total soul tax paid by mercantile peasants up to the level owed by the posad population (120 kopecks).[27] In 1747 this surcharge was raised to 50 kopecks in view of the fact that the peasant soul tax had been lowered to 70 kopecks, albeit more than twenty years earlier.[28] Mercantile peasants were also subject to urban communal services, although new registrants were often exempted from these services for an initial period.[29]

The decree of April 13, 1722, was clearly designed to make possible the enlistment of private and ecclesiastical serfs in the posad without complete abrogation of seigneurial rights, but its cumbersome provisions were also applied to peasants of the court domains and to "black" (chernososhnye) state peasants, as well as to church peasants after the

Materialy dlia istorii moskovskogo kupechestva, Vol. 1 (Moscow, 1883), "Perepisnaia kniga 1747 g.," pp. 10, 15-16, 21, 64; Vol. 2 (Moscow, 1885), "Svodnye vedomosti po III revizii," pp. 23-24, 34, 55, 62, etc. Some urban communes protested to the Legislative Commission of 1767 about the fact that peasants who had registered in the posad as far back as the time of Peter I, and their descendants, continued to be held responsible for peasant obligations. For example, see Sbornik Imperatorskogo russkogo istoricheskogo obshchestva (hereafter Sb. IRIO), Vol. 8 (St. Petersburg, 1871), pp. 331-32; Vol. 93 (St. Petersburg, 1894), p. 421.

[27]PSZ, Vol. 7, No. 4566.

[28]PSZ, Vol. 12, No. 9440.

[29]A. A. Kizevetter, Posadskaia obshchina v Rossii XVIII stoletiia (Moscow, 1903), pp. 337-38.

secularization of 1764 converted them to state "economic" peasants.[30]

Like the serfs, members of these categories remained permanently bound

to peasant status and obligations following enlistment in the posad.

As the Chief Court Chancellery observed in instructions to its estate

administrators, registrants from the court peasantry and their descendants

were "obligated to pay the soul tax, court obligations and communal dues

to their former villages" in perpetuity.[31] The advent of a new census

had no effect on these requirements--in 1776, the court estate adminis-

tration was still demanding dues from peasant families which had en-

listed in the urban classes as early as 1725.[32] Such registrants

sometimes petitioned the authorities for release from peasant status

and obligations, but these petitions were usually ignored.[33] Even

registrants from the small group of court peasants known as "falconers"

(sokol'i pomytchiki), which had the duty of supplying birds of prey for

the imperial hunt, were held responsible for their falconry services

"forever".[34]

---

[30]PSZ, Vol. 11, No. 8608; Vol. 12, Nos. 9216, 9372; Vol. 15, No. 11177; Vol. 18, No. 13326; TsGADA, f. 455 (Iaroslavskaia provintsial'- naia kantseliariia), op. 2, d. 34; E. I. Indova, "Rol' dvortsovoi derevni pervoi poloviny XVIII v. v formirovanii russkogo kupechestva," Istoricheskie zapiski, Vol. 68 (1961), pp. 194-96.

[31]E. I. Indova, Iu. A. Tikhonov, A. A. Preobrazhenskii, "Klassovaia bor'ba krest'ianstva i stanovlenie burzhuaznykh otnoshenii v Rossii," Voprosy istorii, 1964, No. 12, p. 37.

[32]Kizevetter, Posadskaia obshchina, p. 46; Indova, "Rol' dvortsovoi derevni," p. 194.

[33]Indova, "Rol' dvortsovoi derevni," p. 195; S. I. Volkov, Krest'iane dvortsovykh vladenii Podmoskov'ia v seredine XVIII v. (Moscow, 1959), pp. 61-62.

[34]PSZ, Vol. 15, No. 11177.

In the decree of April 13, 1722, as in the 1699-1700 laws which it "clarified," the authorization to register in the posad applied to peasants who already lived in towns and possessed enterprises there. Those who lived in villages were to "sell their goods to urban merchants and not themselves trade in the towns."[35] In 1723, however, the Senate decided that residence in the town was not a prerequisite for posad membership and that "mercantile peasants" could continue to live in villages even after registration.[36] In 1747 the government once again reversed itself on this question, holding that possession of the required capital alone was not sufficient qualification for enlistment. Only those possessing houses, shops or enterprises in the town were eligible, and it once again appeared that a pattern of clearly illegal activity was a prerequisite for entry into the urban commune.[37]

On the other hand, large numbers of peasants who lived in towns or in nearby villages which were essentially suburbs of the town, and who gained their living from small-scale trade or hired labor, were excluded from eligibility by the large capital requirement, even though they differed little in their occupations from the majority of posad members. They were consequently forced to go on seeking their livelihood on the margins of legality, suffering periodic repression as a result of efforts to enforce the exclusive rights of the posad. Occasionally particular groups of peasants received exceptional treatment. In 1742,

---

[35]PSZ, Vol. 7, No. 4312. Apparently peasants engaged in conveying goods to seaports (torgovlia k portam) were allowed to register regardless of their place of residence.

[36]PSZ, Vol. 7, No. 4336.

[37]PSZ, Vol. 12, No. 9372.

for example, the Senate discussed a petition from a large group of court peasants living in Moscow or in the adjacent court villages. These peasants pointed out that the income from which they paid their taxes and dues was derived from small-scale commerce involving a capital of 100 rubles or less and complained that the Moscow municipal authorities were attempting to suppress this trade. Since they could not meet the requirements for enlistment in the posad, the petitioners proposed that they be authorized to engage in trade in return for payment of the 40-kopeck tax but without assessment of other urban obligations. The Senate initially rejected these pleas, deciding that enlistment in the posad must take place strictly in accordance with the decree of April 13, 1722, and that those who did not "wish" to register under these terms must not own urban property or participate in urban business activity.[38] Subsequently these peasants resorted to forcible resistance in defense of their interests. In 1745 they reopened their enterprises in defiance of the law and "by gathering in large crowds" (mnogoliudstvom) prevented officials of the Moscow magistracy from closing them. Eventually, with the backing of the Chief Court Chancellery, these peasants obtained the right to "live in the posad without exclusion from the peasantry" in return for fulfillment of the obligations of both categories.[39]

Another case which contravened the established norms involved peasants of Blagoveshchenskaia Sloboda, a court settlement adjacent to the town of Nizhnii Novgorod which later passed into the hands of a private lord. In 1724, at the time of the First Revision, these peasants were assessed the urban 120-kopeck tax rather than the peasant soul tax

[38]PSZ, Vol. 11, No. 8608.

[39]Indova et al., "Klassovaia bor'ba," p. 38.

on the ground that they were involved in trade and industry. In all other respects, they remained subject to peasant rather than urban obligations. They did not belong to the Nizhnii Novgorod posad and did not participate in its communal service obligations or contribute to local revenues. This anomalous situation apparently continued for half a century.[40]

Peasants who qualified for posad membership under the law of April 13, 1722, cannot have been pleased with the prospect of continued unfree status and responsibility for rural obligations, but these provisions also involved substantial disadvantages from the serfowners' point of view. According to the law, lords could not prevent a qualified serf from enlisting in the posad, nor were they allowed to raise dues above the "customary" level and thus profit from the money-making activities of the enlisted serf. In one of the few instances of state-imposed limitation on seigneurial prerogatives in eighteenth-century Russia, the person, income and property of mercantile peasants were thereby removed from the control of their lords. This limitation was not invariably observed. According to the deputy from the town of Zaraisk to the Legislative Commission of 1767, some mercantile peasants were being forced by their "commands" (nachal'stva) to make heightened dues payments.[41] The court estate administration in particular

---

[40]M. Ia. Volkov, "Materialy pervoi revizii," pp. 303-04; Iu. R. Klokman, Sotsial'no-ekonomicheskaia istoriia russkogo goroda, vtoraia polovina XVIII v. (Moscow, 1967), pp. 270-72; TsGADA, f. 397 (Komissiia o kommertsii), d. 441, 1. 215. In the 1780's the government purchased Blagoveshchenskaia Sloboda from its owner and added it to the Nizhnii Novgorod posad.

[41]Sb. IRIO, Vol. 8, p. 141.

disregarded the provision that mercantile peasants should be charged
only the "customary" dues and collected payments "in proportion to their
commercial enterprises."[42]

However, the physical absence of these peasants from their villages
and their membership in an urban commune attenuated the authority of the
lords and "commands" and sometimes made it difficult to enforce even
those obligations which were sanctioned by the 1722 decree. Mercantile
peasants, understandably resentful of the persistence of rural taxes
and dues, took advantage of the situation to evade payment of them, and
the urban magistracies, which were supposed to enforce these payments,
were mainly interested in collecting urban obligations and not eager to
assist in the imposition of competing claims.[43] Even so powerful a lord
as Arsenii Matseevich, Metropolitan of Rostov and Iaroslavl', found it
difficult to collect taxes and dues from 26 of his peasants who were
registered in the St. Petersburg kupechestvo. In 1762, after an appeal
to the Chief Magistracy failed to bring the desired results, his officials had to petition the Senate in order to obtain satisfaction.[44]
Court peasants registered in the posad also resisted payment of rural
obligations. In the mid-1760's the court estate administration reported that 320 households of peasants from its estates in the Moscow
area, the inhabitants of which had enlisted in the Moscow posad, owed
arrears in taxes and dues of more than 6500 rubles, accumulated over the

[42] Indova, "Rol' dvortsovoi derevni," pp. 194-96.

[43] PSZ, Vol. 12, No. 9216; Vol. 15, No. 11426; Vol. 18, No. 13326.

[44] PSZ, Vol. 15, No. 11426.

preceding twenty-year period.[45]

As a result of these difficulties, the highest administrative
organs of the state sometimes became involved in enforcing the rural
obligations of mercantile peasants and in setting the level of dues to
be collected. In 1736 the Senate dealt with the case of the serf
Maksim Tret'iakov and his brothers, who belonged to Prince Fedor Viazemskii and were registered in the St. Petersburg kupechestvo. It ordered
the magistracy to "collect from them, in addition to the state taxes due
at their former places of residence, an obrok of not more than three
rubles," which was deemed adequate for the satisfaction of seigneurial
interests.[46] In 1760 the Chief Magistracy proposed that seigneurial
dues for serfs registered in the posad be fixed at the level of one
ruble per soul, the same as the obrok currently paid by most categories
of state peasants. This proposal was referred by the Senate to the
commission then attempting to draft a new law code, and the concurrent
case involving the peasants of Metropolitan Arsenii was settled on the
basis of the 1736 precedent.[47]

In 1769 the Senate decreed that state peasants registered in the
posad should pay the same obrok as other state peasants, which by this
time had grown to two rubles per soul. The urban magistracies were made
responsible for collecting these dues and forwarding them to the relevant
instances of the territorial administration.[48] For court peasants, the

---

[45]Indova et al., "Klassovaia bor'ba," p. 37; see also Indova, "Rol'
dvortsovoi derevni," p. 194.

[46]Cited in PSZ, Vol. 15, No. 11426.

[47]Ibid.

[48]PSZ, Vol. 18, No. 13326.

level of dues remained at the discretion of the court estate administration, and the magistracies were to intervene in the collection of these obligations only if their assistance was requested by the Chief Court Chancellery.[49] Mercantile peasants under the authority of this institution who failed to fulfill their rural obligations could forfeit membership in the posad. In 1766 the mercantile peasant Averkii Martynov, who lived in Moscow "in his own house" for 45 years and was registered in the Moscow kupechestvo, was ordered returned to his native village in Kostroma uezd because of arrears in rural taxes and dues of 118 rubles.[50] There is no evidence, however, that private and ecclesiastical lords enjoyed such an option.[51]

The persistent difficulties in enforcing the terms of the decree of April 13, 1722, made the government aware of the shortcomings of this enactment as a means of regulating the absorption of trading peasants into the urban commune. In 1745, while considering the question of how peasants registered in the posad were to be dealt with under the Second Revision, which was then in progress, the Senate took note of the great inconvenience of retaining such individuals in the peasant category and holding them responsible for payment of taxes and dues at some distant

---

[49] PSZ, Vol. 18, Nos. 13301, 13326.

[50] Indova, "Rol' dvortsovoi derevni," p. 190.

[51] Klokman reports a case in which Count I. G. Chernyshev seized 25 mercantile peasants who had been his serfs and forcibly returned them to work in his factories. The Solikamsk magistracy, under which these peasants were registered as merchants, appealed to the higher authorities against this action, but the outcome of the case is not reported. (Klokman, Sotsial'no-ekonomicheskaia istoriia, pp. 98-99.)

location. Nevertheless, it was decided that "pending further consideration and decisions" there was no alternative but to follow the prescriptions of existing legislation.[52] In 1747 the Senate proposed that
mercantile peasants be allowed to buy their freedom from rural obligations for a payment of 500 rubles, with a supplementary charge of 150
rubles for each additional member of the family, but this suggestion
was not enacted. The 1747 proposal was revived in 1762 and sent to the
then deliberating commission on a new law code, where it was again
allowed to die.[53] At the same time, the Senate acted to tighten
seigneurial control over peasants seeking to enter the urban classes,
decreeing that henceforth they could enlist only with the consent of
their lords or "commands" (the institutions supervising their villages).[54]

Several years later, in evaluating the results of the Third Revision,
the Senate again took note of the anomalous status of mercantile peasants.
These individuals, it was pointed out, could not be assigned unequiv-
ocally eitner to tne peasantry or to the kupechestvo, although in terms
of their economic pursuits they clearly belonged to the latter. Consequently, the Senate instructed the Commerce Commission to draw up
proposals for integrating this group more fully with the urban merchant
class while preserving the interests of landlords and specifically their

---

[52]PSZ, Vol. 12, No. 9216.

[53]PSZ, Vol. 15, No. 11426.

[54]Ibid. In effect, this decree seems to allow serfs to enter the
urban classes only after manumission, since it required that they have
otpusknye i uvol'nitel'nye pis'ma (documents of release and manumission).
It is not entirely clear, however, whether lords retained the option of
allowing peasants to register in the posad and continuing to collect
dues from them, which procedure continued to apply to court and state
peasants.

right to receive income from their peasants, but the commission evidently failed to find a way out of this labyrinth.[55] In 1769 the Senate accepted a proposal of the Arkhangel'sk *guberniia* chancellery that state peasants registered in the *posad* be placed exclusively under the authority of urban magistracies and not under rural authorities but continued, as has already been mentioned, to require payment of rural obligations by these peasants.[56] With the minor changes specified, the practices established by the 1722 decree survived up to the reforms of 1775, reflecting a state of affairs not uncommon in the legislative annals of Imperial Russia: the highest organs of the government repeatedly recognized that the existing laws were unsatisfactory, but little was done to improve the situation.

There did remain some other ways for peasants to gain entry to the urban population categories. Freed serfs were allowed to register in the *posad*, and since there could be no question of continuing to assign such individuals to the lords who had dismissed them from service, they were fully absorbed into the town population and placed in the urban 120-kopeck *oklad* (tax assessment). Such registration was most commonly effected at the time of the census, in the course of which the individuals in question would be declared "missing" or "departed" (*ubylyi*) by their former villages and struck off the tax rolls there. The government was naturally eager to enroll these persons in another category bearing obligations toward the state. In 1723, during the course of the First

[55]TsGADA, f. 248, kn. 3676, ll. 791-791 ob.

[56]PSZ, Vol. 18, No. 13326.

Revision, freed serfs who had settled in towns and become involved in trade and crafts were ordered assigned to the posad, while those living by unskilled labor were to be conscripted into military service.[57] The "Instruction" for the implementation of the Second Revision, issued on December 16, 1743, authorized the inscription of freed serfs in the posad "according to their wishes" if they were involved in commercial or craft occupations.[58] In 1744, however, the newly resurrected Chief Magistracy ordered municipal authorities to carry out such registration only with its approval. The local magistracies were to investigate the applicants and report their findings to the Chief Magistracy along with their recommendations.[59] It is possible that the norms of the decree of April 13, 1722, were applied to determine eligibility of freed serfs for membership in the posad. In the four cases reported as pending by the Iaroslavl' magistracy in 1744, all of the applicants claimed a capital of at least 300 rubles, as prescribed by that decree.[60] Two years later local magistracies were given the authority to decide which freedmen were suitable for inclusion in the posad and were no longer required to await the decision of the Chief Magistracy but only to inform it of the number of applicants registered.[61] Subsequent cases in the archives of the Iaroslavl' magistracy and provincial chancellery seldom

---

[57] PSZ, Vol. 7, No. 4318.

[58] PSZ, Vol. 11, No. 8836 (Art. 16).

[59] TsGADA, f. 807 (Iaroslavskii gorodovoi magistrat), op. 1, d. 46, l. 41.

[60] Ibid, ll. 42-53.

[61] Sb. IRIO, Vol. 8, p. 15; TsGADA, f. 807, op. 2, d. 17, ll. 9-9 ob.

refer to specific amounts of capital possessed by the applicants, citing
instead such qualifications as acceptance by the urban commune or guild
and the willingness of some members of the commune to stand as guarantors
for the fulfilment of urban obligations by the applicant.[62] In 1769
the Senate ordered that freed serfs who registered in the posad between
revisions be placed in the 50-kopeck oklad (tax assessment) along with
"mercantile peasants" but transferred to the regular urban 120-kopeck
assessment after the next census.[63]

In practice, local authorities sometimes confused the different
procedures. Sometimes registrants inscribed in the posad under the law
of April 13, 1722, were reported by their villages as "departed" and
were removed from the tax rolls there during the census. If this fact
reached the attention of the government, the registrants in question
would normally be placed in the full urban 120-kopeck oklad. In the
course of the First Revision, some "mercantile peasants" were erroneously
inscribed in the census registers only under the towns where they were
enlisted and not under their lords. These peasants were assigned to the
120-kopeck oklad but required to go on paying seigneurial dues.[64] In
1769 it was reported that of 535 peasants registered in the posad in
towns of Arkhangel'sk guberniia, 197 were paying the urban 50-kopeck
and rural 70-kopeck assessments, 250 were in the urban 120-kopeck oklad
alone, and 88 were in the full urban oklad while continuing to be held

---

[62] TsGADA, f. 807, op. 1, dd. 515, 518, 520; op. 2, d. 17; f. 455,
op. 1, dd. 760, 883, 884, 886, 894, 987.

[63] PSZ, Vol. 18, No. 13326.

[64] PSZ, Vol. 7, No. 4566.

responsible for the rural soul tax.[65]

The Petrine legislation creating craft guilds (tsekhi) allowed peasant craftsmen to become "temporary" members of these guilds, which gave them the right to practice their trade in the towns without hindrance. These registrants had to have seigneurial permission to leave the village and were expected to meet the qualifications of expertise established by the guilds. Peasants not fully qualified could become apprentices or journeymen. Craftsmen producing for the household needs of their lords rather than for sale were not eligible for membership in guilds. "Temporary" guild members, as well as apprentices and journeymen, were not included in the ranks of urban "citizens" but were allowed to live "wherever they want."[66] Like those who inscribed in the posad under the decree of April 13, 1722, "temporary" guild registrants obtained some urban commercial rights without being detached from peasant status and obligations. In theory peasants enrolled in craft guilds were supposed to deal only in goods produced by themselves, but in practice guild membership probably provided a cover for a wider range of commercial activities than that authorized by the law. Peasants made up a very large proportion of the membership of the craft guilds during the first decade of their existence.[67]

Finally, a large number of peasants gained access to the posad when their villages were awarded urban status, either because the

[65]PSZ, Vol. 18, No. 13326.

[66]PSZ, Vol. 6, Nos. 3980, 4054.

[67]Of 6885 guild members registered in Moscow between 1722 and 1726, 3189 (46 percent) were peasants and only 758 were members of the Moscow posad. (K. A. Pazhitnov, Problema remeslennykh tsekhov v zakonodatel'-stve russkogo absoliutizma /Moscow, 1952/, pp. 47-48.) See also below, Chapter IV.

government wished to create new administrative centers or at the request
of a population which had become deeply involved in commercial occupations and wished to enjoy the benefits of municipal rights and institutions. One example of the latter situation is the case of the Ostashkov
slobody (settlements). This group of commercial villages belonged
partially to the Monastery of St. Joseph of Volokolamsk and partially
to the Holy Synod and was located on the Volga near its source in Lake
Seliger. Originally inhabited by fishermen, Ostashkov had by the middle
of the eighteenth century become a thriving center of trade and crafts,
profiting from its favorable location near the water route connecting
Petersburg with Central Russia and in an area containing few major
towns.[68] In 1745, irked by growing restrictions on commercial activities
by peasants, a group of wealthy trading peasants from these settlements
petitioned for inclusion in the kupechestvo as a unit. The government
did not immediately respond to this request, but in 1753 it acted on a
subsequent petition with the same content. After determining that
Ostashkov was in fact a commercial rather than agricultural community,
the Senate authorized the creation of a kupechestvo and urban administrative institutions there, despite the opposition of the Synod and the
monastery. The solution devised by the Senate reflected the influence
of the decree of April 13, 1722. The inhabitants were authorized to
register in the kupechestvo "according to their wishes and their
commercial occupations," and those who did so were placed in the urban
120-kopeck oklad but remained responsible for payment of peasant obligations to the monastery or the Synod. Enlistment in craft guilds was

---

[68]Iu. R. Klokman, Ocherki sotsial'no-ekonomicheskoi istorii gorodov
severo-zapada Rossii v seredine XVIII v. (Moscow, 1960), pp. 123-49.

also permitted. Partly as a result of the imposition of dual obligations, a large segment of the population remained outside the new
kupechestvo, and those who joined were mostly from the wealthier
mercantile element. The newly established Ostashkov kupechestvo then
became the staunchest possible defender of the exclusive rights of the
official merchant class and sought to enforce them against those of
their fellow villagers who remained outside the posad.[69]

In 1761, again acting on a petition from the inhabitants, the
Senate authorized the creation of a kupechestvo and urban institutions
in Sol' Bol'shaia, a settlement in Kostroma uezd belonging to the
Goritskii monastery. Citing the example of Ostashkov, the Senate required the newly registered "merchants" to go on paying dues to their
former lord, but they were otherwise "excluded" from the peasantry and
the authority of the monastery and were placed in the regular urban
oklad.[70] The government did not invariably satisfy petitions from com-
mercialized villages for the introduction of urban institutions and
posad status. In 1745 the Senate refused such a request from the inhabitants of Valdai and Borovichi, two villages belonging to the
Iverskii Monastery and located in northwestern Russia between Tver'
and Novgorod. Despite the fact that these villages were so renowned
for their commerce as to be a special object of complaint by the
Novgorod kupechestvo, the Senate, heeding the objections of their lord,
refused to grant them posad status and instructed the inhabitants instead to inscribe in the kupechestvo as individuals under the terms

---

[69]Klokman has given a detailed account of the creation of the Ostashkov posad (Ibid., pp. 186-210).

[70]PSZ, Vol. 15, No. 11288. This case had the added peculiarity that
the settlement in question had possessed urban status in the sixteenth
century.

of existing legislation.[71]

New towns were created on a massive scale as a result of the Provincial Reform of 1775. Recognizing the existing system of territorial administration as dangerously inadequate, Catherine II and her collaborators designed a panoply of new provincial and local institutions and redrew the internal boundaries of the empire completely. The large gubernii created by Peter I were broken up into smaller gubernii, while the intermediate provintsiia unit was abolished.[72] A similar process took place at the uezd level: the old uezdy were reduced in size and many new ones were created. These changes produced a need for large numbers of new towns to serve as administrative centers, and more than 200 were established between 1775 and 1785.[73] The bulk of these new towns had been peasant settlements of one kind or another.

In 1772, in what amounted to a pilot project for the 1775 reform, Ostashkov, Valdai, Borovichi and the "postal" settlement (iamskaia sloboda) of Vyshnii Volochok were designated uezd towns of Novgorod guberniia. In this instance, the inhabitants were transferred summarily to urban status, with no retention of peasant obligations.[74] Subsequently, the example of the "new towns of Novgorod guberniia" was frequently cited as a precedent in legislation establishing new

---

[71]Klokman, Ocherki, pp. 159-61.

[72]In Catherine's time, the new gubernii were frequently called namestnichestva (viceroyalties). A few gubernii were divided into intermediate units, called oblasti.

[73]Klokman, Sotsial'no-ekonomicheskaia istoriia, p. 202.

[74]PSZ, Vol. 19, No. 13780.

administrative centers in other provinces, and the same benefits were
conferred on their inhabitants. Such was the case, for example, in
Iaroslavl', Kostroma, Tver', Vologda and Pskov gubernii.[75] The right
to full and immediate transfer to the urban classes usually applied
only to native inhabitants of the newly designated towns, but in order
to expand the inadequate population of some of these settlements the
authorities sometimes allowed newcomers to enjoy the same privileges
for a certain period or even compelled nearby villagers to become
"citizens" against their will.[76]

Whether through sheer carelessness or for some other reason which
has not been discovered, the equivalent decrees for many other gubernii
omitted reference to the "new towns of Novgorod guberniia" and did not
deal with the status of the new urban citizens.[77] It is evident that in
some of these provinces at least the inhabitants of the new towns were
subjected to dual obligations, as specified by the existing legislation
on voluntary registration in the posad. This was the case in Vladimir
guberniia, created in 1778, and the protests of the governor-general,
R. I. Vorontsov, against the disadvantages suffered by new towns in his
domain by comparison with those in several neighboring provinces did
not bring prompt relief from the situation.[78] A similar state of affairs

---

[75]PSZ, Vol. 20, Nos. 14400, 14420, 14635, 14636, 14792, 14973.

[76]PSZ, Vol. 20, Nos. 14672, 14991; Vol. 21, No. 15459; Klokman,
Sotsial'no-ekonomicheskaia istoriia, pp. 102-07.

[77]This was the case in Moscow, Vladimir, Kaluga, Nizhnii Novgorod,
Riazan', Orel and Smolensk gubernii, among others. (PSZ, Vol. 20, Nos.
14437, 14525, 14786, 14787, 14793, 14908; Vol. 21, No. 15245.)

[78]TsGADA, Gosarkhiv, r. XVI, d. 638, ll. 93-95 (reference provided
by Prof. Marc Raeff); Klokman, Sotsial'no-ekonomicheskaia istoriia, pp.
101-02. Klokman states incorrectly that the Fourth Revision (1782)
brought an end to the dual obligations imposed on inhabitants of new

existed in Moscow guberniia, where citizens of the new uezd towns created in 1781 were not dropped from the peasant oklad until 1787.[79] Under these circumstances, it is not surprising that many inhabitants of the new towns resisted becoming members of the posad and sought to retain exclusively peasant status.[80] In September 1785 the precedent of the "new towns of Novgorod guberniia" was made applicable retroactively to all new uezd towns, and the peasant obligations of their citizens were cancelled, but the example of Moscow guberniia suggests that the administration took some length of time to put this determination into effect.[81]

In the interim, another reform of 1775 had finally compelled the government to make basic changes in the provisions for voluntary enlistment in the posad. In her "Manifesto" of March 17, 1775, Catherine II divided the posad population into the kupechestvo (merchantry) and the meshchanstvo (townsmen).[82] The kupechestvo was distributed among three guilds according to the amount of capital "declared" by each

---

towns in Vladimir guberniia, an error which stems from his misunderstanding of the legislation governing enlistment in the posad. In reality, Vorontsov raised the matter again in a communication of June 1783.

[79]Tsentral'nyi gosudarstvennyi istoricheskii arkhiv, Leningrad (hereafter TsGIA), f. 558 (Senatskaia ekspeditsiia dlia revizii gosudarstvennykh schetov), op. 2, d. 128, 1. 32.

[80]TsGADA, Gosarkhiv, r. XVI, d. 638, ch. 1, 11. 93-95 (reference provided by Prof. Marc Raeff); Klokman, Sotsial'no-ekonomicheskaia istoriia, pp. 103-04.

[81]PSZ, Vol. 21, No. 16269.

[82]PSZ, Vol. 20, No. 14275 (Art. 47).

merchant and was freed from the "soul" tax, in place of which an
annual tax of one percent of the declared capital was instituted.[83]
Since Catherine insisted that declaration of capital by merchants be
"on their honor," no verification was required, and in practice membership in the three guilds was determined by the ability and willingness
to pay the prescribed tax. Posad members not qualifying for the
kupechestvo were allotted to the meshchanstvo and continued to pay the
soul tax, which was considered a mark of low status.

As the Senate soon discovered, these innovations invalidated the
existing provisions for enlistment of trading peasants in the kupechestvo.
It was obviously not in keeping with the Empress' intention to raise the
status of the urban merchantry and relieve it of the stigma of the soul
tax that newcomers recruited into this category should continue to be
subject to the 70-kopeck peasant oklad and estate dues.[84] Nonetheless,
alternative procedures emerged only gradually over the succeeding
decade. On October 10, 1776, the Senate ordered that mercantile
peasants registered before the 1775 "Manifesto" be distributed among the
three merchant guilds and the meshchanstvo according to their qualifications but said nothing about freeing these individuals from peasant

---

[83]The minimum capital required for membership in each of the three
guilds was as follows (in rubles):

	1775	1785	1794
First Guild	10000	10000	16000
Second Guild	1000	5000	8000
Third Guild	500	1000	2000

(PSZ, Vol. 20, No. 14327; Vol. 22, No. 16188, Art. 102, 108, 114; Vol.
23, No. 17223.)

[84]PSZ, Vol. 20, No. 14516 (Art. 6); No. 14632.

obligations. The procedures for further registration of peasants in
the urban classes, it was added, would be dealt with in a forthcoming
"general statute on the privileges of the kupechestvo" (which did not
in fact materialize for nearly a decade).[85] As a result of this
declaration, lower instances of the administration no longer felt they
had the authority to induct peasants into the urban classes according
to the existing laws and began to refer all such applications to the
Senate. To alleviate this situation, the Senate on July 25, 1777,
established interim rules for the enlistment of peasants in the
kupechestvo. Observing that it would be "appropriate," in the light of
the 1775 "Manifesto," to release such registrants from the soul tax,
the Senate nevertheless decided that it did not have the authority to
set aside the existing laws and therefore ordered that the registrants
continue to pay the "customary" obligations due at their former places
of residence, as well as the tax on capital. They were further required
to have the consent of their lords or "commands" to enrollment in the
urban classes and to fulfil whatever provisions were contained in the
anticipated fundamental legislation on the kupechestvo. Those finding
these provisions unacceptable, it was promised, would be allowed to
return to ordinary peasant status.[86]

Nothing was said in this decree about release from dual obligations after the next revision, but it was clearly implied that these

---

[85] PSZ, Vol. 20, No. 14516 (Art. 6). The accompanying sample graph
for the required reports on the numbers of kuptsy and meshchane in each
town shows that mercantile peasants who were assigned to the guild
kupechestvo paid the percentage tax on capital, while those who were
placed in the meshchanstvo continued to pay the old 50-kopeck oklad.

[86] PSZ, Vol. 20, No. 14632.

obligations would be temporary.[87] Many peasants who registered in the urban classes at this time evidently believed that the double burdens would not endure beyond the new census.[88] The government, despite some gestures in this direction, failed to take the necessary steps to resolve the issue. Sometime in 1781 the Procurator-General of the Senate, Prince Viazemskii, raised the question in a communication to the Empress, as a result of which she ordered the Senate to prepare an "opinion," but the results of this discussion, if any, are not contained in any general enactments.[89] The "Manifesto" of November 16, 1781, which initiated the Fourth Revision, said nothing about the problem.[90] In its instructions on the preparation of census depositions, the Senate required the following information on peasants enlisted in the urban classes: when and under what decrees or authorizations they had been inducted, whether or not they had been released by their lords or "commands," and the place where they were registered in the peasant oklad. It did not, however, state whether they were to remain so registered.[91] In some gubernii, the initiative of particular authorities

---

[87]Release from peasant obligations after the next revision is also unmentioned in a 1780 decree dealing with the enlistment of peasants ascribed to the state factories of the Olonets region in the new town of Petrozavodsk. Subsequent registrants were to be held responsible for factory labor obligations after entry into the urban classes and were not promised any eventual termination of this burden. However, those who had registered between the founding of the town (1777) and the time of the decree were released from factory obligations. (PSZ, Vol. 20, No. 14991).

[88]TsGADA, Gosarkhiv, r. XVI, d. 638, l. 106 (reference provided by Prof. Marc Raeff); Klokman, Sotsial'no-ekonomicheskaia istoriia, p. 95.

[89]TsGIA, f. 558, op. 2, d. 315, ll. 60-61.

[90]PSZ, Vol. 21, No. 15278.

[91]PSZ, Vol. 21, No. 15296.

did result in the release of registrants from peasant obligations under the new revision. On November 16, 1781, the same day she promulgated the new census, Empress Catherine ordered that a register of applicants for membership in the urban classes of St. Petersburg guberniia be submitted to her so that "We may give Our authorization for their enlistment in the towns...and exclusion from the villages."[92] In Vologda guberniia the provincial administration ordered not only that peasants previously registered in the urban classes be eliminated from the peasant oklad in the new revision but that new registrants be charged only urban taxes from the time of their enlistment. These orders reached the attention of the Senate, which reminded the Vologda authorities that only native inhabitants of the newly established uezd towns were eligible for immediate release from peasant status but sanctioned the intention to release all prior registrants under the new census.[93]

If this decision was intended to be generally applicable, the government failed to issue the necessary instructions to other provinces. The Senate did not even respond to a specific request for guidance on this question from Polotsk guberniia, replying only that enlistment of peasants should be carried out "according to the existing laws."[94] As a result, in most provinces peasants registered in the urban classes were left in the peasant oklad under the new revision. Even A. P. Mel'gunov, who as governor-general of both Vologda and Iaroslavl' gubernii was party to the Vologda decision, apparently did not feel that

---

[92]PSZ, Vol. 21, No. 15277.

[93]PSZ, Vol. 21, No. 15459.

[94]PSZ, Vol. 21, No. 15577.

he had the authority to apply this ruling to the other province under
his supervision and in 1783 reported to Prince Viazemskii that in this
province registrants had not been released from peasant status "for lack
of any authorization to do so."[95] The situation was further aggravated
by orders issued in 1782 which required peasants enlisting in the urban
classes to resettle in the towns where they registered and surrender all
peasant holdings.[96] As provincial officials repeatedly pointed out
during the next several years, there could be no justification for continuing to hold such individuals responsible for peasant obligations,
and many of the registrants entangled by this predicament reportedly
saw no way out except a return to unequivocal peasant status.[97]

In the face of such complaints, Viazemskii suggested that the
problem be settled by a "general statute for the whole country," but
apparently no such enactment was issued.[98] The question was dealt with
on a piecemeal basis, as the situation in each guberniia was brought to
the attention of the central authorities. In 1783 peasants registered
in the towns of Ufa guberniia before the Fourth Revision were ordered
eliminated from the rural tax rolls, and in 1785 a similar decision was
issued for Kazan' guberniia.[99] The same relief was granted in 1784 to

---

[95]TsGIA, f. 558, op. 2, d. 315, ll. 60-61.

[96]Ibid.; PSZ, Vol. 21, No. 15459.

[97]TsGADA, Gosarkhiv, r. XVI, d. 638, l. 106; d. 655, ll. 10-12
(reference provided by Prof. Marc Raeff); TsGIA, f. 558, op. 2, d. 315,
ll. 60-61.

[98]TsGIA, f. 558, op. 2, d. 315, l. 62.

[99]PSZ, Vol. 21, No. 16269.

"economic" peasants of the estates formerly belonging to the Predtechev Monastery who had enlisted in the Tula kupechestvo.[100] In 1786 the Senate received a petition from 1224 peasants registered in the Moscow kupechestvo and meshchanstvo, complaining of the continuation of dual obligations in the aftermath of the Fourth Revision.[101] Two years later the Senate finally ruled on the question, deciding that those who had registered in the "first half" of 1782 or earlier should be released from peasant obligations, but these people remained on the rural tax rolls until 1790.[102] In 1787 a report by two senators once again called attention to the fact that many persons registered in the urban classes before the Fourth Revision were still subject to the peasant oklad and recommended that the issue be resolved through a general enactment.[103] The government continued to grapple with the problem, and particularly with the fate of peasants who had enlisted in the "second half" of 1782, up to the time of the next census.[104] In this way the Catherinian solution to the problem of enlisting peasants in the urban classes lurched into existence.

---

[100]Ibid.

[101]Istoriia Moskvy, Vol. 2, p. 319.

[102]TsGADA, f. 248, kn. 4109, 11. 209-12; TsGIA, f. 558, op. 2, d. 128, 1. 32. The significance of the reference to the "first half" of 1782 is that the deadline for the submission of census depositions had been set at the middle of that year. In the present instance, this was designated as the dividing line between those who had registered "before" and "after" the Fourth Revision.

[103]TsGADA, Gosarkhiv, r. XVI, d. 655, 11. 10-12 (reference provided by Prof. Marc Raeff).

[104]TsGIA, f. 558, op. 2, d. 128, 1. 32.

The long-awaited "general statute on the privileges of the
kupechestvo" finally materialized in the form of Catherine's Urban
Charter of 1785, which provided that "anyone of whatever sex, age, birth,
generation, family, status, trade, enterprise, handicraft or skill who
declares a capital of over 1000 rubles...is permitted to register in
/merchant/ guilds." The guild rolls were to be open to new members
every year in the month of December. Incorporating into law what had
already been decided by experience, the Charter stipulated that crown
peasants enlisting in the urban classes bear dual obligations only
until the next census.[105] The government had earlier vacillated somewhat on the question of whether to allow peasants to register in the
meshchanstvo. In its decree of July 25, 1777, establishing interim
rules for enlistment in the kupechestvo, the Senate said nothing about
entry into the lesser category of urban citizens, and in the next
several years it discouraged or even prohibited the process in specific
instances as "not in accord with state interests" and of little benefit
to the towns.[106] Finally, in 1782, enrollment of peasants in the
meshchanstvo was forbidden entirely as not authorized by any existing
legislation.[107] However, the Urban Charter declared that "no one is
forbidden to register in the posad of a town," as a result of which
enlistment of state peasants in the meshchanstvo was again possible.[108]

---

[105]PSZ, Vol. 22, No. 16188, Art. 92, 93, 139.

[106]PSZ, Vol. 20, Nos. 14632, 14991; Vol. 21, No. 15459.

[107]PSZ, Vol. 21, No. 15578.

[108]PSZ, Vol. 22, No. 16188, Art. 138; Vol. 24, No. 18213.

This provision theoretically opened the way for entry into the urban classes of peasants not possessing large amounts of capital or prosperous enterprises.

The Catherinian reforms introduced few changes into the provisions for enlistment of freed serfs in the town population. As before, freedmen were allowed, and indeed obligated, to enlist in another population category according to their preferences and qualifications.[109] This type of registrant was not formally subject to dual obligations. The soul tax for freed serfs had to be paid until the next revision, but this responsibility rested with the former lord.[110] Once manumission was granted, the lord had no further power to claim dues or other obligations. The government did not intervene in the private arrangements made between lord and serf at the time of manumission for the commutation of taxes and dues.[111]

The Urban Charter mentioned as eligible for membership in craft guilds only those who belonged to the meshchanstvo, saying nothing about the "temporary" membership in these guilds which had been authorized by the legislation of Peter I.[112] As a result, this temporary

---

[109] PSZ, Vol. 20, Nos. 14275 (Art. 46), 14294 (Art. 11); Vol. 21, No. 15278 (Art. 11); Vol. 22, No. 16188 (Art. 79); Vol. 23, Nos. 16970, 17021. Catherine firmly prohibited freedmen from becoming serfs of another lord. (See particularly PSZ, Vol. 20, No. 14275, Art. 46; No. 15070.

[110] PSZ, Vol. 20, No. 14294 (Art. 11).

[111] In administrative records dealing with the admission of freed serfs to the urban classes, it is sometimes remarked that the former lord had agreed to pay the soul tax until the next census or that the serf had paid him a lump sum to cover the tax. (TsGADA, f. 807, op. 1, dd. 518, 520; f. 455, op. 1, d. 883; Gosudarstvennyi arkhiv Iaroslavskoi oblasti /GAIaO/, f. 55, op. 1, d. 82.)

[112] PSZ, Vol. 22, No. 16188 (Art. 120).

membership was terminated in Petersburg and probably in many other towns as well.[113] In 1796, citing the need to avoid driving peasant craftsmen into "idleness," the Senate restored the right of such craftsmen to enlist in guilds for the duration of their authorized absence from the village, without the necessity of joining the meshchanstvo.[114] According to the Guild Charter (Ustav tsekhov) of 1799, temporary registrants could obtain only the status of journeyman (podmaster'e) and could not be full-fledged masters.[115] This was the only remaining way for private serfs who could not obtain manumission to gain membership in an official urban category.

After the Urban Charter, the provisions for peasant enlistment in the kupechestvo and meshchanstvo underwent few additional changes during the remaining years of the century. With the arrival of the Fifth Revision, the government determined that only those registrants who had enlisted before the decree announcing the new census (June 23, 1794) would be entitled to release from the peasant oklad, while later registrants would have to wait until the Sixth Revision.[116] The confusion on this issue surrounding the previous census was thus avoided, although much to the resentment, no doubt, of those who had not made the deadline. In 1797 the government acted to tighten the screening of crown peasants seeking to enter the urban classes. Under the existing procedures, applicants had to gain the consent of their "commands" and

---

[113] Pazhitnov, Problema remeslennykh tsekhov, p. 81.

[114] PSZ, Vol. 23, No. 17438.

[115] PSZ, Vol. 25, No. 19187.

[116] PSZ, Vol. 23, No. 17357.

their original peasant communities before their petitions could be
acted upon by the urban authorities. These requirements were intended
to make sure that registrants were not using enlistment as a pretext
for evading military conscription or tax arrears, as well as insuring
their general suitability for urban citizenship. Despite these controls, it was reported that "a great many crown peasants possessing
neither capital nor enterprises" were gaining entry to the urban classes
under existing procedures, and to eliminate this undesirable development authority over the acceptance or rejection of applicants was now
transferred from local urban administrations to the Senate. Henceforth
the peasants were to apply for membership in the urban classes via their
"commands," while the latter were to investigate the suitability of the
candidates and forward the petitions to the Senate with their recommendations.[117]

The history of legislation on enlistment in the posad was in many
ways a reflection of the peculiar class structure of Russian society
and the relationship of individual classes to the state. Demanding
heavy tax payments and burdensome services from the urban commune, the
government was compelled to protect its sources of income by awarding
it exclusive rights in many areas of commerce. But since complete
suppression of trade by peasants was impossible and indeed highly undesirable for economic reasons, the government sought a way to use
these interlopers to strengthen the posad rather than weakening it
through competition. Because of the competing class interests which
impinged on government policy, the various solutions which were tried
have a compromising and ambivalent character which impeded effective

[117]PSZ, Vol. 24, No. 18213.

resolution of the problem. Many of the persons potentially eligible for urban citizenship were private serfs, while most others belonged to obligated communities of other kinds. Neither the serfowners nor the communities wished to surrender control over these individuals so that they might be added to the posad. The latter, on the other hand, wished to incorporate as many new taxpayers as possible and persistently demanded the right to absorb the commercial and industrial population of the country to the fullest possible extent.

In the latter half of the seventeenth century, the government flatly prohibited the infiltration of trading peasants into the urban population, but when an influx occurred nevertheless it periodically ratified these deviations from the law and incorporated the offending peasants into the posad, ignoring the interests of their lords. Voluntary enlistment in the urban classes was introduced by Peter I. The Petrine system, in its ultimate form, assigned such registrants to an intermediate category, sometimes called "mercantile peasants" (kupechestvuiushchie krest'iane), the members of which owed obligations as both peasants and townsmen in perpetuity. Peter's laws also had the unusual feature of sharply limiting seigneurial powers over serfs who could qualify for posad membership, although the provision allowing serfs to enlist without the consent of their lords was withdrawn in 1762. The Petrine procedures functioned poorly and left all the groups and interests involved thoroughly dissatisfied. Mercantile peasants resented the persistence of unfree status and rural obligations and evaded their responsibilities as much as possible. The townsmen objected to the less than complete integration of peasant registrants into the urban commune and the limited efficacy of the system in attracting new recruits. The

serfowners disliked the limitations placed on their control over mercantile peasants and the difficulty of enforcing even those obligations
to which they were legally entitled, while the government was irritated
by recurrent difficulties in administering the cumbersome provisions of
Peter's legislation.

Despite this universal discontent, significant changes were introduced only as a consequence of the reforms of 1775, which rendered the
earlier laws unusable. The Catherinian provisions, which some historians
have mistakenly believed were in effect throughout the century, were
established as the general norm by the Urban Charter of 1785, having
emerged gradually over the preceding decade. For crown peasants
aspiring to urban citizenship, Catherine's legislation offered much
more favorable terms than the Petrine decrees it replaced: it promised
release from peasant status and obligations following a new census, in
place of the perpetual attachment to these burdens prescribed by the
earlier laws. The Urban Charter also lowered barriers to entry into
the posad by authorizing enlistment in the meshchanstvo, which did not
require possession of capital. On the less favorable side, there were
no longer any provisions allowing serfs who could not obtain manumission
to enter the merchantry, although a major category of the serf population had been converted to state peasants through the secularization of
church estates in 1764 and was thus not affected by this disadvantage.
Moreover, as will be demonstrated elsewhere in this study, in the late
eighteenth century a surprisingly large number of serfs did succeed in
extricating themselves from bondage and finding their way into the
urban classes.

CHAPTER III: ENLISTMENT OF PEASANTS IN THE URBAN CLASSES--NATIONWIDE
DATA

Having examined the legal provisions governing enlistment in the
urban classes, we turn to an evaluation of the concrete results of this
enlistment, in terms of the numbers of peasants who were able to acquire
urban citizenship in various periods and places. We begin the discussion
of quantitative results by summarizing the available nationwide data on
this question. Although more limited in scope and completeness than
might be desired, the data to be presented in this chapter do make it
possible to identify major changes in the magnitude and distribution of
enlistment which occurred during the course of the century.

We have at our disposal two principal sources of data for all
"Great Russian" provinces of the empire.[1] These documents include a
"Report on the Number of Souls by Towns," compiled in 1767, which com-
pares the results of the "current" and "previous" censuses for each
territorial unit and population category.[2] Among the information provided by this document is the number of "mercantile peasants" enlisted
in each town at the time of the Second and Third Revisions (the mid-
1740's and early 1760's respectively). The second source to be used,

---

[1]Not included in this assessment are the Baltic provinces, the
Ukraine and Belorussian territories annexed from Poland under the parti-
tions, in all of which urban communities were governed by different
laws and traditions. Also omitted is the Black Sea littoral, where
intensive settlement began only at the end of the eighteenth century.

[2]Gosudarstvennaia publichnaia biblioteka im. Saltykova-Shchedrina,
Leningrad, Rukopisnyi otdel (hereafter GPB RO), Ermitazhnoe sobranie,
No. 242 ("Vedomost' o chisle dush po gorodam"). The document bears no
date, but V. M. Kabuzan has found evidence which assigns it to 1767.
See Kabuzan, Narodonaselenie Rossii v XVIII-pervoi polovine XIX v.
(Moscow, 1963), pp. 24, 111.

a "Tax Register for the Entire State" from the year 1800, gives the
number of crown peasants who had enlisted in the kupechestvo and
meshchanstvo of each guberniia since the Fifth Revision (1795).[3] For
purposes of accurate comparison it must be kept in view that the figures
given by these two sources are far from identical in meaning. Since
"mercantile peasants" were retained permanently in a separate category
and were not merged with the rest of the posad population following
the census, data from the 1767 document represent the cumulative total
of all such registrants remaining in the posad at the time of the census,
and not just those who had enlisted since the previous census.[4] Not
included are those registrants who died or were otherwise removed from
the posad before being counted by a census. The 1800 "Tax Register,"
on the other hand, lists only those who registered in the urban classes

---

Some data on peasant enlistment from this source have been cited
by G. L. Vartanov. However, Vartanov confined his attention to the
towns of Moscow guberniia (in its large pre-1775 configuration). A
recent German monograph reprints Vartanov's figures but attributes them
mistakenly to V. N. Bernadskii. Vartanov, "Kupechestvo i torguiushchee
krest'ianstvo tsentral'noi chasti Evropeiskoi Rossii vo vtoroi polovine
XVIII v.," Uchenye zapiski Leningradskogo gosudarstvennogo pedagogicheskogo instituta im. A. I. Gertsena, Vol. 229 (1962), p. 189; Bernd
Knabe, "Die Struktur der russischen Posadgemeinden und der Katalog der
Beschwerden und Forderungen der Kaufmannschaft," Forschungen zur
osteuropäischen Geschichte, Band 22 (1975), pp. 300-63.

[3]Tsentral'nyi gosudarstvennyi istoricheskii arkhiv, Leningrad
(hereafter TsGIA), f. 571, op. 9, d. 1 ("Okladnaia kniga po vsemu
gosudarstvu o chisle dush po 5-oi revizii po 1 genvariia 1800 g.").

[4]The registrants are listed under a special urban 50-kopeck tax
assessment (oklad), as prescribed by the legislation discussed in the
preceding chapter, and also continue to be listed under the peasant
(70-kopeck) oklad, so that in the guberniia totals for taxable population a second figure, "less mercantile peasants," is given to avoid
duplication. This document thus corroborates the analysis of pre-1775
procedures for enlistment of peasants in the urban classes given in the
preceding chapter. While for most registrants membership in the 50-
kopeck oklad continued indefinitely, it is possible that there was some
leakage into the regular urban (120-kopeck) oklad, particularly if a
registrant managed to gain manumission or was otherwise eliminated from
the rural tax rolls.

from 1795 through 1799.[5] Neither source includes enlistment by freed
serfs, although the 1767 document does include serfs who enlisted in
the posad as mercantile peasants without losing their original status.
The omission of freed serfs is an important one, since evidence to be
presented in subsequent chapters will show that in some towns the influx of such freedmen into the urban classes was at least as great as
that of crown peasants in the late eighteenth century. Data from both
the above sources are in terms of male "souls," the usual unit for
assessment of the taxable population in the eighteenth century.

In addition to the above, there are two other known sources giving
data on peasant enlistment as recorded by the Second and Third Revisions.
These include (1) a 1764 document cited by A. A. Kizevetter, which provides figures from the Second Revision for individual towns, and (2) a
"Report on the Number of Souls According to the Current Revision,"
found among the papers of the First Department of the Senate for the
years 1765-1767 and giving results from the Third Revision for whole
gubernii.[6] However, these sources turn out to be less complete than
the 1767 "Report on the Number of Souls" and add little to the data it
provides. According to the 1767 document 3565 mercantile peasants were

---

[5]Such subtleties have sometimes escaped the attention of scholars
who have cited data from these or similar sources. See Vartanov,
"Kupechestvo i torguiushchee krest'ianstvo," pp. 194-95; Istoriia
Moskvy, Vol. 2 (Moscow, 1953), p. 319.

[6]A. A. Kizevetter, Posadskaia obshchina v Rossii XVIII stoletiia
(Moscow, 1903), pp. 46-47; Tsentral'nyi gosudarstvennyi arkhiv drevnikh
aktov, Moscow (hereafter TsGADA), f. 248 (1 departament Senata), kn.
3676, 11. 769-88 ("Vedomost' o chisle dush po nyneshnei revizii, s
vypiskoiu iz ukazov na kazhdoe zvanie"). Data from the latter source
were published by V. N. Iakovtsevskii, who, however, identified the
registrants only as "trading peasants" and was apparently unaware of
their actual status. Iakovtsevskii, Kupecheskii kapital v feodal'no-
krepostnicheskoi Rossii (Moscow, 1953), p. 50.

enlisted in all towns covered at the time of the Second Revision, while
Kizevetter's source reports only 2055 such registrants.[7] Kizevetter's
figures for individual towns and provinces are often similar or identical to those of the 1767 report, but unlike the latter Kizevetter shows
no data for St. Petersburg or for several towns of Moscow guberniia.
Kizevetter's source also gives a somewhat lower figure for Moscow itself and records much less enlistment in Novgorod guberniia and Siberia.
For the Third Revision the 1767 report gives a total of 3755 mercantile
peasants, while the Senate document lists 3380. The two sources provide identical figures for ten of thirteen gubernii, but the Senate
document omits data on mercantile peasants for Belgorod and Orenburg
gubernii and gives a smaller figure for Moscow guberniia.[8] Of the

---

[7]Kizevetter, presumably citing his documentary source, gives a
total of 1943 registrants, but the figures listed for individual towns
add up to 2055. In addition to 3565 mercantile peasants, the 1767
report mentions 216 "seigneurial peasants registered in the mercantile
oklad" in Nizhnii Novgorod uezd. Unlike mercantile peasants, this
group was included in the regular urban 120-kopeck tax assessment rather
than the special 50-kopeck oklad. These peasants were evidently not
voluntary registrants in the urban classes but rather inhabitants of
Blagoveshchenskaia Sloboda, a peasant settlement adjacent to Nizhnii
Novgorod, who had been placed in the urban oklad at the time of the
First Revision on the ground that they were involved in trade and industry. Despite their urban tax status, they were not members of the
Nizhnii Novgorod posad and did not share in its communal service obligations or contribute to municipal revenues. Kizevetter lists 226 registrants in Nizhnii Novgorod, and all or most of these apparently belong
to the same group. On Blagoveshchenskaia Sloboda and its anomalous
status, see M. Ia. Volkov, "Materialy pervoi revizii kak istochnik po
istorii torgovli i promyshlennosti Rossii pervoi chetverti XVIII v.,"
Problemy istochnikovedeniia, Vol. 11 (1963), pp. 303-04; Iu. R. Klokman,
Sotsial'no-ekonomicheskaia istoriia russkogo goroda, vtoraia polovina
XVIII v. (Moscow, 1967), pp. 270-72; TsGADA, f. 397 (Komissiia o
kommertsii), d. 441, l. 215.

[8]The 1767 report again lists a contingent of seigneurial peasants
registered in the regular urban oklad in Nizhnii Novgorod uezd (187
souls). These are not mentioned by the Senate document.

available sources the 1767 document thus clearly provides the most complete data. On the later period, a document cited by P. G. Ryndziunskii in a recent article evidently contains valuable nation-wide data for the years 1782-1794.[9] Unfortunately, Ryndziunskii chose not to make these data available in any substantial detail and they thus can add little to the present discussion.

The available evidence indicates that the number of peasants absorbed into the urban classes under the legislation of Peter I was not large, despite active efforts by the government during the 1720's to encourage such enlistment. During the prolonged process of verifying and correcting the results of the First Revision (which continued until 1727), government registrars were instructed to seek out and investigate possible candidates, and those unwilling to enlist or found unqualified (as possessing insufficient capital) were ordered deprived of their enterprises and expelled from the towns to their "former places of residence."[10] Nonetheless, at the time of the Second Revision, two decades later, the number of mercantile peasants did not exceed 3600 for the whole empire, and the total increased only slightly between the Second and Third Revisions. These figures suggest not only a generally low level of enlistment but a thorough stagnation of the process following the Second Revision, after which gains from new recruitment were nearly balanced by losses of previous registrants. Mercantile peasants accounted for a maximum of only 1.6 percent of the nationwide posad population during the period covered.

---

[9]P. G. Ryndziunskii, "Osnovnye faktory gorodoobrazovaniia v Rossii vtoroi poloviny XVIII v.," in Russkii gorod (Moscow, 1976), p. 113.

[10]See M. Ia. Volkov, "Materialy pervoi revizii," pp. 302-05.

Not revealed by these figures is the total number of individuals who became mercantile peasants during the years covered. Only those who remained alive and present long enough to be counted by a census are included, and these data also do not distinguish between new registrants since the previous census and survivors from earlier enlistment. Depending on the rate of turnover, the number of peasants who enjoyed posad membership at one time or another could be considerably larger than the figures recorded by the census, although from the standpoint of long-term effect it is the cumulative total of registrants remaining in the urban commune which matters. Information on the total number of peasants who gained posad membership is available only as regards the court peasantry. According to not entirely complete data compiled by E. I. Indova from the records of the court estate administration, from the 1720's through the early 1760's (approximately the same period as that between the First and Third Revisions) 1869 households of court peasants, representing perhaps 3500 male souls, enlisted in the urban classes throughout the empire.[11] If we assume, as seems probable, that the court peasantry contributed no more than half the registrants, the total number enlisted at some point between the First and Third Revisions would have to be at least twice as large as the number remaining at the end of the period.[12]

---

[11]E. I. Indova, "Rol' dvortsovoi derevni pervoi poloviny XVIII v. v formirovanii russkogo kupechestva," Istoricheskie zapiski, Vol. 68 (1961), pp. 191-92. Data to be presented later in this study indicate that households of court peasants absorbed into the Moscow posad between the Third and Fourth Revisions contained an average of 1.8 male souls per household.

[12]The court peasantry was a small population group, comprising less than 10 percent of the peasant population in all "Great Russian" provinces in this period. On the other hand, court peasants were highly active in urban commerce and industry, particularly in the area of

The data provided by the 1767 "Report on the Number of Souls"
show that enlistment by peasants in the posad population was subject to
marked regional and local variations. The distribution of the peasant
registrants by region is shown in Table 1.[13] According to the Second
Revision most of the registrants (85 percent of the nationwide total)
were concentrated in the Central Industrial and Northwest regions,
which contained most of the country's older urban settlements but only
51 percent of its posad population. A substantial number of mercantile
peasants were to be found in Siberia but few in the remaining regions.
As a proportion of the total posad population the mercantile-peasant
element did not exceed 5 percent even where it was most concentrated
(in the Northwest), and it reached a low of 0.1 percent in the Central
Agricultural and Volga-Ural regions. By comparison, the figures from
the Third Revision indicate a certain evening out of the regional distribution. The mercantile-peasant element contracted both relatively
and absolutely in the Central Industrial and Northwest regions--sharply
in the latter case--and these areas now absorbed only 57 percent of all

---

Moscow. Even in Moscow, however, the court peasantry was responsible
for only 40-50 percent of the peasants entering the posad during the
same period. See V. M. Kabuzan, Izmeneniia v razmeshchenii naseleniia
Rossii v XVIII-pervoi polovine XIX v. (Moscow, 1971), pp. 63, 75, 87;
E. I. Indova, "Moskovskii posad i podmoskovnye dvortsovye krest'iane
v pervoi polovine XVIII v.," in Goroda feodal'noi Rossii (Moscow, 1966),
pp. 479-85; Indova, "Les activités commerciales de la paysannerie dans
les villages du tsar de la région de Moscou (première moitié du XVIIIe
siècle)," Cahiers du monde russe et soviétique, Vol. 5, No. 2 (Apr.-
June 1964), pp. 206-28; S. I. Volkov, Krest'iane dvortsovykh vladenii
Podmoskov'ia v seredine XVIII v. (Moscow, 1959), pp. 45-86. On the
role of court peasants in enlistment in the Moscow posad, see below,
Chapter IV.

[13]In this breakdown the pre-1775 territorial units have been grouped
in such a way as to facilitate comparison with later data. The distribution of these units among regions is specified in the footnotes to
the table. Because of the configuration of the data, it has been
necessary to combine the Volga and Ural provinces into a single region
in this instance.

Table 1: Number of "Mercantile Peasants" Enlisted in Urban Classes
According to Second and Third Revisions (Males)

Regions	Second Revision (1744-7)			Third Revision (1762-5)		
	Total urban classes[a]	Merc. peasants	% merc. peasants	Total urban classes[a]	Merc. peasants	% merc. peasants
CIR[b]	81385	1479	1.8	81488	1353	1.7
North[c]	9766	66	0.7	9179	281	3.1
Northwest[d]	31484	1547	4.9	30292	802	2.6
CAR[e]	47380	53	0.1	54010	223	0.4
Volga-Ural[f]	31396	39	0.1	29826	116	0.3
Siberia[g]	21790	381	1.7	24045	980	4.1
Total	223201	3565	1.6	228840	3755	1.6

Source: GPB RO, Ermitazhnoe sobranie, no. 242 ("Vedomost' o chisle
dush po gorodam").

[a]Kupechestvo, tsekhovye (not including "temporary" registrants in
craft guilds) and mercantile peasants.

[b]Central Industrial Region, including the following pre-1775 ter-
ritorial units: Moscow guberniia (Moscow, Kaluga, Kostroma, Iur'ev-
Pol'skoi, Vladimir, Suzdal', Iaroslavl', Uglich and Pereslavl'-
Zalesskii provintsii), Novgorod guberniia (Tver' provintsiia), Nizhnii
Novgorod guberniia (Nizhnii Novgorod and Arzamas provintsii) and
Arkhangel'sk guberniia (Galich provintsiia).

[c]Arkhangel'sk guberniia (Arkhangel'sk, Vologda and Ustiug
provintsii).

[d]St. Petersburg guberniia, Novgorod guberniia (less Tver'
provintsiia) and Smolensk guberniia.

[e]Central Agricultural Region, including Tula and Riazan'
provintsii of Moscow guberniia and Belgorod and Voronezh gubernii.

[f]Alator provintsiia of Nizhnii Novgorod guberniia and Kazan',
Astrakhan' and Orenburg gubernii.

[g]Sibir' (Tobol'sk) and Irkutsk gubernii.

peasant registrants. The share of Siberia rose markedly from 11 to 26 percent of the total, and enlistment also tended to increase in the areas where it had been most weakly developed (the Central Agricultural and Volga-Ural regions and the North), although in the first two it remained at a very low level. As a proportion of the posad population mercantile peasants now had their greatest impact in Siberia but still constituted only 4.1 percent of the urban classes there.

More striking than the variation among regions was the presence of large concentrations of mercantile peasants in individual towns. Thus, although peasant enlistment had a negligible impact on the growth of the posad population on a nationwide basis during this period, it made a substantial contribution to the population of a few towns. Those chiefly affected were the two capitals, Siberian towns and a few others. According to the Second Revision, St. Petersburg contained 1104 mercantile peasants, and these registrants constituted one-quarter of the city's posad population.[14] Ten percent of the Moscow posad (1247 souls) consisted of mercantile peasants.[15] By the Third Revision the number of mercantile peasants in Moscow had dropped to 1087, while that in Petersburg dropped more sharply to 428.[16] Detailed data for Moscow to be presented later in this study indicate that the decline there was due to a diminished influx of newcomers after the Second Revision and a high degree of attrition among the previous registrants, because of

[14]GPB RO, Ermitazhnoe sobranie, No. 242, 11. 92-93.

[15]Ibid., 1. 1.

[16]The losses in the two capitals account for most of the previously observed decline in the numbers of mercantile peasants in the Central Industrial Region and the Northwest between the Second and Third Revisions.

the drastically negative natural growth affecting the Moscow posad
population. It is probable that developments in Petersburg, comparable
to Moscow in size and thus subject to the same poor health conditions
characteristic of such large population centers in the absence of
modern sanitation, were similar.

Despite the declines noted, Moscow and Petersburg together still
claimed an inordinately large share of the country's mercantile peasants.
They had 66 percent of the mercantile peasants according to the Second
Revision and 40 percent according to the following census but only 6 to
8 percent of the nationwide posad population. The capitals also dominated their respective regions, Moscow with 80-84 percent of the regional
total and Petersburg with 53-71 percent. In the Central Industrial
Region no towns other than Moscow boasted large numbers of peasant
registrants, although 22 such towns reported some registrants in one
or both of the specified censuses.[17]

Turning to data from the 1800 tax register (Table 2), we find that
despite the much less inclusive character of these figures a considerably
larger nationwide total of registrants is recorded. From 1795 through
1799, 4700 crown peasants were added to the kupechestvo and 6400 to
the meshchanstvo in all provinces, and these 11,000 registrants represented an increment to the urban classes of about 3 percent. In this
brief period enlistment under the provisions introduced by Catherine II

_____

[17]Ibid., 11. 1-65. The towns were Kolomna (34 registrants according
to the Third Revision), Vereia (9 in the Second Revision and 17 in the
Third Revision), Borovsk (18 and 4 respectively), Serpukhov (0, 13),
Tarusa (0, 3), Romanov (4, 28), Suzdal' (3, 0), Vladimir (26, 19),
Murom (7, 9), Kostroma (4, 5), Pereslavl'-Zalesskii (27, 23), Rostov
(4, 16), Kashin (1, 1), Bezhetsk (1, 1), Tver' (16, 14), Torzhok (40,
31), Rzhev (42, 11), Nizhnii Novgorod (0, 17), Balakhna (21, 16),
Arzamas (1, 1) and Parfen'ev (7, 2). Nerekhta and Ples, listed together as "suburban" settlements (prigoroda) of Kostroma uezd, were
credited with one peasant registrant in each revision.

Table 2: Enlistment of Crown Peasants in Urban Classes, 1795-1799

(Number of Males)

Regions	Total kupechestvo (1800)	Peasant registrants[a]	% peasants	Total meshchanstvo (1800)	Peasant registrants[a]	% peasants	Total in urban classes (1800)	Total peasant registrants[a]	% peasants
CIR[b]	41643	1833	4.4	85013	762	0.9	126656	2595	2.0
North[c]	1810	15	0.8	12462	363	2.9	14272	378	2.6
Northwest[d]	17554	148	0.8	41959	459	1.1	59513	607	1.0
CAR[e]	30065	648	2.2	59659	1169	2.0	89724	1817	2.0
Volga[f]	14309	1535	10.7	35586	2418	6.8	49895	3953	7.9
Ural[g]	4671	484	10.4	16493	659	4.0	21164	1143	5.4
Siberia[h]	2440	51	2.1	33107	544	1.6	35547	595	1.7
Total	112492	4714	4.2	284279	6374	2.2	396771	11088	2.8

Source: TsGIA, f. 571, op. 9, d. 1 ("Okladnaia kniga po vsemu gosudarstvu o chisle dush po 5-oi revizii po 1 genvariia 1800 g."), ll. 1-106.

[a]Crown peasants enlisted since Fifth Revision (1795).

[b]Includes the following post-1775 territorial units: Moscow, Vladimir, Kaluga, Iaroslavl', Tver', Kostroma and Nizhnii Novgorod gubernii.

[c]Arkhangel'sk and Vologda gubernii.

[d]St. Petersburg, Novgorod, Pskov and Smolensk gubernii.

[e]Tula, Riazan', Orel, Kursk, Voronezh and Tambov gubernii.

[f]Kazan', Simbirsk, Saratov and Astrakhan' gubernii.

[g]Viatka, Perm' and Orenburg gubernii.

[h]Tobol'sk guberniia (including former Kolyvan' and subsequent Tomsk gubernii) and Irkutsk guberniia.

thus contributed more to expansion of the urban classes than had the Petrine institution of "mercantile peasants" in the four decades between the First and Third Revisions.

The tax register also reveals striking changes in the regional distribution of peasant enlistment, and it is clear that since the middle of the century this enlistment had diffused much more widely through the provinces of European Russia.[18] With 32 percent of the nationwide posad population, the formerly dominant Central Industrial and Northwest regions now gained only 23 percent of the total number of registrants. As measured by the ratio of peasant registrants to the total in the urban classes, enlistment was in fact at its weakest among all regions in the Northwest. However, the 607 crown peasants added to the urban classes of this region from 1795 through 1799 may still represent a higher per annum influx than the figures reported earlier in the century. In all other regions enlistment unquestionably increased. The most striking growth occurred in the Volga and Ural provinces, which had earlier received very small numbers of registrants but now absorbed 46 percent of the nationwide total. In the Volga Region 11 percent of the kupechestvo and 7 percent of the meshchanstvo consisted of crown peasants who had enlisted during the preceding half-decade, and the figures for the Ural Region were only slightly less impressive. Enlistment had also grown very markedly in the Central Agricultural Region, although not to the same extent as in the Volga

---

[18]The distribution of post-1775 gubernii among regions is shown in the footnotes to Table 2. The area covered by each region approximates closely that of the similarly designated grouping of pre-1775 units in Table 1. Two gubernii created as a result of the 1775 reforms (Olonets and Penza gubernii) are not shown because in 1800 they were temporarily not in existence, having been abolished by the meddlesome Emperor Paul and divided up among the neighboring provinces.

and Ural provinces. This region now claimed 16 percent of the nation-wide total of peasant registrants, as opposed to 6 percent in the results of the Third Revision.

The 1800 "Tax Register" gives data only for whole provinces and thus does not allow us to investigate concentrations of peasant regis-trants in individual towns. The numbers of registrants recorded in each province are shown in Table 3. Sixty percent of the registrants in the Central Industrial Region resided in Moscow guberniia, and as will be demonstrated in forthcoming chapters most of these new urban citizens were to be found in Moscow itself. With one exception, the other provinces of this region reported low levels of enlistment.[19] The apparent disinterest of local villagers in most towns of these pro-vinces possibly reflects the widespread availability of non-agricultural employment in rural commerce and industry and tne strong attraction exerted by Moscow and Petersburg on those who did migrate. The excep-tion was Nizhnii Novgorod guberniia, which was relatively remote from both capitals and unlike the more centrally located provinces, as will be demonstrated by other evidence, did not supply many migrants to either of them.[20] Moreover, this province bordered on the Middle Volga

---

[19]Two of these provinces,Vladimir and Kaluga gubernii, reported no registrants at all. However, the accuracy of this result is open to question, since it is hard to believe that not a single peasant enlisted in any of the towns of these provinces, several of which were large and important. It may be that the provincial treasuries (kazennye palaty) in these gubernii, which were the source of the information contained in the tax register, simply did not separate peasant registrants from the rest of the posad population as was intended by Petersburg. The towns which were later included in Vladimir guberniia reported 63 mercantile peasants at the time of the Second Revision and 51 in the Third Revision, while the corresponding figures for Kaluga guberniia were 18 and 7. Unfortunately, no further investigation of the situa-tion in these provinces is possible with the materials at hand.

[20]See below, Chapters IV, V.

Table 3: Enlistment of Crown Peasants in Urban Classes of Individual Provinces, 1795-1799

Regions and provinces	Total kupechestvo	Peasant registrants	% peasants	Total meshchanstvo	Peasant registrants	% peasants	Total in urban classes	Total peasant registrants	% peasants
CIR									
Moscow	15431	1415	9.2	19846	151	0.8	35277	1566	4.4
Vladimir	5887	-	-	6859	-	-	12746	-	-
Kaluga	4568	-	-	13546	-	-	18114	-	-
Iaroslavl'	3740	51	1.4	11560	25	0.2	15300	76	0.4
Tver'	6692	23	0.3	17120	60	0.4	23812	83	0.3
Kostroma	1849	34	1.8	9459	41	0.4	11308	75	0.7
N. Novgorod	3476	310	8.9	6623	485	7.3	10099	795	7.9
Total	41643	1833	4.4	85013	762	0.9	126656	2595	2.0
North									
Arkhangel'sk	387	1	0.3	4538	10	0.2	4925	11	0.2
Vologda	1423	14	1.0	7924	353	4.5	9347	367	3.9
Total	1810	15	0.8	12462	363	2.9	14272	378	2.6
Northwest									
Petersburg	4734	39	0.8	10430	122	1.2	15164	161	1.1
Novgorod	5544	73	1.3	13247	237	1.8	18791	310	1.6
Pskov	3310	22	0.7	6131	35	0.6	9441	57	0.6
Smolensk	3966	14	0.4	12151	65	0.5	16117	79	0.5
Total	17554	148	0.8	41959	459	1.1	59513	607	1.0

Table 3 (cont.)

Regions and provinces	Total kupechestvo	Peasant registrants	% peasants	Total meshchanstvo	Peasant registrants	% peasants	Total in urban classes	Total peasant registrants	% peasants
CAR									
Tula	3702	108	2.9	12421	292	2.4	16123	400	2.5
Riazan'	4196	-	-	8594	-	-	12790	-	-
Orel	8271	104	1.3	16867	193	1.1	25138	297	1.2
Kursk	5359	221	4.1	9005	421	4.7	14364	642	4.5
Voronezh	1712	205	12.0	3519	250	7.1	5231	455	8.7
Tambov	6825	10	0.1	9253	13	0.1	16078	23	0.1
Total	30065	648	2.2	59659	1169	2.0	89724	1817	2.0
Volga									
Kazan'	2143	407	19.0	8627	1344	15.6	10770	1751	16.3
Simbirsk	1942	244	12.6	8273	467	5.6	10215	711	7.0
Saratov	8126	536	6.6	14400	343	2.4	22526	879	3.9
Astrakhan'	2098	348	16.6	4286	264	6.1	6384	612	9.0
Total	14309	1535	10.7	35586	2418	6.8	49895	3953	7.9
Ural									
Viatka	964	86	8.9	5506	71	1.3	6470	157	2.4
Perm'	1383	38	2.7	9029	357	4.0	10412	395	3.8
Orenburg	2324	360	15.5	1958	231	11.8	4282	591	13.8
Total	4671	484	10.4	16493	659	4.0	21164	1143	5.4

Table 3 (cont.)

Regions and provinces	Total kupechestvo	Peasant registrants	% peasants	Total meshchanstvo	Peasant registrants	% peasants	Total in urban classes	Total peasant registrants	% peasants
Siberia									
Tobol'sk	1509	35	2.3	24566	503	2.0	26075	538	2.1
Irkutsk	931	16	1.6	8541	41	0.5	9472	57	0.6
Total	2440	51	2.1	33107	544	1.6	35547	595	1.7
Total in all provinces	112492	4714	4.2	284279	6374	2.2	396771	11088	2.8

Source: TsGIA, f. 571, op. 9, d. 1, ll. 1-106.

territory and apparently shared the characteristics which produced a
massive influx of registrants in this area: like the "downstream"
towns, Nizhnii Novgorod attracted large numbers of migrants for work in
the Volga transport industry, as well as trading peasants seeking a
share of the thriving commerce associated with Russia's most important
waterway.

According to the tax register, large numbers of registrants
appeared in all the Volga provinces but especially in Kazan' guberniia,
where 16 percent of the urban classes consisted of new recruits from
the peasantry. In the Ural Region, enlistment was heavy in Orenburg
and Perm' gubernii, less so in Viatka guberniia. Four of the six provinces in the Central Agricultural Region reported at least moderately
large totals. In Siberia enlistment took place predominantly in the
western part of the territory (Tobol'sk guberniia), as had been the
case earlier in the century, while in the North the influx into the
urban classes was concentrated in Vologda guberniia. In the Northwest
surprisingly little enlistment was credited to St. Petersburg guberniia,
in contrast to earlier results showing Petersburg to be the main destination of peasant registrants in this region.[21] This result must be
viewed with some suspicion, since the new capital unquestionably continued to be a major attraction for trading peasants and seasonal
migrants in search of work. It is therefore questionable that the
figures from the 1800 tax register accurately reflect the trend of

---

[21] In addition to the figures offered in Table 1, data cited in a
recent study devoted to Petersburg indicate a substantial influx of
peasants (more than 1200 souls) into the urban classes of this city between the Third and Fourth Revisions. See George E. Munro, The Development of St. Petersburg as an Urban Center during the Reign of Catherine
II (1762-1796) (Ph. D. dissertation, University of North Carolina, 1973),
p. 303.

enlistment in Petersburg, but the situation can be clarified only by further detailed research on this city.[22]

Since the middle of the century enlistment of peasants in the urban classes thus not only had grown sharply in terms of nationwide totals but also had spread into regions and provinces where it had formerly been weak or non-existent. In these changes we may detect the influence of the reforms of 1775-1785, which raised the status of the urban kupechestvo, possibly rendering membership in it more attractive to peasants who could qualify, and made such membership available to peasants on much more favorable terms. The reforms also made it possible for peasants not possessing capital or enterprises to enlist in the meshchanstvo, and as we have seen more than half the registrants recorded in the years following the fifth Revision belonged to this lower category of urban citizens. Other factors which undoubtedly contributed to the growth and spread of enlistment were the ongoing commercial and industrial development of the country and the specific characteristics of this development in different regions. The latter relationships can be illuminated only by more detailed research into the processes of urbanization in areas outside the Central Industrial Region, but to some extent economic differences among peasant registrants in various regions and provinces are reflected in the varying proportions in which these registrants belonged to the kupechestvo or the meshchanstvo. During the period covered by the data members of the kupechestvo were supposed to possess a minimum of 2000 rubles in

---

[22]On migration to Petersburg from the Central Industrial Region, see below, Chapter V. One serious shortcoming of the data from the 1800 tax register is that they do not include enlistment by freed serfs. According to figures published by A. I. Kopanev, most of the peasants absorbed into the Petersburg meshchanstvo between 1833 and 1850 were former serfs rather than crown peasants. See Kopanev, Naselenie Peterburga v pervoi polovine XIX v. (Moscow-Leningrad, 1957), p. 43.

capital and pay an annual tax of at least 20 rubles, while the meshchanstvo
paid a head tax of 2 rubles 50 kopecks.[23] It should not be assumed that
the latter consisted entirely of propertyless elements not endowed with
even modestly successful business enterprises, since some persons who
could have qualified for the kupechestvo instead joined the meshchanstvo
to avoid higher taxation.[24] Many members of the meshchanstvo functioned
as small merchants and industrial entrepreneurs or as independent craftsmen. Nevertheless, it is certain that as a whole registrants in the
meshchanstvo constituted a less prosperous group, with a heavy repre-
sentation of laborers, employees and other low-status elements.[25]

The data presented in Table 3 disclose that registrants from the
crown peasantry belonged predominantly to the kupechestvo in Moscow
guberniia, predominantly to the meshchanstvo in Vologda and Perm'
gubernii and in Siberia, and about equally to both in the Central Agricultural and Volga provinces and in Nizhnii Novgorod guberniia. Pre-
ference for the meshchanstvo appears to reflect the balances already
existing in the urban classes of the designated provinces, which heavily
favored this category. The disinclination of crown peasants to enter
the Moscow meshchanstvo (confirmed by more detailed data on Moscow to be
presented later) may be related to the widespread development of trade
and industry in rural areas of the Central Industrial Region and the
availability of seasonal work in the urban economy as well, which relieved the pressure on peasants unable to subsist in the agricultural

---

[23]Polnoe sobranie zakonov Rossiiskoi imperii s 1649 g. (PSZ), Vol.
23, No. 17223; TsGIA, f. 571, op. 9, d. 1, ll. 1 ob.-2.

[24]P. G. Ryndziunskii, "Soslovno-podatnaia reforma 1775 g. i gorodskoe
naselenie," in Obshchestvo i gosudarstvo feodal'noi Rossii (Moscow, 1975),
p. 94.

[25]These contentions are borne out by data on peasants who enlisted in
the Moscow posad between 1782 and 1795, to be presented in the next chapter.

economy to enter the permanent urban population. The Middle and Lower
Volga provinces attracted large numbers of migrant laborers from various
parts of European Russia for work in the important Volga transport industries, which required great quantities of manpower. Since the navigation season was roughly the same as the growing season, work on the
Volga tended to detach peasants completely from agriculture, and many
migrants did not return to their villages in the winter but found work
in the Volga towns.[26] Hence it is not surprising to find substantial
numbers of peasants enlisting in the meshchanstvo of these towns.[27]
However, the importance of the Volga as a commercial artery provided
the opportunities and attractions which assured a major influx of
trading peasants into the kupechestvo as well. Nizhnii Novgorod,
also an important center of the Volga transport industry, shared the

---

[26]On migration to the Volga towns for wage labor during the eighteenth
century, see M. Ia. Volkov, "Materialy pervoi revizii," pp. 289-99; N. B.
Golikova, Naemnyi trud v gorodakh Povolzh'ia v pervoi chetverti XVIII v.
(Moscow, 1965); F. N. Rodin, Burlachestvo v Rossii (Moscow, 1975), pp.
61-97; Klokman, Sotsial'no-ekonomicheskaia istoriia, pp. 280-91; E. N.
Kusheva, "Saratov v pervoi polovine XVIII v.," in Problemy sotsial'no-
ekonomicheskoi istorii Rossii (Moscow, 1971), pp. 28-38; S. I. Arkhangel'-
skii, "Simbileiskaia votchina Vl. Gr. Orlova (1790-1800 gg.)," Trudy
Nizhegorodskogo nauchnogo obshchestva po izucheniiu mestnogo kraia, Vol.
2 (Nizhnii Novgorod, 1929), pp. 176-89.

The Kama, which traversed the Ural provinces, was also the scene
of important labor-intensive water-transport operations.

[27]Another possible source of recruits into the urban classes of the
Volga region was the descendants of the military garrisons which were
the original population of these towns when they were founded in the
sixteenth and seventeenth centuries. These elements, now classified as
state peasants, were the largest population group in many towns of the
region. According to E. N. Kusheva, many members of the urban classes
in Saratov were the descendants of military servitors of an earlier era.
(Kusheva, "Saratov v pervoi polovine XVIII v.," pp. 30-31, 34-36; see
also I. A. Bulygin, "Ob osobennostiakh gorodov Srednego Povolzh'ia vo
vtoroi polovine XVIII v.," in Goroda feodal'noi Rossii, pp. 486-97.
Similar population groups probably existed in many towns of the Central
Agricultural and Ural regions.

indicated characteristics of the "downstream" towns.

The available data allow us to explore to some extent the correlation between peasant enlistment and the growth of the urban classes. Information on this growth can be obtained from data provided by V. M. Kabuzan on the size of the various official population categories according to each revision.[28] These data disclose that in the four decades between the First and Third Revisions, during which enlistment by peasants was very limited, growth of the urban classes was weak and lagged behind general population growth. During the indicated period the posad population grew by only 12 percent in all "Great Russian" provinces while the total male population increased by 33 percent. Growth of the urban classes tended to be somewhat higher in regions of ongoing colonization (Volga, Urals, Siberia) than in the long-settled regions of the country, but even there this growth was greatly exceeded by general population growth. Only in the Central Industrial Region did growth of the urban classes (15 percent) surpass overall growth, which at 12 percent was low by nationwide standards.[29] In the North and Northwest regions posad growth was negative.

The gap between urban and overall growth narrowed in the period between the Third and Fourth Revisions (1764-1782), during which the urban classes increased by 20 percent and the total male population by 24 percent. However, much of the increment to the urban classes probably resulted from the creation of more than 200 new towns in

---

[28]Kabuzan, Izmeneniia v razmeshchenii naseleniia Rossii, pp. 59-127.

[29]There might appear to be some correlation between the growth of the posad population in the Central Industrial Region and the fact that relatively large numbers of mercantile peasants were enlisted there. However, most of these peasants were registered in Moscow, and as will be demonstrated later the Moscow posad did not grow during this period.

connection with the restructuring of the empire's territorial administration and internal boundaries initiated in 1775.[30] Following the Fourth Revision growth of the urban classes continued to accelerate and surpassed overall population growth (which dropped somewhat) by a wide margin. Between the Fourth and Fifth Revisions (1782-1795) the urban classes expanded by 29 percent while the general population grew by only 9 percent. For the period between the Fifth and Sixth Revisions (1795-1811) the figures were 24 and 14 percent respectively. The increase in peasant enlistment which occurred in the late eighteenth century was thus accompanied by a strong surge in the growth of the posad population.

If we examine the results for particular regions and individual provinces, we find that rapid growth of the urban classes and a high level of peasant enlistment are usually although not invariably associated.[31] (See Table 4.) In the Volga and Ural regions, which in the

---

[30]A few new provinces and districts were instituted after the Fourth Revision, and the resulting increment to the urban population presumably appears in the results of the succeeding census.

[31]It is somewhat difficult to devise the proper comparison between the available data on enlistment and those on population growth. The data of the 1800 "Tax Register" fall within the period between the Fifth and Sixth Revisions but cover only the beginning of the period. Other evidence indicates that enlistment by crown peasants tended to cluster around the time of the census. Most of the registrants reported in the 1800 "Tax Register" therefore probably enlisted during the course of the Fifth Revision or in its immediate aftermath, when they may still have had hopes of quick release from peasant status and obligations as a consequence of the new census. (These hopes were frustrated by the government's decision that only those who had enlisted before the announcement of the new census on June 23, 1794, were entitled to these benefits.) Most of the registrants whose membership in the posad was ratified by the Fifth Revision had probably enlisted in the years immediately preceding the census. The influx reported by the "Tax Register" thus probably represents the tail end of a wave of enlistment which appeared before the Fifth Revision and contributed to the posad

Table 4: Peasant Enlistment and Growth of Urban Classes in Late
Eighteenth Century

Regions and provinces	% growth of gen. population[a]		% growth of urban classes[a]		Peasant enlistment[b]
	IV-V Rev.	V-VI Rev.	IV-V Rev.	V-VI Rev.	1795-1799
CIR					
Moscow	8.6	8.1	78.4	20.7	4.4
Vladimir	3.7	5.7	14.7	7.8	-
Kaluga	-2.8	10.2	17.5	25.4	-
Iaroslavl'	2.2	5.6	10.4	8.9	0.4
Tver'	6.9	9.6	16.1	12.1	0.3
Kostroma	0	5.9	8.2	3.8	0.7
N. Novgorod	3.7	8.7	29.4	23.6	7.9
Total	3.4	7.7	28.8	15.8	2.0
North					
Arkhangel'sk	6.9	0.5	10.6	-6.0	0.2
Vologda	5.3	9.8	2.8	3.2	3.9
Total	5.6	7.6	5.4	0	2.6
Northwest					
St. Petersburg	5.4	5.9	49.1	16.0	1.1
Novgorod	7.8	11.7	14.1	7.4	1.6
Pskov	7.0	3.6	28.3	34.7	0.6
Olonets	4.3	11.7	-44.8	1.1	-[c]
Smolensk	5.8	2.2	19.8	6.0	0.5
Total	5.7	5.8	15.3	13.2	1.0

Table 4 (cont.)

Regions and provinces	% growth of gen. population IV-V Rev.	V-VI Rev.	% growth of urban classes IV-V Rev.	V-VI Rev.	Peasant enlistment 1795-1799
CAR					
Tula	2.6	12.1	25.3	22.3	2.5
Riazan'	4.1	14.7	31.6	26.6	-
Orel	3.8	16.0	27.6	26.1	1.2
Kursk	14.9	14.7	46.8	54.9	4.5
Voronezh	12.8	29.7	60.6	145.0	8.7
Tambov	17.2	23.1	66.3	71.0	0.1
Total	9.3	18.3	37.3	44.6	2.0
Volga					
Kazan'	8.1	15.6	50.5	40.1	16.3
Simbirsk	13.2	13.2	45.5	16.1	7.0
Penza	0.3	27.6	59.4	39.6	-c
Saratov	31.3	34.8	38.7	29.9	3.9
Astrakhan'	18.0	15.7	124.4	45.7	9.0
Total	12.9	21.8	51.7	32.2	7.9
Ural					
Viatka	11.8	20.8	34.8	43.1	2.4
Perm'	15.0	18.9	25.8	14.0	3.8
Orenburg	26.7	34.7	198.8	67.2	13.8
Total	17.0	24.2	45.0	33.3	5.4

Table 4 (cont.)

Regions and provinces	% growth of gen. population IV-V Rev.	V-VI Rev.	% growth of urban classes IV-V Rev.	V-VI Rev.	Peasant enlistment 1795-1799
Siberia					
Tobol'sk	13.2	11.1	33.1	3.2	2.1
Irkutsk	-1.4	21.7	-28.7	1.7	0.6
Total	7.7	14.8	11.3	2.9	1.7
Total in all provinces	8.5	14.4	28.8	23.6	2.8

Sources: TsGIA, f. 571, op. 9, d. 1, 11. 1-106; V. M. Kabuzan, _Izmeneniia_ _v_ _razmeshchenii_ _naseleniia_ _Rossii_ _v_ _XVIII_-_pervoi_ _polovine_ _XIX_ _v._ (Moscow, 1971), pp. 95-126.

[a]Percent increase from Fourth to Fifth Revision (1782-1795) and from Fifth to Sixth Revision (1795-1811).

[b]Enlistment of crown peasants, 1795-1799, as percent of total in urban classes in 1800. (See Tables 2-3.)

[c]Olonets and Penza _gubernii_ are not shown in the 1800 data on peasant enlistment because they were temporarily not in existence at the time. (See text.)

closing years of the century were receiving the strongest infusion of peasant registrants (in proportion to the total regional posad population), growth of the urban classes was especially high in the decades following the Fourth Revision. In the Volga Region the posad population grew by 52 percent between the Fourth and Fifth Revisions and by 32 percent in the subsequent intercensus period, and the figures for the Ural provinces are similar. Growth was also very high in the Central Agricultural Region, where peasant enlistment had also increased very markedly. Turning to figures for individual provinces, we find that those which received a strong influx of peasant registrants usually experienced fairly rapid to very rapid growth of the posad population.[32] Such provinces were Moscow, Nizhnii Novgorod, Kursk, Voronezh, Kazan', Simbirsk, Saratov, Astrakhan' and Orenburg gubernii. Likewise, most provinces where peasant enlistment was low recorded low to moderate posad growth (Vladimir, Iaroslavl', Kaluga, Tver', Kostroma, Arkhangel'sk, Novgorod, Smolensk, Irkutsk gubernii). However, a few provinces where enlistment was low experienced at least fairly rapid growth (St. Petersburg, Pskov, Riazan' and especially Tambov gubernii),

---

growth recorded by that census. For this reason the data on enlistment are at least as relevant to the posad growth which preceded this enlistment as to that recorded by the subsequent census, and as is shown by Table 4 the enlistment is in fact more closely correlated with the former.

[32]The boundaries of Novgorod, Arkhangel'sk, Nizhnii Novgorod, Saratov, Simbirsk and Tambov gubernii vary somewhat between the two sources used in this analysis. In the 1800 "Tax Register" these provinces include pieces of the former Olonets and Penza gubernii, which had recently been liquidated by Emperor Paul. Kabuzan, however, uses the configuration of 1806, by which time the two partitioned provinces had been re-established within their former boundaries. However, these changes are not expected to make much difference in the determinations given.

while Vologda guberniia had fairly high enlistment but low growth.[33]
Ample enlistment in Perm' guberniia did not produce particularly rapid
growth, while the neighboring Viatka guberniia had less enlistment but
more growth.

The quantitative increase and geographical expansion of peasant
enlistment in the urban classes which occurred in the late eighteenth
century obviously made an important contribution to the accelerated
growth of the urban classes observed in the same period. The enlistment by crown peasants covered by the available data does not, however,
appear to account for the dynamics of the posad population in their
entirety, nor would it be expected to do so. Other factors involved
in posad growth might include enlistment by freed serfs and members of
other, non-peasant population categories, the resettlement of posad
members from other areas as well as out-migration by native citizens,
administrative reclassification of population groups, and differing
rates of natural growth. The prevailing population dynamics may have
exerted a reciprocal influence on potential registrants, since towns
which were thriving economically and expanding demographically were
probably the most likely to attract a continued stream of migrants.
The elucidation of these relationships and of many other questions
raised by the above discussion requires further archival research.

---

[33]The healthy growth of the urban classes in St. Petersburg
guberniia reinforces doubts expressed earlier regarding the validity
of the enlistment data on this province.

CHAPTER IV: MOSCOW

Role of Peasants in the Population and Economy of Moscow

Eighteenth-century Moscow, although it had lost its political
primacy to Petersburg, remained the undisputed metropolis of Central
Russia and probably the most important individual commercial center in
the country. Surpassed in total population toward the end of the
century by rapidly growing Petersburg, Moscow continued to be by far
the greatest population center of the Russian interior. According to
censuses taken by the church authorities, the total population of Moscow
(not including seasonal migrants) grew from about 140,000 persons of
both sexes in the late 1730's to over 160,000 in 1776, despite the
ravages of the plague which preceded the later census by five years.
Estimates relating to the last two decades of the century range from
175,000 to 217,000 for the permanent population, while in the winter
the population reportedly approached 400,000.[1] Even without this
seasonal expansion Moscow dwarfed all other towns of the Central Industrial Region, the largest of which (Iaroslavl' and Kaluga) were only
about one-tenth the size of the old capital. Nor did any other city
in the empire, excepting Petersburg, approach Moscow in size during
this period.[2]

---

[1]Istoriia Moskvy, Vol. 2 (Moscow, 1953), pp. 306-08; Gilbert
Rozman, Urban Networks in Russia, 1750-1800, and Premodern Periodization
(Princeton, 1976), p. 162; A. Shchekatov, Geograficheskii slovar' Rossiiskogo
gosudarstva, Vol. 4 (Moscow, 1805), pp. 365, 385-87. Another compilation of contemporary geographical descriptions credits Moscow with a
wintertime population of 500,000 to 600,000, but this estimate is
certainly exaggerated. E. Ziablovskii, Zemleopisanie Rossiiskoi
Imperii dlia vsekh sostoianii, Vol. 3 (St. Petersburg, 1810), p. 224.

[2]Rozman, Urban Networks, pp. 162-200.

The composition of Moscow's population, as well as its sheer size, was exceptional. Moscow had the largest posad population of any Russian city, not excluding Petersburg. According to the Second Revision (1744) the Moscow posad contained more than 13,000 male "souls," while the next largest, those of Iaroslavl' and Kaluga, had about 6000.[3] Nevertheless, the difference here was much smaller than the gap in total population, since in Moscow the officially recognized urban classes accounted for a much lower proportion of the total than in most significant urban settlements of the region. According to the ecclesiastical census, the Moscow posad population of the 1730's (24,000 persons of both sexes), was only 17 percent of the total population.[4] Sources relating to the period 1790-1800 credit the posad with 10-15 percent of the total.[5] In contrast, data on the district towns of Moscow guberniia and the towns of Iaroslavl' guberniia indicate that at the end of the eighteenth century the posad typically accounted for 50-90 percent of the population in these settlements.[6] The mammoth size of

[3]A. A. Kizevetter, Posadskaia obshchina v Rossii XVIII stoletiia (Moscow, 1903), p. 102.

[4]Istoriia Moskvy, Vol. 2, pp. 306-07.

[5]Ibid. (posad 21,000 males and females, total 175,000, ratio 12 percent); Shchekatov, Geograficheskii slovar', Vol. 4, pp. 385-87 (posad 15,102 males, total 146,433 males, ratio 10 percent); Tsentral'nyi gosudarstvennyi istoricheskii arkhiv, Leningrad (hereafter TsGIA), f. 558 (Senatskaia ekspeditsiia dlia revizii gosudarstvennykh schetov), op. 2, d. 129, ll. 2 ob.-9 (posad 23,000 males in 1800, ratio 15 percent assuming a total male population of about 150,000, as indicated by Shchekatov). As is suggested by the above figures, the urban classes of Moscow grew rapidly in the last decade of the century, but as a proportion of the total population they apparently did not rise above the level of the 1730's.

[6]See below, Chapter V, Tables 18, 23. The population totals for these lesser towns apparently include only persons officially considered residents of the town and not unofficial peasant settlers. However, as will be evident from the materials to be presented in Chapter V, such

Moscow thus derived not so much from an enlarged posad as from the much more conspicuous presence of members of other population groups. The city was host to unusually large numbers of persons from the tax-exempt categories, including nobles, officials, clergy and military personnel, and from the catch-all category of raznochintsy ("people of miscellaneous status"). The ecclesiastical census of the late 1730's attributed to these groups collectively a 44-percent share of the Moscow population, while data for the early 1790's indicate that nobles made up 5 percent of the population, clergy 2 percent, military personnel 4 percent, and lower officials (prikaznye) and raznochintsy 10 percent--a total of 21 percent for all these groups.[7]

The largest single element in the Moscow population, however, was persons of peasant status. According to the ecclesiastical census the Moscow population of the late 1730's contained 36,000 house serfs (dvorovye liudi) and 18,000 peasants of both sexes, not including seasonal migrants. These peasants comprised 39 percent of the reported total population. Later sources, possibly giving more inclusive data but certainly to some extent reflecting growing peasant immigration, mention considerably larger numbers of peasants. One such source

settlers played a much smaller role in the population of most towns of the Central Industrial Region than in Moscow.

[7]Istoriia Moskvy, Vol. 2, pp. 306-07. Shchekatov's Geographical Dictionary reports figures for these groups which are proportionally comparable to those given by the source for the early 1790's, although Shchekatov reports separately several groups which in the data cited are apparently placed under the heading of raznochintsy. These include retired soldiers, iamshchiki (postmen) and persons attached to various educational, charitable and other institutions. Shchekatov, Vol. 4, pp. 385-87.

(offering data attributed to the period 1788-1795) reports the presence of 61,000 house serfs and 59,000 peasants, constituting 65 percent of the reported total population of 175,000.[8] Shchekatov's Geographical Dictionary, published in the first decade of the nineteenth century and compiled from information collected during the preceding several decades, asserts that a total Moscow population "in normal times" of 217,000 included the following numbers of peasants and serfs:[9]

	Males	Females
House serfs		
"ascribed to /Moscow/ households"	7862	6583
"registered in various provinces"	28683	15743
total	36545	22326
Peasants		
"permanently" living in Moscow	8603	3937
"temporarily" living in Moscow	37698	7457
total	46301	11394

---

[8]Istoriia Moskvy, Vol. 2, pp. 306-07.

[9]Shchekatov, Geograficheskii slovar', Vol. 4, pp. 385-87. It is difficult to date any information given by Shchekatov without tracing it to its source. One item in his population breakdown for Moscow is attributed to an official document of 1804, but the figures given for the urban classes are much too low for that period. According to Shchekatov the Moscow urban classes (including kuptsy, meshchane and "permanent" craft-guild members) totaled 15,102 males, while reports of the Moscow provincial treasury (kazennaia palata) give totals of 15,352 for 1793 and 25,258 for 1802. (TsGIA, f. 558, op. 2, d. 126, ll. 518 ob.-520, 525 ob.-527; d. 129, ll. 382 ob.-388.) Shchekatov's figures on the urban classes at least thus appear to reflect the situation of the early to middle 1790's, just prior the Fifth Revision. Istoriia Moskvy (Vol. 2, p. 306) attributes Shchekatov's data on the Moscow population to the mid-1780's, which seems unlikely, since his figures for the urban classes do not at all correspond to the situation prevailing in that period. On the methods used in compiling the Geographical Dictionary, see L. V. Milov, "K istorii sozdaniia 'Geograficheskogo slovaria' Afanasiia Shchekatova," Arkheograficheskii ezhegodnik za 1968 g. (Moscow, 1970), pp. 166-83.

According to this source the Moscow population thus included 59,000 house serfs and 58,000 peasants of both sexes, and these elements accounted for 54 percent of the total population reported. The above figures do not include the wintertime influx of peasants into Moscow for purposes of trade, craft industry, hired labor and other pursuits.[10] Nor do they include peasants officially registered in the urban classes or "temporarily" enlisted in craft guilds, about whom there will be extensive discussion elsewhere in this chapter.[11] It should also be pointed out that the term "house serfs" does not necessarily denote persons who were actually performing domestic service in seigneurial households and that the distinction between house serfs and seigneurial peasants is vague.[12] Like the latter, such house serfs are frequently encountered living far from their masters, with passports allowing them to roam the country in search of income. The great imbalance between males and females, which was especially characteristic

---

[10]Peasants, of course, were not the only ones who converged on Moscow during the winter. Many nobles moved from their country estates to the city for the winter season, while provincial and foreign merchants also appeared on the scene in the largest numbers at this time. See Shchekatov, Geograficheskii slovar', Vol. 4, p. 365; Ziablovskii, Zemleopisanie, Vol. 3, p. 224; S. Chernov, Statisticheskoe opisanie Moskovskoi gubernii 1811 g. (Moscow, 1812), p. 43.

[11]Between the Fourth and Fifth Revisions (1782-1795) 5100 male souls were inducted into the Moscow urban classes from the various peasant categories. At the end of the eighteenth century there were 11,900 males enlisted as temporary members of Moscow craft guilds, most of whom were undoubtedly peasants.

[12]The group here identified as house serfs is referred to in the sources usually as dvorovye liudi ("people of the master's household") but sometimes as gospodskie liudi ("the lords' people") or as "servants" (sluzhiteli) of lords. Since Russian serfowners were free to do more or less what they wished with their "people," seigneurial peasants could be converted into house serfs or vice versa at the master's wish.

of those identified as peasants but also notable among house serfs
registered for tax purposes in "various provinces" rather than under
Moscow households, suggests a high degree of recent and autonomous
migration from the village.

The Moscow population depended heavily on such immigrants to expand and even maintain its numbers because the disastrous health
conditions characteristic of such large concentrations of population
in the absence of modern sanitation impeded natural growth and often
drove it deep into the negative area. A half-century ago E. A.
Zviagintsev investigated this situation with respect to the Moscow
posad, seeking to explain why this segment of the population not only
failed to grow during the greater part of the eighteenth century but
actually contracted steadily and sharply between the Second and Fourth
Revisions (1744-1782).[13] Zviagintsev found that the decline was due
to an enormous surplus of deaths over births in the native population
and to an influx of newcomers which was insufficient to cover the
resulting deficit. Examining 22 of the 33 subdivisions (slobody and
sotni) which made up the Moscow posad in the eighteenth century, this
investigator determined that of 8114 male "souls" recorded in the
Second Revision, 3621 died before the subsequent census, while new

---

[13]According to the First Revision, the posad population of Moscow
was just under 14,000 male souls. In the Second Revision the posad
population decreased only slightly, by a few hundred souls, but it
thereafter contracted sharply to slightly less than 10,000 souls in
the Third Revision and between 8000 and 9000 in the Fourth Revision.
E. A. Zviagintsev, "Rost naseleniia v moskovskykh slobodakh XVIII v.,"
Moskovskii krai v ego proshlom, Vol. 2 (Moscow, 1930), pp. 137, 141;
Kizevetter, Posadskaia obshchina, pp. 88, 102; Gosudarstvennaia
publichnaia biblioteka im. Saltykova-Shchedrina, Leningrad, Rukopisnyi
otdel (hereafter GPB RO), Ermitazhnoe sobranie, No. 242 ("Vedomost'
o chisle dush po gorodam"), l. 1.

births during the same period contributed only 1777 souls. In addition, 327 persons were conscripted, 106 were removed from the posad for various other reasons, and 523 "disappeared for reasons unknown" (propalo bezvestno). Only 412 newcomers were enlisted, resulting in a total deficit of 2388 males and a 29 percent drop in the population of these slobody.[14]

In the succeeding period, these dismal mortality statistics were further accentuated by the Moscow plague of 1771, which claimed 3346 of the slightly less than 10,000 males registered under the Third Revision; an additional 1136 males died in other "healthy" years up to 1774, 1012 "disappeared for reasons unknown" and 213 were conscripted or left the posad for other reasons.[15] In all, nearly 60 percent of the Moscow posad members recorded in the Third Revision disappeared in the decade following this census. Zviagintsev also traced the fate of individual families belonging to three Moscow slobody and found that while these families contained 817 male souls according to the First Revision they were able to contribute only 554, 367 and 157 souls in the next three censuses.[16] This inexorable decline in the number of old-time Muscovites demonstrates the crucial importance of

---

[14] Zviagintsev, "Rost naseleniia," pp. 136-38. The total posad population dropped by about the same percentage during this period (see above, n. 13), which suggests that the results obtained by Zviagintsev are entirely representative of the posad as a whole.

[15] Zviagintsev, "Dinamika naseleniia dokapitalisticheskoi Moskvy" (manuscript), cited in Istoriia Moskvy, Vol. 2, pp. 312-13.

[16] Zviagintsev, "Rost naseleniia," pp. 140-41.

immigration to the expansion and even survival of the Moscow posad in
the eighteenth century. The spectacular growth which occurred in the
two decades following the Fourth Revision, during which the posad nearly
trebled in size, was due primarily to an unprecedented deluge of new
registrants, although an apparent improvement in the natural growth
rate of the residual population also made some contribution.[17] As will
be demonstrated later in this chapter, the most important contributor
to this influx was the peasantry. While the posad population pursued
the erractic course described, the total population of Moscow apparently
grew steadily throughout the century. The figures cited previously
suggest that this growth was due primarily to the increasing numbers of
peasants who settled in the city without benefit of formal urban
citizenship.

As representatives of the Moscow kupechestvo declared in 1793,
the city "could be considered the focal point of internal Russian
commerce."[18] Moscow was at the hub of a network of trade routes leading from all corners of the Russian Empire and from the foreign lands

---

[17]Between the Fourth and Fifth Revisions the residual population
contracted only slightly (Ibid., p. 143) which suggests that the death
rate had probably dropped below the birth rate for the first time in
the century. The possibility that health conditions in Moscow improved
substantially in the aftermath of the 1771 plague should inspire further
research into the government's efforts to improve urban conditions and
the possible results of these efforts. For some information, see
Istoriia Moskvy, Vol. 2, pp. 332-59; Robert E. Jones, "Urban Planning
and the Development of Provincial Towns in Russia during the Reign of
Catherine II," in J. G. Garrard, ed., The Eighteenth Century in Russia
(Oxford, 1973), pp. 321-44. The work of John T. Alexander on the 1771
epidemic and its impact is also highly relevant to this question.
Alexander, Bubonic Plague in Early Modern Russia: Public Health and
Urban Disaster (Baltimore, 1980).

[18]Istoriia Moskvy, Vol. 2, p. 294.

lying beyond those territories. Eighteenth-century observers tended to
divide the Moscow market into sectors according to the origin of the
goods traded. Besides the "internal Russian" trade in goods produced
by European Russia, these sectors included the "St. Petersburg" or
"European seaborne" trade, the "Polish" or "European overland" trade,
the "Orenburg" trade with Central Asia, and the Siberian, Chinese,
Persian and Turkish trade.[19] The most important types of goods traded
on the Moscow market included (1) food commodities, especially grain
and its derivatives, meat and livestock, fish, fruits and vegetables;
(2) industrial raw materials produced by agriculture and animal husbandry,
such as plant fibers (flax and hemp), wool and other animal fibers,
hides, bristles, lard, tallow and wax; (3) products of Central Russian
craft industries, including textiles, leather goods, articles of clothing, metal goods, wood products, ceramics, soap, candles; and (4) furs
from Siberia and to some extent from European Russia and Central Asia.
The contribution of the neighboring Asian countries consisted principally of silk and cotton fabrics, yarns and fibers but also included
luxury foodstuffs, spices, precious stones and (from Persia) copper.
From Europe Moscow received textiles and articles of clothing, tools,
instruments, crystal and window glass, paints and dyes, other industrial
goods, and wines and other luxury foodstuffs. Moscow also required
large quantities of hay, straw, firewood and building lumber for
internal consumption.

---

[19]Sostoianie stolichnogo goroda Moskvy, 1785 goda (Moscow, 1879),
pp. 7-9; Shchekatov, Geograficheskii slovar', Vol. 4, pp. 366-70. This
perspective was evidently a legacy of the internal-customs system,
abolished in 1753, under which transactions were recorded in separate
registers according to the origin of the goods. See E. N. Kusheva,
"Torgovlia Moskvy v 30-40-kh godakh XVIII veka," Istoricheskie zapiski,
Vol. 23 (1947), pp. 44-75.

Fruits and vegetables, hay, straw and wood were delivered to
Moscow predominantly from nearby districts.[20] In the eighteenth century the Moscow grain market was supplied chiefly by the central black-
soil provinces, located directly to the south of the old capital. This
grain arrived by water (primarily in the spring) via the rivers Oka and
Moskva and was also shipped overland in large quantity during the winter.
The agriculturists of the nearby less fertile districts also contributed
their small surpluses, while toward the end of the century the Middle
Volga provinces began to play a significant role in Moscow's grain
supply. The Moscow grain market not only served the large needs of
the city's own population and the surrounding industrial districts,
which increasingly formed a food-deficit region, but also acted as an
entrepot for transshipment to Petersburg and the Northwest for consumption and export. Grain destined for Petersburg was frequently ground
into flour or meal by mills in the Moscow area before being fed into
the Upper Volga transport system via such nearby tributaries as the
Shosha and Dubna.[21]

---

[20]Kusheva, "Torgovlia Moskvy," pp. 46-47; Shchekatov, Geograficheskii
slovar', Vol. 2, p. 598; Vol. 4, pp. 292, 294, 369-70, 388-89; Sostoianie
stolichnogo goroda Moskvy, 1785 goda, pp. 8-12, 27, 30, 32-33, 35-36, 39,
41; Ziablovskii, Zemleopisanie, Vol. 3, pp. 215-16; S. Chernov,
Statisticheskoe opisanie Moskovskoi gubernii 1811 goda (Moscow, 1812),
pp. 30-31; K. V. Sivkov, "Podmoskovnaia votchina serediny XVIII veka,"
Moskovskii krai v ego proshlom, Vol. 1 (Moscow, 1928), p. 88; Tsentral'
nyi gosudarstvennyi voenno-istoricheskii arkhiv, Moscow (TsGVIA), fond
Voenno-uchenogo arkhiva (VUA), No. 18860 ("Opisanie Moskovskoi gubernii
gorodov, 1776 g."), l. 41 ob.

[21]B. B. Kafengauz, "Khlebnyi rynok v 20-30-kh godakh XVIII stoletiia,"
Materialy po istorii zemledeliia SSSR, Vol. 1 (Moscow, 1952), pp. 459-
510; Istoriia Moskvy, Vol. 2, pp. 294-95; Kusheva, "Saratov v pervoi
polovine XVIII v.," in Problemy sotsial'no-ekonomicheskoi istorii Rossii
(Moscow, 1971), pp. 50-51. Valuable insights into the grain trade in
the second half of the eighteenth century are provided by the observations of I. A. Tolchenov, a merchant of the town of Dmitrov who was
engaged in dispatching grain from various Central Russian markets to
Petersburg--see Zhurnal ili zapiska zhizni i prikliuchenii Ivana
Alekseevicha Tolchenova (Moscow, 1974).

Large herds of cattle reached Moscow from the Ukraine and Don and from the southeastern portions of the Central Agricultural Region. Except for a small number sold for reshipment to Petersburg, these animals were slaughtered in Moscow, where most of the meat was sold retail. Hides, tallow and other by-products of the Moscow slaughter-houses, combined with similar goods received from other Central Russian towns having well developed animal-processing industries, were both used in local industrial production and shipped to Petersburg for export in "large quantities."[22] The largest suppliers of fish to the Moscow market were the Lower and Middle Volga and Iaik (Ural) rivers, but some was also received from the Oka, from the lakes to the north of Moscow at Pereslavl'-Zalesskii and Rostov, from the North and North-west, and from the Don and Khoper' rivers in the south. The higher-grade fish products (sturgeon, salmon, caviar) were destined for export or consumption by the wealthier classes, while others (especially salted fish) were items of mass consumption in Moscow and the surrounding region.[23] Moscow also served as one of the most important markets for the indus-trial production of Central Russia, a role which was in evidence well before the eighteenth century. From Moscow these goods were distributed widely among local and regional markets of the Russian Empire.[24] In

---

[22]Kusheva, "Torgovlia Moskvy," pp. 49-51; Sostoianie stolichnogo goroda Moskvy, 1785 g., pp. 8-9; Shchekatov, Geograficheskii slovar', Vol. 4, p. 369; Kafengauz, Ocherki vnutrennego rynka Rossii pervoi poloviny XVIII v. (Moscow, 1958), pp. 287-317.

[23]Kusheva, "Torgovlia Moskvy," pp. 49-51; Kusheva, "Saratov v pervoi polovine XVIII v.," pp. 44-50; Istoriia Moskvy, Vol. 2, p. 277.

[24]Kusheva, "Torgovlia Moskvy," pp. 58-63, 77-99; Kafengauz, Ocherki vnutrennego rynka, pp. 287-317; Istoriia Moskvy, Vol. 2, p. 296; S. I. Sakovich, "Torgovlia melochnymi tovarami v Moskve v kontse XVII v.," Istoricheskie zapiski, Vol. 20 (1946), pp. 130-49.

the late eighteenth century Moscow received annually from Siberia furs
worth about one million rubles, some of which were made into articles
of clothing by Moscow craftsmen and the rest mostly exported to Europe.[25]
Imported silk and cotton fibers, yarns and unfinished textiles were
used in local industry, while imported finished goods were distributed
for sale among various Russian markets and occasionally re-exported.[26]

The above observations illustrate the size and breadth of Moscow's
role in the commercial life of eighteenth-century Russia. Moscow was
an enormous population center which required large amounts of foodstuffs
and other supplies for internal consumption. Moscow was a major industrial center, particularly in the areas of textile and leather production and the preparation of articles of clothing, and consumed large
quantities of raw materials while producing many of the finished goods
circulating in the Russian market. Moscow was the most important
entrepot for the agriculture, fisheries and industries of the entire
country, as well as for imported goods; from Moscow these commodities
were distributed for consumption throughout the Russian Empire and dispatched to export markets. There were, however, some limits to the
magnetism exerted by the Moscow market, particularly with the rise of
a competing metropolis on the Baltic, and even in Central Russia there
were some important trade routes which bypassed Moscow. The most
obvious of these was the Upper Volga, which in the eighteenth century
connected with an intricate system of rivers, lakes and canals leading to

[25] _Sostoianie stolichnogo goroda Moskvy, 1785 g._, p. 7.

[26] _Ibid._, pp. 7-8; Shchekatov, _Geograficheskii slovar'_, Vol. 4,
pp. 366-68.

Petersburg and conveyed goods from the Lower and Middle Volga and Ural regions directly to the new capital without the mediation of Moscow. Grain purchased in the Central Agricultural Region for direct shipment to Petersburg also circumvented the Moscow market, passing overland through the western part of Moscow guberniia and connecting with the Volga via its tributary, the Gzhat', or descending the Oka from Orel and reaching the Volga at Nizhnii Novgorod.[27] The Petersburg market thus extended its influence into areas quite close to Moscow and in some cases, as we shall learn in later chapters of this study, exerted direct claims on the goods produced by these areas.

A commercial center of Moscow's complexity and magnitude inevitably required the services of a much larger group of merchants than even the large Moscow kupechestvo could provide, and in fact it is evident that important sectors of Moscow commerce were almost entirely in the hands of outsiders. The available evidence suggests that the Moscow kupechestvo was unusually sedentary in its habits and for the most part confined its participation in commerce to administering the vast internal market of the city and to shipment of goods to other wholesale markets, chiefly Petersburg and the major fairs.[28] According to data gathered gathered by the government's Commerce Commission in the 1760's, 56

---

[27] Sostoianie stolichnogo goroda Moskvy, 1785 g., pp. 22, 32; Ziablovskii, Zemleopisanie, Vol. 3, pp. 250-52; Zhurnal ili zapiska zhizni i prikliuchenii Ivana Alekseevicha Tolchenova, pp. 33-35; Sbornik Imperatorskogo russkogo istoricheskogo obshchestva (Sb. IRIO), Vol. 93 (St. Petersburg, 1894), pp. 230-31.

[28] Kusheva, "Torgovlia Moskvy," pp. 54-55, 63, 91-104; Istoriia Moskvy, Vol. 2, pp. 282-83, 291-92; G.L. Vartanov, "Moskovskoe i inogorodnee kupechestvo vo vtoroi polovine XVIII v.," Uchenye zapiski Leningradskogo gosudarstvennogo pedagogicheskogo instituta imeni A. I. Gertsena, Vol. 278 (1965), pp. 272-80.

percent of the Moscow _kupechestvo_ was engaged in trade "within the city,"
while only 3 percent held passports for commercial dealings elsewhere
in Russia.[29] At this time about 10 percent of the entire Russian
kupechestvo and double that proportion in the Central Industrial provinces consisted of such passport-holders.[30]

The Moscow _kupechestvo_ played a weak role in the delivery of goods
to the Moscow market, especially goods of Russian origin, and the most
prominent part in these operations evidently belonged to traders from
settlements located along the routes connecting Moscow with the producing regions. Shipment of grain to Moscow by water was dominated
by merchants from towns of the upper Oka basin, especially Orel and
Kaluga, while Moscow merchants played a comparatively minor role.[31]
Similarly, the cattle trade was largely the property of merchants from
towns to the south of Moscow, particularly Kaluga, Zaraisk and Tula,
while Volga fish was delivered by inhabitants of the producing region
and the intervening territory. Moscow merchants emerged chiefly as
wholesale purchasers of the above goods after their arrival on the
Moscow market, and a similar pattern is observable with respect to the
products of Central Russian craft industry. The Moscow _kupechestvo_

---

[29]Most of the remainder of the Moscow _kupechestvo_ belonged to such
categories as craftsmen, laborers "receiving subsistence from various
work," persons performing state service and the aged and disabled.
According to the same source 19 percent of the Iaroslavl' _kupechestvo_
traded within the town and 13 percent held passports, while comparable
figures for Kaluga were 6 percent and 24 percent. Tsentral'nyi
gosudarstvennyi arkhiv drevnykh aktov, Moscow (TsGADA), f. 397
(Komissiia o kommertsii), d. 441, ll. 10 ob., 15, 21 ob.

[30]Vartanov, "Moskovskoe i inogorodnee kupechestvo," pp. 281-82.

[31]Kafengauz, "Khlebnyi rynok," pp. 471-73, 503-08.

played a more significant role in the procurement of industrial raw
materials (chiefly for use in the purchasers' own industrial enterprises)
and imported goods, but in these instances as well they shared the stage
with traders from settlements occupying a geographically intermediary
position and sometimes with those from the producing regions themselves.[32]
Provincial merchants also handled the shipment of goods from Moscow to
local markets for consumption.[33]

The vast needs of the Moscow market offered opportunities and
attractions to trading peasants as well as provincial merchants, and
the presence of such peasants can be detected in most of the significant
sectors of Moscow commerce in the eighteenth century. Under the prevailing conditions the sector most readily penetrated by peasants was
probably transit trade of the sort which was virtually ignored by
Moscow merchants but which, as we have seen, was of great importance
to the provincial kupechestvo. Despite efforts by the government to
restrict peasant involvement in trade, peasants could participate
fairly freely in transit trade in goods of rural origin, which included
much of the country's industrial production as well as products of
agriculture, animal husbandry and forest industry. Since peasants
were the producers of these goods, they were expected to bring
them to market, and the authorities apparently did not pay close
attention to the question of whether the sellers were in fact the

---

[32]Kusheva, "Torgovlia Moskvy," pp. 50-75; Kafengauz, Ocherki
vnutrennego rynka, p. 200; Kusheva, "Saratov v pervoi polovine XVIII
v.," pp. 47-49. The work of Sakovich suggests that the situation described was already well established in the late seventeenth century.
(Sakovich, "Torgovlia melochnymi tovarami," pp. 139-46).

[33]Kusheva, "Torgovlia Moskvy," pp. 75-88.

primary producers of their wares or had bought them for resale, even where quite large shipments were involved.[34] Consequently, peasants were able to share with merchants of provincial towns the function of delivering goods of internal Russian origin to the Moscow market.

According to the surviving customs registers for the first half of the eighteenth century, which have been studied by B. B. Kafengauz, peasants were responsible for 50 to 60 percent of the grain delivered to the Moscow market via overland shipment. The peasants who participated in this trade originated primarily in Moscow uezd, its immediate southern neighbors (the districts of Kolomna and Serpukhov), and the northern districts of the Central Agricultural Region, especially Riazan' (Pereslavl'-Riazanskii) and Mikhailov.[35] Like the merchants who dominated the water-borne trade in grain, many of these peasant grain traders thus came from areas which occupied a geographically intermediary position between Moscow and the major sources of grain supply. The appearance of such peasants on the Moscow grain market is not to be interpreted simply as the disposal of surpluses by primary agricultural producers or even as the activity of small-scale peasant buyers acquiring the surpluses of their own and neighboring

---

[34]It was the intention of the law that shipments brought by non-resident merchants as well as trading peasants pass into the hands of the local kupechestvo on a wholesale basis. Public sale of small shipments was allowed "from carts" in designated marketplaces. In addition to posing as the primary producers of goods offered for sale, peasants sometimes used the pretext that they were acting on behalf of their lords or as hired agents of merchants to evade attempts at restricting their participation in commerce. (See above, Chapter I.)

[35]Kafengauz, "Khlebnyi rynok," pp. 463-68, 481-90. The remaining grain was shipped by nobles or urban merchants, with the former providing the larger share.

villages for resale. Sale by primary producers was probably a major
factor in deliveries from the nearest areas, chiefly Moscow uezd,
where it was reflected in the very large number of shipments recorded
and their small average size. However, transactions by peasants from
the immediate vicinity of Moscow also included large shipments clearly
involving goods purchased for resale. The average size of shipments
tended to increase markedly with the distance of the seller's home
district from Moscow, suggesting that relatively large commercial
operations were involved with increasing frequency. Thus, the average
size of shipments sent in December 1731 was 19 chetverti for peasants
of Moscow uezd, 39 chetverti for Kolomna uezd, 51 chetverti for Riazan'
uezd, 83 chetverti for Temnikov uezd and 113 chetverti for Arzamas uezd.[36]

There is evidence that peasant grain traders sometimes traveled
long distances to major sources of supply to acquire their shipments.
In the first half of the eighteenth century the court village of
Dedinovo (Kolomna uezd) included among its inhabitants large-scale
grain merchants who dispatched shipments worth thousands of rubles
from Orel or Mtsensk to Moscow by water.[37] By the middle of the century
peasants of Miachkovo volost', another court estate to the south of

---

[36]Kafengauz, Ocherki vnutrennego rynka, pp. 251-52. (One chetvert'=
5.95 bushels or 2.099 hectolitres.)

[37]Kafengauz, "Khlebnyi rynok," pp. 505-07; G. D. Kapustina, "K
istorii khlebnogo rynka Moskvy v nachale XVIII v.," in Goroda feodal'-
noi Rossii (Sbornik statei pamiati N. V. Ustiugova) (Moscow, 1966),
pp. 384-85. In 1737 trading peasants of this village shipped more
grain to Moscow by water than any other group of graders except for
merchants of Orel. In the middle of the seventeenth century peasants
of Dedinovo and other court villages in the districts of Kolomna and
Riazan' were already prominent as buyers of grain in Orel for resale
elsewhere. (V. S. Bakulin, "Orel kak khlebnyi rynok vo vtoroi polovine
XVII v.," in Goroda feodal'noi Rossii, pp. 256-63.

Moscow, had already made their appearance in the emerging Middle Volga breadbasket region, buying grain for resale in Moscow.[38] Observers in the second half of the century reported that peasants of various districts in the vicinity of Moscow traveled to the Ukraine or "the steppe regions" to purchase grain, which they resold in Moscow and elsewhere.[39]

Peasants also played a major role in the shipment of Volga and Iaik fish to the Moscow market. The peasants active in the fish trade once again were primarily those from settlements located on or near the routes connecting Moscow with the producing regions, along with some from the latter areas themselves. These settlements included court estates in the southern part of Moscow uezd and villages in the districts of Vladimir, Balakhna, Nizhnii Novgorod, Makar'ev, Ardatov, Arzamas, Alatyr' and Simbirsk.[40] Peasants bringing Volga and Iaik fish to the Moscow market included both primary producers and middlemen who purchased their shipments in the markets of the producing areas. In 1740, for example, a peasant of Novinskaia hamlet (derevnia) in Moscow uezd shipped to Moscow via Samara a cargo of fresh fish and caviar which, according to the customs declaration, he "bought in the Cossack town of Iaik."[41] Likewise, many seigneurial peasants of

---

[38]E. I. Indova, "Les activités commerciales de la paysannerie dans les villages du tsar de la région de Moscou (première moitié du XVIIIe siècle)," Cahiers du monde russe et soviétique, Vol. 5, No. 2 (Apr.-June 1964), p. 218.

[39]Ziablovskii, Zemleopisanie, Vol. 3, pp. 218, 244, 246, 258; Shchekatov, Geograficheskii slovar', Vol. 5, p. 434; S. I. Volkov, Krest'iane dvortsovykh vladenii podmoskov'ia v seredine XVIII v. (Moscow, 1959), pp. 51, 67.

[40]Kusheva, "Torgovlia Moskvy," pp. 53-54; L. F. Zakharova, Pomeshchich'i krest'iane Nizhegorodskoi gubernii i ikh klassovaia bor'ba vo vtoroi polovine XVIII v. (dissertation, Gor'kii, Gor'kovskii gosudarstvennyi universitet, 1954), pp. 117, 127.

[41]Kusheva, "Torgovlia Moskvy," p. 54.

Nizhnii Novgorod guberniia bought up fish in the markets of the Lower Volga and Iaik and hauled it away for sale in Moscow.[42]

Peasant communities were prominent participants in the industries of the Central Industrial provinces, and peasants involved in commerce thus enjoyed ready access to the sources of many industrial goods appearing on the Russian market. Deliveries of such goods by peasants were already a common occurrence in Moscow in the late seventeenth century.[43] The surviving customs registers from the early 1740's indicate that industrial goods were generally delivered to the Moscow market by inhabitants of the areas which produced them, either peasants or townsmen, and that direct sale by primary producers was again intermixed with sale of purchased goods by middlemen. Metal goods, including, nails, knives, scissors, locks, hinges, pots, pans, crampirons and many other articles, were brought by peasants of such Upper Volga districts as Tver', Kashin, Iaroslavl' and Nizhnii Novgorod uezdy, as well as the districts Poshekhon'e and Belozersk to the north of the Volga, where these same articles were produced.[44] Wooden utensils and articles were made and sold in Moscow by peasants of the Moscow, Kolomna, Klin, Iaroslavl', Romanov and Belozersk districts.[45] According to a

---

[42]Zakharova, p. 127.

[43]Sakovich, "Torgovlia melochnymi tovarami," pp. 141-47.

[44]In the case of metal goods the customs registers indicate a significant amount of activity by Moscow merchants as well. (Kusheva, "Torgovlia Moskvy," pp. 60-61.) On shipment of metal goods to Moscow by peasants of Poshekhon'e uezd, see also K. N. Serbina, Krest'ianskaia zhelezodelatel'naia promyshlennost' severo-zapadnoi Rossii XVI-pervoi poloviny XIX v. (Leningrad, 1971), pp. 81-90.

[45]Kusheva, "Torgovlia Moskvy," p. 61.

contemporary observer, peasants of Romanov uezd also specialized in the

processing of sheepskins and the making of sheepskin coats, which they

sold in "various places, including Moscow and Petersburg."[46] Peasants

of Gzhel'sk volost', a court estate located a short distance south of

Moscow, were famous for their production of pottery, which they both

sold in Moscow and sent to more distant markets.[47]

Probably the most widespread form of industrial activity among

the Central Russian peasantry was textile production. The "economic

notes" (ekonomicheskie primechaniia) to the general land survey conducted

by the government of Catherine II indicate that in the early 1770's

62 percent of the peasant population of Moscow uezd (in its large pre-

1775 configuration) engaged in household textile production, while

about 40 percent sold at least part of their production on the market.[48]

The peasant textile industry also included many small enterprises

employing a few hired workers as well as some large manufactories.

The latter were located principally in a cluster of industrial villages

in the northeastern part of Vladimir guberniia, among which was the

[46]"Svedeniia o Iaroslavskom namestnichestve," Uedinennyi poshekhonets (ezhemesiachnyi zhurnal) (Iaroslavl', 1786), p. 441.

[47]S. I. Volkov, Krest'iane dvortsovykh vladenii, pp. 48-49; Kusheva, "Torgovlia Moskvy," p. 61; Ziablovskii, Zemleopisanie, Vol. 3, p. 258.

[48]I. V. Meshalin, Tekstil'naia promyshlennost' krest'ian Moskovskoi gubernii v XVIII i pervoi polovine XIX v. (Moscow-Leningrad, 1950), pp. 26-31.

famed serf textile center of Ivanovo.[49] The serf entrepreneurs of
Ivanovo and similar industrial villages frequently maintained stores
in Moscow through which they disposed of their production, while other
trading peasants bought up the output of small-scale textile industry
for resale in Moscow and sometimes contracted with such producers on a
"putting-out" basis.[50]

Trading peasants of Moscow uezd and the surrounding districts also
appeared in Moscow as suppliers of firewood, lumber, hay, fruits and
vegetables produced by those districts.[51] These goods were sometimes
brought to market by the primary producers but were often purchased
locally for resale by merchants and trading peasants.

In their participation in delivery of goods of internal Russian
origin to the Moscow market, trading peasants were comparable more to
the provincial kupechestvo than to that of Moscow itself. Like the
former, these peasants served as intermediaries between the producing
regions and the Moscow market, benefiting from their close connections
with these regions or the favorable location of their home settlements
astride the routes leading from Moscow to the sources of goods. Participation in this transit trade, involving brief sojourns in Moscow inter-
spersed with long periods of travel, would not necessarily or even

---

[49]Ibid., pp. 127-43; A. M. Razgon, "Promyshlennye i torgovye sela
i slobody Vladimirskoi gubernii vo vtoroi polovine XVIII v.,"
Istoricheskie zapiski, Vol. 32 (1950), pp. 133-51.

[50]Razgon, p. 157; Meshalin, pp. 44, 107-12, 127-43.

[51]Sostoianie stolichnogo goroda Moskvy, 1785 g., pp. 11-12, 33-34,
39, 41; Ziablovskii, Zemleopisanie, Vol. 3, pp. 215-16, 248, 261;
Shchekatov, Geograficheskii slovar', Vol. 2, p. 598, Vol. 4, p. 621,
Vol. 5, p. 433; S. I. Volkov, Krest'iane dvortsovykh vladenii, p. 52.

usually lead to permanent settlement and formal citizenship in the
city, although it probably did so in individual cases. Conceivably,
a peasant who acquired capital, experience and familiarity with the
Moscow market through successful participation in the transit trade
might eventually turn to commercial activity on the internal Moscow
market, involving the disposal of goods after their arrival in Moscow.
Such activity was subject to much tighter restriction than the transit
trade and according to laws prevailing during most of the eighteenth
century was supposed to be the exclusive prerogative of the Moscow
urban classes, but peasants nevertheless succeeded in infiltrating the
internal commerce of Moscow under a variety of pretexts.[52] Documents
of the court estate administration reveal that hundreds of peasants
from the court properties in the vicinity of Moscow participated
extensively in the internal trade of the city, occupying stores in
the officially sanctioned markets or "rows" and selling silk, fabrics,
lace, garments, footwear and other leather goods, foodstuffs, silver
articles and other products, with individual turnovers in the hundreds
or even thousands of rubles.[53]

Court peasants appear to have occupied a particularly prominent
role in internal Moscow commerce, possibly because the backing of a
powerful state institution made their activities less vulnerable to

---

[52]Government restrictions on peasant participation in commerce and
the means employed by peasants to evade these restrictions are discussed
in the first chapter of this dissertation.

[53]S. I. Volkov, Krest'iane dvortsovykh vladenii, pp. 55-56, 65, 71-
72; Indova, "Les activités commerciales," pp. 214-28; Indova, "Moskovskii posad i podmoskovnye dvortsovye krest'iane v pervoi polovine XVIII
v.," in Goroda feodal'noi Rossii, pp. 479-85.

interference by the urban authorities and because of the proximity of
many court estates to the city.[54] However, other groups of peasants
also participated in these activities, and in documents on seigneurial
estates one often finds reference to peasants who were living in Moscow
and engaged in some sort of commercial enterprise.[55] Of the nearly
300 peasant households belonging to Prince M. M. Shcherbatov's estates
in the districts of Iaroslavl' and Borisoglebsk, 23 were reported in
1793 to be keeping taverns or inns in Moscow, three to be trading in
Moscow on the Okhotnyi riad, one to be engaged in unspecified trade in
the city and three to be "in Moscow" for reasons not given.[56] The
ownership of stores in Moscow by the serf textile entrepreneurs of
Ivanovo has already been mentioned. Peasants not occupying stores or
other facilities in the official markets sold goods from their houses
or peddled them on the street or door-to-door (v raznos).[57] Peasants
also served urban merchants in the capacity of hired shopkeepers,
itinerant salesmen and other employees.[58] Some peasants served as

---

[54]Another possible reason for the apparently heightened role of
court peasants in these activities is that the sources on this segment
of the peasantry are fairly concentrated and have been comparatively
well studied.

[55]Sivkov, "Podmoskovnaia votchina," p. 68; K. N. Shchepetov,
Krepostnoe pravo v votchinakh Sheremetevykh (Moscow, 1947), pp. 96-97.

[56]TsGADA, f. 1289 (M. M. Shcherbatov), op. 1, d. 595, ll. 1-35.
Okhotnyi riad: a marketplace in the center of Moscow adjoining Red
Square to the northeast, which at one time specialized in the sale of
poultry. See P. V. Sytin, Iz istorii moskovskikh ulits (3rd edition,
Moscow, 1958), pp. 148-57.

[57]Indova, "Moskovskii posad," p. 482; Istoriia Moskvy, Vol. 2,
p. 288; Kafengauz, "Khlebnyi rynok," p. 474.

[58]Istoriia Moskvy, Vol. 2, p. 288; S. I. Volkov, Krest'iane
dvortsovykh vladenii, p. 52; K. German, Statisticheskoe opisanie
Iaroslavskoi gubernii (St. Petersburg, 1808), pp. 91-92.

commercial intermediaries, in the eighteenth century known as "kulaks," buying up arriving shipments for quick resale to Moscow storeowners. These individuals lacked substantial capital of their own but profited by their knowledge of the market and their ability to bridge the gap between the seller and the eventual purchaser.[59]

Trading peasants apparently played a particularly large role in the sale of foodstuffs within Moscow. In 1730 court peasants owned 245 butcher shops spread over twelve districts of the city. One peasant owned ten such shops, with additional outlets in various marketplaces for sale of meat, while another had nine shops.[60] During the same period Spiridon Astaf'ev, a peasant of the Avram'ev (St. Avramii) Monastery of Galich, "resided in Moscow and traded in meat."[61] In the mid-1720's, of 1440 persons recorded by the authorities as dealing in grain and bread products within Moscow, 605 were members of the Moscow posad and 832 were peasants, of whom the largest contingent (401) came from Iaroslavl' uezd, while Moscow uezd and several other districts of the Upper Volga area (Romanov, Kostroma, Poshekhon'e) also contributed substantial numbers.[62] Most of these peasants were evidently

[59]Such activity was observable chiefly in the grain trade. Kafengauz, "Khlebnyi rynok," pp. 496-97; Indova, "Moskovskii posad," p. 482; S. I. Volkov, Krest'iane dvortsovykh vladenii, p. 80.

[60]Indova, "Les activités commerciales," p. 226.

[61]Materialy po istorii krest'ianskoi promyshlennosti (hereafter MPIKP), Vol. 2 (Moscow-Leningrad, 1950), p. 67.

[62]Kafengauz, "Khlebnyi rynok," pp. 474-76. Participation in retail trade in foodstuffs was authorized by the government, which collected an annual fee (obrok) from the traders. There is indication that the government consistently took a more permissive attitude toward commercial activity by peasants in this area than in others.

small-scale sellers of baked goods who peddled their wares v raznos, but larger operations and ownership of stores by peasants were also observed. In 1729 the brothers Vasilii and Ivan Grigor'ev, court peasants of Khatun volost' (Moscow uezd), sold grain in stores they rented from urban merchants, while their fellow villager Afanasii Aksenov had such a store "in his yard" in Moscow.[63] In 1800 it was reported that peasants in Moscow conducted an "impressive" wholesale and retail trade in grain and flour, possessing 200 large stores.[64] Other peasants dealt in fish, fruits, vegetables and various other foodstuffs.[65]

Peasants were equally active in the industrial sectors of the Moscow economy, working as independent artisans, founding large and small enterprises using hired labor, and providing a large proportion of the industrial labor force. A description of Moscow in the mid-1780's observed that crafts and artisanry were the predominant occupation of serfs and peasants "arriving from the countryside," who "perform all the needed crafts."[66] An official document of the same period reported the presence of nearly 44,000 peasants living in Moscow "temporarily, with passports, for the purpose of artisanry,

---

[63]Indova, "Moskovskii posad," p. 482.

[64]Istoriia Moskvy, Vol. 2, p. 302. An ordinance of 1799 allowed peasants to gain the legal right to engage in such trade through payment of an "excise".

[65]S. I. Volkov, Krest'iane dvortsovykh vladenii, p. 80; Indova, "Moskovskii posad," p. 482; Indova, "Les activités commerciales," pp. 218-221; Kafengauz, "Khlebnyi rynok," p. 475.

[66]Sostoianie stolichnogo goroda Moskvy, 1785 g., p. 6.

labor and personal service."[67] Peasant industrial activity was widespread in Moscow earlier in the century as well, despite government
sanctions against "unauthorized" industrial production.[68]

The available evidence suggests that among industrial occupations
pursued by peasants in Moscow the production of textiles and leather
goods and the construction industry played a particularly large role.
Peasant contractors entered into agreements for the delivery of building
materials (stone, bricks, lumber and other materials) and for the
execution of construction work in Moscow. Especially prominent as construction contractors were court peasants of Miachkovo volost', whose
home territory contained the quarries which provided most of Moscow's
supply of building stone, but peasants of other court estates in the
vicinity of Moscow and of other categories and more distant districts
also participated.[69] In 1756 and 1757 court peasants of Gzhel'sk
volost' contracted to make repairs on the Semenovskii Palace and the
old imperial palace at Kolomenskoe, receiving 225-235 rubles for each
job. Ivan Loginov, another peasant of the same estate, in collaboration

---

[67]Istoriia Moskvy, Vol. 2, p. 324.

[68]These prohibitions derived from the government's efforts to protect large-scale industry founded with government authorization. They
were withdrawn in the reign of Catherine II, which both encouraged the
expansion of peasant industrial activity and reduced the amount of information available to historians about it, since much of this information emerges from applications to found "authorized" enterprises and
arrests of "unauthorized" producers. The relevant decrees are listed
and described in MPIKP, Vol. 1 (Moscow-Leningrad, 1935), pp. 369-75.

[69]Sostoianie stolichnogo goroda Moskvy, 1785 g., p. 45; S. I.
Volkov, Krest'iane dvortsovykh vladenii, pp. 49-50; "Primechaniia,
sluzhashchie k poznaniiu do domostroitel'stva i sostoianiia mest po
rekam Kliaz'me, Moskve i Oke lezhashchikh," Akademicheskie izvestiia
na 1780 g., Vol. 4, pp. 483-86.

with Petr Sushchev and Dmitrii Pashinin, church peasants of Pereslavl'-
Zalesskii and Iaroslavl' uezdy respectively, in 1757 undertook to build
a brewery for the court administration for the sum of 4420 rubles.[70]
In 1754 the Moscow first-guild merchant Filat Lukin Shestakov contracted
"together with his partner,.../Count/ Sheremetev's peasant Nikifor
Artem'ev Sezonov...and with his own building materials and his artisans
and workmen," to make repairs on the Moscow Cathedral of the Kazan'
Virgin "with good, durable workmanship."[71]

Since such contracts were awarded through competitive bidding,
we sometimes find several peasant entrepreneurs competing against one
another for business. In 1769 the court peasants Fedor Ushakov and
Petr Garenshikov lost a contract worth in the neighborhood of 2000
rubles because they were underbid by a partnership of economic peasants
from the districts of Epifan' and Olonets.[72] The peasantry also
supplied many of the skilled artisans who carried out the work provided
for in such contracts. One major source of stonemasons was again
Miachkovo volost', where local quarries naturally bred specialists in
this trade. Prince M. M. Golitsyn's estate in Peremyshl' uezd, in the
province of Kaluga, also contained many peasant stonemasons, who spent
much of the year away from home performing construction work under
contract. Some of these artisans worked in Moscow.[73] According to

[70]S. I. Volkov, Krest'iane dvortsovykh vladenii, p. 49.

[71]I. E. Zabelin, Materialy po istorii, arkheologii i statistike
goroda Moskvy, Vol. 2 (Moscow, 1891), pp. 928-29.

[72]S. I. Volkov, Krest'iane dvortsovykh vladenii, p. 51.

[73]E. I. Drakokhrust, "Rassloenie krepostnogo krest'ianstva v
obrochnoi votchine XVIII v.," Istoricheskie zapiski, Vol. 4 (1938),
p. 134.

contemporary descriptions, at the end of the eighteenth century peasants of Iaroslavl' uezd migrated to Moscow "primarily to work as stonemasons, plasterers and carpenters."[74]

Textile production, so widespread in the countryside, was also carried on extensively by peasants within the bounds of Moscow. The city and its environs were particularly noted for the silk industry, although the woolen sector was also strong.[75] In 1766 an investigation by the Manufactures College determined that of 416 small-scale textile producers in two slobody on the outskirts of Moscow, 337 were peasants.[76] Some peasants arrived in Moscow fully qualified for work as a result of their experience in the rural textile industry, while others received their first experience and training in the city. The latter was particularly true in the earlier part of the century, during which silk-weaving and some other specialties were novelties only recently introduced into Russia via large government-sponsored enterprises. Arrested in 1739 for working in a small "unauthorized" silk-weaving enterprise, the monastery peasant Savelii Markov Losev, a native of Pereslavl'-Zalesskii uezd, told the authorities that he had come to

---

[74]German, Statisticheskoe opisanie Iaroslavskoi gubernii, pp. 90-91; "Svedeniia o Iaroslavskom namestnichestve," Uedinennyi poshekhonets (Iaroslavl', 1786), p. 190. According to the investigation of the Imperial Free Economic Society in the 1760's, peasants of Galich provintsiia, in the northern part of what was to become Kostroma guberniia, also "resided in Moscow and other towns to engage in carpentry and other work." "Otvety na ekonomicheskie voprosy po Galitskoi provintsii," Trudy Vol'nogo ekonomicheskogo obshchestva (hereafter Trudy VEO), Vol. 10 (1768), p. 93.

[75]Meshalin, pp. 66, 128-39; MPIKP, Vol. 2, pp. 90-102; A. P. Doroshenko, "Rabota na domu v tekstil'noi promyshlennosti Moskvy v seredine XVIII v.," Istoricheskie zapiski, Vol. 72 (1962), pp. 268-73. The Moscow silk industry was founded at the beginning of the century, expanded rapidly, and spread extensively into the surrounding countryside.

[76]Meshalin, pp. 65-66.

Moscow with a passport a decade or so earlier "upon coming of age" and
had begun to "learn the weaving of galloons /pozumenty/under the peasant
Afanasii Mikhailov of Bratovshchino village." After serving an apprenticeship of five years under this artisan, Losev lived briefly in his
native village but then returned to Moscow and went to work as a hired
weaver.[77] Another peasant arrested at the same time for similar
reasons belonged to a different ecclesiastical estate in Pereslavl'-
Zalesskii uezd and had come to Moscow to "learn the weaving of galloons
under the court peasant Andrei Ivanov Murinov," thereafter working in
several "unauthorized" enterprises.[78] The monastery peasant Artemon
Luk'ianov Mandyrev learned silk-weaving through apprenticeship to a
Moscow merchant, subsequently acquired his own looms and made galloons
and ribbons "without the permission of the Commerce College" in quarters
he rented from several Moscow citizens.[79] Nefed Beliaev, from an
estate of the Kaliazin Monastery in Kashin uezd, left his village at
the age of fifteen and lived eight years in Petersburg and Moscow,
where he learned the weaving of galloons, worked for various employers
and subsequently turned to independent production.[80]

---

[77]MPIKP, Vol. 2, pp. 66-68. The "unauthorized" enterprise in which
Losev worked at the time of his arrest was operated by the widow of
another peasant silk-weaver who had pursued his craft in Moscow. The
woman in question was also the daughter of another Moscow trading
peasant, the church peasant Spirodon Astaf'ev, identified above as a
meat merchant. Bratovshchino: a court village in the vicinity of
Moscow.

[78]Ibid., p. 70.

[79]Ibid., p. 71.

[80]A. L. Shapiro, "Krest'ianskie otkhody i krest'ianskii naem v
Petrovskoe vremia," Uchenye zapiski Leningradskogo gosudarstvennogo
pedagogicheskogo instituta im. M. N. Pokrovskogo, Vol. 5, No. 1 (1940),
p. 40. Silk ribbons and galloons (a kind of braid) were extensively
produced in eighteenth-century Russia and were apparently in great
demand for use as trimmings in clothing and for other decorative purposes.

As the above cases indicate, peasant textile artisans worked independently, performed hired labor and founded small enterprises using
a few hired workers, probably moving back and forth among these alternatives according circumstances. Some peasants used the skills they
gained from work in the Moscow textile industry to found successful
enterprises in their villages, and there are cases recorded in which
large numbers of peasants from a particular village apparently set
about this process with the specific intention of turning their home
village into a center of textile production.[81] Some peasants went
beyond small-scale craft production and opened large enterprises with
government sanction. These ambitious entrepreneurs had already enriched
themselves in other ways, usually through trade. In 1738-9 Timofei
Nazarov, a peasant from the estates of Tsarevna (later Empress)
Elizabeth, applied for permission to open a silk-weaving enterprise
with fifteen looms in Moscow, claiming possession of 1000 rubles in
capital and stores in the silk and muslin "rows".[82] Another peasant
of similar origins, Semen Polianskii, in 1738 did receive permission
to open a "factory" for the weaving of silk kerchiefs and ribbons,
also with 1000 rubles of his own capital. In 1744 this enterprise
employed seventeen hired workers and produced goods valued at 515
rubles, but its production did not meet the standards of the Manufactures College and it was ordered closed that same year.[83]

---

[81] M. N. Artemenkov, "Naemnye rabochie moskovskikh manufaktur v 40-
70-kh godakh XVIII v.," Istoriia SSSR, 1964, No. 2, pp. 135, 144;
Meshalin, pp. 60-61.

[82] MPIKP, Vol. 2, pp. 296-98.

[83] Ibid., pp. 298-306. Despite their commercial attainments, both
Nazarov and Polianskii were illiterate and could not sign their names.

The industrial career of the court peasant E. S. Zaitsev, from the
suburban Moscow village of Pokrovskoe, was different if ultimately
also unsuccessful. In 1749 Zaitsev leased a silk-weaving enterprise
from a Moscow merchant for three years at a cost of 700 rubles. Subsequently Zaitsev became the manager of another such enterprise owned by
a Moscow merchant, and in 1756, following the death of his employer,
he received permission to found his own "factory," for which purpose
he evidently appropriated some of the resources of the defunct enterprise he formerly managed. In 1757 Zaitsev's factory produced goods
valued at 7000 rubles on thirty looms. The following year, however,
Zaitsev himself died, and because he had accumulated large debts,
possibly in acquisition of the above enterprise, it was quickly sold
by his widow. During his rise to industrial proprietorship. E. S.
Zaitsev apparently participated in trade as well. In 1750 he acquired
five stores and a number of other commercial facilities in Moscow's
Novonemetskii Market.[84]

It was of course far more common for peasants to perform hired
labor in large-scale textile enterprises than to own them. Although
the labor force of authorized manufactories consisted partially of
workers "ascribed" to the enterprise or purchased by it and bound to
work for it as serfs, these workers were supplemented extensively by
hired labor, the importance of which grew as the century progressed.[85]

---

[84]Ibid., pp. 307-10, 430-32; S. I. Volkov, Krest'iane dvortsovykh
vladenii, pp. 72-73.

[85]On the role of hired labor in large-scale Moscow industry see
Artemenkov, pp. 133-44; Meshalin, pp. 58-59, 95; Istoriia Moskvy, Vol.
2, pp. 258-61, 326; E. I. Zaozerskaia, Rabochaia sila i klassovaia
bor'ba na tekstil'nykh manufakturakh v 20-60-kh gg. XVIII v. (Moscow,
1960), esp. pp. 110-79, 255-312; A. P. Doroshenko, "Rabochaia sila v
ukaznoi legkoi promyshlennosti Moskvy v 1730-1760 gg.," Istoriia SSSR,
1958, No. 5, pp. 144-67.

Much of this labor was provided by peasant migrants in search not only

of income but of industrial training.[86] M. N. Artemenkov, examining

documents on more than 14,000 workers hired by Moscow textile manufac-

tories in the period 1740-1780, found that nearly all these workers

were peasants.[87] The labor force hired by Semen Polianskii to staff

the silk-weaving enterprise described above consisted almost entirely

of court and monastery peasants of Pereslavl'-Zalesskii uezd, along

with some from the districts of Vladimir and Iaroslavl'.[88] The largest

---

In 1762 the government withdrew the right of factory owners to purchase peasant villages for use as industrial labor. Henceforth additions to the labor force had to be supplied by hired labor. The Moscow plague of 1771 seriously depleted the remaining cadres of ascribed and purchased workers and further encouraged the use of hired labor. However, the precise status of factory workers was subject to some ambiguities. In the first half of the century individuals who began as hired workers often became permanently attached to the factory, particularly as the result of a 1736 decree. In the same period hired workers were often bound by contractual or legal obligations to remain in the service of a particular employer for a given number of years, which might be regarded as a temporary enserfment. Seigneurial peasants were frequently "hired" through contracts between their lord and the factory owner, under which seigneurial prerogatives were transferred to the latter.

[86]Artemenkov, pp. 133-44; Doroshenko, "Rabochaia sila," pp. 146, 165; Zaozerskaia, Rabochaia sila, pp. 145, 161 (Table 29); Meshalin, pp. 58-59; Istoriia Moskvy, Vol. 2, pp. 256-57, 325-26. According to Zaozerskaia, of 1668 cases documented by a survey of the factory labor force in the late 1730's, 1003 workers stated that they had originally taken up factory work "for subsistence /prokormlenie/ and for training /obuchenie/."

[87]Artemenkov, p. 134. However, this researcher used a category of documents dealing with the registration of persons who had received permission to depart from their official places of residence for work in Moscow (pokormezhnye dela). These materials would not include persons who were legally permanent residents of the city. A. P. Doroshenko, on the basis of documents relating to 6366 workers hired from the late 1730's through the early 1760's, concluded that 84 percent of these workers were peasants. Other sources of hired factory labor included the lower strata of the Moscow posad and raznochintsy, especially former soldiers and their families.

[88]MPIKP, Vol. 2, pp. 302-05.

numbers of peasants in the factory labor force apparently came from

Moscow uezd, the surrounding districts and the districts of the Upper

Volga area (particularly Iaroslavl', Poshekhon'e, Kashin, Kostroma).[89]

Moscow textile manufacturers also dealt with peasant craftsmen under

the putting-out system, the latter being an expedient widely adopted in

the mid-eighteenth century to increase production, overcome bottlenecks

and solve the problem of "cramped premises." As Ivan Zhuravlev, one

of the most important woolen manufacturers, reported to the Commerce

Commission in the 1760's, some phases of production in his enterprise

were performed "outside the factory" by "people who have come from the

villages." Small enterprises of which peasants were the proprietors

or in which they served as hired laborers were also recipients of

putting-out work.[90]

Peasants were active not only in the basic phases of textile pro-

duction (spinning and weaving) but in the conversion of cloth into

colored fabrics, articles of clothing and other finished goods. Petr

Petrov Linev, arrested in 1751 for operating an "unauthorized" dyer's

shop, was a peasant of Count M. M. Saltykov's estate in Dmitrov uezd

who had lived in Moscow on passports for twenty years. After working

as a hired laborer in "various places," Linev had learned his trade

from a Moscow merchant and become an independent artisan, receiving

much business from Moscow textile merchants.[91] During the middle

---

[89]Doroshenko, "Rabochaia sila," p. 166; Istoriia Moskvy, Vol. 2, pp. 258, 326; S. I. Volkov, Krest'iane dvortsovykh vladenii, pp. 57-58; Sostoianie stolichnogo goroda Moskvy, 1785 g., p. 11; Shchekatov, Geograficheskii slovar', Vol. 4, p. 1195; Vol. 5, p. 434.

[90]Doroshenko, "Rabota na domu," pp. 259-75.

[91]MPIKP, Vol. 1, pp. 229-42.

decades of the eighteenth century much illegal activity by peasants was discovered in the production of gold and silver tinsel, lace and braid-work.[92] Another popular occupation among peasants settled in Moscow was tailoring.[93] Some peasants specialized in the making of felts and felt hats, which they sold to merchants or themselves offered to the public on Red Square and other marketplaces.[94] Among the court peasants of nearby villages living in Moscow there were furriers (skorniaki) and makers of fur hats (shaposhniki).[95]

Peasants also excelled in the leather trades and particularly in the production of finished goods (shoes, boots, soles, gloves, breeches and other articles) from leather, crafts which were widespread in rural areas as well. A local observer, replying to the inquiry of the Imperial Free Economic Society in the late 1760's, asserted that in Kashin uezd "nearly half the district, and especially the villages of Kimry and Medveditskoe..., consists of bootmakers /sapozhniki/ and shoemakers /bashmachniki/," who "for the most part live in Moscow during the winter and sometimes the summer as well."[96] Ivan Semenov and Vasilii

---

[92]Ibid., pp. 60-129. The crafts indicated (susal'noe, mishurnoe delo), involving the production of metallic filament or leaf or the gilding of textile thread and the interweaving of these materials with textile yarns, contained features of both textile and metallurgical crafts. The resulting articles were widely used as trimmings in women's clothing and for other decorative purposes.

[93]Shchekatov, Geograficheskii slovar', Vol. 5, p. 434; Shapiro, "Krest'ianskie otkhody," p. 40; S. I. Volkov, Krest'iane dvortsovykh vladenii, pp. 56-57.

[94]MPIKP, Vol. 1, pp. 12-16.

[95]S. I. Volkov, Krest'iane dvortsovykh vladenii, pp. 46-47, 55-56.

[96]"Otvety na ekonomicheskie voprosy po Kashinskomu uezdu," Trudy VEO, Vol. 26 (1774), p. 70. This observer also alleged that life in Moscow turned the peasants into "drunkards and spendthrifts, eventually rendering them unsuitable for either cultivation or the bootmaker's craft."

Matveev, monastery peasants of Iaroslavl' _uezd,_ settled in Moscow in 1761 and began to produce suede gloves and breeches, buying raw hides from "incoming peasants" and having them processed by a worker of an "authorized" tannery who was taking business on the side.[97] As in the textile field, peasants in the leather industry sometimes went beyond craft production to found large "authorized" enterprises. In 1723 the court peasant Vasilii Zaitsev of Pokrovskoe village received permission from the Manufactures College to open a factory for the production of various kinds of leather in Moscow. Upon the death of the founder in 1727 this enterprise passed to his son and continued to function until 1744, when it was closed by the government, along with a large number of other enterprises, "to avoid the proliferation of factories and because of poor workmanship."[98] The court peasant Ivan Koz'min Smirnov of Kolychevo village, Miachkovo _volost',_ in 1757 applied for authorization to "establish in Moscow, in my own house,...as well as in Petersburg, in a suitable location, factories for the production of suede and the dyeing...of this suede and of elk and deer hides," claiming to possess 4000 rubles in capital.[99]

---

[97]_MPIKP,_ Vol. 1, pp. 6-12.

[98]_Ibid.,_ pp. 1-6; S. I. Volkov, _Krest'iane dvortsovykh vladenii,_ p. 69. Vasilii Zaitsev was related to E. S. Zaitsev, the peasant of Pokrovskoe village who was previously identified as the owner of an "authorized" silk-weaving enterprise in Moscow. (See _MPIKP,_ Vol. 2, p. 432.) Earlier Vasilii Zaitsev participated in a partnership which aimed to found a leather enterprise in Narva. He also dealt in furs at the Makar'ev Fair (near Nizhnii Novgorod) and enlisted in the Moscow _kupechestvo,_ becoming a member of the first guild.

[99]_MPIKP,_ Vol. 1, p. 6. Elk and deer hides were used in large quantities by the army. (_Ibid.,_ p. 247, n. 9.)

Peasants were represented among Moscow's metal craftsmen, including blacksmiths, locksmiths, tinsmiths, silversmiths, goldsmiths, and makers of brass and tin buttons.[100] Peasants also worked as carpenters, wheelwrights, ceramists and makers of brooms.[101] In the second half of the eighteenth century peasants provided virtually the entire skilled labor force in Moscow's thirty-odd brick factories, which in 1778 produced twenty million bricks, and a few peasants owned such factories.[102] It appears doubtful that there were many industrial occupations in Moscow which were not penetrated by peasants.

The available materials give the impression that in the mid-eighteenth century peasants of the church properties (later "economic" peasants) were especially prominent among small-scale industrial producers in Moscow. In the documented cases of "unauthorized" production of gold and silver tinsel, lace and braid-work in the period 1742-1763, three-quarters of the producers were church peasants.[103] Among 390 peasants discovered by a 1766 investigation to be engaged in small-scale industrial production (mostly in various textile fields) in Moscow's Preobrazhenskaia and Semenovskaia slobody, there were 235

[100]Ibid., pp. 175-79; Sivkov, "Podmoskovnaia votchina," pp. 83-84; S. I. Volkov, Krest'iane dvortsovykh vladenii, pp. 55-56; Indova, "Moskovskii posad," p. 482; Indova, "Les activités commerciales," p. 219; Shchekatov, Geograficheskii slovar', Vol. 4, p. 390; TsGADA, f. 455 (Iaroslavskaia provintsial'naia kantseliariia), op. 2, d. 34, l. 1.

[101]Indova, "Moskovskii posad," p. 482; S. I. Volkov, Krest'iane dvortsovykh vladenii, pp. 52-56, 70-71; Shchekatov, Geograficheskii slovar', Vol. 4, p. 390; Vol. 5, p. 434.

[102]N. V. Voronov, "Stachka moskovskikh kirpichedel'tsev letom 1779 g.," Istoricheskie zapiski, Vol. 37 (1951), pp. 292-93; Materialy dlia istorii moskovskogo kupechestva, Vol. 4 (Moscow, 1886), pp. 226 (No. 515), 264 (No. 936)

[103]MPIKP, Vol. 1, pp. 60-129.

economic peasants, 38 court peasants and 117 private serfs.[104] The
apparent lesser involvement of court peasants is perhaps attributable
to the fact that such crafts were carried on extensively in the home
villages of these peasants, the proximity of which to the city assured
rural producers of ready access to the Moscow market.[105] The tightening
strictures against "unauthorized" industrial production during the
reigns of Anna and Elizabeth may have further motivated craftsmen from
the court peasantry to work in their villages, where the likelihood of
interference from the authorities was much less, rather than in the
city itself. On the other hand, court peasants were well represented
in such legal forms of industrial activity as factory labor and "temporary" membership in craft guilds, as were peasants of the other major
categories.[106] Court peasants seem to predominate in the few documented
cases of large-scale "authorized" production by peasants in Moscow.

    Among other, miscellaneous occupations in which the participation
of peasants can be documented are innkeeping and commercial vegetable

---

[104]Ibid., Vol. 2, pp. 90-102. These totals include independent
artisans, small entrepreneurs with a few employees, and hired workers
in such enterprises. Preobrazhenskaia and Semenovskaia were soldatskie
slobody, quarters occupied largely by soldiers and other military
personnel. The significance of such areas in regard to peasant infiltration of the city is discussed below.

[105]S. I. Volkov, Krest'iane dvortsovykh vladenii, pp. 45-52.

[106]Artemenkov, pp. 134, 142; Doroshenko, "Rabochaia sila," pp. 146,
165; Zaozerskaia, Rabochaia sila, p. 161 (Table 29); Istoriia Moskvy,
Vol. 2, p. 257; MPIKP, Vol. 2, p. 65. A more precise determination of
the contribution of the various peasant categories to the factory labor
force is not possible because of the partial character of the available
data and the contradictory results deriving from various sources. The
data do suggest, however, a substantial increase in the role of seigneurial peasants as the century progressed. The membership of craft
guilds is treated in more detail later in this chapter.

gardening and orchardry.[107] Many peasants worked as teamsters
(izvozchiki), and peasants apparently dominated the local transport
industry.[108] Peasants performed unskilled labor (chernaia rabota)
and personal service for commercial and industrial enterprises and for
households.

We have seen that in "normal times" eighteenth-century Moscow contained 50,000 to 100,000 persons of peasant status, with many more
passing through for purposes of trade or seasonal work. Despite the
tangle of regulations restricting their right to live and trade in the
city and to engage in some forms of industrial production, peasants
readily found employment in the vast Moscow economy. Notwithstanding
the clamor of the urban kupechestvo for tighter restrictions on commercial activity by peasants, individual merchants did not hesitate to
establish business relationships with peasants where it was economically
advantageous to do so. Urban merchants took trading peasants as
partners in commercial and industrial enterprises, sold goods to
peasant retail traders and peddlers operating within the city, often
on credit, and accepted the service of peasants as intermediaries in
the wholesale purchase of goods. Merchants bought from "unauthorized"

---

[107]TsGADA, f. 1289, op. 1, d. 595, ll. 1-35; German, Statisticheskoe
opisanie Iaroslavskoi gubernii, pp. 91-92; S. I. Volkov, Krest'iane
dvortsovykh vladenii, p. 84. The growing of fruits and vegetables for
sale was a common occupation in towns and other large settlements of
Central Russia, probably because the concentration of population made
adequate manuring possible. See L. V. Milov, "O tak nazyvaemykh
agrarnykh gorodakh Rossii XVIII v.," Voprosy istorii, 1968, No. 6, pp.
54-64; A. Ia. Artynov, Vospominaniia krest'ianina sela Ugodich A. Ia.
Artynova (Moscow, 1882), pp. 7-8, 13-14, 34, 39, 44-48, 59, 77-83.

[108]Ziablovskii, Zemleopisanie, Vol. 3, p. 252; Chernov, Statisticheskoe
opisanie Moskovskoi gubernii, p. 43; Sivkov, "Podmoskovnaia votchina,"
p. 88; I. Tokmakov, Istoriko-statisticheskoe i arkheologicheskoe opisanie
goroda Dmitrova (Moskovskoi gubernii) (Moscow, 1893), p. 58.

peasant producers and brought them goods to be processed, while authorized manufactories used such producers for putting-out work. Peasants
were accepted as apprentices, skilled workers, managers, hired shopkeepers and in other subordinate capacities. Many peasant migrants
arrived in Moscow without skills and learned a craft or specialty
through apprenticeship or hired labor, while others brought previously
acquired skills with them into the city. Some migrants subsequently
returned to their villages, spreading new skills through rural areas,
while others remained in Moscow for decades with passports authorizing
their absence from the village. Such long-term settlers had effectively
cut their ties with the rural milieu and become a permanent part of the
urban population.

In overcoming the legal barriers to urbanization, peasants thus
benefited greatly from the economic collaboration of members of the
urban classes. The assistance of urban merchants, nobles and members
of other population categories also enabled peasants to acquire commercial and residential property in Moscow, despite legal prohibitions.
Barred from direct possession of stores and other commercial facilities
in the officially sanctioned markets or "rows," peasants gained control
of such property by purchasing it under the names of "merchants of
their acquaintance."[109] Many large noble landowners looked benignly
upon the enrichment of their serfs through trade and industry and
willingly abetted these serfs in acquiring urban property. In censuses
and other surveys of Moscow households one finds numerous references

---

[109]In this manner E. I. Grachev, the textile manufacturer of
Ivanovo village, acquired his Moscow stores. (Istoriia Moskvy, Vol. 2,
p. 301.) The widespread existence of such a practice in Russian towns
is documented by the complaints of many urban communes to the Legislative Commission of 1767 and has been discussed in the first chapter
of this dissertation.

to houses owned by such lords but occupied by their peasants, and it was reported that in certain quarters of Moscow there were streets on which nearly all the houses were listed as belonging to Count Sheremetev, Count Orlov or other great lords.[110] There were also cases in which serfs made use of property genuinely in the possession of their lords for the furtherance of their own urban activities. Thus, the peasant Ivan Alekseev in 1766 lived in "separate quarters" in the Moscow household of his master, Major-General M. M. Ivinskii, and engaged there in "unauthorized" production of silk ribbons.[111]

In the surreptitious acquisition of urban property, peasants were not dependent on their own lords alone for assistance. In 1766 a house in the Preobrazhenskaia sloboda nominally belonging to the "senatorial secretary" Vasilii Travkin was occupied by ten peasants engaged in the dyeing of cloth, none of whom were serfs of Travkin himself.[112] A house in the Semenovskaia sloboda belonging to "the late Admiral Vasilii Alekseevich Miatlev" was occupied by a peasant of a different serfowner who operated a silk-weaving "factory" on the premises.[113] A house belonging to Count P. S. Saltykov was in the possession of an economic

---

[110]MPIKP, Vol. 2, pp. 93 (No. 49), 96 (No. 81), 100 (No. 146); Materialy dlia istorii moskovskogo kupechestva (hereafter MDIMK), Vol. 4, pp. 298 (No. 253), 480 (No. 77), 534 (Nos. 404, 408), 701 (No. 107), etc.; V. I. Semevskii, Krest'iane v tsarstvovanii imperatritsy Ekateriny II, Vol. 1 (St. Petersburg, 1903), p. 327; N. I. Tourgenieff (Turgenev), La Russie et les russes, Vol. 2 (Brussels, 1847), p. 89.

[111]MPIKP, Vol. 2, p. 97 (No. 93).

[112]Ibid., p. 96 (No. 80).

[113]Ibid., p. 101 (No. 155).

peasant of Borovsk uezd who was engaged in the weaving of woolen goods
with the help of three hired workers.[114] Peasants were also sometimes
found to be in occupation of houses nominally belonging to merchants,
soldiers and priests.[115] In the same documents, however, peasants are
frequently identified as the owners of Moscow houses without qualification, which suggests either that they could sometimes acquire property
without the assistance of the above parties, perhaps under some other
pretext or due to lax enforcement, or that the legal fiction of ownership by silent partners drawn from classes authorized to possess urban
property was so well established and understood that it was not invariably necessary to make reference to it.[116]

For those not able or inclined to purchase property, rented
quarters were widely available. Much of the population of eighteenth-
century Moscow lived in such quarters, and according to a description
of Moscow in the 1780's the leasing of both residential and commercial

---

[114]Ibid., p. 101 (No. 151). Additional examples unearthed by the
aforementioned 1766 investigation of "unauthorized" industrial activity
in the Semenovskaia and Preobrazhenskaia slobody: Ibid., pp. 99 (Nos.
124-26, 100 (No. 140), 101 (No. 152). In the cases cited the exact
arrangements under which the peasants possessed these properties cannot
be determined. The nobles may have sold property they owned to peasants
while remaining the owners of record to avoid legal complications or
may have allowed peasants to use their names in the purchase of property
as a favor or paid service. Rental of property by peasants from its
noble owners is another possibility. Probably all of these alternatives
occurred.

[115]Ibid., pp. 100 (No. 141), 101 (Nos. 147-48, 152), 102 (Nos. 156,
161-62).

[116]In the 1766 survey of the Preobrazhenskaia and Semenovskaia
slobody peasants are listed as the owners of houses in 11 out of 162
cases. (Ibid., pp. 90-102.) The skazki of the Fifth Revision (1795)
for Moscow also make reference to houses owned by peasants, although
since these peasants were not officially part of the urban population
they are mentioned here only as landlords supplying rented quarters to
members of the urban classes. See MDIMK, Vol. 4, pp. 227 (No. 528),
231 (No. 575), 240 (No. 670), 241 (Nos. 678-79), etc.

property was a major source of income for the local urban classes.[117] There is evidence that such leasing was widely practiced by Moscow householders of other categories as well.[118] Rented quarters commonly consisted of separate "cottages" (izby), often located in the landlord's yard adjacent to his own house, or of rooms or parts of rooms (ugly) and "cellars" (podklet'i) in dwellings occupied by several households.[119] Some peasants rented vacant land and erected their own structures on it.[120] The same rented quarters frequently served as both residence and the headquarters of a commercial or craft enterprise. Peasants performing hired labor often lived with their employers under contracts (zhilye zapisi) which specified that the worker was to be housed, fed and sometimes clothed by the employer.[121] Of the twenty-one peasant households from the court Khatun volost' living in Moscow in 1736, seven were living in their own houses, three in rented "cottages," seven in rented rooms, three with their employers, and one had no permanent residence.[122]

---

[117]Sostoianie stolichnogo goroda Moskvy, 1785 g., p. 6.

[118]The documents of the Fourth and Fifth Revisions indicate that members of the Moscow urban classes frequently lived in quarters rented from householders belonging to all of the major categories of the city's population. (MDIMK, Vols. 3-4.)

[119]S. I. Volkov, Krest'iane dvortsovykh vladenii, pp. 55, 80; Istoriia Moskvy, Vol. 2, p. 59.

[120]MPIKP, Vol. 1, p. 233; Istoriia Moskvy, Vol. 2, p. 59.

[121]Istoriia Moskvy, Vol. 2, pp. 59-60, 326.

[122]S. I. Volkov, Krest'iane dvortsovykh vladenii, p. 80.

Another circumstance which assisted peasants arriving in Moscow
in infiltrating urban life was the existence of enclaves within the
city where the control of the urban authorities was loose or absent
entirely. On such territories, which included quarters (slobody)
occupied by soldiers and iamshchiki (servitors of the state postal
system) and land belonging to monasteries, peasants could pursue
illegal economic activities and acquire property with less danger of
detection and interference by the authorities. A case in point is the
career of Ekim Afanas'ev Repin, a peasant from the estates of the
Novodevichii Convent, who about 1740 possessed a house in Moscow built
on land rented from the convent and sold goods on the woolen "row".
In 1745 Repin "purchased a building near the Andreevskii Monastery
on land belonging to the monastery" and there began the production of
silver tinsel.[123] The large number of "unauthorized" peasant producers
operating in the Preobrazhenskaia and Semenovskaia soldiers' slobody
and their acquisition of property in these quarters have already been
discussed.[124]

The suburban peasant villages belonging to the imperial court
played a similar mediating role in urban settlement by peasants arriving
from elsewhere. Many court villages in the immediate vicinity of Moscow,
such as Pokrovskoe, Taininskoe, Izmailovo and Kolomenskoe, were themselves centers of trade and industry, and contemporary observers found
that "for a significant distance /from the city/ the inhabitants appear

[123]MPIKP, Vol. 1, pp. 68-69, 73-74.

[124]Ibid., Vol. 2, pp. 90-102. On the use by peasants of property in
areas of the types mentioned, see also Ibid., Vol. 1, p. 75; MDIMK,
Vol. 4, pp. 240 (No. 670), 241 (No. 679); Istoriia Moskvy, Vol. 2,
pp. 59, 310, 312.

to be urban rather than rural."[125] Commercial activity in these settlements functioned under the protection of the court estate administration, which did not observe the restrictions prevailing on posad territory. Because of these favorable conditions the most centrally located of these villages, Pokrovskoe, which in the eighteenth century was already physically if not legally a part of tne city, attracted not only peasants of more distant court properties but those of other categories entirely and even provincial merchants seeking access to the Moscow market. The monastery peasant Ivan Shchedrinin, for example, in 1746 lived in Pokrovskoe and engaged in "unauthorized" production of silk ribbons with the assitance of hired workers.[126] As a result of this situation property in Pokrovskoe became, in the words of E. I. Indova, a "genuine object of commerce," and inhabitants who gained a foothold on the territory of the city itself and were therefore relinquishing their holdings in the village, or were forced to do by economic difficulties, readily found buyers.[127] Another court possession within Moscow which was useful to trading peasants was the Novonemetskii Market, where trade took place under explicit authorization but without the supervision of the posad authorities. This market was operated by the court estate administration, usually through a "farmer" (otkupshchik)

---

[125]Sostoianie stolichnogo goroda Moskvy, 1785 g., pp. 9, 11-12; S. I. Volkov, Krest'iane dvortsovykh vladenii, pp. 46-48, 67-68; Indova, "Les activités commerciales," pp. 213, 219.

[126]MPIKP, Vol. 2, p. 73.

[127]Indova, "Les activités commerciales," pp. 219-24. See also Indova, "Moskovskii posad," pp. 484-85; S. I. Volkov, Krest'iane dvortsovykh vladenii, pp. 66, 72-73. The authorities attempted to prevent property in Pokrovskoe and other court possessions from passing into alien hands, but apparently without much success. Late in the eighteenth century, Pokrovskoe was legally incorporated into the city.

drawn from the court peasantry. Its stores and other facilities were
in the hands of trading peasants, primarily those of Pokrovskoe and
other court villages but to some extent of other categories as well.[128]

Even the protection of the court administration did not render
trading peasants immune to periodic offensives by the urban authorities
against illicit trade. The peasants of Pokrovskoe complained in a 1761
petition that "the Moscow magistracy is prohibiting trade /by peasants/
not only in Moscow but in Pokrovskoe village and at the /Novo/nemetskii
market...and is seizing trading peasants and holding them under arrest
at the magistracy."[129] "Unauthorized" industrial producers, when discovered, could be arrested in Pokrovskoe and throughout the city on
the authority of the Manufactures College. Nevertheless, the confused
structure of urban government in Moscow and the attenuation of urban
authority in outlying areas of the city unquestionably assisted peasants
in evading barriers to settlement in the "center of the all-Russian
market" and participation in its commerce and industry.

Enlistment in the Urban Classes: First, Second and Third Revisions

Having examined the available evidence concerning the overall
peasant presence in the population and economy of eighteenth-century
Moscow, we turn to the more systematic documentation on those settlers
who gained legal sanction for their entry into the urban population
through enlistment in the urban classes or in craft guilds. Data on
enlistment in the urban classes have been gathered principally through

[128]Indova, "Les activités commerciales," pp. 219-25; S. I. Volkov,
Krest'iane dvortsovykh vladenii, pp. 62, 66.

[129]S. I. Volkov, Krest'iane dvortsovykh vladenii, p. 85.

analysis of census depositions (<u>revizskie</u> <u>skazki</u>) from the five
"revisions" which took place in the eighteenth century.[130] Because of
the voluminous character of this material it has been possible to
accord the documents from the first three revisions only a cursory
analysis, aimed at determining the total amount of peasant enlistment
during the period covered and the salient features of this influx.
The results of the Fourth and Fifth Revisions (1782, 1795) have been
given a comprehensive analysis, while enlistment in craft guilds is
treated on the basis of separate sources.

The Moscow Census Register (<u>Perepisnaia</u> <u>kniga</u>) of 1725, incorporating the results of the First Revision, divides peasants enlisted
in the Moscow posad into three categories: (1) those registered "since
1719" in the special 40-kopeck tax assessment (<u>oklad</u>); (2) those registered "since 1719" in the regular urban 120-kopeck <u>oklad</u>; and (3) those
registered "before 1719."[131] The first category consists of "mercantile
peasants" enlisted under the provisions of the decree of April 13, 1722,
and continuing to pay the rural "soul tax" and seigneurial dues as well
as the urban tax.[132] The second group would include both freed serfs,
who were dropped from peasant status entirely, and some "mercantile
peasants" who had been omitted from the rural tax assessments through
confusion over the complex new regulations governing enlistment in the

---

[130]<u>MDIMK</u>, Vols. 1-4 (Moscow, 1883-86).

[131]<u>Ibid.</u>, Vol. 1 (Moscow, 1883), "Perepisnaia kniga 1725 g.," pp.
1-240.

[132]<u>Polnoe</u> <u>sobranie</u> <u>zakonov</u> <u>Rossiiiskoi</u> <u>imperii</u> <u>s</u> <u>1649</u> <u>g.</u> (hereafter
<u>PSZ</u>), Vol. 7, Nos. 4312, 4566. See also above, Chapter 2.

posad but continued to be held responsible for estate dues.[133] The

third group probably consists for the most part of registrants who

appeared before 1719 but after the authorization of voluntary enlistment

by Peter I in 1699-1700, although no initial date is specified.[134]

By the conclusion of the First Revision about 250 male "souls"

had enlisted as mercantile peasants in the 40-kopeck oklad, while an

additional 150 peasants were registered in the regular urban tax assess-

ment between 1719 and 1725.[135] Peasants listed in the census register

as having entered the posad "before 1719" amount to about 600 souls.[136]

---

[133]The decree of September 16, 1724 (PSZ, Vol. 7, No. 4566) specified
that such individuals remain in the urban 120-kopeck oklad but continue
to pay estate dues.

[134]In the census register peasants who enlisted before 1719 are
listed along with registrants from other categories under the heading
of those who entered the posad "before 1700 and from 1700 through 1719."
New registrants of all types are juxtaposed to starinnye tiagletsy
(taxpayers "of old"), a term probably signifying those families which
belonged to the given Moscow sloboda or sotnia according to the preceding
general census of 1678. Some peasants who were added to the posad
through involuntary enrollment of migrants in the late seventeenth
century may thus be included among the new registrants, but probably
not many. On the involuntary attachment of peasants to the urban
commune in seventeenth-century Russia, see above, Chapter 2.

[135]The 1725 register actually lists only 157 souls as belonging to
the 40-kopeck oklad. However, the Census Register of 1747, containing
the results of the Second Revision, names 256 souls belonging to this
category "according to the previous census," including 108 still present in the posad and 148 no longer present. (MDIMK, Vol. 1,
"Perepisnaia kniga 1747 g.," pp. 1-165.) The later source probably
includes persons who enlisted too late for inclusion in the 1725
register but not long afterward or who were overlooked in the initial
compilation of results. None of the figures cited can be considered
complete, since information on three subdivisions of the Moscow posad
(out of a total of 33) is missing wholly or partially from the surviving registers.

[136]This figure, rather than being determined directly from the source,
is extrapolated from figures cited above and from findings made by E. A.
Zviagintsev and E. I. Zaozerskaia on the basis of the same source.
(Zviagintsev, "Rost naseleniia," p. 139; Zaozerskaia, "Moskovskii posad
pri Petre I," Voprosy istorii, 1947, No. 9, p. 28.) It may be considered a reliable approximation.

The Moscow posad at the conclusion of the First Revision thus contained
about 1000 male souls absorbed from the peasantry during the previous
quarter-century, and these registrants constituted about seven percent
of the total posad population of nearly 14,000 males. According to the
determinations of E. I. Zaozerskaia, the Census Register of 1725 lists
as newcomers to the Moscow posad 1441 households of provincial townsmen,
511 households of peasants and 256 households of raznochintsy.[137] The
peasant influx, which contributed 23 percent of all newcomers, was thus
dwarfed by that of the provincial urban classes, which contributed 65
percent. About half the peasant registrants derived from the court
peasantry, while the remainder came from the estates of church institutions or private lords.[138]

According to the Census Register of 1747, containing the results
of the Second Revision, of the nearly 14,000 souls registered in the
regular urban (120-kopeck) tax assessment under the previous census
more than 7800 (56 percent) disappeared in the two succeeding decades.[139]
Mercantile peasants enlisted in the 40-kopeck oklad (which in 1747 was
raised to 50 kopecks) suffered an almost identical degree of attrition,
losing 58 percent of their original number, while new births made up
only one-third of this deficit. As a result, this group contracted
from 256 to 162 males (including survivors and the newborn) during the
intercensus period.[140] However, the enlistment of nearly 1100 newcomers

---

[137]Zaozerskaia, "Moskovskii posad," p. 28. Zaozerskaia's figures
would not include the additional peasants shown by the Census Register
of 1747 to have been enlisted in the 40-kopeck oklad "according to the
previous census," but this omission affects the results only slightly.

[138]Ibid.

[139]MDIMK, Vol. 1, "Perepisnaia kniga 1747 g.," pp. 153-54.

[140]Ibid., pp. 1-154.

during the same period boosted the total number of mercantile peasants registered in Moscow to 1247 by the conclusion of the Second Revision.[141] An additional 200 peasants were added to the regular urban oklad during this period. Between the First and Second Revisions Moscow also gained about 700 new registrants from the provincial kupechestvo and 400 from other, miscellaneous population categories.[142] Of the 2400 new members added to the Moscow posad during this period more than half thus derived from the peasantry, although the increased relative importance of the peasant contribution was due not so much to a sharp rise in enlistment by peasants as to a decrease in the number of provincial townsmen re-settling in Moscow. At the conclusion of the Second Revision the Moscow posad population stood at about 13,500 males and thus registered only a slight decline since the previous census.[143] Despite the heavy losses experienced by the residual population the decline was held to a minimum by a substantial influx of newcomers. Peasants enlisted since the

---

[141] The 1767 "Report on the Number of Souls" cited extensively in the preceding chapter records the presence of 1247 mercantile peasants in Moscow according to the Second Revision. (GPB RO, Ermitazhnoe sobranie, No. 242, l. 1.) The Census Register of 1747 lists only 1006 mercantile peasants, but the discrepancy can be accounted for by the fact that in this source documentation for three Moscow slobody is missing. Also, the 1767 source probably lists some peasants who registered too late for inclusion in the census register but were still considered enlisted "under" or "before" the Second Revision. According to the census register about 850 new registrants were added to the 50-kopeck oklad between the two revisions, but if the higher total of the 1767 document is accepted the number of new registrants was closer to 1100. Registrants who died or otherwise were removed from the posad before the census are of course not included in either of these figures.

[142] MDIMK, Vol. 1, "Perepisnaia kniga 1747 g.," pp. 1-153. The 1747 register lists 588 registrants from the provincial kupechestvo and 319 from other categories. To compensate for the incompleteness of the register as it survives, these figures have been raised by a factor of 25 percent, on the analogy of the results obtained above for mercantile peasants.

[143] GPB RO, Ermitazhnoe sobranie, No. 242, l. 1.

previous census comprised slightly less than 10 percent of the Moscow

posad in the results of this census, while about 13 percent probably

consisted of peasants who had entered the posad over the entire period

since the beginning of the century, or their descendants.[144]

The 1747 census register discloses that of the peasants added to

the posad since the First Revision 41 percent derived from the court

peasantry, 39 percent from the church peasantry and 18 percent from

the ranks of private serfs. In the serf contingent 10 percent was con-

tributed by house serfs and 8 percent by seigneurial peasants. The

house serfs consisted exclusively of freedmen who were placed in the

regular urban oklad, having been relieved of rural taxes through manu-

mission, while the seigneurial peasants were predominantly although not

exclusively in the 50-kopeck oklad intended for mercantile peasants.

The census register also makes it possible to trace the geographical

origins of the peasant newcomers. To facilitate comparison with later

data, these findings are expressed here in terms of post-1775 territorial

units. Not surprisingly, the largest contributor was Moscow guberniia,

which accounted for 44 percent of the registrants. The other major

contributors were provinces to the north and east of Moscow guberniia,

including Iaroslavl' (19 percent), Kostroma (13 percent), Vladimir

(12 percent) and Vologda (4 percent).

The Moscow posad population underwent its sharpest contraction be-

tween the Second and Third Revisions (from the mid-1740's to the early

---

[144]This latter estimate assumes that peasants enlisted in the 120-
kopeck oklad between 1719 and 1725 and those enlisted before 1719
maintained the same rate of survival and reproduction as mercantile
peasants registered in the 40-kopeck oklad. On this basis we would
expect to find about 500 souls deriving from the first two groups in
the Moscow posad at the time of the Second Revision.

1760's), falling by nearly 30 percent from about 13,500 to slightly under 10,000 males.[145] The findings of E. A. Zviagintsev on the dynamics of the posad population in this period, which have already been mentioned, indicate that the contraction resulted from continued massive attrition among the residual population and a pronounced reduction in the influx of newcomers.[146]

Zviagintsev's conclusion is supported by other evidence. According to an official document summarizing the results of the Second and Third Revisions, the number of mercantile peasants enlisted in the Moscow posad fell from 1247 to 1087 souls between the two censuses, indicating that the number of new registrants added to this category was insufficient even to cover its concurrent losses.[147] Data gathered from documents of the Third Revision for ten Moscow slobody provide further insight into this unfavorable trend.[148] At the time of the Second Revision these slobody contained 360 mercantile peasants, of whom only 174 remained at the subsequent census. Of the other 186 registrants, 140 died, 10 were conscripted, 2 were transferred to other categories, 1 fled and 23 disappeared "for reasons unknown" during the intervening period. New births added only 68 souls, so that the mercantile-peasant population recorded by the Second Revision suffered a net loss of 33 percent and fell to 242 souls. Peasants enlisted in the Moscow posad

[145] GPB RO, Ermitazhnoe sobranie, No. 242, 1. 1.

[146] Zviagintsev, "Rost naseleniia," pp. 138-39.

[147] GPB RO, Ermitazhnoe sobranie, No. 242, 1. 1.

[148] MDIMK, Vol. 2 (Moscow, 1885), "Svodnye vedomosti po III revizii," pp. 23-216.

thus did not escape the fate of native burghers and experienced the
same disastrous surplus of deaths over births which Zviagintsev found
to be characteristic of the latter. New enlistment after the Second
Revision contributed only 78 additional mercantile peasants to the
population of these slobody, not enough to cover the resulting deficit.

In the ten slobody investigated the remainder of the Second
Revision population (i.e. those in the 120-kopeck oklad) contracted
by virtually the same proportion as did the group of mercantile peasants
(35 percent). Between the Second and Third Revisions 202 new registrants, of whom only a handful were peasants, were added to the 120-
kopeck oklad. After inclusion of all gains and losses, the total population of these slobody fell by 28 percent, from 3811 to 2740 souls,
which is proportionally almost identical to the loss suffered by the
posad as a whole (27 percent).[149]   If the slobody studied are representative of all 33 slobody, as they appear to be, it is possible to
estimate that the entire posad contained in the neighborhood of 300 new
registrants from the peasantry and 700 from all other sources.[150]
Enlistment by peasants had thus dropped very sharply by comparison
with the preceding period, while the influx from other population categories dropped less sharply.

The evidence gathered thus far on peasant enlistment in the Moscow
posad from the beginning of the eighteenth century through the Third

[149]The contraction of the mercantile-peasant group in these ten
slobody (11 percent) also corresponds closely to the decrease in mercantile peasants in the posad as a whole (13 percent).

[150]If anything, the estimates given are probably too generous.
Zviagintsev, investigating 22 slobody containing 58 percent of the
Moscow posad population, found 412 new registrants from all sources.
(Zviagintsev, "Rost naseleniia," p. 138.) This figure can be extrap-
olated to a total of about 700 registrants for the entire posad.

Revision allows several tentative conclusions. During the designated
period a total of between 2000 and 3000 peasant "souls" were incorporated into the posad.[151] From the early 1720's on enlistment took
place primarily through the institution of "mercantile peasants"
(kupechestvuiushchie krest'iane) created by the laws of Peter I.
Registrants placed in this category did not lose their membership in
the peasantry and remained permanently responsible for rural taxes
and estate dues while paying a reduced urban tax of 40 kopecks (later
50 kopecks). From the 1720's through the Third Revision between 1500
and 2000 souls enlisted in the Moscow posad as mercantile peasants,
while a much smaller number of freed serfs and other peasant registrants
(300 to 400) were added to the regular urban (120-kopeck) oklad during
this period. At the time of the Second and Third Revisions about ten
percent of the Moscow posad population consisted of mercantile peasants.
However, new enlistment dropped sharply following the Second Revision
and in the succeeding decades failed even to cushion substantially the
sharp decline suffered by the posad population due to other forces.
To explain this decline in peasant enlistment we can at present resort
only to speculation. The cumbersome features of the Petrine system
for absorbing trading peasants into the posad, particularly the prospect of continued unfree status and responsibility for rural obligations
may increasingly have deterred peasants from seeking entry into the
urban classes. Moreover, the decline in peasant enlistment coincided
with the period when government repression of participation by peasants

---

[151]These figures, like all the preceding data, include only registrants who remained in the posad long enough to be counted by a census,
omitting those who died or otherwise disappeared before their presence
was so recorded.

in urban trade and industry was most severe. Such activity was usually
a prerequisite for enlistment in the posad.[152]

Once they became members of the Moscow posad peasant registrants
suffered the same rapid attrition--due primarily to natural decrease--
as did other urban citizens, which is understandable since they faced
the same unfavorable health conditions. On the other hand, mercantile
peasants apparently were not subject to any other important forces of
attrition, such as removal from the posad because of business failure
or for reasons connected with their continued legal ties to the
peasantry.[153] Rather, the ravages experienced by Moscow's mercantile-
peasant population appear to be virtually identical in quantity and
in source to those inflicted on the posad as a whole. In practice,
enlistment in the category of mercantile peasants thus conferred a
membership in the urban classes which was as permanent as any other
kind.

The available evidence also demonstrates that court peasants
played a particularly strong role in the influx of peasants into the
Moscow posad during this period. They contributed 50 percent of the
registrants recorded by the First Revision and more than 40 percent of

---

[152]It will be recalled that under the Petrine decrees possession of
300-500 rubles was required for entry into the category of mercantile
peasants. Moreover, in 1747 the Senate decided that only peasants who
already possessed houses, stores or enterprises in the town (paradoxi-
cally, in violation of the law) were eligible for posad membership.
(PSZ, Vol. 12, No. 9372.)

[153]It was mentioned earlier (Chapter II) that court peasants enlisted
in the posad who defaulted on their obligation to pay estate dues were
sometimes reclaimed by the court estate administration but that there
is no evidence for such a practice on the part of secular or ecclesiastical lords. The data on Moscow suggest that such removal from the
posad occurred rarely regardless of the origin of the registrant.

those added by the Second Revision.[154] With 11 percent of the peasant
population in the Central Industrial Region, according to the First
Revision, the court peasantry was clearly very much overrepresented
among newcomers to the Moscow posad.[155] The explanation for this
heightened role perhaps lies in the precocious involvement of these
peasants in trade and industry in Moscow and its environs, in which
activities they benefited from the proximity of many court estates to
the city and the relatively high degree of freedom and encouragement
accorded such activities by the court estate administration. The
peasants of the church estates (21 percent of the peasant population
in the same region) were another major contributor to the replenishment
of the Moscow posad in this period. The role of private serfs (68
percent of the peasant population) seems surprisingly small in view of
the size of this group and the stipulation of Peter I that such
peasants could enlist "freely," without the consent of their masters,
if they met the specified requirements.

---

[154]On enlistment by court peasants in the Moscow posad during this
period, see also E. I. Indova, "Rol' dvortsovoi derevni pervoi poloviny
XVIII v. v formirovanii russkogo kupechestva," Istoricheskie zapiski,
Vol. 68 (1961), pp. 191-93. Indova's data, derived from the records
of the court estate administration, indicate that 577 households of
court peasants were added to the Moscow urban classes between the First
and Third Revisions. Other evidence suggests that these households
probably included about 1000 male souls. (See Zaozerskaia, "Moskovskii
posad," p. 28; Zviagintsev, "Rost naseleniia," p. 139; see also the
data from the Fourth and Fifth Revisions discussed below.) However,
these figures are not strictly comparable to census data, since they
indicate the total number of registrants entering the posad during
the indicated period rather than the number remaining at the time of
the census.

[155]On the size of the different peasant groups, see V. M. Kabuzan,
Izmeneniia v razmeshchenii naseleniia Rossii v XVIII-pervoi polovine
XIX v. (Moscow, 1971), pp. 59-61.

Enlistment of Peasants in Craft Guilds

As has been explained in a previous chapter, peasants arriving in
the city with passports authorizing departure from their villages
could enlist "temporarily" in craft guilds (tsekhi). Such enlistment
did not require large amounts of capital, nor did the registrant incur
urban obligations other than those of the guilds themselves. "Temporary"
registrants in craft guilds were not considered members of the posad
but did have official sanction for residence in the city and pursuit
of some forms of commercial activity there. Reports of the Moscow city
authorities on the membership of craft guilds in 1726, 1730 and 1737
indicate that in this period thousands of peasants took advantage of
the above opportunities.[156] Peasants consistently comprised 50 to 60
percent of the craft-guild membership, far outstripping the contribution
of any other population group. (See Table 5.) In this case the court
peasantry was not the dominant element among peasant registrants and
in fact played a smaller role than did the other major peasant categories,
although court peasants were still substantially overrepresented with
respect to their small share of the total peasant population. Peasants
of secular lords and house serfs together made up one-quarter of the
craft-guild membership, while peasants of the church estates comprised
14-16 percent and court peasants 10 percent.

Much interest attaches to the distribution of peasant artisans
among particular crafts, since this is one of the few sources of quantitative data on the occupations pursued by peasants living in Moscow.

---

[156]MPIKP, Vol. 2, pp. 54-65; Istoriia Moskvy, Vol. 2, pp. 322-23.

Table 5: Membership of Moscow Craft Guilds, 1726-1737

	1726	1730	1737[a]
Urban classes	1451 (21.1%)	1873 (21.9%)	794 (20.9%)
of Moscow	758 (11.0%)	-	502 (13.2%)
of other towns	693 (10.1%)	-	292 (7.7%)
Peasants	3609 (52.4%)	4453 (52.0%)	2330 (61.3%)
church	-[b]	1371 (16.0%)	513 (13.5%)
court	-	892 (10.4%)	380 (10.0%)
seigneurial	-	1657 (19.3%)	836 (22.0%)
house serfs	420 (6.1%)[c]	533 (6.2%)	141 (3.7%)
unspecified	-	-	460 (12.1%)
Other	1825 (26.5%)	2240 (26.1%)	676 (17.8%)
clergy, church servitors	-	273 (3.2%)	-
retired soldiers	-	241 (2.8%)	-
state artisans	-	299 (3.5%)	-
servitors of court adm.	-	240 (2.8%)	-
foreigners	-	487 (5.7%)	-
other and unidentified	-	700 (8.2%)	-
Total guild membership	6885	8566	3800

Sources: Materialy po istorii krest'ianskoi promyshlennosti, Vol. 2 (Moscow-Leningrad, 1950), pp. 54-65 (1726, 1730); Istoriia Moskvy, Vol. 2 (Moscow, 1953), pp. 322-3 (1737).

[a]The 1737 data is given by the source in terms of percentages of an approximate total. In the interest of compatibility with the remaining data, these percentages have been supplemented here by equivalent absolute figures.

[b]3189 members from church, court and seigneurial peasantry.

[c]Including "servants" of monasteries (monastyrskie sluzhki).

The 1731 report of the Moscow municipal authorities lists 149 separate
guilds, many of which had only a few members or even a single member.[157]
Peasants figured in 110 of these guilds, and it is difficult to find a
major profession in which peasants were not significantly represented.
(Few peasants, it must be admitted, were members of the icon-painters'
guild.) Table 6 lists the guilds which contained a substantial repre-
sentation of peasants.[158] These data reveal that peasants thoroughly
dominated the guilds concerned with preparation of food products, and
these occupations absorbed nearly a quarter of the peasant guild membership. An even larger segment (42 percent) was occupied with the production of articles of clothing and fur and leather goods, chiefly in the
huge cobblers' and tailors' guilds. Peasants were strongly represented
in some textile trades (those involving cloth-printing and the production of braid-work and tinsel), but in many of the basic textile
sectors guilds were weakly developed altogether. These data thus
greatly underestimate the importance of the textile trades among
occupations of peasants settling in Moscow, which is well known from
other sources. Metallurgical trades absorbed about 13 percent of the
peasant guild membership, and of these artisans more than half worked
with precious metals. Another substantial segment of peasant craftsmen was involved in construction-related professions, and peasants
also figured prominently in guilds concerned with the making of candles,

---

[157]MPIKP, Vol. 2, pp. 58-65. On the basis of additional documentation,
S. I. Sakovich asserts that this report reflects the membership of the
guilds as it stood in 1730. (Sakovich, "Sotsial'nyi sostav moskovskikh
tsekhovykh remeslennikov 1720-kh gg.," Istoricheskie zapiski, Vol. 42
/1953/, pp. 238-39.

[158]These guilds contained 93 percent of the peasant guild registrants
according to the 1731 document.

Table 6:   Distribution of Peasants in Moscow Craft Guilds, 1730

Membership

Occupational groupings and guilds[a]	Church peasants	Court peasants	Seigneurial peasants	House serfs	Total peasants	Total membership	% peasants
Preparation of food products							
bakers (bread)	66	17	215	1	299	311	96.1
bakers (rolls)	28	11	172	-	211	226	93.4
sutlers[b]	51	38	179	2	270	286	94.4
kvas-brewers	24	15	51	-	90	96	93.8
millers of hempseed oil	30	-	63	-	93	97	95.9
total	199	81	680	3	963	1016	94.8
% of category	15.7	9.8	43.0	0.6	23.2	13.8	
Textile production							
cloth-printing (2 guilds)	57	80	43	5	185	270	68.5
braid-work (2 guilds)	20	50	3	-	73	125	58.4
tinsel (2 guilds)	17	29	14	-	60	122	49.2
total	94	159	60	5	318	517	61.5
% of category	7.4	19.2	3.8	1.1	7.7	7.0	

Table 6 (cont.)

	Church peasants	Court peasants	Seigneurial peasants	House serfs	Total peasants	Total membership	% peasants
Articles of clothing, fur and leather goods							
tailors	112	39	125	228	504	955	52.8
hatters	37	18	21	4	80	184	43.5
furriers	63	62	28	22	175	499	35.1
makers of fur hats	20	20	12	11	63	190	33.2
makers of fur coats	14	-	1	-	15	21	71.4
tanners	6	4	10	2	22	43	51.2
cobblers	341	49	339	85	814	1546	52.7
glovers	31	16	9	6	62	220	28.2
total	624	208	545	358	1735	3658	47.4
% of category	49.2	25.2	34.5	76.0	41.8	49.8	
Metallurgy							
blacksmiths	10	15	17	7	49	137	35.8
tinsmiths	13	8	8	10	39	87	44.8
coppersmiths (2 guilds)	23	31	13	7	74	168	44.0
button-makers (copper)	12	26	3	1	42	71	59.2
locksmiths	3	2	5	4	14	29	48.3
goldsmiths[c]	5	3	2	16	26	116	22.4
gilders[d]	2	49	18	-	69	73	94.5

Table 6 (cont.)

	Church peasants	Court peasants	Seigneurial peasants	House serfs	Total peasants	Total membership	% peasants
Metallurgy (cont.)							
silversmiths (2 guilds)	66	82	15	15	178	402	44.3
gold and silver wire or leaf[e]	7	27	5	2	41	66	62.1
total	141	243	86	62	532	1149	46.3
% of category	11.1	29.4	5.4	13.2	12.8	15.6	
Construction							
stonemasons	60	19	13	11	103	157	65.6
bricklayers	5	3	2	-	10	13	76.9
carpenters[f]	54	51	48	-	153	216	70.8
joiners[g]	15	10	11	18	54	146	37.0
wood-carvers	6	4	4	7	21	61	34.4
total	140	87	78	36	341	593	57.5
% of category	11.0	10.5	4.9	7.6	8.2	8.1	
Other							
saddlers	15	11	11	1	38	89	42.7
harness-makers	9	9	10	3	31	74	41.9
carriage-makers	15	6	8	2	31	46	67.4
makers of carts, sleighs	13	2	10	1	26	34	76.5
candle-makers (tallow)	6	14	73	-	93	100	93.0

Table 6 (cont.)

	Church peasants	Court peasants	Seigneurial peasants	House serfs	Total peasants	Total membership	% peasants
Other (cont.)							
candle-makers (wax)	12	7	20	–	39	66	59.1
total	70	49	132	7	258	409	63.1
Total	1268	827	1581	471	4147	7342	56.5

Source: Materialy po istorii krest'ianskoi promyshlennosti, Vol. 2 (Moscow-Leningrad, 1950), pp. 58-65.

[a]This listing does not include guilds with few peasant members or very few members altogether. (See text.)

[b]Markitanty.

[c]Zolotoe masterstvo.

[d]Zolotarnoe masterstvo.

[e]Masterstvo volochenogo i pliushchil'nogo zolota i serebra.

[f]Plotniki.

[g]Stoliary.

horse gear and vehicles. There is a noticeable degree of differentiation
in the occupational preferences of the various peasant categories.
Seigneurial peasants dominated the guilds devoted to food products and
the candle-makers' guilds and also contributed many tailors and cobblers.
However, this category was notably weak in the textile guilds, in most
metal trades and in the construction trades (except carpentry). House
serfs were most prominent in the tailors' guild--nearly half of all
house serfs enlisted in Moscow craft guilds belonged to this one profession. Most of the remainder was occupied in other clothing trades
and secondarily in metallurgy and construction. Court peasants were
prominent in textiles and metallurgy, and especially in the working of
precious metals, but they were weak in the clothing trades, except
those involving fur goods. Church peasants were distributed more evenly
among the major sectors of craft production than were the other groups.

Documents studied by S. I. Sakovich provide some additional information on the origins of peasants registered in Moscow craft guilds.[159]
These documents indicate that peasants of the Iaroslavl' area predominated in the guilds concerned with preparation of food products.[160]
Of 509 peasant members of the bakers' guilds 265 came from Iaroslavl'

[159]Sakovich, "Sotsial'nyi sostav," pp. 253-55. The documents referred to are registers of craft-guild members compiled by the Moscow
municipal authorities (ratusha) in 1729. Unfortunately, Sakovich chose
not to make this information available in other than a vague and
limited way.

[160]This information is in accord with data compiled by B. B.
Kafengauz and cited here earlier which show that peasants of Iaroslavl'
uezd played an especially large role in trade in grain and bread products
in Moscow in the 1720's. Data to be presented later in this chapter
indicate that among peasants of Iaroslavl' guberniia newly enlisted in
the Moscow urban classes according to the Fifth Revision (1795), trade
in foodstuffs was the most important occupation and attracted a much
larger proportion of the registrants from this province than from
other provinces.

uezd, as did 90 of 93 processors of hempseed oil. Kvas brewers came primarily from the neighboring Romanov _uezd_. Other guilds in which immigrants from particular areas predominated include the gilders (from Pereslavl'-Zalesskii _uezd_) and the carpenters (from several Upper Volga districts and the region of Olonets in the Northwest). Two-thirds of the seigneurial peasants enlisted in Moscow craft guilds came from the estates of large landowners. Peasants of smaller landlords belonged to a comparatively narrow range of guilds, chiefly those of food processors and cobblers.

At the end of the 1730's the Moscow craft guilds experienced a precipitous decline. Inadequately supported by the government and shunned by many urban artisans, who had no desire for additional regulation, obligations and fees and wished to avoid the possibility of being conscripted for involuntary work on government projects, the guilds suffered a drastic reduction in membership, and many were liquidated entirely.[161] By 1737 the total membership of Moscow guilds had already declined by more than half since the beginning of the decade.[162] At the time of the Second Revision the Moscow urban classes contained only 117 craft-guilds members, and in the subsequent census only 96 members were counted.[163] These figures presumably include only permanent

---

[161]K. A. Pazhitnov, _Problema remeslennykh tsekhov v zakonodatel'stve russkogo absoliutizma_ (Moscow, 1952), pp. 56-60; S. I. Volkov, _Krest'-iane dvortsovykh vladenii_, pp. 56-57.

[162]Some of this decline may be a result of the great Moscow fire of 1737, which preceded the gathering of the 1737 data on guild membership. See _Istoriia Moskvy_, Vol. 2, pp. 322-23.

[163]GPB RO, Ermitazhnoe sobranie, No. 242, l. 1; _MDIMK_, Vol. 1, "Perepisnaia kniga 1747 g.," p. 1.

members and not "temporary" peasant registrants, and there is some
evidence of continued peasant enlistment in craft guilds even in the
period of their decline. The peasant Petr Petrov Linev, who had been
active as a dyer in Moscow for many years, learned in 1750 of a police
order that "no one practice the dyer's craft except guild masters" and
consequently applied to the Moscow magistracy for guild membership.[164]
In 1754 there were 90 peasants from the estates of Count P. B. Sheremetev
alone enlisted in Moscow craft guilds.[165] Among the 379 peasants found
in 1766 to be active in small-scale textile production in Moscow's
Semenovskaia and Preobrazhenskaia slobody, four had enlisted in craft
guilds.[166] However, it is unlikely that in the middle decades of the
eighteenth century peasant enlistment in Moscow craft guilds approached
its earlier level. According to data collected by the Commerce Commission, Moscow in the mid-1760's contained a total of 396 "permanent"
and "temporary" craft-guild members.[167] A description of Moscow in the
year 1785 states that the city's guilds had 314 "permanent" and 123
"temporary" members.[168] There is little information on what happened

[164]MPIKP, Vol. 1, pp. 229-42. Linev was accepted into the guild but
was nevertheless arrested as an "unauthorized" producer on the authority
of the Manufactures College. The latter, defending the interests of
large-scale government-authorized industry, disputed the peasant's
qualifications and eventually had him barred from his occupation on a
technicality. This case suggests one probable reason for the weakness
of craft guilds in this period. In consequence of the government's
efforts to promote large-scale "authorized" enterprises, the competing
small-scale production fostered by the guilds was deprived of support
and even repressed.

[165]Shchepetov, Krepostnoe pravo, p. 92.

[166]MPIKP, Vol. 2, pp. 100 (No. 142), 101 (No. 151), 102 (Nos. 161-62).

[167]TsGADA, f. 397, d. 441, 1. 10 ob.

[168]Sostoianie stolichnogo goroda Moskvy, 1785 goda, p. 9.

to the thousands of peasant guild members of earlier decades. Many
probably continued to work at their trades in Moscow without official
sanction, despite greater interference from the authorities.

At the end of the eighteenth century craft guilds in Moscow revived and "temporary" peasant membership in them once again burgeoned.
According to Shchekatov's Geographical Dictionary the guilds contained
2183 "permanent" and 11,931 "temporary" members.[169] Since the households of the latter included only 2697 females, it is probable that
recent migrants from the countryside predominated in this group.

Enlistment in the Urban Classes: Fourth Revision

The period between the Third and Fourth Revisions (1764-1782)
was witness to several important developments regarding the future
of the Moscow posad. On the unfavorable side, the plague of 1771
raised the normally high death rate in the city to staggering levels.
The Moscow magistracy reported in 1774 that about one-third of the
posad population recorded in the Third Revision had died in the plague
year alone, and in addition the disease probably left many weakened
survivors who died prematurely in subsequent years.[170] On the other hand,
Catherine II's reforms of 1775 raised the status of the kupechestvo,
lightened its burdens somewhat, and led to an improvement in the conditions under which crown peasants were allowed to register in the
urban classes. These changes, although instituted late in the period

---

[169]Shchekatov, Geograficheskii slovar', Vol. 4, p. 386.

[170]Zviagintsev, "Dinamika naseleniia dokapitalisticheskoi Moskvy"
(manuscript), p. 59, cited in Istoriia Moskvy, Vol. 2, pp. 312-13.
According to Zviagintsev, of those recorded in the Third Revision and
their offspring only 4620 souls remained in 1782--a contraction of
about 50 percent. (Zviagintsev, "Rost naseleniia," p. 141.)

and not fully worked out until after the Fourth Revision, promised a favorable effect on the recruitment of new urban citizens.

In the final outcome, the Moscow posad population contracted from slightly under 10,000 to between 8000 and 9000 souls (i.e. by 9-16 percent) between the Third and Fourth Revisions, a decline which was surprisingly small under the circumstances and in comparison to that recorded in the previous intercensus period (27 percent).[171] The enormous deficit resulting from the combined effects of the plague and the high rate of attrition which pressed the Moscow population downward even in "healthy" years was partially covered by an accelerated influx of newcomers. Analysis of census depositions (revizskie skazki) for 32 of the 33 Moscow slobody and sotni discloses that between the Third and Fourth Revisions 753 peasant households, which in 1782 contained 1463 male souls, were added to the population of these subdivisions.[172] During the same period 670 households of provincial townsmen and 445 households from other population categories (including state and factory artisans, clergy and servitors of church institutions, retired soldiers and other former military personnel, refugees returned from abroad and foreigners) enlisted in the urban classes of Moscow, and these groups added about 2100 souls to the Moscow posad population.[173]

---

[171]Zviagintsev, working with the published census documents of the Fourth Revision, counted a total of 8170 souls in the Moscow urban classes. (Zviagintsev, "Rost naseleniia," p. 141.) However, it is not clear (and indeed appears doubtful) that Zviagintsev included in his total an estimate for Sadovaia Bol'shaia sloboda, the Fourth Revision documents for which are missing. Other materials allow us to deduce that this sloboda contained about 800 additional souls. (See below, n. 174.)

[172]MDIMK, Vol. 3 (Moscow, 1885), pp. 1-460.

[173]The number of souls contributed by these groups is estimated under the assumption that the households contained the same average number of males as did households of peasant registrants (1.9 souls per household).

Missing from the surviving Fourth Revision materials are documents on the Sadovaia Bol'shaia sloboda--a serious omission, since this sloboda was apparently the largest of all subdivisions of the Moscow posad at the time and probably contained hundreds of additional registrants. On the basis of other materials it is possible to estimate the number of these registrants as between 300 and 400 households.[174] The total number of these registrants who appeared in the Moscow urban classes in this period thus amounted to about 2200 households or 4200 male souls, and these newcomers constituted nearly half the Moscow posad in 1782.[175] Of the newcomers 40 percent, or about 900 households and 1700 souls, derived from the peasantry.[176]

The geographical origins of the 1463 peasant registrants for whom we have direct documentation are analyzed by Table 7. As the focal

_____

[174]According to the Fifth Revision skazki for Sadovaia Bol'shaia (MDIMK, Vol. 4, pp. 184-277), this sloboda in 1795 contained 338 households which had been recorded in the previous census. An additional 98 households which had been present at the time of the Fourth Revision had since disappeared. Thus, according to the later census Sadovaia Bol'shaia sloboda contained 436 households at the time of the Fourth Revision. In the Third Revision only 122 households were recorded. (MDIMK, Vol. 2, "Skazki otdel'nykh lits," pp. 39-42.) Consequently, at least 300 households of new registrants must have entered this sloboda between the Third and Fourth Revisions, and in view of the enormous mortality which prevailed during this period we are entitled to push the estimate somewhat higher.

[175]Zviagintsev, working with the same Fourth Revision materials, determined the number of registrants from all categories to be 3550 souls. (Zviagintsev, "Rost naseleniia," p. 141.) Elsewhere the author states that in general he attempted to compensate for incomplete documentation through use of estimates, but the basis of these estimates is not discussed, nor is it stated whether one was made in this particular case. Zviagintsev's total is very close to the determination made here for the 32 documented slobody.

[176]These estimates assume that the distribution of registrants among various categories was the same in Sadovaia Bol'shaia sloboda as in the remainder of the posad.

Table 7: Enlistment of Peasants in Urban Classes of Moscow, 1764-1782 (Number of Males)

Province of origin	Crown peasants: Econ.	Court	Other	Total	Seigneurial peasants: Peasants	H. serfs	Total	All peasants	%
Moscow	354	200	6	560	67	43	110	670	54.3
Vladimir	145	8	5	158	3	14	17	175	14.2
Iaroslavl'	51	-	4	55	37	33	70	125	10.1
Tver'	54	-	1	55	3	8	11	66	5.3
Kaluga	29	-	-	29	-	8	8	37	3.0
Kostroma	12	-	2	14	16	13	29	43	3.5
Tula	24	5	1	30	5	4	9	39	3.2
Riazan'	24	1	4	29	-	5	5	34	2.8
Other[a]	9	1	4	14	14	18	32	46	3.7
Total	702	217	25	944	145	146	291	1235	100
Undetermined	68	17	8	93	8	127	135	228	-
Total	770	234	33	1037	153	273	426	1463	-
%	52.6	16.0	2.3	70.9	10.5	18.7	29.1	100	

Source: Materialy dlia istorii moskovskogo kupechestva, Vol. 3 (Moscow, 1885), pp. 1-460.

[a]Nizhnii Novgorod 2, Orel 7, Voronezh 4, Tambov 7, Kazan' 1, Penza 4, Simbirsk 3, Perm' 1, Vologda 10, Novgorod 1, Pskov 4, Smolensk 2.

point of the national market, with manifold commercial ties extending
throughout Russia, Moscow might have been expected to draw migrants
from widely scattered areas of the empire, and to some extent this
was in fact the case. However, what is striking about these results is
the high degree of concentration and localization evidenced by Moscow's
sources of immigration. Ninety-six percent of the peasant registrants
for whom geographical origin can be determined came from six provinces
of the Central Industrial Region or two neighboring Central Agricultural
provinces, while only 46 souls derived from more distant parts of the
empire. More than half the registrants came from Moscow guberniia
itself. For nearly 16 percent of the total number of registrants
geographical origin cannot be determined with certainty from the information given in the skazki, but the bulk of these registrants probably
originated in Moscow guberniia as well, and the actual contribution of
this province may thus have exceeded 60 percent.[177] Aside from Moscow
guberniia the outstanding contributors were Vladimir and Iaroslavl'
gubernii, while the provinces of Tver', Kostroma, Kaluga, Tula and
Riazan' delivered more modest contingents. Of the Central Industrial
provinces only the relatively distant Nizhnii Novgorod guberniia made
no significant contribution. In this connection it may be significant
that Nizhnii Novgorod was one of the few provincial towns in Central
Russia which itself received substantial numbers of peasant registrants.
Furthermore, this province bordered on the region of the Middle Volga,
the towns of which also attracted large numbers of registrants in the

---

[177]House serfs for whom no place of origin is specified probably had
in most cases been attached to the Moscow households of their masters.
In the case of crown peasants placed in the indeterminate category, the
name of a village or volost' is usually given without mention of the
uezd, and it is likely that Moscow uezd is understood.

late eighteenth century. Peasants of Nizhnii Novgorod guberniia
apparently found attractive opportunities for urban settlement closer
to home.

If we examine the origin of Moscow's peasant registrants at the
uezd level we find that the city's sources of immigration were even
more concentrated than is indicated by the above data. For the districts of Moscow guberniia it is useful to supplement the census
materials with a 1787 report of the Moscow provincial treasury
(kazennaia palata) giving the numbers of crown peasants of Moscow
guberniia who enlisted in the urban classes from the Third Revision
through 1782.[178] The latter source is more suitable for comparison
with later (Fifth Revision) results since it gives data according to
the post-1782 configuration of Moscow guberniia, under which five new
districts were created and the boundaries of the remaining districts
redrawn completely. The 1787 report gives more complete data on crown
peasants but does not cover freed serfs, necessitating the use of both
sources in conjunction.[179] According to the census documents, 82 percent of the registrants for whom geographical origin can be determined
came from Moscow uezd alone (in its large pre-1782 configuration).
(See Table 8.) According to the 1787 report, 84 percent of the

---

[178]TsGADA, f. 248 (1 departament Senata), d. 4109, 11. 213-19 ob.

[179]The 1787 report covers the entire Moscow posad, not omitting any
subdivisions, and also includes a large number of registrants who enlisted in the "second half" of 1782, after the deadline for submission
of revizskie skazki. Although the government decided in 1787 that only
those peasants who had enlisted through the "first half" of 1782 were
to be considered registered "before" the Fourth Revision and therefore
entitled to immediate release from peasant status and obligations,
other materials make clear that this decision was not strictly observed and that at least some of the later registrants were dropped
from the peasant oklad before the next census.

Table 8: Enlistment of Peasants of Moscow Guberniia in Urban Classes
of Moscow, 1764–1782 (Number of Males)

District of origin	Crown peasants:				Seigneurial peasants:			All peasants	%
	Econ.	Court	Other	Total	Peasants	H. serfs	Total		
Moscow	277	191	2	470	53	27	80	550	82.1
Dmitrov	24	-	-	24	-	3	3	27	4.0
Kolomna	36	2	-	38	11	9	20	58	8.7
Serpukhov	4	7	-	11	-	-	-	11	1.6
Zvenigorod	4	-	3	7	-	1	1	8	1.2
Vereia	-	-	-	-	-	1	1	1	0.1
Ruza	4	-	-	4	-	-	-	4	0.6
Mozhaisk	5	-	1	6	3	2	5	11	1.6
Volokolamsk	-	-	-	-	-	-	-	-	-
Klin	-	-	-	-	-	-	-	-	-
Total	354	200	6	560	67	43	110	670	100

Source: Materialy dlia istorii moskovskogo kupechestva, Vol. 3
(Moscow, 1885), pp. 1–460.

crown-peasant registrants from Moscow guberniia came from the reduced

Moscow uezd or the surrounding districts (Bogorodsk, Bronnitsy, Nikitsk,

Podol , Voskresensk, Zvenigorod), which to a large extent occupied

territory formerly belonging to Moscow uezd. (See Table 9.) Aside

from Moscow uezd, the districts which made the most plentiful contribu-

tions were those to the east and southeast of Moscow (Bogorodsk,

Bronnitsy, Nikitsk). Dmitrov uezd and the southern Serpukhov uezd made

some contribution, but immigration from the western part of the province

(the districts of Vereia, Mozhaisk, Ruza, Volokolamsk and Klin) was

weak.[180]

Registrants from outside Moscow guberniia also tended to come from

a well defined area of their respective provinces or even from a single

district. Most of the registrants from Vladimir guberniia came from

According to the 1787 report 784 crown peasants of Moscow guberniia
enlisted in the Moscow posad from the Third Revision through the first
half of 1782 and 418 in the second half of 1782. The revizskie skazki
for the 32 documented slobody list only 560 registrants from the crown
peasantry of Moscow guberniia. Inclusion of an estimated figure for the
missing sloboda (100 souls) brings the total closer to the figure given
by the 1787 report for enlistment through the first half of 1782. This
comparison suggests that the procedures used above to estimate the
composition of Sadovaia Bol'shaia sloboda do not exaggerate the number
of peasant registrants to be found there. The revizskie skazki naturally
do not include most registrants who enlisted in the second half of 1782.
(A few who were "added" in the summer months and submitted skazki late
are included.) Many additional registrants from other provinces and
from the seigneurial peasantry of Moscow guberniia may also have appeared
in the second half of 1782, and if one includes this overflow the total
number of peasants added to the Moscow posad from the Third Revision
through 1782 may have been as much as 50 percent higher than what is
indicated by the revizskie skazki.

[180]Discrepancies between the two sources regarding the relative contributions of individual districts are attributable mainly to radical
changes in district boundaries. Two-thirds of the new Serpukhov uezd
consisted of territory formerly belonging to Moscow and Kolomna uezdy.
More than half of Zvenigorod uezd was territory annexed from the former
Moscow uezd.

Table 9: Enlistment of Crown Peasants of Moscow <u>Guberniia</u> in Urban

Classes of Moscow, 1764-1782 (Number of Males)

<u>Districts</u>	<u>Econ.</u>	<u>Court</u>	<u>Other</u>	<u>Total</u>	<u>%</u>
Moscow	154	162	-	316	26.3
Bogorodsk	155	20	-	175	14.6
Bronnitsy	15	106	-	121	10.1
Nikitsk	40	141	-	181	15.1
Podol	67	-	-	67	5.6
Voskresensk	86	-	-	86	7.2
Zvenigorod	57	3	-	60	5.0
Dmitrov	54	-	-	54	4.5
Kolomna	6	-	-	6	0.5
Serpukhov	-	51	-	51	4.2
Vereia	14	-	-	14	1.2
Ruza	8	-	-	8	0.7
Mozhaisk	9	-	3	12	1.0
Volokolamsk	21	-	-	21	1.7
<u>Klin</u>	<u>24</u>	<u>-</u>	<u>6</u>	<u>30</u>	<u>2.5</u>
Total	710	483	9	1202	100

Source: TsGADA, f. 248, kn. 4109, ll. 213-219 ob.

the western part of the province (principally Vladimir and Pereslavl'-Zalesskii uezdy), which was adjacent to Moscow guberniia. Immigrants from Iaroslavl' guberniia came principally from the southeastern portion of the province (the districts of Iaroslavl' and Rostov) and secondarily from districts adjacent to it (Uglich, Romanov), with little contribution from the northern half of the province. In Tver' guberniia it was the Volga districts in the southeastern corner of the province (Kashin, Kaliazin), adjoining Moscow, Vladimir and Iaroslavl' gubernii, which sent peasant immigrants into the Moscow urban classes.[181] Registrants from the provinces to the south of Moscow (Kaluga, Tula and Riazan' gubernii) came almost exclusively from a single district of each province (Borovsk, Kashira and Egor'evsk uezdy respectively). These districts were adjacent to the southern part of Moscow guberniia and had in fact been part of the pre-1775 Moscow provintsiia. Peasant registrants from the neighboring provinces thus tended to come from the parts of those provinces which were nearest to Moscow. The exception to this rule was Kostroma guberniia, immigrants from which came in equal measure from Kostroma uezd and the remote northern districts of Galich and Chukhloma. Notwithstanding this deviation, the principal area of recruitment for the Moscow posad was a compact territory roughly bounded by the Volga and Oka rivers and by Vladimir in the east and Zvenigorod in the west. Significantly, many of the same districts (particularly Moscow, Pereslavl'-Zalesskii, Iaroslavl', Romanov, Kashin) were also frequently mentioned as the source of peasant immigrants living in Moscow without inscription in the urban classes.

---

[181]Kaliazin uezd was created following the 1775 reforms largely from territory formerly belonging to Kashin uezd. The area described is thus largely equivalent to the pre-1775 Kashin uezd.

Of the peasant registrants reported in the census documents, 71 percent were crown peasants and 29 percent were freed serfs. Since private serfs comprised 73 percent of the peasant population in the eight provinces which provided the bulk of the registrants, they are relatively very much underrepresented among the newly enlisted townsmen.[182] This is hardly surprising, in view of the much greater obstacles faced by serfs in changing their status, and it is noteworthy that contrary to the beliefs of some scholars a substantial number of serfs did succeed in extricating themselves from bondage and entering the urban classes.[183] Moreover, the role of serfs had clearly increased since the Second Revision, despite the fact that serfs could no longer enlist without the consent of their masters. Most of this growth resulted from increased enlistment by former house serfs. More than half the registrants came from the former church peasantry, now converted to state "economic" peasants, while only 16 percent came from the court peasantry.[184] The latter had thus declined in importance as a source of recruits for the Moscow posad, as the tempo of enlistment rose

---

[182]Kabuzan, Izmeneniia v razmeshchenii naseleniia Rossii, pp. 95-97.

[183]Misinterpreting one item in the 1787 report of the Moscow kazennaia palata cited above, G. L. Vartanov asserts that only 11 seigneurial peasants enlisted in the Moscow posad between 1742 and 1782 and that freed serfs thus constituted an "insignificant proportion" of the peasant influx into the urban classes. See Vartanov, "Kupechestvo i torguiushchee krest'ianstvo tsentral'noi chasti Evropeiskoi Rossii vo vtoroi polovine XVIII v.," Uchenye zapiski Leningradskogo gosudarstvennogo pedagogicheskogo instituta im. A. I. Gertsena, Vol. 229 (1962), pp. 187-93.

[184]Included under this heading are court peasants proper (dvortsovye krest'iane, those subject to the court estate administration), peasants of the court stables administration (koniushennye krest'iane), "Her Majesty's own" peasants and "falconer" peasants (sokol'i pomytchiki). According to the two available sources 55-65 percent of the registrants from the court peasantry were dvortsovye and 35-45 percent were koniushennye. The other two categories delivered only a few registrants.

among other groups but remained stationary among the court peasantry.
However, almost all of the registrants from this category came from
Moscow guberniia, and in this province court peasants were still notably
overrepresented among peasants enlisting in the Moscow urban classes:
they comprised 15 percent of the crown peasantry and 35-40 percent of
the registrants from the crown peasantry.[185] Peasants from the suburban court estates thus remained very active in the immigration to the
city, but few of the substantial numbers of court peasants in Vladimir,
Tver', Kostroma, Tula and Riazan' gubernii appeared as registrants in
the Moscow posad. Registrants from the economic peasantry, in contrast,
came from a much broader area, and freed serfs were still less concentrated in terms of geographical origin. Most of the registrants from
the more distant parts of the empire were former serfs, and freedmen
also predominated among immigrants from Iaroslavl' and Kostroma gubernii.

The data of the Fourth Revision indicate that peasant registrants
tended to cluster in the middle ranks of urban society and on the average
possessed a higher economic status than the posad population as a whole.
(See Table 10.) Eighty percent of the households of peasant registrants
belonged to the kupechestvo in 1782, as opposed to 58 percent of all
posad households. Only two families of new peasant registrants belonged
to the first merchant guild, but peasants were only slightly less likely
to belong to the first or second guild than were all posad members.[186]

---

[185]Kabuzan, Izmeneniia v razmeshchenii naseleniia Rossii, pp. 95-97.

[186]Another scholar has found that in the late eighteenth century 21
percent of the Moscow first guild was of peasant origin--i.e. consisted
of peasants who had entered the posad sometime during the eighteenth
century, or their descendants. A. I. Aksenov, Moskovskoe kupechestvo
v XVIII v. (Opyt genealogicheskogo issledovaniia) (dissertation, Moscow,
Institut istorii SSSR AN SSSR, 1974), pp. 93-96, 204-05.

Table 10: Enlistment of Peasants in Urban Classes of Moscow, 1764-1782
--Distribution among Urban Strata

	Econ. peasants	Court peasants	Other crown peasants	Seigneurial peasants	House serfs	Total peasants	%	Souls/household
Kupechestvo								
1st guild								
households	1	1	-	-	-	2	0.3	-
male souls	3	2	-	-	-	5	0.3	2.5
2nd guild								
households	42	19	1	9	20	91	12.1	-
male souls	118	41	1	19	48	227	15.5	2.5
3rd guild								
households	255	78	10	54	93	490	65.1	-
male souls	537	154	19	111	165	986	67.4	2.0
unspecified								
households	11	2	-	2	5	20	2.7	-
male souls	15	-	-	-	3	18	1.2	0.9
total								
households	309	100	11	65	118	603	80.1	-
male souls	673	197	20	130	216	1236	84.5	2.0
Meshchanstvo								
households	59	28	10	12	41	150	19.9	-
male souls	97	37	13	23	57	227	15.5	1.5
Total								
households	368	128	21	77	159	753	100	-
male souls	770	234	33	153	273	1463	100	1.9

Source: Materialy dlia istorii moskovskogo kupechestva, Vol. 3
(Moscow, 1885), pp. 1-460.

Two-thirds of the peasant registrants were members of the third guild, which contained only 30 percent of the Moscow posad population, and more than a third of the membership of this guild consisted of peasant registrants. This general distribution was characteristic of immigrants from all peasant categories, but economic and seigneurial peasants showed the greatest tendency to congregate in the middle ranks while court peasants and former house serfs displayed a somewhat greater degree of differentiation. These variations are minor, however, and do not indicate any sharp differences in the character of the recruits coming from the various peasant groups at this stage. On the other hand, family size varied substantially with economic status. The average number of males per household was 2.5 for peasant registrants belonging to the second guild, 2.0 for the third guild and 1.5 for the meshchanstvo.

Concluding our discussion of the results of the Fourth Revision, we turn to the chronological profile of peasant enlistment in the Moscow posad during the period covered (Table 11). In view of the poor survival rate of persons resident in the Moscow posad and the exceptionally large mortality caused by the 1771 plague, these data must be considered biased against the earlier period. Many peasants who enlisted in the 1760's were subsequently killed off and do not appear in the census results. Nevertheless, the likelihood that entire families would disappear in this manner is much less than for individual souls, and a chronological profile based on the number of households enlisted should therefore portray the trend with approximate accuracy. According to the census documents 126 households of peasants entered the posad between 1764 and 1769, 102 between 1770 and 1775, 326 between

2
80

Table 11: Enlistment of Peasants in Urban Classes of Moscow, 1764-1782
--Chronological Profile (Number of Households)

Year enlisted	Crown peasants: econ.	court	other	total	Seigneurial peasants: peasants	h. serfs	total	Total
1764	8	3	-	11	8	8	16	27
1765	5	2	-	7	-	1	1	8
1766	14	3	1	18	4	4	8	26
1767	3	4	-	7	5	1	6	13
1768	10	18	-	28	2	7	9	37
1769	7	3	-	10	-	5	5	15
1770	9	1	1	11	-	2	2	13
1771	9	1	-	10	3	4	7	17
1772	2	2	-	4	1	7	8	12
1773	14	3	1	18	1	6	7	25
1774	12	1	-	13	-	5	5	18
1775	8	3	3	14	1	3	4	18
1776	18	7	2	27	3	3	6	33
1777	28	8	1	37	1	5	6	43
1778	30	9	1	40	2	10	12	52
1779	22	1	4	27	3	7	10	37
1780	31	18	2	51	5	6	11	62
1781	40	19	1	60	23	16	39	99
1782	96	22	4	122	15	59	74	196
Undated	2	-	-	2	-	-	-	2
Total	368	128	21	516	77	159	236	753

Table 11 (cont.)

Year enlisted	Crown peasants: econ.	court	other	total	Seigneurial peasants: peasants	h. serfs	total	Total
Average per year:								
1764-9	7.8	5.5	0.2	13.5	3.2	4.3	7.5	21.0
1770-5	9.0	1.8	0.8	11.7	1.0	4.5	5.5	17.2
1776-81	28.2	10.3	1.8	40.3	6.2	7.8	14.0	54.3

Source: Materialy dlia istorii moskovskogo kupechestva, Vol. 3
(Moscow, 1885), pp. 1-460.

1776 and 1781, and 196 in 1782. Peasant enlistment thus did not increase between the 1760's and the early 1770's and indeed dropped somewhat, and for reasons already stated this decrease was probably greater than is shown by the data. Enlistment expanded after 1775 and peaked sharply in 1782, the year of the census, and in fact the 1782 peak is probably much understated in these data.[187]

In this accelerated influx it is tempting to see the influence of the 1775 reforms, which raised the status of the kupechestvo and relieved it of some of the more onerous state obligations, such as military conscription, possibly rendering membership more attractive to trading peasants who could meet the requirements. These reforms also appeared to offer registrants from the crown peasantry eventual release from dual status and obligations, in place of the permanent attachment to them prescribed by earlier legislation. The hope of prompt release from peasant status under the new revision partially explains the clustering of enlistment around the time of the census, although this expectation was not altogether borne out by the government's action.[188]

Since revisions were known to occur roughly every other decade, this motivation may also have played a role in elevating the level of enlistment during the several preceding years. Enlistment by freed serfs, who were not subject to dual obligations, also accelerated at the time of the census, possibly because such registrants did not wish to incur urban taxation until absolutely necessary and because serfowners

---

[187]As previously indicated, a large number of peasant registrants who appeared in the "second half" of 1782 are not included in the census documents.

[188]The complex situation surrounding the issue of releasing registrants from peasant status following the census has been discussed in Chapter II.

were most likely to grant manumission when a new census was imminent.

Peasants who in 1782 belonged to either the second merchant guild or the meshchanstvo were more likely than the average registrant to have been in the posad a relatively long time. Thirty-four percent of the households enlisted in the second guild had entered the Moscow posad between 1764 and 1769, as opposed to 17 percent of all households of registrants. Fifty-one percent of those belonging to the meshchanstvo but only 30 percent of all registrants had enlisted from 1764 through 1775. These figures suggest that economic differentiation among peasant registrants tended to increase following their entry into the urban classes and that the great majority of registrants were persons of middling economic attainments at the time of their enlistment. On the other hand, some registrants attained prosperity before their enlistment and entered the posad at a higher level. Thus, both peasant families which in 1782 belonged to the first merchant guild had enlisted in the posad after 1775, as had half of those belonging to the second guild.

Enlistment in the Urban Classes: Fifth Revision

The period between the Fourth and Fifth Revisions (1782-1795) was a time of spectacular and unprecedented growth for the Moscow posad, during which it doubled in size to more than 17,000 souls.[189] This growth resulted from a massive influx of new registrants combined with

---

[189]Zviagintsev, using the published revizskie skazki, determined that the Moscow posad at the time of the Fifth Revision consisted of 17,100 male souls. (Zviagintsev, "Rost naseleniia," p. 143.) In September 1796 the Moscow kazennaia palata reported a considerably higher figure (19, 650 souls), although this includes a substantial number of persons enlisted after the census. (TsGIA, f. 558, op. 2, d. 128, ll. 2-7, 17-24.)

an apparent improvement in the survival rate of the residual population.
Analysis of census depositions from the Fifth Revision discloses that
during the indicated period 2509 peasant households, containing about
5100 male souls enlisted in the Moscow kupechestvo and meshchanstvo.[190]
About 2650 souls entered the Moscow posad from the urban classes of
other towns, and 1300 enlisted from the remaining categories of the
population.[191] The contributions of all the above groups increased
substantially with respect to the preceding period, but the peasantry
recorded the sharpest gains and thus continued to grow in relative
importance as a source of new members for the Moscow urban classes.
The more than 9000 newcomers from all sources were added to a residual
population which declined only slightly between the Fourth and Fifth
Revisions, in contrast to its more pronounced contractions in earlier
periods.

---

[190]MDIMK, Vol. 4, pp. 1-868. As in the case of all the earlier revisions, the available documents of the Fifth Revision are incomplete.
In this case the incompleteness results from the decision by the editor
of the above publication, N. A. Naidenov, not to print the complete
skazka for households belonging to the meshchanstvo. It is thus possible to determine exactly only the number of households and not the
number of souls belonging to this stratum of the urban classes. However,
the documents for some slobody include a "register" which summarizes
the census results, listing the number of souls in each household.
From this partial information it is possible to calculate the average
number of male souls per meshchanstvo household and thereby reach a
reliable estimate of the total number of souls these households contained. Detailed breakdowns, on the other hand, must be given in terms
of households rather than souls.

The total given for peasant registrants includes only households
headed by males or which were apparently so headed at the time of enlistment. The documents of the Fifth Revision also reveal for the first
time the existence of substantial enlistment by unattached women (widows
and the unmarried), and this phenomenon is accorded a separate discussion
below.

[191]For groups other than the peasantry the determinations of Zviagintsev
from the published revizskie skazki are used. Zviagintsev, "Dinamika
naseleniia dokapitalisticheskoi Moskvy" (manuscript), p. 64, cited in
Istoriia Moskvy, Vol. 2, p. 316.

These greatly increased numbers of peasant registrants were drawn
from essentially the same area as those recorded by the preceding census,
although some broadening is to be noted in the geographical pattern of
recruitment. (See Table 12.) As before, the great majority of registrants (in this case 92 percent of those for whom geographical origin
can be determined) came from the provinces of the Central Industrial
Region or two adjoining Central Agricultural provinces (Tula and Riazan'
gubernii). The influx from more distant provinces, however, grew from
4 to 8 percent. Within the principal area of recruitment the pattern
of distribution changed significantly in the direction of decentraliza-
tion. A greater proportion of the registrants came from the neighboring
provinces rather than from Moscow guberniia, and within these provinces
recruitment was somewhat less concentrated in the areas closest to
Moscow. If the comparison is extended to data from the Second Revision,
an additional trend comes into view: during the course of the century
recruitment from areas north of the city (especially Kostroma and Vologda
gubernii) declined in relative importance, although Iaroslavl' guberniia
remained one of the principal sources. There was a corresponding increase in the shares contributed by the provinces adjoining Moscow
guberniia to the south (Kaluga, Tula, Riazan').[192]

---

[192]Data on immigration to Moscow in the mid- and late nineteenth
century show that with the addition of Smolensk guberniia (the province
bordering Moscow guberniia to the west), the provinces making the
largest contributions were the same in the later period as in the
earlier, although their ranking order changed markedly. These data also
indicate a continued trend toward a less centralized pattern of recruitment and a general southward shift in that pattern. See A. G. Rashin,
"Dinamika chislennosti i protsessy formirovaniia gorodskogo naseleniia
Rossii v XIX-nachale XX vv.," Istoricheskie zapiski, Vol. 34 (1950),
pp. 72-73.

Table 12: Enlistment of Peasants in Urban Classes of Moscow, 1782-1795
(Number of Households)

Province of origin	Crown peasants:				Seigneurial peasants:			All peasants	
	Econ.	Court	Other	Total	Peasants	H. serfs	Total		%
Moscow	394	152	19	565	132	209	341	906	39.8
Vladimir	173	6	41	220	27	63	90	310	13.6
Iaroslavl'	47	-	3	50	127	81	208	258	11.3
Tver'	68	-	6	74	15	33	48	122	5.4
Kaluga	120	-	5	125	12	52	64	189	8.3
Kostroma	10	5	-	15	14	21	35	50	2.2
Nizhnii Novgorod	-	-	-	-	7	39	46	46	2.0
Tula	3	1	4	8	14	72	86	94	4.1
Riazan'	50	1	10	61	18	49	67	128	5.6
Other[a]	10	3	10	23	18	134	152	175	7.7
Total	875	168	98	1141	384	753	1137	2278	100
Undetermined	11	6	4	21	15	195	210	231	-
Total	886	174	102[b]	1162	399	948	1347	2509	-
%	35.3	6.9	4.1	46.3	15.9	37.8	53.7	100	

Source: Materialy dlia istorii moskovskogo kupechestva, Vol. 4
(Moscow, 1886), pp. 1-868.

[a]Orel 40, Kursk 2, Voronezh 3, Tambov 11, Kazan' 3, Simbirsk 10,
Saratov 7, Penza 11, Ufa 25, Perm' 1, Viatka 1, Vologda 10, Olonets 7,
Arkhangel'sk 2, St. Petersburg 4, Novgorod 20, Pskov 4, Smolensk 14.

[b]Includes 93 households of unspecified affiliation or identified
only as kazennye krest'iane (crown peasants).

As before, the bulk of the registrants from Moscow _guberniia_ originated in the part of the province nearest to Moscow, i.e. in Moscow _uezd_ or the surrounding districts which had for the most part been carved from the territory of the large pre-reform Moscow _uezd_. (See Table 13). However, the degree of this concentration was somewhat reduced, chiefly because of the decreased importance of Moscow _uezd_ itself.[193] Of the surrounding districts, the largest contributors to the Moscow _posad_ continued to be those to the east and southeast (Bogorodsk, Bronnitsy, Nikitsk), which now rivaled Moscow _uezd_ in this respect. At the same time, the share of the outlying districts of the province, including those on the southern fringe (Kolomna, Serpukhov), the western districts (Vereia, Ruza, Mozhaisk, Volokolamsk, Klin) and Dmitrov _uezd_ in the north, increased somewhat from 16 to 23 percent of the registrants from the crown peasantry.

In the remaining provinces the corresponding changes can be determined only with a lesser degree of exactitude because of the confusion caused by extensive changes in district boundaries resulting from the 1775 reforms. In Vladimir _guberniia_ the bulk of the registrants (73 percent) continued to come from the western part of the province, adjoining Moscow _guberniia_, but this proportion was reduced somewhat from 85 percent in the previous census. In Iaroslavl' _guberniia_ the locus of emigration to Moscow appears to have moved somewhat northward.

---

[193]Earlier data suitable for comparison with the Fifth Revision results (i.e. given according to the post-1782 configuration of Moscow _guberniia_) are provided by the 1787 report of the Moscow _kazennaia palata_ cited previously, which covers only crown peasants. Moscow _uezd_ and the six surrounding districts produced 84 percent of the registrants from the crown peasantry of Moscow _guberniia_ who enlisted between the Third and Fourth Revisions and 77 percent of those who enlisted between the Fourth and Fifth Revisions. The share of Moscow _uezd_ fell from 26 to 16 percent.

Table 13: Enlistment of Peasants of Moscow _Guberniia_ in Urban Classes
of Moscow, 1782-1795 (Number of Households)

District of origin	Crown peasants:				Seigneurial peasants:			All peasants	% (crown peasants)	% (all peasants)
	Econ.	Court	Other	Total	Peasants	H. serfs	Total			
Moscow	57	29	1	87	5	23	28	115	15.8	13.2
Bogorodsk	70	5	4	79	35	19	54	133	14.3	15.3
Bronnitsy	14	52	3	69	44	13	57	126	12.5	14.4
Nikitsk	45	57	5	107	4	24	28	135	19.4	15.5
Podol	15	-	-	15	4	16	20	35	2.7	4.0
Voskresensk	29	1	1	31	1	10	11	42	5.6	4.8
Zvenigorod	37	1	-	38	13	19	32	70	6.9	8.0
Dmitrov	26	-	2	28	5	11	16	44	5.1	5.0
Kolomna	14	3	-	17	6	15	21	38	3.1	4.4
Serpukhov	26	2	1	29	4	15	19	48	5.3	5.5
Vereia	12	-	-	12	2	3	5	17	2.2	1.9
Ruza	9	-	-	9	1	12	13	22	1.6	2.5
Mozhaisk	6	-	1	7	-	9	9	16	1.3	1.8
Volokolamsk	13	-	-	13	-	1	1	14	2.4	1.6
Klin	10	-	1	11	3	3	6	17	2.0	1.9
Total	383	150	19	552	127	193	320	.872	100	100
Unknown	11	2	-	13	5	16	21	34	-	-
Total	394	152	19	565	132	209	341	906	-	-

Source: _Materialy dlia istorii moskovskogo kupechestva_, Vol. 4
(Moscow, 1886), pp. 1-868.

The largest contribution was provided by the central section of the province, consisting of three districts perched on the Volga above Iaroslavl' (Rybinsk, Romanov, Borisoglebsk). These districts collectively provided 54 percent of the registrants, while the northeastern districts (Danilov, Liubim, Poshekhon'e), which formerly had a negligible impact, now contributed 19 percent. The southern part of the province (Iaroslavl', Uglich, Rostov and Petrovsk uezdy), which contained the largest towns and was also the section closest to Moscow, also contributed 19 percent, apparently much less than in the earlier period. Seventy-seven percent of the registrants from Tver' guberniia came from the southeastern portion of the province (Kaliazin, Korcheva, Kashin uezdy), results which are comparable to those of the previous census. Likewise, little change is observable in the pattern of recruitment from Kostroma guberniia, immigrants from which continued to emerge from Kostroma uezd and the remote northern parts of the province (in this case Chukhloma uezd) in roughly equal measure. The contribution of Nizhnii Novgorod guberniia was made up of small numbers from many districts.

The Fourth Revision indicated that most of the registrants from the three contributing provinces to the south of Moscow came in each case from a single district adjacent to Moscow guberniia. In the results for the Fifth Revision this pattern is again noticeable, although to a somewhat lessened degree. Most (60 percent) of the registrants from Kaluga guberniia continued to originate in Borovsk uezd, but a significant number now came from the neighboring Maloiaroslavets uezd as well. Emigration from Riazan' guberniia continued to be predominantly from Egor'evsk uezd, but in Tula guberniia, while Kashira uezd continued to provide the largest number of registrants it now contributed only 30 percent of the provincial total. The remainder came in small numbers from many more remote districts.

The results of the Fifth Revision thus show that the intensity of recruitment into the Moscow posad was rising most rapidly in areas beyond the immediate vicinity of the city and that Moscow was increasingly able to draw relatively large numbers of immigrants from these more distant localities. Nevertheless, the largest individual contributors to the influx continued to be the districts closest to Moscow. The five most prolific districts, which delivered between 108 and 135 households of peasants apiece into the Moscow posad, consisted of four districts of Moscow guberniia (Moscow, Bogorodsk, Bronnitsy and Nikitsk) and Borovsk uezd of Kaluga guberniia. (See Table 14.) A second group of districts, each contributing 52-88 households, included two districts of western Vladimir guberniia (Vladimir, Aleksandrovsk), Zvenigorod uezd of Moscow guberniia, Borisoglebsk uezd (Iaroslavl' guberniia) and Egor'evsk uezd (Riazan' guberniia). The third group of significant contributors, each of which provided 28-50 households, included five districts of Moscow guberniia, three each of Vladimir and Iaroslavl' gubernii, two of Tver' guberniia and one each of Kaluga and Tula gubernii.

Between the Fourth and Fifth Revisions much more striking changes occurred in the distribution of enlistment among the various peasant categories. As measured by the average annual number of households entering the Moscow posad during the specified period, the overall rate of enlistment was about four times greater in 1782-1795 than in the previous intercensus period. However, enlistment by court peasants increased only 1.4 times, while that of economic peasants trebled and

Table 14:   Enlistment of Peasants in Urban Classes of Moscow, 1782-1795

--Districts Contributing Largest Numbers of Registrants

District	Province	No. households
A. Over 100 households		
Moscow	Moscow	115
Bogorodsk	Moscow	133
Bronnitsy	Moscow	126
Nikitsk	Moscow	135
Borovsk	Kaluga	108
Total		617
B. 51-100 households		
Zvenigorod	Moscow	70
Vladimir	Vladimir	60
Aleksandrovsk	Vladimir	52
Borisoglebsk	Iaroslavl'	64
Egor'evsk	Riazan'	88
Total		334
C. 25-50 households		
Voskresensk	Moscow	42
Podol'	Moscow	35
Dmitrov	Moscow	44
Kolomna	Moscow	38
Serpukhov	Moscow	48
Pokrov	Vladimir	48
Kirzhach	Vladimir	28
Pereslavl'-Zalesskii	Vladimir	30
Romanov	Iaroslavl'	28
Rybinsk	Iaroslavl'	47
Liubim	Iaroslavl'	28
Kaliazin	Tver'	50
Kashin	Tver'	33
Maloiaroslavets	Kaluga	29
Kashira	Tula	28
Total		556

Source: Materialy dlia istorii moskovskogo kupechestva, Vol.4
(Moscow, 1886), pp. 1-868.

that of freed serfs grew sevenfold.[194] The most spectacular growth occurred among house serfs, but the growth of enlistment by seigneurial peasants was only slightly less startling. The extremely rapid rise in the number of serfs who succeeded in extricating themselves from bondage and entering the urban classes now placed such freedmen in a slight majority among all peasant registrants.[195] The role of the court peasantry relative to other peasant categories, on the other hand, continued to decline.

As before, registrants from the several peasant categories differed greatly in their patterns of geographical origin. Most of the court peasants who enlisted continued to come from Moscow guberniia. Of the economic peasants, only 44 percent came from this province but 99 percent came from the provinces of the Central Industrial Region or Tula and Riazan' gubernii. The pattern for freed serfs was again the most diversified, and the trickle of registrants emerging from the more distant parts of the empire consisted largely of former serfs (particularly house serfs). Thirty percent of the freed serfs for whom geographical origin can be determined came from Moscow guberniia, while

---

[194]In these determinations the absence of Fourth Revision data for Sadovaia Bol'shaia sloboda has been taken into account, and compensatory estimates have been introduced under the assumption that the same proportional relationships among peasant categories prevailed in this subdivision as in the rest of the posad of that time.

[195]Freed serfs contributed 54 percent of the peasant households which were added to the Moscow urban classes between the Fourth and Fifth Revisions. In terms of numbers of male souls (which cannot be determined exactly for reasons stated above), the proportion contributed by freed serfs was less, since more of the former serfs belonged to the meshchanstvo, where average family size was somewhat smaller. Freed serfs and crown peasants each contributed about half the total number of souls. The possible reasons for this rapid rise in enlistment by freed serfs are discussed in a later chapter.

87 percent came from the nine central provinces specified above.[196]
The registrants from Iaroslavl' and Kostroma gubernii again consisted
predominantly of former serfs, as did the current contingents from
Nizhnii Novgorod and Tula gubernii.

We have previously noted a tendency for enlistment of peasants in
the urban classes to cluster about the time of the census, and this
pattern was evident to an even greater degree than before in the results
of the Fifth Revision. (See Table 15.) As before, the pattern was most
pronounced among economic peasants. In the 1780's, following the Fourth
Revision, enlistment by these peasants dropped back to the modest levels
of the middle 1770's. A marked rise is discernible in the early 1790's,
but nearly 50 percent of the registrants from this category enlisted
during the census year itself. Among court peasants the 1795 peak was
less pronounced. Enlistment by freed serfs also peaked in the census
year, but to a lesser extent than that of crown peasants--about one-third
of the serfs registered in 1795. Moreover, the influx of freed serfs
tended to grow more steadily with time. The level of enlistment for this
group was already considerably higher in the 1780's than it had been
before the Fourth Revision, and in the early 1790's it rose precipitously.[197]

---

[196]If we assume that the large number of former house serfs for whom
geographical origin is not specified in the skazki (195 households)
originated mainly in Moscow guberniia (i.e. were registered under the
Moscow households of their lords), the proportion contributed by this
province can rise as high as 40 percent. This does not change the fact
that freed serfs were much more likely than crown peasants to come from
outside the nine central provinces which contributed most of the registrants.

[197]Only 46 households of new registrants were identified in the Fifth
Revision as having enlisted in 1782. Thus, no more than a few of the
large number of registrants who had enlisted in the "second half" of
1782 were still being counted as new registrants subsequent to the Fourth
Revision, despite the 1787 decision requiring this. There is some

Table 15: Enlistment of Peasants in Urban Classes of Moscow, 1782-1795
--Chronological Profile (Number of Households)

Year enlisted	Crown peasants: econ.	court	other	total	Seigneurial peasants: peasants	h. serfs	total	Total
1782	12	14	1	27	6	13	19	46
1783	21	2	2	25	11	9	20	45
1784	15	5	1	21	18	19	37	58
1785	23	3	2	28	10	41	51	79
1786	11	9	2	22	7	15	22	44
1787	23	8	1	32	7	9	16	48
1788	10	6	1	17	17	52	69	86
1789	21	5	3	29	16	36	52	81
1790	33	6	2	41	31	49	80	121
1791	52	13	5	70	19	45	64	134
1792	89	25	12	126	46	51	97	223
1793	60	5	10	75	46	159	205	280
1794	68	7	8	83	36	114	150	233
1795	438	65	52	555	127	332	459	1014
Undated	10	1	-	11	2	4	6	17
Total	886	174	102	1162	399	948	1347	2509

Average per year:

1783-6	17.5	4.8	1.8	24.0	11.5	21.0	32.5	56.5
1787-90	21.8	6.3	1.8	29.8	17.8	36.5	54.3	84.0
1791-4	67.3	12.5	8.8	88.5	36.8	92.3	129.0	217.5

Source: Materialy dlia istorii moskovskogo kupechestva, Vol. 4 (Moscow, 1886), pp. 1-868.

In the results of the Fifth Revision significant changes are observable in the distribution of peasant registrants among the officially defined ranks of the urban citizenry. (See Table 16.) Few registrants now belonged to the second merchant guild, a change which reflects the sharp increases in the capital required for membership in this guild decreed by the government in 1785 and 1794.[198] The proportion of registrants belonging to the meshchanstvo, on the other hand, was enlarged from 20 percent to 34 percent. These registrants now consisted predominantly of former serfs, especially house serfs, while in the previous census serf registrants had been only slightly more likely than those from the crown peasantry to belong to the meshchanstvo. These results indicate that many serfs were being released from bondage and allowed to enter the urban classes for reasons other than a proven capacity for business activity or an ability to buy their freedom. However, the influx of freed serfs into the Moscow urban classes cannot be ascribed solely to such propertyless elements, since more than half of these former serfs belonged to the kupechestvo, and among registrants enlisted in the kupechestvo the proportion which was of serf origin rose

---

evidence that this decision was later modified. A 1796 report of the Moscow kazennaia palata indicates that some such registrants from the crown peasantry of Moscow guberniia were released from the peasant oklad in the early 1790's, pursuant to newly issued decrees. (TsGIA, f. 558, op. 2, d. 128, 1. 32.) In any case, few registrants who enlisted in the second half of 1782 are identified in the skazki of either census. These registrants have therefore gone largely uncounted in our analysis, except for those from the crown peasantry of Moscow guberniia reported by the kazennaia palata in 1787.

[198]The capital required for membership in the second guild increased from 1000 rubles in 1775 to 5000 rubles in 1785 and to 8000 rubles in 1794. The requirements for the remaining guilds increased less spectacularly--from 10,000 to 16,000 rubles for the first guild and from 500 to 2000 rubles for the third guild between 1775 and 1794. (PSZ, Vol. 20, No. 14327; Vol. 22, No. 16188, Art. 102, 108, 114; Vol. 23, No. 17223.)

Table 16: Enlistment of Peasants in Urban Classes of Moscow, 1782-1795
--Distribution among Urban Strata

	Econ. peasants	Court peasants	Other crown peasants	Seigneurial peasants	House serfs	Total peasants	%	Souls/household
Kupechestvo								
1st guild								
households	-	-	-	1	2	3	0.1	-
male souls	-	-	-	3	4	7	-	2.3
2nd guild								
households	6	4	-	5	6	21	0.8	-
male souls	10	7	-	11	7	35	-	1.7
3rd guild								
households	723	132	78	256	441	1630	65.0	-
male souls	1766·	266	167	669	934	3802	-	2.3
total								
households	729	136	78	262	449	1654	65.9	-
male souls	1776	273	167	683	945	3844	-	2.3
Meshchanstvo								
households[a]	157	38	24	137	499	855	34.1	-
Total								
households	886	174	102	399	948	2509	100	-

Source: Materialy dlia istorii moskovskogo kupechestva, Vol. 4
(Moscow, 1886), pp. 1-868.

[a]The exact number of souls in these households cannot be determined from the source. A partial sample indicates that such households contained an average of 1.5 souls per household and thus a
total of between 1200 and 1300 souls. (See text.)

substantially (from 30 to 43 percent) by comparison with the results of the Fourth Revision. Four-fifths of the registrants from the crown peasantry belonged to the kupechestvo and one-fifth to the meshchanstvo --the same proportion as was observed in the Fourth Revision results, which suggests that there was little change in the economic character of recruits from this source. Relatively few crown peasants gravitated to the meshchanstvo, possibly because such peasants found it difficult to obtain releases from their communities and the institutions controlling them without the financial and business successes which would entitle them to membership in the kupechestvo, or because they saw little advantage in becoming members of the meshchanstvo.[199]

One particularly valuable feature of the skazki from the Fifth Revision is that they, unlike the materials of previous revisions, contain data on the occupations of the population surveyed. This information consists of a one-sentence statement naming the occupation of the household (or in a few cases several occupations being practiced by different members of the family) and sometimes giving the location where this activity was pursued.[200] Occupational information is provided for 1639 of the 2509 households of peasant registrants, including 58 cases in which the respondent was declared to have "no commerce or enterprises" (torgov i promyslov ne imeet). The nearly 900 remaining

---

[199]However, in some other parts of the country larger numbers of crown peasants enlisted in the meshchanstvo. (See above, Chapter III, Table 2.) A decree of 1797 complained that despite controls many crown peasants were enlisting in the urban classes without possessing capital or enterprises of any kind. (PSZ, Vol. 24, No. 18212).

[200]Examples: "torg imeet v muchnom riadu na Bolote" ("trades in the flour row on Boloto Square"); "masterstvo imeet shelkovoe" ("silk weaver"); "soderzhit postoialyi dvor" ("operates an inn").

skazki mostly provide no information whatever on these registrants'
source of livelihood, although in some cases it is indicated that the
respondent did not live in Moscow but in some other town or in a village
(about 30 cases). Sometimes (in about 50 cases) the living arrangements
of the registrants indicate a possible source of sustenance. In these
cases the registrants usually lived with relatives or in-laws or "in
the house of" their former lord under an unspecified relationship.
A few such registrants lived in Old Believer communities or in asylums
or poorhouses (bogadel'ni).[201]

The available occupational data on peasant registrants is presented
in Table 17. As might be expected, the registrants participated in a
broad range of occupations but showed a strong predilection for some
occupations in particular. Forty-five percent of the total engaged in
trade, 29 percent in craft industry and 23 percent in other occupations,
mostly involving the provision of services. The largest single
occupational grouping (18 percent of the total) consisted of those

---

[201]Persons living "in the house of" their former lord under unspecified conditions were almost always former house serfs. As noted
below, other ex-serfs were "in the service of" their former lords as
hired employees (v usluzhenii). The absence of occupational information for a large proportion of the registrants leads us to wonder
about the significance of this omission. In many cases the information
was probably left out through negligence, or perhaps deliberately, if
the respondent wished to avoid the scrutiny of the authorities. Some
registrants for whom no occupation is specified may have participated
in enterprises owned by relatives or been otherwise dependent on them.
Many probably pursued menial occupations such as unskilled day labor
(chernaia rabota). Such activity is known to have been widespread in
the Moscow posad of the eighteenth century, but among the registrants
only a few cases of it are cited specifically. Another possible
source of income is the rental of living space and other property.

Table XX. Occupations of Peasants Enlisting in Urban Classes of
Moscow, 1782-1795 (Number of Households)

Occupations	Belonging to:			From crown peasantry:			From seigneurial peasantry:		Province of origin:										
	Kupechestvo	Meshchanstvo	Total	Econ.	Court	Other	Peasants	House serfs	Moscow	Vladimir	Iaroslavl'	Tver'	Kaluga	Kostroma	N. Novgorod	Tula	Riazan'	Other	Undetermined
I. Trade																			
Foodstuffs																			
grain	127	19	146	60	35	8	34	9	77	11	39	5	3	-	-	-	8	1	2
meat	26	6	32	16	-	4	7	5	10	10	6	1	-	3	-	-	2	-	-
fish	18	7	25	8	3	3	9	2	10	3	7	-	-	-	-	-	2	1	2
vegetables, fruits	24	4	28	11	2	-	6	9	8	3	11	-	2	-	-	-	-	2	2
other	45	17	62	20	6	2	16	18	17	2	15	2	2	1	-	-	8	6	6
total	240	53	293	115	46	17	72	43	122	30	78	9	8	4	-	-	20	10	12
% of category	20.7	11.1	17.9	18.8	34.8	24.6	28.3	7.5	20.8	13.3	42.9	11.0	6.5	10.8	-	-	22.2	9.0	10.0
Textiles, articles of clothing, fur and leather goods																			
textiles	42	8	50	19	4	2	12	13	27	5	2	1	1	6	-	-	2	3	3
garments	16	2	18	10	5	-	-	3	9	4	2	-	-	-	-	-	-	1	2
fur goods	25	4	29	10	2	2	8	7	13	-	11	-	-	-	-	-	4	1	-
footwear	10	3	13	5	-	1	1	6	4	-	-	4	3	-	-	1	-	1	-
leather goods	34	4	38	19	5	1	8	5	19	5	15	-	-	-	-	2	9	-	2
total	127	21	148	63	16	6	29	34	72	14	15	5	4	6	-	3	15	6	8
% of category	10.9	4.4	9.0	10.3	12.1	8.7	11.4	5.9	12.3	6.2	8.2	6.1	3.2	16.2	-	5.5	16.7	5.4	6.7

Table 17 (cont.)

Occupations	Belonging to:			From crown peasantry:			From seigneurial peasantry:		Province of origin:										
	Kupechestvo	Meshchanstvo	Total	Econ.	Court	Other	Peasants	House serfs	Moscow	Vladimir	Iaroslavl'	Tver'	Kaluga	Kostroma	N. Novgorod	Tula	Riazan'	Other	Undetermined
Metal goods																			
iron goods	11	6	17	11	1	3	1	1	8	4	1	1	-	1	-	-	1	-	1
silver goods	4	2	6	1	2	1	-	2	2	-	-	-	-	-	1	1	-	1	1
other	8	1	9	3	2	-	1	3	4	-	-	-	-	2	-	-	2	-	1
total	23	9	32	15	5	4	2	6	14	4	1	1	-	3	1	1	3	1	3
% of category	2.0	1.9	2.0	2.5	3.8	5.8	0.8	1.0	2.4	1.8	0.5	1.2	-	8.1	3.7	1.9	3.3	0.9	2.5
Wood	35	1	36	19	3	2	9	3	18	8	2	-	-	-	-	-	5	1	2
Wooden articles[a]	9	4	13	3	2	3	1	4	4	4	1	-	1	-	-	-	1	-	2
Vehicles[b]	20	3	23	6	-	-	3	14	2	2	5	4	4	4	-	1	-	2	3
Assorted consumer goods[c]	47	14	61	25	7	1	9	19	16	12	10	5	4	2	2	2	3	1	4
Other and unspecified goods	62	13	75	28	8	3	15	21	33	6	6	-	9	1	2	4	6	1	7
"Contractual" trade	9	-	9	4	-	1	2	2	3	2	-	-	-	-	1	2	-	1	-
Transit trade[d]	33	6	39	11	1	2	11	14	14	8	4	3	1	-	-	2	2	4	1
Total engaged in trade	605	124	729	289	88	39	153	160	298	90	122	27	27	20	6	15	55	27	42
% of category	52.2	25.9	44.5	47.2	66.7	56.5	60.2	28.0	50.8	40.0	67.0	32.9	21.8	54.1	22.2	27.8	61.1	24.3	35.0

Occupations	Kupechestvo	Meshchanstvo	Total	Econ.	Court	Other	Peasants	House serfs	Moscow	Vladimir	Iaroslavl'	Tver'	Kaluga	Kostroma	N. Novgorod	Tula	Riazan'	Other	Undetermined
	Belonging to:			From crown peasantry:			From seigneurial peasantry:		Province of origin:										

II. Industrial crafts

Textiles

Occupations	Kupechestvo	Meshchanstvo	Total	Econ.	Court	Other	Peasants	House serfs	Moscow	Vladimir	Iaroslavl'	Tver'	Kaluga	Kostroma	N. Novgorod	Tula	Riazan'	Other	Undetermined
wool	7	-	7	6	1	-	-	-	3	-	-	-	4	-	-	-	-	-	-
silk	30	11	41	29	5	1	5	1	16	11	-	6	6	-	-	-	2	-	-
kerchiefs, ribbons	34	8	42	23	4	3	6	6	13	14	1	1	8	1	-	-	-	1	3
sashes	25	1	26	24	-	1	1	-	4	-	-	-	22	-	-	-	-	-	-
braid-work, tinsel	17	10	27	18	2	1	2	4	16	4	2	-	2	-	-	-	1	-	2
cloth-printing	4	-	4	2	1	-	1	-	2	1	-	-	1	-	-	-	-	-	-
dyeing, bleaching	12	1	13	10	-	1	1	1	6	2	-	-	4	-	-	-	1	-	-
other	4	2	6	2	1	1	-	2	4	-	-	1	-	-	-	-	-	1	-
total	133	33	166	114	13	8	17	14	64	32	3	8	47	1	-	-	4	2	5
% of category	11.5	6.9	10.1	18.6	9.8	11.6	6.7	2.4	10.9	14.2	1.6	9.8	37.9	2.7	-	-	4.4	1.8	4.2

Articles of clothing, fur and leather goods

Occupations	Kupechestvo	Meshchanstvo	Total	Econ.	Court	Other	Peasants	House serfs	Moscow	Vladimir	Iaroslavl'	Tver'	Kaluga	Kostroma	N. Novgorod	Tula	Riazan'	Other	Undetermined
tailors	19	22	41	9	-	2	3	27	7	9	11	1	2	-	-	5	-	4	2
furriers[e]	4	-	4	1	-	-	1	2	2	-	1	-	-	-	-	1	-	-	-
tanners	1	2	3	1	1	-	1	-	3	-	-	-	-	-	-	-	-	-	-
cobblers[f]	14	13	27	12	-	1	3	11	6	7	1	4	-	-	1	1	-	4	3
glovers	5	1	6	2	1	-	-	3	-	1	-	-	1	-	-	1	2	-	1

Table 17 (cont.)

Occupations	Belonging to:			From crown peasantry:				From seigneurial peasantry:		Province of origin:										
	Kupechestvo	Meshchanstvo	Total	Econ.	Court	Other		Peasants	House serfs	Moscow	Vladimir	Iaroslavl'	Tver'	Kaluga	Kostroma	N. Novgorod	Tula	Riazan'	Other	Undetermined
Articles of clothing, fur and leather goods (cont.)																				
other	2	2	4	2	1	-		-	1	2	-	-	1	-	-	-	-	-	1	-
total	45	40	85	27	3	3		8	44	20	17	13	6	3	-	1	8	2	9	6
% of category	3.9	8.4	5.2	4.4	2.3	4.3		3.1	7.7	3.4	7.6	7.1	7.3	2.4	-	3.7	14.8	2.2	8.1	5.0
Metallurgy																				
blacksmiths	7	5	12	3	-	-		1	8	3	3	1	1	1	-	-	1	-	1	1
silversmiths	21	1	22	13	2	1		1	5	7	1	1	2	6	2	-	2	-	-	1
goldsmiths, gilders[g]	2	2	4	1	-	-		-	3	1	1	-	-	-	-	-	1	-	1	1
coppersmiths	20	10	30	15	2	-		3	10	9	8	2	3	1	-	-	1	2	2	2
tinsmiths	1	1	2	1	-	-		-	1	1	-	-	-	1	-	-	-	-	-	-
other	2	2	4	1	-	1		-	2	1	1	1	-	-	-	-	-	-	1	1
total	53	21	74	34	4	1		5	30	22	14	4	6	9	2	-	4	2	5	6
% of category	4.6	4.4	4.5	5.6	3.0	1.4		2.0	5.2	3.7	6.2	2.2	7.3	7.3	5.4	-	7.4	2.2	4.5	5.0
Woodworking																				
carpenters[h]	13	13	26	4	1	-		3	18	8	3	-	3	4	-	1	-	-	1	5
wood-carvers[i]	4	2	6	1	-	1		-	4	1	-	-	1	-	-	1	-	-	2	1
wheelwrights	2	1	3	1	-	-		-	2	-	1	-	-	-	-	-	-	2	-	-
builders of carriages, carts, sleighs	6	11	17	11	-	-		2	4	4	4	3	5	-	-	-	-	-	1	-

Occupations	Belonging to:			From crown peasantry:			From seigneurial peasantry:		Province of origin:										
	Kupechestvo	Meshchanstvo	Total	Econ.	Court	Other	Peasants	House serfs	Moscow	Vladimir	Iaroslavl'	Tver'	Kaluga	Kostroma	N. Novgorod	Tula	Riazan'	Other	Undetermined
Woodworking (cont.)																			
other	4	-	4	2	-	-	-	2	1	1	1	-	-	-	-	-	-	-	1
total	29	27	56	19	1	1	5	30	14	9	4	9	4	-	2	-	3	4	7
% of category	2.5	5.6	3.4	3.1	0.8	1.4	2.0	5.2	2.4	4.0	2.2	11.0	3.2	-	7.4	-	3.3	3.6	5.8
Other crafts	73	22	95	36	4	1	21	33	35	11	12	6	10	8	1	6	4	1	2
Total in industrial crafts	333	143	476	230	25	14	56	151	155	83	36	35	73	11	3	18	15	21	26
% of category	28.7	29.9	29.0	37.6	18.9	20.3	22.0	26.4	26.4	36.9	19.8	42.7	58.9	29.7	11.1	33.3	16.7	18.9	21.7
III. Misc. occupations																			
Innkeepers	36	1	37	24	4	2	4	3	22	11	-	1	1	-	-	-	1	1	-
Millers	8	-	8	3	1	3	1	-	3	3	-	1	-	-	-	-	1	1	-
Operators of public baths	5	-	5	2	-	-	2	1	1	-	-	1	1	-	-	-	2	-	-
Watchmen	6	10	16	3	4	-	1	8	9	1	-	-	-	-	-	2	-	-	4
Gardeners, orchard-keepers	9	4	13	3	-	-	1	9	4	1	3	-	-	-	-	1	-	2	2
Teamsters, coachmen	3	3	6	2	-	-	-	4	4	-	-	-	1	-	-	-	-	1	2
Barbers	6	-	6	-	-	-	-	6	2	1	-	-	-	-	-	1	-	1	1
Cooks	-	3	3	-	-	-	-	3	2	-	-	-	-	-	-	-	-	1	-
Employed by merchants, townsmen																			
stewards, shopmen	23	3	26	10	3	2	2	9	12	1	-	1	2	-	-	-	4	5	1

Table 17 (cont.)

	Belonging to:			From crown peasantry:			From seigneurial peasantry:		Province of origin:										
	Kupechestvo	Meshchanstvo	Total	Econ.	Court	Other	Peasants	House serfs	Moscow	Vladimir	Iaroslavl'	Tver'	Kaluga	Kostroma	N. Novgorod	Tula	Riazan'	Other	Undetermined
Employed by merchants (cont.)																			
factory workers																			
	1	2	3	-	-	1	-	2	-	-	-	-	-	-	-	1	-	2	-
other^j	24	56	90	26	1	5	14	44	19	12	4	6	9	2	2	4	5	11	16
total	58	61	119	36	4	8	16	55	31	13	4	7	11	2	2	5	9	18	17
% of category	5.0	12.7	7.3	5.9	3.0	11.6	6.3	9.6	5.3	5.8	2.2	8.5	8.9	5.4	7.4	9.3	10.0	16.2	14.2
Employed by nobles, officers, officials																			
stewards	6	1	7	-	-	-	-	7	1	1	1	1	1	-	-	-	-	-	2
other^k	23	64	97	4	-	-	8	85	22	11	7	4	4	3	9	5	3	14	15
total	39	65	104	4	-	-	8	92	23	12	8	5	5	3	9	5	3	14	17
% of category	3.4	13.6	6.3	0.7	-	-	3.1	16.1	3.9	5.3	4.4	6.1	4.0	8.1	33.3	9.3	3.3	12.6	14.2
Employed by persons of other or unspecified status	9	24	33	-	2	-	5	26	10	1	3	3	1	-	1	3	-	8	3
Employed by institutions	3	7	10	-	-	-	-	10	1	-	1	1	1	-	-	1	2	1	2
Unskilled day laborers	2	4	6	1	-	-	-	5	2	1	1	-	-	-	-	-	-	1	1
Other	6	4	10	5	-	1	1	3	2	-	1	1	1	1	-	1	1	2	1
Total in misc. occupations	190	186	376	83	15	14	39	225	116	44	21	20	22	5	12	19	18	51	48
% of category	16.4	38.8	22.9	13.6	11.4	20.3	15.4	39.3	19.8	19.6	11.5	24.4	17.7	13.5	44.4	35.2	20.0	45.9	40.0
"No commerce or enterprises"	32	26	58	10	4	2	6	26	18	8	3	-	2	1	6	2	2	12	4
Total in all occupations	1160	479	1639	612	132	69	254	572	587	225	182	82	124	37	27	54	90	111	120

Table 17 (cont.)

Source: <u>Materialy</u> <u>dlia</u> <u>istorii</u> <u>moskovskogo</u> <u>kupechestva</u>, Vol. 4
(Moscow, 1886), pp. 1-868.

[a]Wooden articles and vessels, furniture.

[b]Carriages, carts, sleighs.

[c]<u>Melochnoi</u> <u>tovar</u>, <u>shchepetil'nyi</u> <u>tovar</u>.

[d]<u>Ot"ezdnyi</u> <u>torg</u>.

[e]<u>Skorniashnoe</u>, <u>shubnoe</u> <u>masterstva</u>.

[f]<u>Sapozhnoe</u>, <u>bashmachnoe</u> <u>masterstva</u>.

[g]<u>Zolotoe</u>, <u>zolotarnoe</u> <u>masterstva</u>.

[h]<u>Plotnichnoe</u>, <u>stoliarnoe</u> <u>masterstva</u>.

[i]<u>Masterstvo</u> <u>reznoe</u> <u>dereviannoe</u>.

[j]"In service of" employer (<u>v</u> <u>usluzhenii</u>) or "serving as laborers"
(<u>v</u> <u>rabotnikakh</u>).

[k]In most cases "in service of" employer.

trading in foodstuffs, of whom half dealt in grain and bread products.[202]
Nine percent of the registrants traded in textiles, articles of clothing
or fur and leather goods. Of less importance but still significant was
trade in metal goods, wood, wooden articles, vehicles (carriages, carts,
sleighs) and assortments of small consumer goods (melochnoi tovar,
shchepetil'nyi tovar). Small numbers of registrants sold glassware,
pottery, candles, soap, combs, horse gear, icons, books, wallpaper and
other goods, while 21 households traded in goods not identified. Nine
households engaged in "contractual" trade (torg podriadnyi), presumably
involving the delivery of goods to government and other institutions.
Of the registrants engaged in commerce the overwhelming majority operated
within the Moscow market, while 39 households engaged in transit trade
or trade in other markets (torg ot"ezdnyi).

In the industrial sector the most important professional grouping
was the textile trades, which absorbed 10 percent of the total number
of registrants surveyed. The most important forms of textile activity
were the production of silk fabrics and of articles which were usually
made of silk (kerchiefs, ribbons), while a much smaller number of these

---

[202]The data on trade specialties must be used with some caution.
In the majority of cases the skazki name not the commodity traded but
rather the "row" where the store was located. In the eighteenth century
the old system of specialized markets was beginning to fall into dis-
use, and trade in a given row was not always confined to the indicated
goods. Some merchants used their stores to sell other commodities in
addition to those authorized and others dealt in different goods altogether. Unfortunately, there is little detailed information on these
practices.

The present data are analyzed on the assumption that in most
cases the name of the row indicates the type of goods sold. The
grouping together of similar kinds of goods will help to reduce the
possible error. Moreover, the skazki themselves sometimes introduce
the necessary corrections, stating that a particular respondent trades
in a certain row but in goods other than would be expected.

artisans worked with wool.[203] Other important craft occupations included the production of fur and leather goods and articles of clothing
(5 percent of the total), the metal trades (5 percent) and woodworking
of various kinds (3 percent). The remaining craftsmen were scattered
in small numbers over a variety of unclassified trades and included
candle-makers, harness-makers, hoopers, stonemasons, house-painters,
stove-builders, icon-painters and other artists, printers, book-binders,
clock-makers, jewelers and makers of umbrellas, brooms, wallpaper and
combs. Seven registrants possessed brick-making enterprises and nine
owned beer breweries.

Of the remaining registrants most were employed by merchants, by
nobles, officers and officials, and more rarely by persons of other
categories or by institutions. Some of these employees worked as
stewards (prikazchiki) or shopmen (sidel'tsy), but most were identified
as being "in the service of" their employers (v usluzhenii) without
further specification or served these employers as laborers (v rabotnikakh).
Innkeeping was the occupation of 37 households, while a few operated
such facilities as mills, public baths and ferries. Also included among
the registrants were gardeners and orchard-keepers, watchmen, teamsters
and coachmen, barbers and cooks.

The data presented in Table 17 permit us to explore the differentiation in occupational patterns of peasant registrants with respect to
their origins and the stratum of the urban classes to which they now

---

[203]Sashes (kushaki) were also sometimes made of silk but more frequently of wool. Tinsel and braid-work also frequently involved the
use of silk. As was noted above, Meshalin found that silk was also
the predominant sector in the rural textile industry of the area surrounding Moscow. (Meshalin, Tekstil'naia promyshlennost' krest'ian,
pp. 128-39.)

belonged. In view of the unequal size of the categories considered, this differentiation is best assessed in terms of the proportion of each category which participated in a given occupation or group of occupations.[204] Predictably, registrants belonging to the kupechestvo were twice as likely as those enrolled in the meshchanstvo to be involved in trade, while members of the latter category were much more likely to be earning their living as employees. Nevertheless, meshchanstvo members were active in most sectors of commerce, while a healthy minority of the employees, including almost all of those working as stewards or shopmen, belonged to the kupechestvo. Craft occupations absorbed members of both urban categories in equal proportions.

Registrants from individual peasant categories and particular provinces usually participated in a broad range of occupations as well, but the patterns of occupational distribution for these various sub-groups differed markedly. Registrants from the economic peasantry and from Moscow and Vladimir gubernii were broadly and relatively evenly distributed among the important commercial and craft sectors. Immigrants from the court and seigneurial peasantry and from Iaroslavl' and Riazan' gubernii were predominantly (60-67 percent) engaged in trade, while those from Kaluga guberniia were predominantly craftsmen and those from Tver' guberniia were also more likely than the average registrant to be engaged in craft industry. Court peasants exhibited a particularly strong inclination toward trade in grain and bread products, which

---

[204]Nevertheless, the limits of this approach must be kept in mind. Where the absolute numbers involved are very small, proportions or percentages cease to be meaningful, since a certain random element in the distribution must be acknowledged. The percentages are useful mainly in connection with larger categories or groupings, while in the smaller ones only a very pronounced concentration can be considered significant.

activity absorbed one-quarter of the registrants from this source but
only 9 percent of all registrants. Trade in foodstuffs was also highly
developed among registrants from the seigneurial peasantry and especially
among immigrants from Iaroslavl' guberniia, of whom 43 percent were involved in this one sector of commerce.[205]

Textile artisans derived principally from the economic peasantry,
and textile production was the most important occupation among immigrants
from Kaluga guberniia, who were nearly four times as likely as the
average registrant to be involved in this industry. Nearly half the
textile producers from this province were concentrated in a single
branch of the industry, the production of sashes, which they had virtually to themselves. Other large contingents of textile producers came
from Moscow and Vladimir gubernii. In the remaining craft occupations,
a relatively large degree of participation by former house serfs is to
be noted in such occupations as tailoring, shoemaking and carpentry
(all potentially related to personal or household service) and to a
lesser extent in the metal trades.

When we turn to the remaining, mostly service-oriented occupations,
we find that most innkeepers were former economic peasants and came
from Moscow or Vladimir guberniia. Economic peasants also contributed
substantially to the ranks of those employed by merchants, but otherwise
former house serfs dominated the scene. Registrants found in the employ
of nobles, officers and officials came overwhelmingly from the ranks of
house serfs, and such employment was the most important single occupation

---

[205]Most of the seigneurial peasants engaged in this trade (50 of 72
households) actually came from Iaroslavl' guberniia. On the other hand,
peasants of other categories emerging from this province also displayed
a strong inclination toward trade in foodstuffs, so that it is clearly
the geographical affiliation which is most significant in this case.

among these freedmen. In one-third of these cases the freed serfs were employed by their own former lords. Many former house serfs worked for merchants or other parties as well, while some made their living as watchmen, teamsters, gardeners, barbers and cooks. The occupational pattern of immigrants from Tula and Nizhnii Novgorod gubernii and the assorted group of more remote provinces, as well as those of undetermined geographical origin, reflects the presence of relatively large numbers of former house serfs in these contingents. These registrants made a weak contribution to trade and to the textile industry and tended to be employees, although they were also to be found in such craft occupations as tailoring, shoemaking, woodworking and metallurgy.

The data on occupations of peasants who enlisted in the Moscow urban classes in the late eighteenth century have much in common with information introduced earlier on the pursuits of peasants living in Moscow without official sanction or registered "temporarily" in craft guilds, suggesting that the registrants were in some ways representative of this larger influx into the urban economy and population. We consistently find that large numbers of urbanized peasants were engaged in trade in foodstuffs and the production and sale of textiles, leather goods and articles of clothing. However, some occupations known to have been pursued by peasants living in Moscow were weakly represented among registrants in the urban classes. Only a few registrants worked as teamsters, vegetable gardeners, stonemasons or factory laborers, and the number of registrants who were tailors or cobblers was much less than one might expect from the large peasant membership enrolled in the corresponding craft guilds earlier in the century. The existence of such an occupational differential between peasants registered in the urban classes and those residing in Moscow without such registration comes as no surprise. The registrants presumably were drawn for the most part from those peasants who were most thoroughly and permanently integrated into urban life, and occupations differed in the degree to which they encouraged or necessitated such integration.[206] Some occupations, such as trade, were capable of producing relatively high levels of income and facilitating enlistment in the _kupechestvo,_ while others provided little more than subsistence. Occupations such as tailoring, shoemaking and transport could be and were pursued on a seasonal basis, while construction work and gardening were inevitably seasonal and encouraged a return to the village during the slack season. Other occupations encouraged or required permanent residence in the city.

Also consistent with previous observations are several salient features of the distribution of occupations among registrants of particular peasant categories or individual provinces. Once again we find that economic peasants displayed the broadest range of occupational choices and were more likely than immigrants from other groups to be involved in small-scale industrial production, particularly in the textile field, while former court and seigneurial peasants made comparatively heavy contributions to the trade in foodstuffs. Interestingly, the commercial specializations of peasants permanently settled in Moscow and engaged in trade on the internal market frequently cannot be

---

[206]However, in many cases involving freed serfs it is apparent that enlistment in the urban classes was primarily a consequence of their release from their former status for reasons having nothing to do with participation in commerce. (Such freedmen had to join one of the population categories bearing taxes or other state obligations.) In these cases enlistment should have little to do with occupational characteristics.

attributed to close connections with the regions producing the goods
traded or to a prior involvement in the shipment of these goods from
the producing regions to Moscow. The provinces to the south of
Moscow straddled the routes leading to major food-producing regions,
and their inhabitants were heavily involved in the transit trade in
food commodities, but the evidence consistently shows that it was instead peasants of the northerly Iaroslavl' guberniia who specialized
in trade in foodstuffs on the internal Moscow market. Similarly, we do
not find large numbers of dealers in metal goods emanating from Tver'
and Iaroslavl' gubernii, where the peasant population was heavily involved in the production of such goods. These instances support the
supposition made in earlier discussion that involvement in the transit
trade supplying the Moscow market and permanent urban settlement were
not strongly interrelated.[207]

Enlistment of Unattached Peasant Women in the Moscow Urban Classes

In addition to the more than 2500 peasant households headed by
males, the Fifth Revision recorded the enlistment in the Moscow urban
classes of 801 households of unattached peasant women (widows and unmarried women of various ages). This influx represented a new phenomenon, very few cases of which had been detected by the previous census
and which had possibly been encouraged by the provisions of Catherine II's

---

[207] There are, admittedly, a few instances in which such a relationship might be inferred from the data. Most of the peasant registrants
dealing in wood did come from the provinces containing the city's
principal source of supply of this commodity (Moscow and Vladimir
gubernii), which in this case were very close at hand. Eleven of 29
registrants trading in fur goods came from Iaroslavl' guberniia, which
was astride the main route connecting Moscow with Siberia. Unfortunately,
in most cases the numbers of registrants from individual provinces who
were engaged in particular occupations are too small to allow any
meaningful inference.

Urban Charter of 1785 specifically authorizing women to enlist in the
kupechestvo and meshchanstvo.[208] Most of these "households" consisted
of a single individual, but occasionally they contained two or more related women or widows with young children.[209] Forty-two female registrants were enlisted in the kupechestvo (including one in the second
guild), with the remainder, constituting an overwhelming majority,
belonging to the meshchanstvo. The female registrants came predominantly
(77 percent) from the ranks of freed serfs, and 60 percent (483 households) consisted of former house serfs. Also included were 132 households from the seigneurial peasantry, 120 from the economic peasantry
and 41 from the court peasantry. More than 70 percent of the female
registrants acquired urban status in 1795, the census year, while before
1793 there appeared only a trickle of such registrants (an average of
8 cases per year). For a large proportion of the female registrants
(47 percent) geographical origin cannot be determined. Those for whom
such information is available fall into a pattern similar to that of
male-headed households, with 95 percent emanating from the provinces
of the Central Russian heartland as previously defined. Forty-four
percent of the females originated in Moscow guberniia, while other
substantial contributors to this influx were Vladimir, Kaluga, Iaroslavl',
Tver', Tula and Riazan' gubernii.

---

[208]PSZ, Vol. 22, No. 16188, Art. 92, 138.

[209]We do not include among female registrants cases in which enlistment was originally accomplished by a husband or other male family member who was deceased by the time of the census but only those in which
a woman enlisted apparently unaccompanied by mature male family members.

Occupational information is available for only 272 cases, or one-third of the female registrants. The range of occupations here was much narrower than for households headed by males. In nearly half the cases surveyed the former peasant women were employed in domestic service or other work by individuals or institutions. Of these employees 57 worked for merchants or other members of the urban classes, 44 for nobles, 28 for members of other or unidentified population categories, and 4 for institutions. In 15 cases the women were employed by the individuals or families which formerly possessed them as serfs. About one-third of the women gained their livelihood in the textile and clothing trades--in spinning, weaving, sewing, knitting, tailoring, embroidery and similar pursuits. Women who had belonged to the economic or seigneurial peasantry were somewhat more likely than former house serfs to be engaged in the above crafts, while the house serfs predictably showed the strongest predilection for domestic service. A few women engaged in trade, mostly in textile goods and articles of clothing, or were involved in other crafts, and 23 women reportedly had "no commerce or enterprises." As in the case of households headed by males, women for whom no occupational information is provided were sometimes reported to be living with relatives or in-laws, in Old Believer communities, in asylums, or in the houses of their former masters under unspecified relationships.[210]

The influx of unattached females into the Moscow urban classes provides further evidence of the fact that in the late eighteenth century fairly large numbers of serfs were being released from bondage

---

[210]About 80 such cases, of which half consisted of those residing with relatives or in-laws, were observed in a not necessarily complete count.

and allowed to enter the "free" population categories for reasons
having little to do with any economic attainments on their part. Regarding the female registrants who did not derive from house serfs, it
is likely that the superfluous position of unmarried women in the
village economy and social structure made it comparatively easy for
such women to gain release from peasant status, as well as motivating
them to seek their fortune elsewhere.[211]

Enlistment following the Fifth Revision

In the aftermath of the Fifth Revision peasants continued to pour
into the Moscow posad, sustaining its rapid growth. Information on
this continued influx is available from semi-annual reports of the
Moscow provincial treasury (kazennaia palata) on changes in the number
of "souls" in each tax category.[212] These reports disclose that from
the Fifth Revision through 1802 an additional 1785 crown peasants,
including 1354 economic peasants, 384 court peasants and 47 peasants
of other categories, enlisted in the Moscow urban classes.[213] Of these

---

[211]On this factor, see B. N. Mironov, "Traditsionnoe demograficheskoe
povedenie krest'ian v XIX-nachale XX vv." in Brachnost', rozhdaemost'
i smertnost' v Rossii i SSSR (Moscow, 1977), pp. 86-87.

[212]TsGIA, f. 558, op. 2, d. 128, ll. 2 ob.-3, 7, 24, 38-40, 56 ob.-
63, 98 ob.-104; d. 129, ll. 2 ob.-5, 43 ob.-44 ob., 99-102, 273 ob.-278,
287 ob.-288, 347 ob.-353, 382 ob.-388. These reports do not include
changes due to births and deaths (which were taken into account only by
the subsequent census) but do deal with transfers from one population
category to another and with souls "omitted" from the census (propisany)
through error or accident and subsequently added to the oklad.

[213]It is possible that these data overlap somewhat with the previously
discussed data of the Fifth Revision. According to a decree of July 13,
1795 (PSZ, Vol. 23, No. 17357), only peasants who had registered in the
urban classes prior to the announcement of the new census (June 23, 1794)
were to be relieved of peasant status and obligations by the census.

registrants 1608 enlisted in the kupechestvo and 177 in the meshchanstvo --as before, crown peasants showed little inclination to join the lesser category of urban citizens. The bulk of these registrants appeared in the immediate aftermath of the census, when they may still have had hoped of prompt release from dual status and obligations, after which the level of enlistment declined. From the Fifth Revision through the beginning of 1797 registrants from the crown peasantry numbered 1333, while in the succeeding six years only 452 enlisted. Still, the latter figure was higher than that for the comparable period following the Fourth Revision by about 50 percent.

On the surface, it would appear that the large number of peasants re-corded in the census documents as having enlisted in 1795 were not eligible for this benefit and would continue to be carried on the rolls as new registrants enlisted "after" the Fifth Revision. However, it is not known what constituted the effective date of enlistment for the purpose of the above determination--whether it was the date when the peasant applied for membership in the urban classes, or the much later date when the lengthy administrative process involved was completed and the applicant was added to the roster of urban taxpayers, or perhaps some other juncture. The dates given in the revizskie skazki probably refer to the final stages of the process.

Moreover, some features of the data make a substantial overlap appear unlikely. On the basis of the skazki for the Fifth Revision Zviagintsev determined the size of the Moscow posad to be 17,100 males. (Zviagintsev, "Rost naseleniia," p. 143.) This total includes 555 households or about 1200 souls of crown peasants who enlisted in 1795 (Table 15), and if these registrants are excluded the total falls to less than 16,000. In 1796 the Moscow kazennaia palata, reporting the results of the Fifth Revision, gave the much higher total of 19,650 souls, including 841 crown peasants of Moscow guberniia enlisted after the census, or 18,809 souls without those subsequent registrants. (TsGIA, f. 558, op. 2, d. 128, ll. 2 ob.-3, 7.) The gap between the totals provided by these two sources would seem to indicate that no substantial number of individuals listed in the revizskie skazki were excluded from the kazennaia palata figure. We may therefore assume that additional registrants reported by the kazennaia palata are not the same as those appearing in the skazki. Discrepancies in the com-position of the two groups of registrants could also be cited to support this conclusion.

The influx of freed serfs was still larger and continued without any abatement into the early years of the nineteenth century. From 1797 through 1802 registrants from the serf population numbered 2430, of whom 1022 enlisted in the kupechestvo and 1408 in the meshchanstvo.[214] Thus, according to the not entirely complete data of the Moscow kazennaia palata more than 4200 peasants enrolled in the Moscow urban classes in the half-dozen years following the Fifth Revision, maintaining the high rate of enlistment prevalent in the period immediately preceding the census.[215] From 1797 through 1802 the Moscow posad gained 918 immigrants from the ranks of provincial townsmen and 477 from other categories of the population. The importance of the peasantry as a source of new urban citizens thus continued to increase both absolutely and relatively.

The Pattern of Immigration to Moscow

In the eighteenth century, Moscow was by far the most frequent destination of peasants migrating to urban settlements in the Central Industrial Region. The attraction exerted by the old capital is easy to explain. Moscow dwarfed all other towns of Central Russia and as a commercial and industrial center of unrivaled importance offered a vast

---

[214]The reports of the kazennaia palata do not contain information on enlistment from groups other than the crown peasantry before 1797, and the data for these groups are therefore less complete.

[215]In view of the lengthy administrative process involved and the inherent delays in communicating its results from one government institution to another, it is probable that enlistment reported by these documents of the kazennaia palata had been initiated and recorded by the urban authorities somewhat earlier. Thus, reports of the kazennaia palata for 1794 and 1795 do not include the deluge of registrants which appeared at the time of the census but apparently focus on the preceding years. (TsGIA, f. 558, op. 2, d. 126, ll. 518-27.) The results cited therefore overlap only slightly, if at all, into the first years of the nineteenth century.

array of opportunities to newcomers in search of income from business
activity or hired labor. Moreover, the size and complexity of the city
and the diversity of its population rendered enforcement of the restrictions on settlement and economic activity particularly difficult, while
the largely non-native origin of the local posad population, a by-
product of the continuing stream of immigration, further reduced barriers
to assimilation of newcomers. As a result, Moscow was able to draw
immigrants in large numbers from an area which extended far beyond the
immediately adjacent countryside, although there were definite limits
to this orbit.

As has been demonstrated, the Moscow urban classes consisted to an
unusual extent of recent immigrants and their descendants. This situation was the result both of heavy immigration and enlistment and of the
disastrous health conditions and rapid natural decrease which removed
native elements from the scene. The peasantry was the most important
source for the replenishment and growth of the Moscow posad: the data
presented in this chapter indicate that in the eighteenth century about
13,000 male souls were absorbed from various peasant categories, while
the urban classes of other towns contributed about 8000 and other
population groups 4000. The rate at which peasants infiltrated the
posad was far from uniform and underwent a steep rise in the last two
decades of the century, during which two-thirds of the total number of
registrants made their appearance. In the first half of the century,
peasant enlistment added an average of only about 50 souls per year to
the Moscow posad population. In the period between the Third and Fourth
Revisions (1764-1782), the rate increased somewhat to about 90 souls,
but by the 1790's it had grown explosively to nearly 700 souls per year.

As a result of this deluge the Moscow urban classes, now growing rapidly after more than a half-century of stagnation and decline, contained a large and rapidly expanding contingent of persons of very recent peasant origin. According to the first two revisions between 7 and 10 percent of the total posad population of 13,000 to 14,000 males consisted of peasants enrolled during the preceding two decades. By the beginning of the nineteenth century the Moscow posad had grown to more than 25,000 souls, of whom more than a third consisted of such recent peasant recruits, while a large part of the remainder was descended from peasants who had enlisted earlier in the century or consisted of new-comers from other groups and their descendants.

The growing influx of peasants into the Moscow urban classes reflects legal, economic and social changes which occurred in Russia during the eighteenth century. The reforms of 1775, which raised the status of the urban kupechestvo and improved tne conditions under which crown peasants were allowed to become members of it, probably made a substantial contribution to the rapid growth of peasant enlistment in the succeeding period. Other factors of equal importance probably contributed to the increasing peasant influx: the relaxation under the government of Catherine II of attempts to suppress commercial and in-dustrial activity by peasants, the growing involvement of peasants in such activity, and the increasing willingness of serfowners to free some serfs for enlistment in the urban classes.

These changes also affected the relative contributions of the various peasant categories to the replenishment and growth of the Moscow posad. The court peasantry was precocious in its involvement in trade and industry in Moscow and the surrounding territory and in enlistment in the urban classes, but recruitment from this category did not increase sharply in the later decades of the century while that from other, larger categories of peasants expanded greatly. The rapid rise in the number of freed serfs entering the Moscow urban classes in this period is particularly notable. In the four decades from the end of Peter I's reign to the beginning of that of Catherine II only a few hundred freed serfs at most were added to the Moscow posad, although in this period serfs could also enlist in the urban commune as mercantile peasants without losing their original status. In the remaining four decades of the century more than 5000 such freedmen appeared in the Moscow posad, which by the end of the period was receiving more recruits from the serf population than from the crown peasantry. Moreover, the former serfs were to be found predominantly at the middle and lower economic levels of the posad population, and two-thirds of them derived from the category of house serfs, commonly regarded as the poorest and most degraded element of the Russian peasantry. These results belie the widespread assumption that only a few wealthy serfs capable of "buying their way out of bondage" were able to obtain manumission and gain entry to the urban classes.[216]

Peasant immigrants absorbed into the Moscow urban classes during the eighteenth century came predominantly from Moscow guberniia and the adjacent provinces to the east, north and south, and these results presumably reflect the overall patterns of peasant immigration to the city. In general, recruitment was most intense in the area nearest to Moscow and thinned out with increasing distance from it, but toward the end of

---

[216]See, for example, Vartanov, "Kupechestvo i torguiushchee krest'ianstvo," pp. 187-93.

the century this concentration was evidently lessening, as a growing proportion of the immigrants arrived from districts well beyond the immediate vicinity of the city. Another trend which was apparent in the eighteenth century and continued into the nineteenth was a gradual southward shift in Moscow's sources of immigration, as provinces to the south of the old capital gained in importance at the expense of those to the north.

The peasants absorbed into the Moscow posad were engaged predominantly in trade or small-scale industry within the city and were usually entrepreneurs of modest attainments rather than possessors of great wealth. As was evidently the case with peasant immigrants in general, large numbers of registrants were involved in trade in foodstuffs and the production and sale of textiles, leather goods and articles of clothing, but trade in a wide variety of other goods and many additional industrial crafts were also practiced. Some registrants were employees in enterprises and households rather than independent entrepreneurs, although in this occupational group former house serfs predominated.

A few registrants engaged in transit trade or operated some sort of enterprise in their native villages or some other rural locality, but for the most part there is little evidence that successful commercial and industrial activity pursued outside an urban context would lead to permanent urban settlement and enlistment in the urban classes. Individuals who became very wealthy in this manner might well be motivated to become members of the Moscow kupechestvo--thus E. I. Grachev, the well known textile manufacturer of Ivanovo village, in 1795 enlisted in the city's first guild.[217] However, Grachev was one of the few

---

[217]MDIMK, Vol. 4, p. 411 (No. 536).

registrants to emerge from the vicinity of Ivanovo (the eastern part of Vladimir guberniia), where local commercial and industrial development apparently absorbed most peasants in need of non-agricultural employment. Likewise, we have been able to discover little relation between participation in transit trade involving the shipment of goods to the Moscow market and permanent settlement in the city. For the area in the immediate vicinity of Moscow, however, the distinction between urban and rural economic activity probably loses its validity. Trading peasants of this area could infiltrate the internal Moscow economy without straining their ties to the original base of their commercial success.

CHAPTER V: PROVINCIAL AND DISTRICT TOWNS OF THE CENTRAL INDUSTRIAL
REGION

Data presented in the two preceding chapters have indicated that
among the towns of the Central Industrial Region Moscow was the principal destination of peasant immigrants in the eighteenth century. These
data have given no reason to believe that any of the lesser towns of
the region, with the exception of Nizhnii Novgorod or possibly other
towns of Nizhnii Novgorod guberniia, attracted substantial numbers of
peasant registrants, even in proportion to their much smaller populations. In the present chapter we will take a closer look at the situation and investigate more thoroughly the extent to which these towns
were able to compete with Moscow for immigrants.

Detailed data have been gathered for three provinces of the Central
Industrial Region, Moscow guberniia (i.e. the uezd towns of this province)
and Iaroslavl' and Nizhnii Novgorod gubernii. These provinces provide
a sampling of various zones within the region. Moscow guberniia, of
course, represents the area immediately surrounding the metropolis and
under its most intense influence. At a farther remove from the old
capital, Iaroslavl' guberniia was also subject to the economic influence
of the Upper Volga, which linked it directly to Petersburg, the "downstream" provinces and the Urals without the mediation of Moscow.
Nevertheless, the impact of the Moscow economy was strongly felt in
this province, as is demonstrated by the relatively heavy flow of
peasant immigration from Iaroslavl' guberniia experienced by the city.
In Nizhnii Novgorod guberniia, located farther downstream on the Volga
and at the easternmost extremity of the Central Industrial Region, the
influence of Moscow was further diluted by distance and the countervailing

influence of the Volga economy. This province, it will be recalled, contributed the fewest peasant registrants to the Moscow posad of any in the Central Industrial Region. Beyond these considerations, the towns of Nizhnii Novgorod guberniia demand further scrutiny because of their already demonstrated ability to attract peasant immigrants.

In investigating each province, prior to considering the data on enlistment in the urban classes, we shall examine briefly the degree and character of economic development in the towns involved, the participation of peasants in these urban economies and the development of commercial and industrial activities in the surrounding countryside, in the hope of relating these various factors to the observed patterns of migration. Another significant question to be dealt with in this chapter is the effect of immigration or the lack of it on the population dynamics of these lesser urban centers of the Central Industrial Region --the Moscow posad, it will be recalled, was dependent on substantial immigration for its very survival.

Moscow Guberniia

The restructured Moscow province instituted in 1781-82 included, in addition to the old capital, nine previously existing district towns (Dmitrov, Kolomna, Serpukhov, Zvenigorod, Vereia, Ruza, Mozhaisk, Volokolamsk, Klin) and five district centers newly awarded urban status. Of the latter towns, two (Bronnitsy, Nikitsk) had been villages belonging to the court properties, two (Voskresensk, Podol) were former "economic" villages and one (Bogorodsk) was formerly a settlement of iamshchiki (servitors of the state postal system).[1] An additional "non-administrative"

---

[1] Polnoe sobranie zakonov Rossiiskoi imperii s 1649 goda (hereafter PSZ), Vol. 21, Nos. 15245, 15398. In 1796 Paul I abolished all five

town was created in 1782 from settlements formerly belonging to the
Trinity-St. Sergei Monastery and located beneath its walls.[2] This town
was given the name Sergiev Posad and was located in Bogorodsk uezd.
The five new districts of Moscow guberniia were created largely from
territory formerly belonging to Moscow uezd, although the neighboring
Kolomna uezd also yielded a substantial amount of territory, and the
new districts thus formed a ring around the much reduced Moscow uezd.[3]
Also part of this ring was Zvenigorod uezd, which received at least
two-thirds of its area from the former Moscow uezd while relinquishing
a comparable segment of its previous territory. Beyond this inner
core of the province were the districts of Kolomna and Serpukhov to the
south of Moscow, Dmitrov and Klin to the north, and Vereia, Ruza,
Mozhaisk and Volokolamsk to the west. These outer districts also
experienced drastic changes in boundaries as a result of the territorial
reforms and in some cases (Serpukhov, Ruza, Vereia) resembled their

---

new districts and demoted their towns to "non-administrative" status.
(See below, n. 2.) In 1802 the districts of Bogorodsk, Bronnitsy and
Podol were reestablished, but within different boundaries than those in
effect from 1782 through 1796. Voskresensk remained a "non-administrative" town, while Nikitsk reverted to its pre-1781 status as the court
village of Kolychevo. See PSZ, Vol. 27, No. 20143; V. E. Den, Naselenie
Rossii po V revizii, Vol. 1 (Moscow, 1902), pp. 292-93.

[2]PSZ, Vol. 21, No. 15371. Known variously as zashtatnyi gorod,
posad or sloboda, such "non-administrative" towns had populations bearing
urban status and were governed by the usual urban institutions but were
not used as headquarters for the administration of the surrounding territory. Official statistics on the posad population frequently combine
the uezd town and any "non-administrative" urban settlements within the
district boundaries in a single figure.

[3]See Materialy po istorii krest'ianskoi promyshlennosti (MPIKP),
Vol. 2 (Moscow-Leningrad, 1950), maps following p. 460. The new districts also included small amounts of territory formerly belonging to
Serpukhov, Dmitrov, Zvenigorod, Ruza and Borovsk districts (the latter
transferred to Kaluga guberniia as a result of the reforms).

former incarnations in little more than the retention of the same administrative center.[4]

Information provided by contemporary descriptive surveys makes it possible to assess the size and economic importance of the towns of Moscow guberniia in the late eighteenth century.[5] The quantitative information provided by these sources is summarized in Table 18, and data on Moscow offered by the same sources are included for purposes of comparison. The largest uezd towns in this province (Kolomna, Serpukhov, Vereia) were located along its southern fringes. These

---

[4]For this reason caution must be exercised in the comparative use of descriptive sources dating from before and after the reform.

[5]Tsentral'nyi gosudarstvennyi voenno-istoricheskii arkhiv, Moscow (TsGVIA), f. Voenno-uchenogo arkhiva (VUA), No. 18859, ch. 2 ("Ekonomicheskie primechaniia po Dmitrovskomu uezdu"); No. 18860 ("Opisanie Moskovskoi gubernii gorodov, 1776 g."); Sostoianie stolichnogo goroda Moskvy, 1785 g. (Moscow, 1879); S. Chernov, Statisticheskoe opisanie Moskovskoi gubernii 1811 g. (Moscow, 1812); "Primechaniia, sluzhashchie k poznaniiu do domostroitel'stva i sostoianiia mest po rekam Kliazme, Moskve i Oke lezhashchikh," Akademicheskie izvestiia na 1780 g., Vol. 4, pp. 472-95; E. Ziablovskii, Zemleopisanie Rossiiskoi Imperii dlia vsekh sostoianii, Vol. 3 (St. Petersburg, 1810), pp. 214-63; A. Shchekatov, Geograficheskii slovar' Rossiiskogo gosudarstva, Vols. 1-7 (Moscow, 1801-09); I. Tokmakov, Istoriko-statisticheskoe i arkheologicheskoe opisanie goroda Dmitrova (Moskovskoi gubernii) s uezdom i sviatyniami (Moscow, 1893). The Tokmakov book reprints the section on Dmitrov and its district from various eighteenth-century descriptive surveys of Moscow guberniia.

In addition to the above, reports of the Moscow provincial treasury (Tsentral'nyi gosudarstvennyi istoricheskii arkhiv, Leningrad, /TsGIA/, f. 558, op. 2, d. 126, ll. 518 ob.-527, 571 ob.-581; d. 128, ll. 2 ob.-7) provide information on the size of the posad population and its distribution between the kupechestvo and meshchanstvo during the 1790's. Data on urban populations collected by the Commerce Commission in the 1760's is a further source of information on the development of craft industry (i.e. the numbers of craftsmen) in the towns. (Tsentral'nyi gosudarstvennyi arkhiv drevnikh aktov, Moscow /TsGADA/, f. 397, dd. 441, 445.) A digest of the data gathered by the Commerce Commission has recently been published in Bernd Knabe, "Die Struktur der russischen Posadgemeinden und der Katalog der Beschwerden und Forderungen der Kaufmannschaft," Forschungen zur osteuropäischen Geschichte, Band 22 (1975), pp. 300-63.

Table 18: Demographic and Economic Characteristics of Towns of
Moscow <u>Guberniia</u>, Late Eighteenth Century

Towns	Houses	Total pop.	Males	Urban classes (males)	% in urban classes	No. of merchants	% urban classes in kupechestvo	Declared capital
Moscow	9000	217000	146000	15000	10	6-8000	40-53	5.4 mln.
Kolomna	900	7000	3500[a]	1900	54	8-900	42-47	220000
Serpukhov	800	5500	2800	2300	82	700-1000	30-43	220000
Vereia	750	5000	2500	2000	80	900-1000	45-50	230-360000
Mozhaisk	700	3900	1900	700	37	100	14	29-36000
Dmitrov	600	3000	1500	1400	93	2-300	14-21	91000
Ruza	300	2400	1200	800	67	1-200	13-25	24-39000
Volokolamsk	250	2500	1400	400	29	30-200	8-50	10-31000
Klin	150	1100	600	300	50	100	33	25000
Zvenigorod	100	1000	500	300	60	100-150	33-50	32-45000
Bronnitsy	200	1500	800	600	75	300	50	?
Voskresensk	150	800[a]	400	300	75	100	33	24000
Podol	100	900	400	300	75	100	33	32000
Nikitsk	100	700	400	100	25	50	50	10000
Bogorodsk	50	600	300	?	?	?	?	?

[a]Estimated, assuming equal numbers of males and females.

Table 18 (cont.)

Towns	No. of stores	Ratio to pop.	Inns	Weekly markets	Fairs	Industrial enterprises	No. of craftsmen	Craft specialties	% of urban classes engaged in crafts
Moscow	11000	1:20	400	–	–	400	2200[b]	?	15
Kolomna	370	1:19	?	2	–	44–108	50–70	11	3–4
Serpukhov	157	1:35	30	3	3/1 d.	19–34	140–170	23	6–7
Vereia	63	1:79	4	1	1/3 d.	13–27	120–210	5	6–11
Mozhaisk	190	1:20	?	1	1/9 d.	1	10–20	?	1–3
Dmitrov	132	1:23	45	2	1/7 d.	22–26	60–80	7	4–6
Ruza	48	1:50	2	1	2/1 d.	4	20	?	3
Volokolamsk	7	1:357	12	2	1	–	10	?	3
Klin	21	1:52	70	1	1	8	?	?	?
Zvenigorod	14	1:71	2	1	–	1	2–7	?	1–2
Bronnitsy	26	1:58	?	2	1/1 d.	5	?	?	?
Voskresensk	10	1:80	1	2	1/2 d.	–	50	6	17
Podol	13	1:69	?	1	–	3	10	?	3
Nikitsk	–	–	?	–	1/1 d.	–	?	?	?
Bogorodsk	?	?	?	?	2/1 d.	?	?	?	?

Sources: See text (Ch. V, n. 5).

[b]"Permanent" craft-guild members.

towns each contained 750-900 houses and a total population of 5000-7000

persons of both sexes and also displayed such signs of substantial

commercial development as a numerous merchant class (kupechestvo) with

comparatively large amounts of "declared" capital.[6] The economies

of these towns, favorably located astride major trade routes connecting

the productive agriculture and fisheries of the southern parts of

---

[6]Except in the case of Moscow, where a large contingent of "temporary" peasant residents was identified, the population figures from descriptive surveys apparently include only the "permanent" population—those officially regarded as residents of the town. It is probable that temporary peasant migrants and even peasants permanently but unofficially settled in the towns were not credited to the urban population because these individuals officially remained residents of villages. Peasants listed as part of the town population were usually those belonging to peasant communities within or adjacent to the town. In Moscow, however, the presence of migrant peasants was too large to ignore.

The proportion of the posad population belonging to the kupechestvo and the amount of declared capital are at best rough measures of the wealth, prosperity and economic importance of the citizenry in any town. The Urban Charter of 1785 (PSZ, Vol. 22, No. 16188) defined the types of commercial activity permitted to the members of each of the three merchant guilds and the meshchanstvo, but these stipulations were apparently little enforced and usually observed in the breach. Theoretically, the kupechestvo included the more prosperous members of the posad whose enterprises and income enabled them to pay higher taxes in return for the enhanced status and privileges which went with membership in this category. While this was certainly true on the average, some members of the kupechestvo performed hired labor or engaged in other lowly occupations, while some members of the meshchanstvo engaged in the same kinds of commercial activities as did the average kupets. (See above, Chapter IV, Table 17.) Sometimes merchants deliberately reverted to the meshchanstvo to escape rising taxation. (See P. G. Ryndziunskii, "Soslovno-podatnaia reforma 1775 g. i gorodskoe naselenie," in Obshchestvo i gosudarstvo feodal'noi Rossii /Moscow, 1975/, p. 94.) The amount of capital "declared" by a merchant was determined by the requirements of the guild to which he wished to belong and the level of taxation he was able and willing to bear rather than the amount he actually possessed. Since the Urban Charter (Art. 105, 109, 115) provided that merchants be ranked according to their declared capital, some merchants declared more than the minimum necessary to qualify for membership in the desired guild, but most claimed the minimum or an amount slightly above it. The total amount of capital declared by merchants of a particular town thus reflects the size of the kupechestvo and its distribution among the three guilds.

European Russia with the markets of Moscow and Petersburg, were to a large extent based on transit trade. Merchants from the indicated towns purchased grain, fish, livestock and animal products (meat, hides, tallow, wool, sheepskins), hemp and hempseed oil, honey, beeswax and other agricultural products in the producing regions for resale in Moscow, Petersburg, Riga, Arkhangel'sk and to some extent other markets in the central and northwestern provinces of Russia.[7]

The transit trade of Vereia, in keeping with its more westerly location, in proximity to trade routes bypassing Moscow and proceeding directly to Petersburg, was oriented more toward the Northwest and Baltic, while Kolomna and Serpukhov dealt with Moscow and Petersburg on a roughly equal basis.[8] The large number of stores in Kolomna indicates the presence of a domestic market serving a clientele much wider than the local urban inhabitants and probably including the surrounding rural population and merchants and other travelers passing through on the busy route traversing the town.[9] These stores sold a wide variety of foodstuffs, textiles, articles of clothing and footwear, metal goods, chandlery, small household and personal items (shchepetil'nyi tovar) and other products, many of which had been brought from Moscow or Petersburg for local distribution. Unlike most towns in the province, Kolomna had no annual fair, perhaps because the extensive development of permanent

---

[7]Livestock usually passed through the local slaughterhouses and was sent on to market in the form of meat, hides, tallow, and so forth.

[8]Vereia also participated in the overland trade between Russia and its western neighbors (Poland, Prussia). TsGVIA, f. VUA, No. 18860, ll. 19 ob.-20; Sostoianie stolichnogo goroda Moskvy, 1785 g., pp. 22-23.

[9]However, according to a survey dated 1776, 267 of these stores had burned down in a recent fire. TsGVIA, f. VUA, No. 18860, l. 38.

trade in the local market rendered such a gathering superfluous. Vereia,
in contrast, had few stores for a town of this size but a relatively
elaborate fair attended by merchants from Moscow, Tula, Kaluga, Serpukhov,
Mozhaisk, Borovsk and other nearby towns as well as by the neighboring
peasantry. Weekly markets in all three towns attracted "only peasants,"
who brought agricultural and craft products (grain, hemp, homespun
cloth, pottery, wooden utensils, and so forth). For the twice-weekly
Kolomna market such peasants arrived in "substantial numbers" and came
from several different districts.

The three towns all exhibited substantial industrial development.
They possessed enterprises producing textiles, leather, bricks, pottery,
ceramic tiles, tallow and malt, partly for sale in Moscow, Petersburg,
Riga, Arkhangel'sk, the Ukraine and other internal and export markets
and for state procurement. The available sources indicate that the
craft sector in Kolomna, which had the largest number of "factories,"
was relatively small and consisted mainly of smiths. Larger numbers of
craftsmen were to be found in Serpukhov (chiefly smiths and potters,
but with a large number of specialties represented) and Vereia (predominantly glovers, also cobblers, tailors, smiths, carpenters).
Commercial vegetable gardening and orchard-keeping (ogorodnichestvo,
sadovodstvo) were another major source of income in Kolomna and Vereia.[10]

Dmitrov, lying about 70 kilometers due north of Moscow, was also a
significant commercial and industrial center, although inhabited by a
kupechestvo considerably less numerous and wealthy than that of the
largest uezd towns. In the sixteenth century Dmitrov had been a

---

[10]TsGVIA, f. VUA, No. 18860, ll. 19-20, 25-27, 37 ob.-38; Sostoianie
stolichnogo goroda Moskvy, 1785 g., pp. 13-14, 18-24; Ziablovskii,
Zemleopisanie, Vol. 3, pp. 250-55, 259-60; Shchekatov, Geograficheskii
slovar', Vol. 1, pp. 806-08; Vol. 5, pp. 926-29.

prosperous intermediary in the trade between Moscow and northern Russia, but the town had fallen into stagnation following a shift in trade routes which left it largely isolated from major commercial currents.[11] Dmitrov experienced a revival in the eighteenth century, benefiting from the founding of Petersburg and the development of export trade via the Baltic—the town was well situated to exploit the possibilities opened by the new system of waterways linking Petersburg to the Upper Volga.

The transit trade of Dmitrov concentrated heavily on grain, which was purchased in the black-soil provinces and shipped to Petersburg via the Oka and Volga or hauled overland to connect with the Volga system via one of its upper tributaries (Gzhat', Dubna, Shosha). Some grain was ground into flour in Dmitrov or Dmitrov uezd before being sent on to Petersburg.[12] According to one contemporary estimate the grain trade of the Dmitrov kupechestvo was valued at 100,000 rubles annually.[13] The domestic market of Dmitrov was substantial, and the large number of inns suggests that a considerable amount of traffic passed through the town, adding to the clientele of local merchants. In addition to its two weekly market days, attracting "only peasants," Dmitrov was notable for a week-long annual fair (later extended to two weeks), which was

---

[11]M. N. Tikhomirov, "Gorod Dmitrov, ot osnovaniia goroda do poloviny XIX v.," Trudy Muzeia dmitrovskogo kraia, Vol. 2 (Dmitrov, 1925), pp. 15-26.

[12]Much detailed information on the grain trade of the Dmitrov kupechestvo is provided by the "journal" of one eighteenth-century Dmitrov merchant: Zhurnal ili zapiska zhizni i prikliuchenii Ivana Alekseevicha Tolchenova (Moscow, 1974), e.g. pp. 33-39, 50-52. See also TsGVIA, f. VUA, No. 18859, ch. 2, l. 2 ob.; No. 18860, ll. 5 ob.-6; Sostoianie stolichnogo goroda Moskvy, 1785 g., p. 26.

[13]Sostoianie stolichnogo goroda Moskvy, 1785 g., p. 26.

attended by merchants from a large number of nearby towns, bringing silk, woolen and linen textiles and other assorted consumer goods (melochnye tovary). Dmitrov boasted a substantial number of industrial enterprises, although these were not very large. The "factories" produced woolen textiles, braid-work, leather, malt, tallow and wax for sale in Moscow and Petersburg as well as for local distribution. The craft sector in Dmitrov was modest but visible and included blacksmiths, furriers, glovers, cobblers, tailors, candlemakers and carpenters. As in Kolomna and Vereia, the raising of vegetables was also a significant source of income. However, according to one source most members of the Dmitrov urban classes "live in poverty," gaining their livelihood by working for merchants in Moscow, Petersburg and other towns.[14]

Mozhaisk, located in the southwestern corner of the province on a tributary of the Moscow River, was larger than Dmitrov in total population but had a smaller posad. The small Mozhaisk kupechestvo participated to some extent in the transit trade in grain, animal products, flax, hemp and hempseed oil. Another important enterprise of the Mozhaisk posad was the shipment of locally produced lumber and firewood downstream to Moscow. The most striking economic feature of the town, however, was the size of its local market--in the number of stores it contained, Mozhaisk was surpassed only by Kolomna, which was much larger, among the district towns of Moscow guberniia. The merchants of Mozhaisk derived much business from the provisioning of travelers passing through on the Moscow-Smolensk highway. The town also conducted a major annual fair, lasting nine days. The Mozhaisk fair was attended by merchants

---

[14] TsGVIA, f. VUA, No. 18859, ch. 2, ll. 2 ob.-3; No. 18860, ll. 5-6 ob.; Sostoianie stolichnogo goroda Moskvy, 1785 g., pp. 25-27; Ziablovskii, Zemleopisanie, Vol. 3, pp. 238-39; Tokmakov, Istoriko-statisticheskoe i arkheologicheskoe opisanie goroda Dmitrova, pp. 4-12, 51-53; Tikhomirov, "Gorod Dmitrov," pp. 50-54.

from many nearby towns with fancy textiles "not ordinarily sold in the town," articles of clothing, tools, foodstuffs and other goods, as well as by peasants with locally produced linen cloth and other rural products. The fair also attracted a large influx of buyers from the surrounding rural area. The town had little industry of any kind—the available sources list only one brick "factory" and a few craftsmen. As in many other Central Russian towns, commercial vegetable gardening was also practiced—Mozhaisk specialized in cucumbers and "supplied" a number of nearby towns with this commodity.[15]

The remaining long-established towns of Moscow guberniia (Ruza, Volokolamsk, Klin, Zvenigorod) were of less importance. The merchants of Ruza, Volokolamsk and Klin participated to some extent in the transit trade in grain, animal products, hemp and flax, although these goods were mostly obtained from local sources rather than the more distant and abundant producing regions and were handled in small quantities. As in several other towns located upstream from Moscow, the inhabitants of Ruza derived substantial income from supplying locally produced lumber and firewood to meet the huge demands of the old capital. Some merchants of Ruza sold goods for local consumption in stores or brought them to nearby rural fairs for disposal. Many of the merchants of Volokolamsk were engaged in purchasing industrial products and foodstuffs in Moscow and some other towns of Central Russia and selling them in nearby towns and districts. The economy of Klin was stimulated by the heavy traffic passing through the town en route between Moscow and Petersburg, and many inhabitants derived a living from innkeeping and

---

[15]Sostoianie stolichnogo goroda Moskvy, 1785 g., pp. 31-33; Shchekatov, Geograficheskii slovar', Vol. 4, pp. 287-91; Ziablovskii, Zemleopisanie, Vol. 3, pp. 248-50.

the sale of foodstuffs and other supplies to travelers. The commerce of
Zvenigorod was strictly local and did not benefit from such stimuli,
since the town stood aside from major overland routes and had little
in the way of facilities for servicing travelers. The merchants of
Zvenigorod supplied the town population and nearby villages with various
foodstuffs, textiles and woven articles, beads, rings, crosses and
"other goods needed by the peasantry," which were mostly brought from
Moscow. Klin and Ruza had a few industrial enterprises, producing
leather, pottery, bricks, malt and tallow. "Many inhabitants" of Klin
engaged in craft industry, working as blacksmiths, coppersmiths, potters,
brick-makers, tailors and cobblers, while some citizens of Zvenigorod
made their living from the spinning of silk. Other occupations of the
posad population in these towns included transport services (izvoz),
hired labor in Moscow and other towns, vegetable gardening and even
grain cultivation.[16]

Of the newly established towns, several showed at least the beginnings of an urban economy. Bronnitsy and Podol, to the south of
Moscow and located on major overland routes (Moscow-Kolomna-Riazan'-
Saratov and Moscow-Serpukhov-Tula-Voronezh respectively), derived substantial income from servicing itinerant merchants and other travelers.
However, the local population apparently did not participate directly
in the transit trade along these routes. The two towns had some stores

---

[16]TsGVIA, f. VUA, No. 18860, ll. 41-41 ob.; Sostoianie stolichnogo
goroda Moskvy, 1785 g., pp. 15-16, 29, 35, 37-38; Ziablovskii,
Zemleopisanie, Vol. 3, pp. 240-48; Shchekatov, Geograficheskii slovar',
Vol. 1, pp. 1018-20; Vol. 2, pp. 596-97; Vol. 3, pp. 570-72; Vol. 5,
pp. 429-31.

and a few industrial enterprises producing textiles, bricks and malt.[17]
Voskresensk showed some development as a center of craft industry, with
a population including blacksmiths, stonemasons, plasterers, carpenters,
stove-makers, potters and even icon-painters.[18] Nikitsk, on the other
hand, differed little from an ordinary village of the court _volost'_ to
which it had formerly belonged. This town reportedly had no stores or
weekly market, and the inhabitants gained their livelihood from agriculture, quarrying and "the most minimal trade."[19] In 1802, no longer
a district center, Nikitsk was returned to its former status as Kolychevo
village, because of "the poverty of its inhabitants" and its inability
to sustain the obligations of urban status.[20] Bogorodsk, apparently
the smallest town in Moscow _guberniia_, was located on the overland route
connecting Moscow with Vladimir, Nizhnii Novgorod and points farther
east but derived only modest benefits from this favorable situation--
some inhabitants made their living as innkeepers, while others engaged
in "petty" trade, principally in foodstuffs. The town had no weekly
market and although located in an area of highly developed rural textile
industry apparently did not serve as a marketing point for this

---

[17]_Sostoianie stolichnogo goroda Moskvy, 1785 g._, pp. 43, 45-46;
Ziablovskii, _Zemleopisanie_, Vol. 3, pp. 255-57; Shchekatov, _Geograficheskii
slovar'_, Vol. 1, pp. 573-74; Vol. 4, pp. 1193-94.

[18]_Sostoianie stolichnogo goroda Moskvy, 1785 g._, p. 40; Ziablovskii,
Zemleopisanie, Vol. 3, p. 262; Shchekatov, _Geograficheskii slovar'_,
Vol. 1, pp. 1153-55. The development of craft industry in this settle-
ment possibly reflects its relationship with the adjacent Voskresenskii
Monastery, to which it formerly belonged.

[19]_Sostoianie stolichnogo goroda Moskvy, 1785 g._, pp. 44-45;
Ziablovskii, _Zemleopisanie_, Vol. 3, pp. 261-62; Shchekatov, _Geograficheskii
slovar'_, Vol. 4, pp. 618-20.

[20]_PSZ_, Vol. 27, No. 20143.

production, nor did the local posad population play a role in distributing it to other markets.[21]

More significant as a commercial and industrial center was the "non-administrative" town of Sergiev Posad, with a population probably exceeding 2000 by the end of the century, a central marketplace (gostinnyi dvor) built of stone and long-established craft industries emphasizing the production of wooden articles, which were sold in Moscow and at other Russian markets.[22] This town held two week-long fairs attracting merchants from Moscow and other towns, who brought a wide assortment of textiles (including "German" and "Russian" woolen cloth, cotton and linen goods and such luxury fabrics as satins, brocades, taffeta and other silks), specialty foodstuffs (coffee, tea, sugar) and various small household and personal articles (shchepetil'nye melochi).[23]

This brief survey of the towns of Moscow guberniia indicates that these towns covered a broad range in terms of size and economic importance. The major towns of the province participated extensively in long-distance transit trade serving not only the Moscow market but those of Petersburg and other Baltic and northern ports. In addition, these towns generally

[21]Sostoianie stolichnogo goroda Moskvy, 1785 g., pp. 41-42; Ziablovskii, Zemleopisanie, Vol. 3, pp. 235-36; Shchekatov, Geograficheskii slovar', Vol. 1, p. 476.

[22]According to a 1796 report of the Moscow provincial treasury (TsGIA, f. 558, op. 2, d. 128, ll. 2 ob.-7), the posad population of Bogorodsk uezd, including Bogorodsk and Sergiev Posad, totaled somewhat over 1300 males. The Geographical Dictionary (Vol. 1, p. 476) credits Bogorodsk with a population of about 300 males, which suggests that Sergiev Posad had about 1000 males in its urban classes alone.

[23]Sostoianie stolichnogo goroda Moskvy, 1785 g., p. 42; Ziablovskii, Zemleopisanie, Vol. 3, p. 237.

were significant domestic markets, served by a hundred or more permanent stores as well as the usual periodic commercial gatherings, and displayed substantial industrial development. Some commercial or industrial pursuits were in evidence in most of the lesser towns as well. Nevertheless, the staggering size and economic breadth of Moscow in comparison to even the largest uezd towns is readily apparent. To what extent, therefore, did these towns attract the interest of trading peasants and other rural migrants in search of non-agricultural sources of income, when the metropolis beckoned from only a short distance?

Peasant encroachments on urban commerce are documented in the complaints about these activities submitted by urban communes to the Legislative Commission of 1767. Of the eight uezd towns in what was to become Moscow guberniia which sent deputies to the commission, all but one (Dmitrov) mentioned commercial activities of the peasantry as a threat to the well-being of the local posad population in their "instructions" to these deputies.[24] Many of the trading peasants who attracted the unfavorable attention of merchants in Serpukhov, Vereia and Mozhaisk were apparently rural middlemen (skupshchiki), who bought up the production of the surrounding countryside and brought it to town for sale, preventing direct contact between urban merchants and the primary producers and thus increasing the prices merchants had to pay to acquire these goods for resale as well as encroaching on their retail business. However, some peasants penetrated further into the internal

---

[24]Dmitrov submitted an "instruction" stating that the town had no complaints about present conditions. See Sbornik Imperatorskogo russkogo istoricheskogo obshchestva (hereafter Sb. IRIO), Vol. 93 (St. Petersburg, 1894), p. 91. Klin was not represented as an urban community in the Legislative Commission because it had no posad at the time and was populated chiefly by iamshchiki (servitors of the state postal system). The remaining uezd towns, of course, were created only in 1781.

commerce of these towns, renting stores and buying their stocks from wholesale merchants or setting up inns and restaurants in houses rented from local nobles or raznochintsy ("people of various ranks").[25] In Serpukhov peasants selling foodstuffs on the town market square dealt not only in goods hauled in from the countryside, as was authorized by long-standing legislation, but in goods acquired on the spot.[26] The large Kolomna market was claimed to be heavily infested with peasants and raznochintsy who sold "all kinds of goods" purchased by them for resale, although it is not clear to what extent these were goods of rural origin hauled in by the sellers themselves.[27] Even in tiny Zvenigorod peasants competed with local merchants in the sale of assorted consumer goods (melochnye tovary).[28] The merchants of Zvenigorod and Ruza also complained that peasants were buying up grain in these towns and carting it away for sale elsewhere.[29]

---

[25] Sb. IRIO, Vol. 93, pp. 193-201, 250-52, 383-85. The merchants of Vereia and Mozhaisk expressed their views on the subject in virtually identical language. Such similarities in the "instructions" of several different towns are common and indicate that in many cases these documents were partly a result of collaboration among several nearby towns. See A. A. Kizevetter, "Proiskhozhdenie gorodskikh deputatskikh nakazov v Ekaterininskuiu komissiiu 1767 g.," in Kizevetter, Istoricheskie ocherki (Moscow, 1912), pp. 209-41.

[26] In the mid-eighteenth century urban merchants were barred from making wholesale purchases of foodstuffs hauled in from the countryside until noon. (See PSZ, Vol. 14, No. 10191.) The aim of this regulation was to encourage direct contact between urban consumers and peasants bringing goods for sale, thus holding down urban food prices. However, some urban communes complained that trading peasants took advantage of the situation to buy up the available supplies for resale.

[27] Sb. IRIO, Vol. 93, pp. 138-39.

[28] Ibid., p. 487.

[29] Ibid., pp. 379, 488; see also above, n. 26.

The urban communities did not confine their objections to peasant activities within the towns themselves but also complained about rural commerce which bypassed the towns and competed with their business. In the late eighteenth century Moscow guberniia was studded with rural markets--villages conducting weekly markets, annual fairs or both. The descriptive surveys cited above, in a not necessarily complete listing, mention more than a dozen villages with weekly markets and a total of 70 rural fairs.[30] Significantly, the only districts completely lacking in rural markets were Moscow and Kolomna, which had the largest urban markets, and rural markets were most numerous in the northwestern districts (Ruza, Volokolamsk, Klin), where the urban markets were weakly developed--each of these latter districts boasted a dozen or more rural fairs. Rural markets could have a complementary relationship to the urban economy, serving as collection points for the agricultural and industrial production of the surrounding area and allowing urban merchants to sell consumer goods to the rural population. The many fairs in Ruza uezd, for example, were attended by merchants mainly from the district town, who brought various textiles and foodstuffs as well as such goods as beads, silver earrings, rings, copper, and tin crosses, mirrors and chandlery for sale to the peasants, while purchasing locally produced grain, hemp and hides.[31]

---

[30]Sostoianie stolichnogo goroda Moskvy, 1785 g., pp. 1-46; Ziablovskii, Zemleopisanie, Vol. 3, pp. 214-63.

[31]Sostoianie stolichnogo goroda Moskvy, 1785 g., pp. 35-36; Ziablovskii, Zemleopisanie, Vol. 3, pp. 247-48; Shchekatov, Geograficheskii slovar', Vol. 5, p. 431.

However, in such rural markets the merchants had even less protection against competition from trading peasants than they did elsewhere, and if their complaints are to be believed they were often forcibly barred from participation by the peasants, presumably in retaliation for their own efforts to exclude peasants from urban commerce. At rural markets local production often passed into the hands of trading peasants and sometimes of merchants from other towns for resale elsewhere, and these interlopers also brought in the consumer goods needed by the peasant population, obviating the functions of the local urban market and its merchants. Among the towns of Moscow guberniia, Serpukhov, Vereia, Ruza, Volokolamsk and Zvenigorod complained to the Legislative Commission about competition from rural markets.[32]

The peasantry of Moscow guberniia engaged in a variety of other commercial activities which paralleled those of the posad population without involving direct participation in local urban economies. Peasants from the districts of Bronnitsy, Nikitsk, Dmitrov, Zvenigorod, Ruza and Volokolamsk participated in the transit trade in grain, purchasing stocks in the black-soil provinces and bringing them northward for sale in Moscow, Petersburg, local urban and rural markets and various transshipment points (Gzhatsk, Tver', Torzhok).[33] Like many local merchants,

---

[32] Sb. IRIO, Vol. 93, pp. 201, 251, 376-77, 487-88; Vol. 107 (St. Petersburg, 1900), pp. 93-94.

[33] Sostoianie stolichnogo goroda Moskvy, 1785 g., p. 44; Ziablovskii, Zemleopisanie, Vol. 3, pp. 218, 240, 244, 246, 258; Tokmakov, Istoriko-statisticheskoe i arkheologicheskoe opisanie goroda Dmitrova, p. 58; Zhurnal ili zapiska zhizni i prikliuchenii Ivana Alekseevicha Tolchenova, pp. 38-39; S. I. Volkov, Krest'iane dvortsovykh vladenii Podmoskov'ia v seredine XVIII v. (Moscow, 1959), p. 67. Some peasants brought grain supplies from the black-soil provinces to their own districts, where what was not needed for local consumption was sold for shipment to Petersburg.

peasants of districts located upstream from Moscow on the Moscow River
or its tributaries (Moscow, Zvenigorod, Voskresensk, Ruza and Mozhaisk
uezdy) traded in lumber and firewood, shipping these supplies to the city
by water, while inhabitants of Dmitrov and Volokolamsk districts also
participated in this trade, sending their shipments overland "by the
winter route."[34] Peasants of Moscow, Bronnitsy, Podol, Dmitrov and
Klin uezdy, like merchants of the nearby towns, took advantage of the
proximity of major transit routes to make money through innkeeping and
the sale of provisions to travelers.[35]

Rural industrial production was another major source of income for
the peasantry of Moscow guberniia. Village textile industry was highly
developed in the eastern portion of the province. According to the
"economic notes" to the General Land Survey, in the 1760's 62 percent
of the peasant population of Moscow uezd (in its large pre-reform
dimensions, encompassing the greater part of seven post-1782 districts)
engaged in the spinning and weaving of wool or linen at least on a part-
time basis, while about 40 percent produced to some extent for the market.[36]

---

[34] Sostoianie stolichnogo goroda Moskvy, 1785 g., pp. 11, 27, 33-34,
36, 39, 41; Ziablovskii, Zemleopisanie, Vol. 3, pp. 246-50; Shchekatov,
Geograficheskii slovar', Vol. 2, p. 598; Vol. 4, p. 294; Tokmakov,
Istoriko-statisticheskoe i arkheologicheskoe opisanie goroda Dmitrova,
p. 58; K. V. Sivkov, "Podmoskovnaia votchina serediny XVIII v.,"
Moskovskii krai v ego proshlom, Vol. 1 (Moscow, 1928), p. 88.

[35] Sostoianie stolichnogo goroda Moskvy, 1785 g., pp. 11, 17;
Ziablovskii, Zemleopisanie, Vol. 3, pp. 241, 258; Shchekatov, Geograficheskii slovar', Vol. 5, p. 1195; V. A. Fedorov, Pomeshchich'i krest'-
iane tsentral'no-promyshlennogo raiona Rossii kontsa XVIII-pervoi poloviny
XIX v. (Moscow, 1974), p. 93.

[36] I. V. Meshalin, Tekstil'naia promyshlennost' krest'ian Moskovskoi
gubernii v XVIII i pervoi polovine XIX v. (Moscow-Leningrad, 1950),
pp. 26, 31.

The second half of the eighteenth century witnessed the rapid emergence
of a silk-weaving industry in the districts of Moscow and Bogorodsk,
where in addition to independent craftsmen many peasant-owned enterprises employing a few to several dozen hired workers appeared.[37]
Textile production was also widespread in the villages of Dmitrov uezd,
which in 1796-97 were reported to contain 17 peasant enterprises producing woolen cloth and 24 producing braid-work.[38] Peasants of Dmitrov
uezd also worked as blacksmiths, while those of Serpukhov uezd painted
icons and produced leather footwear and reeds for looms.[39] Other rural
crafts in eastern Moscow guberniia noted by contemporary descriptions
include carpentry (Moscow and Kolomna uezdy) and the production of
pottery (Moscow, Bronnitsy uezdy), ceramic tiles (Voskresensk uezd)
and rope (Kolomna uezd).[40] A wide variety of crafts was practiced in
several of the western districts (Ruza, Mozhaisk, Volokolamsk), where
peasants worked as tailors, cobblers, carpenters, wheelwrights, hoopers,
blacksmiths, stove-makers, and potters, and also produced wooden articles,
vehicles, brooms, rope and homespun woolen and linen cloth, selling

---

[37]Ibid., pp. 65-77, 125-44; MPIKP, Vol. 2, pp. 260-85, 448-53;
Sostoianie stolichnogo goroda Moskvy, 1785 g., p. 11, Shchekatov,
Geograficheskii slovar', Vol. 4, p. 390; Fedorov, pp. 85-88.

[38]MPIKP, Vol. 2, pp. 288-91, 451-53; Sostoianie stolichnogo goroda
Moskvy, 1785 g., p. 27; Tikhomirov, "Gorod Dmitrov," pp. 54-55.

[39]Sostoianie stolichnogo goroda Moskvy, 1785 g., p. 27; Ziablovskii,
Zemleopisanie, Vol. 3, p. 255; Shchekatov, Geograficheskii slovar',
Vol. 5, pp. 932-33.

[40]Sostoianie stolichnogo goroda Moskvy, 1785 g., pp. 11, 15, 41;
Ziablovskii, Zemleopisanie, Vol. 3, pp. 258, 261; Shchekatov, Geograficheskii slovar', Vol. 4, p. 390.

their goods in towns and at rural markets and fairs.[41]

Peasant craftsmen of Moscow guberniia sometimes migrated to towns to practice their trades or to learn them in the first place. According to the limited evidence available, such activities occurred "in Moscow and other towns" but "especially in Moscow."[42] Of the more than 1000 peasants of Moscow uezd (which at that time included most of the later Bogorodsk, Bronnitsy, Nikitsk, Podol and Voskresensk districts) and also of Kolomna, Dmitrov, Zvenigorod and Vereia uezdy who received government licences to operate looms between 1771 and 1774, virtually all worked either in Moscow and its suburban settlements or in villages and none in any of the uezd towns.[43] Moscow also received by far the greatest share of peasants who migrated to towns for wage labor in industrial enterprises, but district towns with well developed industries, particularly Kolomna and Serpukhov, also drew substantial numbers of workers from the countryside. The labor force of Kolomna's many "factories" consisted of peasants from the surrounding district, while the textile industries of Serpukhov employed 600 permanent workers drawn from both urban and rural populations and offered work on a putting-out basis to many other peasants, thus providing a major source

[41]Sostoianie stolichnogo goroda Moskvy, 1785 g., pp. 15, 41, 44; Ziablovskii, Zemleopisanie, Vol. 3, pp. 255, 258; Shchekatov, Geograficheskii slovar', Vol. 4, p. 619, 1195; Vol. 5, p. 932.

[42]Sostoianie stolichnogo goroda Moskvy, 1785 g., p. 36; Ziablovskii, Zemleopisanie, Vol. 3, pp. 248-50; Shchekatov, Geograficheskii slovar', Vol. 4, pp. 294, 619; Vol. 5, p. 434; Tokmakov, Istoriko-statisticheskoe i arkheologicheskoe opisanie goroda Dmitrova, p. 58. The unspecified "other towns" were of course not necessarily confined to Moscow guberniia and might include Petersburg and other major urban centers elsewhere in the empire.

[43]MPIKP, Vol. 2, pp. 144-237.

of income for the population of the district.[44]

The use of peasant labor in Russian towns was not confined to industrial enterprises. In Moscow, as we have already learned, peasants frequently worked for urban merchants as stewards (_prikazchiki_), storekeepers (_sidel'tsy_) and other commercial employees. The use of peasants in such capacities is mentioned by the 1767 "instructions" of Serpukhov, Ruza and Vereia, suggesting that these towns were familiar with the practice.[45] These "instructions" also make reference to the employment of peasants as household servants and unskilled laborers and to perform guard duty and other service obligations of the _posad_ population.[46] There is no reason to believe that such employment was confined to these particular towns. Russian merchants of the eighteenth century, particularly those engaged in long-distance trade, had great need for hired subordinates in conducting their operations, and other evidence indicates that peasants were frequently hired for such duties.[47] However, the

---

[44]_Sostoianie stolichnogo goroda Moskvy, 1785 g._, pp. 13-14, 19-20; Ziablovskii, _Zemleopisanie_, Vol. 3, p. 254; Shchekatov, _Geograficheskii slovar'_, Vol. 5, p. 928.

[45]_Sb. IRIO_, Vol. 93, pp. 193-201, 252, 377.

[46]The "instructions" of Serpukhov and Ruza (_Sb. IRIO_, Vol. 93, pp. 200, 378) declared the hired peasant workers to be unreliable, unwilling to remain on the job for an extended period and frequently prone to thievery. These claims were made in the context of an argument for allowing merchants to purchase serfs.

[47]As has already been mentioned, many towns elsewhere in the empire referred to the employment of peasants in commercial capacities in their "instructions," usually calling for prohibition of the practice on the ground that these jobs should be reserved for the poorer members of the _posad_ population and that such employment was sometimes a pretext under which peasants engaged in trade on their own account, in contravention of the law. Examples of employment of peasants by urban merchants, relating to several towns of Iaroslavl' guberniia and to Nizhnii Novgorod, are cited later in this chapter and also in Chapter VI.

fragmentary references at hand do not allow us to judge the importance of such employment as a factor in peasant immigration.

Finally, another major occupation which brought peasants into contact with urban markets was overland transport (izvoz), which was virtually monopolized by the peasantry and was practiced by peasants throughout Moscow guberniia.[48] The peasant teamsters were normally in transit between various urban and other markets with their cargoes, and their presence in particular towns was therefore sporadic, except in the case of huge market centers such as Moscow and Petersburg, where much work was available shifting goods about within the spacious confines of the city. Among those working as teamsters "in Moscow" were peasants of Bronnitsy, Nikitsk, Voskresensk, Vereia, Ruza and Mozhaisk districts.[49]

The foregoing review of commercial and industrial activity of the peasantry in Moscow guberniia, although admittedly based on limited evidence, discloses few signs of a large influx of peasant settlers into the uezd towns comparable to that experienced by Moscow itself. Some peasants lived in these towns and operated stores or otherwise participated in local commerce, engaged in craft industry or worked in various capacities for urban merchants, craftsmen or factories. For those seeking urban employment or involvement in urban commerce, however, Moscow clearly had much more to offer. In addition, many non-agricultural

---

[48]In the available surveys, only the descriptions of Bogorodsk and Volokolamsk uezdy fail to mention izvoz as an occupation of the rural population.

[49]Ziablovskii, Zemleopisanie, Vol. 3, pp. 248-50, 252, 258; Shchekatov, Geograficheskii slovar', Vol. 4, p. 294; Sivkov, "Podmoskovnaia votchina," p. 88.

pursuits of the peasantry involved only an intermittent presence in the urban milieu (such as the sale of goods hauled in from the countryside and izvoz) or paralleled the activities of the urban population without impinging directly on local urban economies (transit trade, trade in rural markets, rural industry).

The available data on enlistment in the urban classes in the towns of Moscow guberniia also reflect a generally low level of peasant immigration. These data cover the period between the First Revision and the end of the eighteenth century, and while by no means as complete as the figures assembled for Moscow itself, they do permit a reliable assessment of the peasant influx. The 1767 "Report on the Number of Souls" already cited extensively in previous chapters, incorporating data of the Second and Third Revisions (1744-47, 1762-65), gives the number of "mercantile peasants" registered in each town according to the provisions established by Peter I, with retention of peasant status and obligations. Of the towns later included in the post-reform Moscow guberniia, only Vereia included any such registrants in its population at the time of the Second Revision, while in the subsequent census some registrants were recorded in Kolomna and Serpukhov as well.[50] The numbers of registrants--reflecting, it should be recalled, the cumulative total of all mercantile peasants remaining in the posad at the indicated time--were insignificant. Vereia had 9 mercantile peasants according to the earlier census, while the later one credited Kolomna with 34 registrants, Vereia with 17 and Serpukhov with 13. In towns with a total posad population of 1500 to 2100 male souls, these numbers of registrants

[50]Gosudarstvennaia publichnaia biblioteka imeni Saltykova-Shchedrina, Leningrad, Rukopisnyi otdel (hereafter GPB RO), Ermitazhnoe sobranie, No. 242, ll. 1-3.

represented an increment of only 0.6 to 1.8 percent. Not reported by the source is the number of freed serfs who enlisted in these and other towns of Moscow guberniia during the indicated period, but such registrants are unlikely to have been substantially more numerous than the mercantile peasants.

Data on enlistment in the towns of Moscow guberniia up to the time of the Fourth Revision (1782) are provided by the 1787 report of the Moscow provincial treasury (kazennaia palata) already cited in connection with the contemporary influx into the Moscow posad.[51] This document is limited in its coverage, dealing only with crown peasants originating within the province, but since it is unlikely that many peasants came from more distant areas of the country to settle in these towns, the data may be considered roughly complete as regards registrants from the crown peasantry. According to the 1787 document the uezd towns of Moscow guberniia received 275 registrants from the crown peasantry of their province, while 1202 such peasants joined the Moscow posad and 125 enlisted in the urban classes of towns elsewhere in Russia.[52] Only 2 to 3 percent of the posad population of Moscow guberniia (excluding Moscow) consisted of such registrants in 1782.[53]

[51]TsGADA, f. 248 (1 departament Senata), kn. 4109, ll. 213-219 ob.

[52]Of those enlisting in towns outside Moscow guberniia 60 enlisted in Petersburg and small numbers in Sofiisk, Narva, Tver', Vyshnii Volochok, Korcheva, Gzhatsk, Pereslavl'-Zalesskii, Tarusa, Kashira, Epifan', Orel, Kursk, Tambov, Kozlov, Saratov, Kremenchug and Iakutsk. These registrants included 27 court peasants and 98 economic peasants.

[53]V. M. Kabuzan, Izmeneniia v razmeshchenii naseleniia Rossii v XVIII-pervoi polovine XIX v. (Moscow, 1971), p. 98.

The registrants, emanating predominantly (90 percent) from the economic peasantry, were distributed among ten of the fourteen uezd towns, but more than 80 percent of the total was concentrated in only two towns. (See Table 19.) The Kolomna posad absorbed more than 100 crown peasants, who comprised about 5 percent of its population. A slightly larger number of registrants was credited to the new town of Bogorodsk. However, it was the practice of the provincial treasury to cite a single figure for the posad population in each district, making no distinction between the uezd town and any "non-administrative" urban settlements located within the district boundaries. The information given for Bogorodsk thus applies to Sergiev Posad as well, and it is likely that the latter, larger and far more developed economically than the tiny district town, received most or all of the reported registrants.[54] The peasant registrants were predominantly natives of the district surrounding the town where they settled. Bogorodsk and/or Sergiev Posad attracted some registrants from the districts of Moscow, Bronnitsy, Serpukhov, Zvenigorod, Vereia and Klin, but two-thirds of the reported influx originated in Bogorodsk uezd. Registrants in Kolomna came mostly from Kolomna uezd, with a few from the neighboring districts of Bronnitsy and Serpukhov. The remaining towns drew their few registrants from the surrounding district exclusively, except in one case where a neighboring district was involved.

For the period between the Fourth and Fifth Revisions (1782-1795), data can be obtained from reports of the Moscow provincial treasury on the numbers of taxpayers in each district of the province in the years

---

[54]Both Bogorodsk and Sergiev Posad, of course, were given urban status only in 1781-82, and the indicated enlistment thus occurred entirely at the end of the period under consideration.

Table 19: Enlistment of Crown Peasants of Moscow Guberniia in Towns of Moscow Guberniia (without Moscow), 1764-1782 (Number of Males)

Towns	Econ. peasants	Court peasants	Other groups	Total peasants
Kolomna	102	2	-	104
Serpukhov	6	-	-	6
Vereia	1	-	-	1
Mozhaisk	-	-	3	3
Dmitrov	12	-	-	12
Ruza	1	-	-	1
Volokolamsk	10	-	4	14
Zvenigorod	11	-	-	11
Bronnitsy	-	4	-	4
Bogorodsk/S. Posad	111	8	-	119
Total[a]	254	14	7	275

Source: TsGADA, f. 248, kn. 4109, ll. 213-219 ob.

[a]No enlistment reported in the remaining towns (Klin, Podol, Voskresensk, Nikitsk).

1794 and 1795.[55] These documents give the number of male souls in the kupechestvo and meshchanstvo of each town, specifying any changes which occurred since the previous year due to enlistment of newcomers or the departure of local citizens to other towns or other population categories. The reports thus give information on registrants from the crown peasantry of Moscow guberniia and of other provinces, from the ranks of freed serfs and from other population groups who were added to the roster of taxpayers in 1794 and 1795. In addition, they state the cumulative total of previous registrants from the crown peasantry of Moscow guberniia since the Fourth Revision.[56] The data provided on registrants from the latter source are thus considerably more inclusive than those on the remaining groups.[57]

---

[55]TsGIA, f. 558, op. 2, d. 126, ll. 518 ob.-527, 571 ob.-581.

[56]G. L. Vartanov, citing data from this source, construes the figures on crown peasants of Moscow guberniia as applying only to the years 1794 and 1795. This interpretation appears unjustified and moreover is directly contradicted by another document of the provincial treasury, listing a total number of registrants for the entire period between the two censuses which is nearly identical to that provided by the 1794 and 1795 reports. TsGIA, f. 558, op. 2, d. 128, l. 32; Vartanov, "Kupechestvo i torguiushchee krest'ianstvo tsentral'noi chasti Evropeiskoi Rossii vo vtoroi polovine XVIII v.," Uchenye zapiski Leningradskogo gosudarstvennogo pedagogicheskogo instituta im. A. I. Gertsena, Vol. 229 (1962), pp. 192-93.

[57]Although encompassing enlistment by the local crown peasantry since the Fourth Revision, the reports apparently stop short of the enlistment clustered around the time of the new census of 1795. These documents, it is true, refer to increments to the posad population which took place "in the course of" 1794 and 1795, but these dates represent the time when the registrants appeared in the records of the treasury rather than in the posad itself, a significant difference given the legendary inertia of administrative processes in eighteenth-century Russia. The provincial treasury credited Moscow with 1042 registrants from all peasant categories in the years 1794 and 1795, while the analysis of census depositions carried out in the preceding chapter demonstrates that more than twice that number actually enlisted in those years. However, since in the data on the uezd towns there are no signs of a strong surge in enlistment toward the end of the period, such as occurred in Moscow, the absence of late results for these towns may be unimportant.

According to these reports, a total of 353 crown peasants from Moscow guberniia enlisted in the towns of the province (excluding Moscow) from the Fourth Revision through 1795. (See Table 20.) Nearly all of these registrants came from the economic peasantry and all entered the kupechestvo--no enlistment of crown peasants in the meshchanstvo of these towns was reported, although the Moscow meshchanstvo was credited with more than 200 such registrants by the same documents. Nearly three-quarters of the registrants were absorbed by the urban settlements of Bogorodsk uezd (Bogorodsk and/or Sergiev Posad), where the newcomers comprised about half the kupechestvo and one-fifth of the total urban classes. The remaining registrants were distributed in small numbers among six other towns. In none of these did the posad population as a whole gain significantly in size as a result of enlistment by crown peasants. However, 8-12 percent of the small kupechestvo in Dmitrov, Zvenigorod and Voskresensk consisted of such registrants. Once again Bogorodsk/Sergiev Posad demonstrated an ability to attract registrants from many different districts of the province, although the largest numbers continued to come from Bogorodsk uezd.[58] Registrants in the other towns came from the surrounding district and in a few cases from a neighboring district. There are no signs of a marked surge in enlistment toward the end of the period, such as occurred in Moscow. Almost all the reported registrants were added to the posad before 1795, with only a few newcomers, even in Bogorodsk/Sergiev Posad, credited to that year.

---

[58]Bogorodsk/Sergiev Posad drew registrants from the districts of Moscow guberniia as follows: Bogorodsk 127, Vereia 48, Bronnitsy 22, Zvenigorod 16, Moscow 14, Voskresensk 14, Klin 7, Serpukhov 4, Kolomna 2, unspecified 6.

Table 20: Enlistment of Peasants in Towns of Moscow <u>Guberniia</u>
(without Moscow), 1782-1795 (Number of Males)

Peasant registrants:

Towns	Total in urban classes (1795)	econ. peasants of Moscow guberniia (1782-95)	court peasants of Moscow guberniia (1782-95)	econ. peasants of other gubernii (1794-5)	freed serfs (1794-5)
Kolomna					
kupechestvo	1099	28	-	-	16
meshchanstvo	870	-	-	-	2
total	1969	28	-	-	18
Serpukhov					
kupechestvo	1229	9	-	-	10
meshchanstvo	1052	-	-	-	4
total	2281	9	-	-	14
Dmitrov					
kupechestvo	273	24	-	-	3
meshchanstvo	1131	-	-	-	-
total	1404	24	-	-	3
Zvenigorod					
kupechestvo	132	11	-	-	-
meshchanstvo	173	-	-	-	-
total	305	11	-	-	-
Bronnitsy					
kupechestvo	455	4	-	-	-
meshchanstvo	143	-	-	-	-
total	598	4	-	-	-
Voskresensk					
kupechestvo	139	17	-	-	-
meshchanstvo	142	-	-	-	-
total	281	17	-	-	-
Bogorodsk/S. Posad					
kupechestvo	539	247	13	4	-
meshchanstvo	680	-	-	-	4
total	1219	247	13	4	4

Table 20 (cont.)

Towns	Total in urban classes (1795)	econ. peasants of Moscow guberniia (1782-95)	court peasants of Moscow guberniia (1782-95)	econ. peasants of other gubernii (1794-5)	freed serfs (1794-5)
		Peasant registrants:			
Other[a]					
kupechestvo	2111	-	-	-	-
meshchanstvo	2575	-	-	-	-
total	4686	-	-	-	-
Total					
kupechestvo	5977	340	13	4	29
meshchanstvo	6766	-	-	-	10
total	12743	340	13	4	39

Source: TsGIA, f. 558, op. 2, d. 126, 11. 518 ob.-527, 571 ob.-581.

[a]No peasant enlistment reported in these towns (Vereia, Mozhaisk, Ruza, Volokolamsk, Klin, Podol, Nikitsk).

As reported by the provincial treasury, enlistment from groups other than the local crown peasantry in 1794 and 1795 was also limited. Four economic peasants from outside Moscow guberniia joined the kupechestvo of Bogorodsk/Sergiev Posad, while 39 former serfs entered the kupechestvo and meshchanstvo of various towns, chiefly Kolomna and Serpukhov. Registrants from non-peasant categories consisted of 4 posad members from other towns and 12 "churchmen" (tserkovniki). On the other hand, the towns of Moscow guberniia lost 129 of their own citizens through emigration, principally to Moscow, during these same years. Slightly less than half the emigrants came from Serpukhov and the remainder from nine other towns.[59]

Information on the continuation of enlistment in the aftermath of the Fifth Revision can be obtained from a later series of reports of the Moscow provincial treasury on the number of "souls" in each tax category, covering the years 1797-1802.[60] The reports indicate the number of registrants from all peasant categories and from other population groups added to the treasury's tax rolls during the period specified. According to these documents, only 88 male souls from all categories of the peasantry were absorbed into the urban classes of Moscow guberniia (without Moscow) in these years. (See Table 21.) Even Bogorodsk/

---

[59]The following numbers of emigrants were reported: Serpukhov 59, Kolomna 14, Ruza 11, Mozhaisk 10, Zvenigorod 8, Dmitrov 7, Ruza 7, Volokolamsk 6, Bogorodsk/Sergiev Posad 5, Voskresensk 2.

[60]TsGIA, f. 558, op. 2, d. 128, ll. 56 ob.-63, 98 ob.-104; d. 129, ll. 2 ob.-5, 43 ob.-44, 99-102, 273 ob.-278, 287 ob.-288, 347 ob.-353, 382 ob.-388. These documents were cited earlier in connection with enlistment in Moscow.

Table 21: Enlistment of Peasants in Towns of Moscow Guberniia
(without Moscow), 1797-1802 (Number of Males)

Towns	Total in urban classes (1802)	Peasant registrants: econ. peasants	freed serfs	total peasants
Kolomna				
kupechestvo	935	12	3	15
meshchanstvo	1063	3	5	8
total	1998	15	8	23
Vereia				
kupechestvo	1293	1	2	3
meshchanstvo	820	-	-	-
total	2113	1	2	3
Mozhaisk				
kupechestvo	190	-	-	-
meshchanstvo	509	-	9	9
total	699	-	9	9
Dmitrov				
kupechestvo	359	-	-	-
meshchanstvo	1034	-	9	9
total	1393	-	9	9
Ruza				
kupechestvo	114	-	-	-
meshchanstvo	578	-	1	1
total	692	-	1	1
Volokolamsk				
kupechestvo	38	-	-	-
meshchanstvo	275	-	6	6
total	313	-	6	6
Klin				
kupechestvo	101	1	-	1
meshchanstvo	261	-	-	-
total	362	1	-	1
Voskresensk				
kupechestvo	156	-	1	1
meshchanstvo	140	-	-	-
total	296	-	1	1

Table 21 (cont.)

Towns	Total in urban classes (1802)	Peasant registrants: econ. peasants	freed serfs	total peasants
Bogorodsk/S. Posad				
kupechestvo	513	9	-	9
meshchanstvo	751	4	22	26
total	1264	13	22	35
Other[a]				
kupechestvo	1778	-	-	-
meshchanstvo	1853	-	-	-
total	3631	-	-	-
Total				
kupechestvo	5477	23	6	29
meshchanstvo	7284	7	52	59
total	12761	30	58	88

Source: TsGIA, f. 558, op. 2, d. 128, ll. 56 ob.-63, 98 ob.-104; d. 129, ll. 2 ob.-5, 43 ob.-44, 99-102, 273 ob.-278, 287 ob.-288, 347 ob.-353, 382 ob.-388.

[a]No enlistment reported in these towns (Serpukhov, Zvenigorod, Bronnitsy, Podol, Nikitsk).

Sergiev Posad now failed to attract a substantial influx.[61] The registrants included 30 economic peasants, who enlisted mostly in the
kupechestvo of Kolomna and Sergiev Posad, and 58 former serfs, who enlisted mainly in the meshchanstvo and in various towns. Registrants
from non-peasant categories totaled 69 and included citizens of other
towns, "churchmen," returned runaways (iavivshiesia iz begov), a few
foreigners, and members of various other groups. These migrants settled
principally in Kolomna and Serpukhov and to a lesser extent in Vereia,
Bogorodsk/Sergiev Posad and Mozhaisk. The total influx from all sources
thus amounted to 157 souls, while in the half-dozen years under consideration these towns lost 338 posad members through emigration, in the
overwhelming majority of cases to Moscow. The heaviest emigration was
from Bogorodsk and/or Sergiev Posad (102 souls) and Nikitsk (68 souls),
while Kolomna, Serpukhov and Ruza lost 24-36 citizens apiece and the
remaining towns lost smaller numbers.[62]

The available data demonstrate adequately that the posad population
in the district towns of Moscow guberniia did not receive substantial
numbers of recruits from the peasantry during most of the eighteenth
century. The "non-administrative" town of Sergiev Posad apparently absorbed several hundred registrants around the time of the Fourth Revision

---

[61]As was explained at the beginning of this chapter, from 1796
through 1802 Bogorodsk lost its status as a district town and therefore
ceased to be the administrative center for the district containing
Sergiev Posad. Nevertheless, the reports of the Moscow provincial
treasury continued to treat the two towns as a unit, giving a single
population figure for Bogorodsk "with Sergiev Posad." In this instance,
however, thirteen registrants from the economic peasantry were explicit-
ly credited to Sergiev Posad in an explanatory note.

[62]In 1802 most of the small Nikitsk kupechestvo transferred to
Moscow in connection with the liquidation of the posad in this settlement and its return to village status.

and in the immediately following years. However, the failure of this influx to sustain itself in the mid-1790's and the years following the Fifth Revision suggests that the results should be interpreted as an exceptional burst of enlistment following the creation of the town, in which native inhabitants and peasants from other villages who had earlier migrated to this long-established commercial and craft settlement were absorbed into the newly instituted posad. Kolomna, the largest of the district towns, attracted a substantial number of registrants in the period between the Third and Fourth Revisions, but enlistment fell off in subsequent years. The remaining towns, even such important and prosperous ones as Serpukhov and Vereia, received only occasional registrants. Data for the 1790's indicate that enlistment by members of other population categories also did not make a significant contribution to the posad population in these towns. When the outflow of population due to resettlement in Moscow and occasionally in other places is taken into account, it becomes evident that the uezd towns often experienced a net loss from such population transfers.

Despite limited and even negative immigration, the posad population of the uezd towns not only succeeded in maintaining itself but tended to creep upwards. Table 22 offers data on the growth of the posad in eight uezd towns of Moscow guberniia between the Second and Fifth Revisions (1744-1795).[63] In Kolomna, the town receiving the most registrants from the peasantry and other sources, the population remained stationary. Otherwise, the posad increased by varying degrees in the larger towns of the province--most notably in Vereia--and contracted

---

[63]Not included are the towns which were created in 1781-82 and also the older town of Klin, which had no posad at the time of the Second Revision.

Table 22: Growth of Urban Classes in Towns of Moscow <u>Guberniia</u>, 1744-1795 (Number of Males)

Towns	2nd Revision (1744)	5th Revision (1795)	% growth
Kolomna	1950	1950	0
Serpukhov	1900	2250	18
Vereia	1500	2100	40
Dmitrov	1200	1400	17
Mozhaisk	500	650	30
Ruza	650	700	8
Volokolamsk	400	300	-25
Zvenigorod	350	300	-14
Total	8450	9650	14

Sources: GPB RO, Ermitazhnoe sobranie, No. 242 ("Vedomost' o chisle dush po gorodam"), ll. 1-3; TsGIA, f. 558, op. 2, d. 128, ll. 2 ob.-7; A. A. Kizevetter, <u>Posadskaia</u> <u>obshchina</u> <u>v</u> <u>Rossii</u> <u>XVIII</u> <u>stoletiia</u> (Moscow, 1903), pp. 102-11.

somewhat in the smaller ones (Volokolamsk, Zvenigorod). These differences in growth might be accounted for by varying balances of immigration and emigration and variations in the rate of natural increase,
relating to differing economic and health conditions in individual
towns. It is clear, however, that these smaller towns did not experience
the disastrous health conditions which decimated the Moscow posad and
were usually able to sustain a neutral or somewhat positive rate of
natural growth.

Iaroslavl' Guberniia

Iaroslavl' guberniia as instituted in 1777 consisted of twelve districts, of which five (Iaroslavl', Uglich, Rostov, Romanov, Liubim)
were headed by towns which had earlier served as administrative centers
of districts or provinces (provintsii) and three (Rybinsk, Borisoglebsk,
Mologa) by former "non-administrative" urban settlements. The remaining
four district towns were converted villages. The settlement now known
as Poshekhon'e, although already the administrative center of an uezd
of the same name, had earlier been classified as an "economic" village
and had been without a posad population. The towns of Myshkin and
Petrovsk were also former economic villages, while Danilov had been a
court village.[64] Norskaia Sloboda, a small "non-administrative" town
in Iaroslavl' uezd, continued in its former status. Eight of these

---

[64]PSZ, Vol. 20, No. 14635; Iu. R. Klokman, Sotsial'no-ekonomicheskaia
istoriia russkogo goroda, vtoraia polovina XVIII v. (Moscow, 1967), pp.
156-60; K. German, Statisticheskoe opisanie Iaroslavskoi gubernii (St.
Petersburg, 1808), pp. 13-17. In 1796 the districts of Borisoglebsk
and Petrovsk were abolished and absorbed into the surrounding districts,
while their towns were relegated to "non-administrative" status. Den,
Naselenie Rossii, Vol. 1, pp. 375-76.

thirteen towns were located on the Volga, which pursued a meandering

course through the province. Proceeding upstream from Iaroslavl', the

traveler would encounter Norskaia Sloboda, Romanov and Borisoglebsk

(facing each other from opposite sides of the river), Rybinsk, Mologa,

Myshkin and Uglich in that order. Two towns, Rostov and Petrovsk,

were located south of the river, in a sector of the province bordering

on Vladimir guberniia. The remaining three towns (Liubim, Danilov,

Poshekhon'e) were beyond the Volga to the north, in an area adjacent

to Kostroma, Vologda and northern Tver' gubernii.

For information on the size and economic development of these

towns, we turn once again to the "topographical descriptions" and other

contemporary descriptive surveys.[65] The quantifiable demographic and

economic characteristics revealed by these sources are summarized in

[65]TsGVIA, f. VUA, No. 19176 ("Topograficheskoe opisanie Iaroslavskoi
gubernii," 1783); Topograficheskoe opisanie Iaroslavskogo namestnichestva,
sochinennoe v Iaroslavle v 1794 g. (Iaroslavl', 1794); GPB RO, Ermitazhnoe
sobranie, No. 288 ("Topograficheskoe opisanie Iaroslavskoi gubernii,
sochinennoe v Iaroslavle v 1798 g."); GPB RO, F IV, No. 640 ("Topograficheskoe opisanie Iaroslavskoi gubernii," 1803); "Svedeniia o Iaroslavskom
namestnichestve," Uedinennyi poshekhonets (ezhemesiachnyi zhurnal)
(Iaroslavl', 1786).

The entries on Iaroslavl' guberniia in Shchekatov's Geographical
Dictionary and in the "Svedeniia o Iaroslavskom namestnichestve" (serial-
ized in a short-lived local monthly magazine) are nearly identical in
text and figures to the 1783 topograficheskoe opisanie. (See L. V. Milov,
"K istorii sozdaniia 'Geograficheskogo slovaria' Afanasiia Shchekatova,"
Arkheograficheskii ezhegodnik za 1968 g. /Moscow, 1970/, p. 174.) The
later versions of the topograficheskoe opisanie show some variations in
descriptive details as well as updated figures. Also drawing heavily
on the topograficheskoe opisanie, as well as on other documents and publications, are Karl German's Statisticheskoe opisanie Iaroslavskoi
gubernii and Ziablovskii's Zemleopisanie Rossiiskoi Imperii (Vol. 4, pp.
1-35). The 1776 "Opisanie Moskovskoi gubernii gorodov" (TsGVIA, f. VUA,
No. 18860) remains relevant, since it embraces Moscow guberniia in its
immense pre-reform dimensions, encompassing all of the later Iaroslavl'
guberniia. Additional descriptive materials on Iaroslavl' guberniia
include Opisanie goroda Rybinska (Rybinsk, 1910), taken from a manuscript
composed in 1811; Topograficheskie izvestiia, sluzhashchie dlia polnogo
geograficheskogo opisaniia Rossiiskoi Imperii, Vol. 1, Part 4 (St.
Petersburg, 1774); "Primechaniia, sluzhashchie k poznaniiu domostroitel'-

Table 23. In addition to the provincial capital, with a total "permanent" population of more than 20,000, Iaroslavl' guberniia at the end of the eighteenth century included two fairly large towns with populations of between 5000 and 6000 persons of both sexes, five towns with populations of 2000 to 3000, three with populations of 1000 to 2000 and two with less than 1000.[66] Taken together, these towns had a population of more than 51,000, or 6-7 percent of the total population of the province.[67] Two-thirds of this urban population consisted of members of the urban classes, while other elements included "ascribed" factory workers (mostly in Iaroslavl'), nobles, officials, clergy, house serfs attached to urban households, retired soldiers, iamshchiki and other raznochintsy.[68]

---

stva i sostoianiia mest v verkh po reke Volge, ot eia vershiny do Nizhnego Novagoroda /sic/ lezhashchikh," Akademicheskie izvestiia na 1780 g., Vol. 5, pp. 284-311. Iu. R. Klokman (Sotsial'no-ekonomicheskaia istoriia, pp. 222-28) cites useful data from the materials of the General Land Survey, particularly on the size of the population in the uezd towns of this province. Further information on the size of the posad population is provided by reports of the Iaroslavl' provincial treasury, particularly one giving the results of the Fifth Revision (TsGIA, f. 558, op. 2, d. 317, ll. 37 ob.-38).

[66]The available sources do not provide detailed information on the population of Norskaia Sloboda, although in two descriptions it is credited with a posad population of 217-243 males, apparently according to the Third Revision. (TsGVIA, f. VUA, No. 18860, l. 149; "Svedeniia o Iaroslavskom namestnichestve," p. 189.) The total population thus was certainly below 1000.

[67]According to the 1798 topograficheskoe opisanie, the total population of Iaroslavl' guberniia was about 796,000 persons, including 381,000 males. (GPB RO, Ermitazhnoe sobranie, No. 288, l. 12.) The latter figure accords closely with Kabuzan's data from the Fifth Revision (384,000). (Kabuzan, Izmeneniia v razmeshchenii naseleniia Rossii, p. 107.)

[68]For reasons already explained (see above, n. 6), peasant migrants are not included among the enumerated population groups. Whether these migrants constituted a substantial addition to the urban population, as they apparently did not in the uezd towns of Moscow guberniia, remains to be determined.

Table 23: Demographic and Economic Characteristics of Towns of

Iaroslavl' Guberniia, Late Eighteenth Century

Towns	Total pop. (both sexes)	Urban classes (both sexes)	% in urban classes	Kupech- estvo (both sexes)	% urban classes in kupech- estvo
Iaroslavl'	22000	11600	53	2400	21
Uglich	6000	4600	77	2300	50
Rostov	5400	3900	72	1800	46
Rybinsk	2700	1900	70	700	37
Mologa	2700	2400	89	150	6
Romanov	2400	1900	79	600	32
Poshekhon'e	2200	1800	82	400	22
Borisoglebsk	2100	1900	90	300	16
Danilov	1900	1200	63	400	33
Liubim	1600	1200	75	200	17
Petrovsk	1200	1000	83	700	70
Myshkin	900	600	67	400	67
Total	51,100	34,000	67	10350	30

Table 23 (cont.)

Towns	No. of stores	Ratio to pop.	Weekly markets	Fairs	Industrial enterprises
Iaroslavl'	700-800	1:31-1:28	3	3	92
Uglich	300	1:20	3	2/2-3 d.	21
Rostov	400-600	1:14-1:9	3	1/3 w.	17
Rybinsk	220	1:12	1	2/1 d.	11
Mologa	35	1:77	?	2/3 d.	2
Romanov	150	1:16	1	2/2 d.	5
Poshekhon'e	80	1:28	?	2/1 w.	4
Borisoglebsk	100	1:21	1	2/1 d.	-
Danilov	120	1:16	1	-	-
Liubim	100	1:16	?	2/1 d.	2
Petrovsk	15	1:80	?	2/1 d.	-
Myshkin	60	1:15	?	1/2 d.	-

Sources: See text (Ch. V, n. 65).

Sharp variations are to be noted among these towns in the proportion of the posad population belonging to the kupechestvo. In the mid-1790's, two-thirds of the posad in the small towns of Petrovsk and Myshkin (formerly villages of economic peasants) was included in the merchant guilds, as was about half the posad in Uglich and Rostov. As a result, the kupechestvo in each of the latter two towns was nearly as large as that of Iaroslavl', despite the much greater overall size of the provincial capital. At the opposite extreme, only a minute proportion of the sizeable Mologa posad consisted of persons with merchant status.

In the seventeenth century, Iaroslavl' had been the largest city in Russia after Moscow. It was still one of the country's major urban centers in the time of Catherine II, although it had been surpassed by rapidly growing cities in some other parts of the country and was now rivaled in size by several other towns in Central Russia. The economic importance of Iaroslavl' rested to a large extent on its role as an industrial center. The city had long been known for its leather industry, which continued to be an important sector of the local economy in the late eighteenth century.[69] This traditional Iaroslavl' industry, however, was in the process of contraction due to competition resulting from the growth of leather production in other towns.[70] Moreover, it had been greatly surpassed in size by the newer large-scale textile

---

[69]On the leather industry of Iaroslavl' in the seventeenth and early eighteenth centuries, see N. V. Ustiugov, "Ekonomicheskoe razvitie russkogo gosudarstva v XVII v. i problema skladyvaniia vserossiiskogo rynka," in Ustiugov, Nauchnoe nasledie (Moscow, 1974), pp. 27, 37; G.L. Vartanov, Kupechestvo gorodov Moskovskoi gubernii vo vtoroi polovine XVIII v. (kandidat dissertation, Leningrad, Gosudarstvennyi pedagogicheskii institut im. A. I. Gertsena, 1966), pp. 289-94.

[70]TsGVIA, f. VUA, No. 18860, l. 146.

industry. The city was the site of two large linen manufactories employing 4000-5000 workers and annually producing goods valued at 300,000 to 500,000 rubles, while four silk-weaving enterprises had a production worth a total of 90,000 rubles.[71] Other "factories" in Iaroslavl' included several additional enterprises in the textile sector (involved in the dyeing of cloth and the production of braid-work and tinsel-cloth) and 50-70 enterprises producing felt and felt hats, paper, glue, vitriol, starch, copper and tin wares, pottery, ceramic tiles, bricks, candles and food products.

Craft industry also was a major factor in the economy of Iaroslavl'. In the mid-1760's the municipal authorities reported to the Commerce Commission the presence of 1100 craftsmen (constituting 22 percent of the male posad population), who were involved in 50 different craft specialties, and other sources also attest to the large numbers of craft professions and individual craftsmen functioning in Iaroslavl'.[72] Among these artisans coppersmiths and tinsmiths were especially important --their products were sent to other towns for sale in "substantial quantities."[73] Also well represented were other metallurgical trades

---

[71]"Svedeniia o Iaroslavskom namestnichestve," pp. 178-81; Topograficheskoe opisanie Iaroslavskogo namestnichestva (1794), pp. 19-21; Ziablovskii, Zemleopisanie, Vol. 4, pp. 14-16; Klokman, Sotsial'no-ekonomicheskaia istoriia, pp. 222-24. By contrast, "Svedeniia o Iaroslavskom namestnichestve" credits the city's tanneries with production worth only 48,000 rubles. The 1794 topograficheskoe opisanie mentions nine silk-weaving enterprises, but several of these were very small.

[72]TsGADA, f. 397, d. 441, l. 15; Knabe, "Die Struktur der russischen Posadgemeinden," p. 310; Topograficheskie izvestiia, Vol. 1, Part 4, pp. 292-93; Topograficheskoe opisanie Iaroslavskogo namestnichestva (1794), p. 22; Shchekatov, Geograficheskii slovar', Vol. 7, p. 389. The materials of the Commerce Commission refer to 404 craft-guild members and 695 craftsmen not belonging to guilds.

[73]Topograficheskoe opisanie Iaroslavskogo namestnichestva (1794), p. 22.

(blacksmiths, silversmiths), the leather and clothing trades (cobblers, glovers, saddlers, furriers, hatters, tailors) and craftsmen involved in the preparation of foodstuffs.

The commerce of Iaroslavl', valued by the "topographical descriptions" at one million rubles annually, was influenced by the city's location on the great Volga waterway as well as its role as an industrial producer. Like those of many other Volga towns, the merchants of Iaroslavl' participated extensively in the water-borne grain trade supplying the Petersburg market, acquiring their stocks in various "downstream" ports. Iaroslavl' merchants also dealt in the goods produced by local "factory" and craft industry, selling them at various towns and fairs. In particular, they did "much business" in the shipment of footwear, hats and gloves down the Volga as far as Astrakhan' as well as to "other towns of the realm." Some merchants purchased silk textiles and other domestic and imported goods in the capitals for resale in Iaroslavl' and elsewhere.[74] The city itself was a market center of large proportions, with 700-800 stores reportedly in operation at the end of the eighteenth century. These stores were apparently occupied in the wholesale marketing of the town's industrial production and in serving the consumption needs of the large urban population and the surrounding rural area. In addition to the permanent trade in stores, the Iaroslavl' market was served by three annual fairs. These events attracted merchants of nearby towns, who brought domestic and imported goods for sale and also made purchases for resale in their own communities. The

---

[74]"Svedeniia o Iaroslavskom namestnichestve," pp.176-77; Topograficheskoe opisanie Iaroslavskogo namestnichestva (1794), pp.21-22 TsGVIA, f. VUA, No. 18860, l. 146.

nobility of the surrounding districts also attended, in "large numbers,"
to buy for their consumption needs, while the peasantry of these districts
arrived to sell agricultural and craft products and purchase needed
goods.[75]

Like Iaroslavl', the town of Uglich had a diversified economy
based on transit trade, a large domestic market and substantial industry.
In addition to participating in the Volga grain trade, the merchants
of Uglich delivered linen cloth, leather goods, furs, wool felt and
meat to the markets of both Moscow and Petersburg and also dealt in
silver, copper and tin wares. In the town itself, a large number of
stores offered goods produced by local industry, brought from the
capitals, purchased in other towns or at fairs, and acquired from the
neighboring rural population. The annual turnover of Uglich merchants
in the late eighteenth century was estimated at 700,000 to 800,000
rubles, a level not much below that credited to Iaroslavl'.[76] As in
the larger city, leather production was an important industry. In
the late eighteenth century eight sizeable tanneries were reported
to be in operation, producing goods valued at 30,000 rubles annually.[77]

---

[75] "Svedeniia o Iaroslavskom namestnichestve," pp. 177-78; Ziablovskii,
Zemleopisanie, Vol. 4, p. 14. However, several other sources claim that
these fairs were attended only by peasants of nearby villages. GPB RO,
Ermitazhnoe sobranie, No. 288, 1. 25; G.L. Vartanov, "Gorodskie iarmarki
tsentral'noi chasti Evropeiskoi Rossii vo vtoroi polovine XVIII v.,"
Uchenye zapiski Leningradskogo gosudarstvennogo pedagogicheskogo instituta
im. A.I. Gertsena, Vol. 194 (1958), p. 149.

[76] Shchekatov, Geograficheskii slovar', Vol. 6, pp. 535-36; Ziablovskii,
Zemleopisanie, Vol. 4, p. 23. In the 1803 topograficheskoe opisanie,
however, the estimate is reduced to 500,000 rubles. GPB RO, F IV, No. 640,
11. 27 ob.-28.

[77] Shchekatov, Geograficheskii slovar', Vol. 6, p. 535; GPB RO, F IV,
No. 640, 1. 28. Another source reports 11 tanneries. Ziablovskii,
Zemleopisanie, Vol. 4, p. 24.

Other enterprises included one "major" paper mill, several linen
manufactories, glue and candle "factories" and malthouses. The goods
produced by these industries were sold "primarily" in Petersburg and
Moscow but also in various other towns and at fairs.[78] In the 1760's
the local magistracy reported that more than 400 individuals, nearly
a quarter of the town's male posad population, were engaged in craft
industry and that they participated in 25 different craft professions.[79]
The craft industry of Uglich, like its large-scale enterprises,
emphasized the production of leather goods, especially footwear and
saddles, which were sent to other markets for sale in large quantities.[80]

Rostov, the third-largest town of Iaroslavl' guberniia, owed its
economic significance primarily to the fact that it was the site of one
of the most important trade fairs in Russia. Lasting three weeks, the
Rostov fair in the late eighteenth century reportedly was attended by
up to 7000 merchants, including not only those from all parts of Russia
but also Armenians, Tatars and Greeks, and did business worth more than
three million rubles.[81] The fair was also a stimulus to the trade of

---

[78] GPB RO, F IV. No. 640, 1. 28.

[79] TsGADA, f. 397, d. 441, 1. 24 ob.; Knabe, p. 311.

[80] Shchekatov, Geograficheskii slovar', Vol. 6, p. 535; Ziablovskii,
Zemleopisanie, Vol. 4, p. 23.

[81] Shchekatov, Geograficheskii slovar', Vol. 5, p. 402; Topograficheskoe
opisanie Iaroslavskogo namestnichestva (1794), pp. 37-38; Ziablovskii,
Zemleopisanie, Vol. 4, pp. 20-21; /M. Chulkov/, "Slovar' uchrezhdennykh v
Rossii iarmarok i torgov," in Novyi i polnyi geograficheskii slovar'
Rossiiskogo gosudarstva, Vols. 4, 6 (Moscow, 1788-9), p. XCII.

the local kupechestvo, which not only brought goods from various markets for sale to the large clientele in attendance but was in a favorable position to acquire goods from far-flung sources for transshipment to Petersburg, sale in local stores or distribution among the towns and local fairs of Central Russia.[82] Trade in Rostov was not confined to the fair, however, but remained active throughout the year. The town contained an unusually large number of stores for a settlement of this size, as many as one for every nine inhabitants, according to one source.[83] At the end of the eighteenth century Rostov was emerging as a significant industrial center as well and was the site of four textile manufactories producing linen and cotton goods valued at 150,000 rubles and employing several hundred workers.[84] Textiles made in Rostov were shipped to the Baltic ports and sold at various Russian fairs. Other enterprises produced bricks, leather, tallow and chemicals, for local sale and to some extent for shipment to other towns. Another important feature of the Rostov economy was commercial vegetable gardening, which

---

[82] "Svedeniia o Iaroslavskom namestnicheste," p. 258; Topograficheskoe opisanie Iaroslavskogo namestnichestva (1794), pp. 37-38; Ziablovskii, Zemleopisanie, Vol. 4, p. 20.

[83] "Svedeniia o Iaroslavskom namestnichestve" (p. 252) and Shchekatov (Vol. 5, p. 401) mention 383 stores. Klokman (Sotsial' no-ekonomicheskaia istoriia, p. 226) cites a reference to 570 stores. It is not entirely clear whether all these stores were in operation throughout the year or whether some were in use only during the fair, although Klokman assumes the former to be the case.

[84] GPB RO, Ermitazhnoe sobranie, No. 288, l. 39; Topograficheskoe opisanie Iaroslavskogo namestnichestva (1794), pp. 38-40. An earlier version of the topograficheskoe opisanie, probably reflecting conditions of the late 1770's, mentions only one textile enterprise, of modest size and output, which suggests that Rostov experienced rapid industrial development at the end of the eighteenth century. See "Svedeniia o Iaroslavskom namestnichestve," pp.255-56; the same data are in Shchekatov, Geograficheskii slovar', Vol. 5, p. 482.

occupied a large number of inhabitants of "middling" economic status. Vegetables and seeds grown in Rostov were sold widely in other markets.[85]

Among the smaller towns of Iaroslavl' guberniia, Rybinsk deserves particular attention. Despite its modest population, this town was perhaps the most important port of the Upper Volga--it was at Rybinsk that cargoes proceeding upstream were usually reloaded onto smaller boats which could negotiate the shallower waters of the river's upper reaches as well as the tortuous system of natural and artificial waterways connecting the Volga with Petersburg. According to a description of the town composed in 1811, 2500 vessels arrived annually from "downstream" ports, bringing shipments of grain, salt, iron and other goods valued at 30 million rubles.[86] Most of this cargo was intended for onward shipment in the direction of Petersburg, but much of it changed hands at Rybinsk before proceeding further, and merchants from many towns located farther upstream and to the north and northwest converged on this port to buy grain for sale in their own towns or other markets. The inhabitants of Rybinsk participated extensively in the grain trade, buying and selling from arriving shipments or dispatching grain to Petersburg from the local port and from "downstream" points. The local population also profited from the Volga traffic in other

---

[85] Topograficheskoe opisanie Iaroslavskogo namestnichestva (1794), pp. 37-38; Ziablovskii, Zemleopisanie, Vol. 4, p. 20.

[86] Opisanie goroda Rybinska, pp. 35-36. On the role of Rybinsk in Volga shipping, see also Klokman, Sotsial'no-ekonomicheskaia istoriia, p. 227; V. I. Snezhnevskii, "Opis' delam i dokumentam Nizhegorodskogo gorodcvogo magistrata (1787-1861)," Deistviia Nizhegorodskoi gubernskoi uchenoi arkhivnoi komissii (hereafter Deistviia NGUAK), Vol. 2, No. 15 (Nizhnii Novgorod, 1895), Part 3, pp. 12-19.

ways--through the milling of grain shipments, boatbuilding, the sale of
provisions and nautical supplies and innkeeping--while those without
commercial ability or resources could readily find employment on the
piers, in the warehouses and on the boats headed upstream.[87]

The remaining Volga towns (Romanov, Borisoglebsk, Mologa, even
tiny Myshkin and Norskaia Sloboda) also participated in the Petersburg-
bound grain trade.[88] Another common characteristic of most of these
towns was a large number of stores per capita, a situation which
perhaps resulted, as in the case of Rybinsk, from the stimulus of the
passing river traffic.[89] Except in the case of Norskaia Sloboda the
indicated towns held annual fairs of local significance, attended by
peasants with agricultural and craft products and (in the case of
Romanov, Mologa and Myshkin) by merchants of neighboring towns, bringing
principally textiles. As for industrial development, Romanov had
several textile enterprises and tanneries and a few other "factories,"
the production of which was sold in nearby towns, at fairs and to some
extent shipped to Petersburg.[90] Borisoglebsk and Norskaia Sloboda

---

[87] Opisanie goroda Rybinska, pp. 25-38; Ziablovskii, Zemleopisanie,
Vol. 4, pp. 29-30; Klokman, Sotsial'no-ekonomicheskaia istoriia, pp. 227-28.

[88] TsGVIA, f. VUA, No. 18860, ll. 152-152 ob.; "Svedeniia o
Iaroslavskom namestnichestve," pp. 189, 434-35, 444-45; Shchekatov,
Geograficheskii slovar', Vol. 1, p. 526; Vol. 4, pp. 305-06, 457;
Vol. 5, pp. 64-65; Vol. 7, p. 394; GPB RO, Ermitazhnoe sobranie, No. 288,
l. 12; GPB RO, F IV, No. 640, ll. 2 ob., 32 ob.; Ziablovskii, Zemleopisanie,
Vol. 4, pp. 18, 25-33. The merchants of Romanov also dispatched to
Petersburg rural craft products purchased in their own and the neighboring
districts (homespun cloth, cured sheepskins and sheepskin coats).

[89] An exception was Mologa, where only 35 stores were permanently
in operation. It may be significant in this regard that the town was
located not far upstream from Rybinsk. Nothing is known about the
number of stores in Norskaia Sloboda, but because of this small settlement's
proximity to Iaroslavl' it was probably of little account as a market.

[90] "Svedeniia o Iaroslavskom namestnichestve," pp. 434-36; GPB RO,
F IV, No. 640, l. 33; Ziablovskii, Zemleopisanie, Vol. 4, p. 32.

were well known as centers of metallurgical crafts, producing chiefly

iron cauldrons (in Borisoglebsk) and nails and tin articles (in Norskaia

Sloboda). These products reportedly enjoyed a wide distribution.[91]

Commercial vegetable gardening was a major source of income in Romanov,

while many members of the population of Mologa, Borisoglebsk and

Myshkin earned their living by working on river transport; some citizens

of Myshkin, like their peasant forbears, went to Petersburg, Moscow

and other towns in search of jobs.[92]

Overland transit trade was a significant factor in the economies

of the four smaller towns situated inland from the Volga. The merchants

of Poshekhon'e, for example, acquired textile goods and foodstuffs in

such major markets as Moscow, Petersburg and the great Makar'ev fair

near Nizhnii Novgorod, selling them in the towns of Iaroslavl' guberniia

and the neighboring provinces of Tver' and Vologda and at rural fairs

and markets.[93] Merchants of the new town of Petrovsk had "no trade

whatever" within the town itself but bought goods in Iaroslavl', Rostov,

Uglich and Pereslavl'-Zalesskii and at fairs for resale elsewhere.

Among their business was the shipment of linen cloth to Petersburg

and other Baltic ports.[94] Significant local markets existed in

---

[91] "Svedeniia o Iaroslavskom namestnichestve," pp. 444-45; Ziablovskii, Zemleopisanie, Vol. 4, pp. 18, 33; GPB RO, Ermitazhnoe sobranie, No. 288, 1. 12.

[92] Topograficheskie izvestiia, Vol. 1, Part 4, pp. 298-99; Shchekatov, Geograficheskii slovar', Vol. 4, p. 306; Ziablovskii, Zemleopisanie, Vol. 4, pp. 25-26; GPB RO, F IV, No. 640, 1. 33.

[93] Shchekatov, Geograficheskii slovar', Vol. 4, p. 1277; Ziablovskii, Zemleopisanie, Vol. 4, p. 28. Also in the inventory of traveling merchants of Poshekhon'e were leather goods produced by local industry.

[94] Shchekatov, Geograficheskii slovar', Vol. 4, p. 1111; Ziablovskii, Zemleopisanie, Vol. 4, pp. 21-22. The inhabitants of Petrovsk also earned money by operating inns for travelers moving between Moscow and Iaroslavl'.

Danilov, Liubim and Poshekhon'e, which in the late eighteenth century
had 80-100 stores each with only modest numbers of urban dwellers to
supply. The two fairs at Poshekhon'e were evidently events of major
local significance--they lasted one week each and attracted merchants
from the capital cities, bringing "German" and other imported goods
for local distribution, as well as merchants from nearby towns.
Poshekhon'e and Liubim each boasted several tanneries, while craftsmen
of various specialties (including blacksmiths, locksmiths, cobblers,
glovers, hatters, tailors, carpenters, glass-blowers, stove-builders
and bakers) were noted in all four towns. Some craftsmen from Petrovsk
(cloth-dyers, wood-carvers, gilders and upholsterers) went to Moscow
or Petersburg to pursue their trades.[95]

Although in the late eighteenth century it supported a relatively
dense rural population, Iaroslavl' guberniia was considered one of the
least fertile provinces of Central Russia and one chronically afflicted
with a grain deficit.[96] The degree of infertility was not uniform, of
course, and some districts (for example Iaroslavl', Danilov, Liubim,
Myshkin) normally managed to grow enough to cover the needs of the

---

[95]Shchekatov, Geograficheskii slovar', Vol. 3, p. 1229; Vol. 4,
pp. 1111-12, 1277; Ziablovskii, Zemleopisanie, Vol. 4, pp. 28-35.

[96]GPB RO, Ermitazhnoe sobranie, No. 288, ll. 5-6; Ziablovskii,
Zemleopisanie, Vol. 4, pp. 5-7; German, Statisticheskoe opisanie
Iaroslavskoi gubernii, pp. 3, 6. See also L. V. Sretenskii, "Pomeshchich'ia
votchina Iaroslavskoi gubernii vo vtoroi polovine XVIII v.," Uchenye
zapiski Iaroslavskogo gosudarstvennogo pedagogicheskogo instituta im.
K.D. Ushinskogo, Vol. 25/35 (1958), pp. 478-82.

rural population and even produced salable surpluses.[97] At the other extreme, the soil of Rybinsk uezd produced a "poor" harvest, and the inhabitants of this district relied to a large extent on outside sources of grain.[98] Many of the river towns (Rybinsk, Romanov, Borisoglebsk, Mologa) relied on Volga grain for their food supply, receiving little or nothing from the surrounding districts.[99] Overall, the province normally although not invariably ran a substantial deficit in grain production and imported up to one-fifth of its needs from outside sources.[100] Even in the relatively favored districts the small and unevenly distributed surpluses did not suffice to cover the subsistence needs of most individual peasant households or pay their taxes and dues.[101]

Although agriculture and animal husbandry in Iaroslavl' guberniia were "weak," the rural population was considered to be relatively prosperous, an anomaly attributed by contemporary observers to the

---

[97]GPB RO, Ermitazhnoe sobranie, No. 288, ll. 5-6; Ziablovskii, Zemleopisanie, Vol. 4, pp. 25, 34-35.

[98]Ziablovskii, Zemleopisanie, Vol. 4, p. 30.

[99]Shchekatov, Geograficheskii slovar', Vol. 1, p. 526; Vol. 4, p. 306; Vol. 5, p. 65. According to our sources, of the remaining Volga towns Iaroslavl' and Uglich were supplied partly by Volga shipments and partly by local production, while Myshkin was fully supplied by its district, as were the towns not situated on the Volga (Rostov, Petrovsk, Danilov, Liubim, Poshekon'e). Ibid., Vol. 3, p. 1230; Vol. 4, pp. 457, 1112, 1277; Vol. 6, p. 536; Ziablovskii, Zemleopisanie, Vol. 4, p. 16; GPB RO, Ermitazhnoe sobranie, No. 288, ll. 25-36, 38; GPB RO, F IV, No. 640, l. 28.

[100]Ziablovskii, Zemleopisanie, Vol. 4, pp. 5-7. According to data of the Ministry of the Interior cited by Ziablovskii, the province registered a deficit of 311,000 chetverti in 1802, while in the two subsequent years it produced surpluses of 124,000 and 71,000 chetverti respectively. (1 chetvert'=5.95 bushels.) The poor year was apparently considered more typical, however. Consumption needs were estimated at about 1.5 million chetverti.

[101]GPB RO, Ermitazhnoe sobranie, No. 288, l. 11.

widespread development of non-agricultural occupations among the peasants.[102] Such pursuits, as one observer pointed out, were in some cases merely a supplement to agriculture but "in a great many cases must be considered the chief occupation" of the peasants.[103] To some extent the villages themselves were the site of this activity, since rural markets and craft industries were well developed in many parts of the province. Parts of Iaroslavl' uezd were noted for metallurgical industries, particularly the production of nails and other iron articles, and such industries were also widespread in the districts of Mologa and Poshekhon'e.[104] The inhabitants of villages located along the Volga or its tributaries, in Iaroslavl', Mologa, Poshekhon'e and Myshkin uezdy, sometimes became boatbuilders.[105] Many peasants in the districts of Rybinsk and Romanov occupied themselves with the curing of sheepskins and the production of sheepskin coats, which were sold "everywhere".[106] Also noted by contemporary descriptive surveys were household production of linen and woolen textiles (especially in Iaroslavl', Rostov, Romanov and Uglich uezdy) and the

---

[102]Ziablovskii, Zemleopisanie, Vol. 4, pp. 7-9.

[103]German, Statisticheskoe opisanie, p. 90.

[104]TsGIA, f. 1350 (Mezhevoi departament), op. 312, d. 198 ("Ekonomicheskoe primechanie Iaroslavskogo uezda"), ll. 14-15 ob., 20 ob.-27; Sb. IRIO, Vol. 93, p. 300; MPIKP, Vol. 1, p. 337; Klokman, Sotsial'no-ekonomicheskaia istoriia, pp. 224-25; K. N. Serbina, Krest'ianskaia zhelezodelatel'naia promyshlennost' severo-zapadnoi Rossii XVI-pervoi poloviny XIX v. (Leningrad, 1971), pp. 81-108.

[105]Ziablovskii, Zemleopisanie, Vol. 4, pp. 25-27; German, Statisticheskoe opisanie, p. 93; Klokman, Sotsial'no-ekonomicheskaia istoriia, pp. 225-27.

[106]Ziablovskii, Zemleopisanie, Vol. 4, pp. 31-33.

production of wooden articles (Rostov, Romanov uezdy) and pottery
(Rostov uezd).[107] Some peasants in the districts of Rostov and Romanov
even turned to icon-painting for a livelihood.[108]

Descriptive surveys of Iaroslavl' guberniia disclose that in the
late eighteenth century 16 villages in Iaroslavl', Rostov, Uglich and
Danilov uezdy conducted weekly markets, while more than 60 annual fairs
took place in villages throughout the province. The outstanding event
among these fairs was that in Velikoe village (Rostov uezd), which
lasted one week, attracted "great numbers" of merchants from both
nearby and faraway towns, and reportedly did business worth 200,000
rubles.[109] A. P. Mel'gunov, who as governor-general of the province
visited Velikoe in 1777, reported that the inhabitants were engaged
"exclusively" in commerce and did not participate in agriculture.[110]
The remaining fairs and markets were less impressive, but many nevertheless attracted substantial numbers of buyers and sellers, including
merchants of various towns bringing silk and cotton textiles and other

---

[107]Shchekatov, Geograficheskii slovar', Vol. 5, p. 67; Ziablovskii,
Zemleopisanie, Vol. 4, p. 24; Topograficheskoe opisanie Iaroslavskogo
namestnichestva (1794), pp. 43-44; GPB RO, F IV, No. 640, 1. 23; German,
Statisticheskoe opisanie, pp. 90-91.

[108]Topograficheskoe opisanie Iaroslavskogo namestnichestva (1794),
p. 43; Ziablovskii, Zemleopisanie, Vol. 4, pp. 32-33.

[109]"Svedeniia o Iaroslavskom namestnichestve," pp. 262-63; GPB RO,
Ermitazhnoe sobranie, No. 288, 11. 12, 31-32; Ziablovskii, Zemleopisanie,
Vol. 4, p. 22. Some sources place Velikoe in Iaroslavl' uezd, reflecting
changes in district boundaries instituted in 1796.

[110]TsGADA, Gosarkhiv, r. XVI, No. 1012, ch. 1, 1. 7 ob.

goods "needed by the peasantry." At these fairs rural craft and agricultural production passed into the hands of urban merchants and more often of trading peasants for resale elsewhere.[111]

More striking than the development of trade and craft industry in the villages of Iaroslavl' guberniia, however, was the widespread practice of temporary migration (otkhod) for the purpose of earning income. Contemporary observers perceived that the peasants of this province had an "extreme predilection" for the "itinerant mode of life" and for "long absences in distant territories."[112] From 1778 through 1802 the government annually issued between 55,000 and 75,000 passports to inhabitants of Iaroslavl' guberniia (mostly peasants), a number equivalent to 15-20 percent of the total male population and perhaps as high as one-third of the adult males.[113] Many peasants, particularly those from districts abutting on the Volga, found work on the barges and wharves, while others (from Iaroslavl', Rostov and Petrovsk uezdy) gained a living from overland transport (izvoz).[114] The involvement

---

[111] The merchants of Romanov, Mologa, Liubim and Norskaia Sloboda, as well as those of many towns elsewhere in Russia, complained to the Legislative Commission of 1767 that trade in rural markets was monopolized by peasants, who obstructed, sometimes by force, the efforts of urban merchants to acquire rural products without dealing with peasant middlemen. Sb. IRIO, Vol. 8, pp. 117-18; Vol. 93, pp. 215, 398-400; Vol. 107, pp. 75-78.

[112] Ziablovskii, Zemleopisanie, Vol. 4, pp. 8-9; German, Statisticheskoe opisanie, p. 99.

[113] V. A. Fedorov, Pomeshchich'i krest'iane tsentral'no-promyshlennogo raiona Rossii kontsa XVIII-pervoi poloviny XIX v. (Moscow, 1974), pp. 200-01; M. Tugan-Baranovskii, Russkaia fabrika v proshlom i nastoiashchem, Vol. 1 (7th ed., Moscow, 1938), pp. 42-43; Kabuzan, Izmeneniia v razmeshchenii naseleniia Rossii, pp. 95, 107. Since some passports were effective for more than one year, the total number of persons with valid passports was even higher than the number issued annually.

[114] Shchekatov, Geograficheskii slovar', Vol. 4, p. 1113; Vol. 5, pp. 404, 450; Vol. 6, p. 394; German, Statisticheskoe opisanie, pp. 90-93;

of peasants in the long-distance transit trade traversing the province
was not limited to their role in transport work. Many participated in
the Volga grain trade, as their competitors, the merchants of Rybinsk
(then known as Rybnaia Sloboda) had occasion to note with displeasure
in 1767, and the records of the Iaroslavl' provincial chancellery
identify some local peasants as owners of large vessels plying the
river with cargoes of grain.[115] Peasants of the inland Rostov uezd
dealt in such foodstuffs as meat, fish, poultry, butter and honey,
which were purchased mostly in the "downstream" provinces and brought
overland for sale in various towns of the central and northwestern
provinces.[116] Peasants of Iaroslavl' and Poshekhon'e districts were
known in Moscow as dealers in metal goods produced by their home
territory and were the subject of strenuous complaints by their competitors
in the kupechestvo of Norskaia Sloboda.[117] The extensive role of the
local peasantry in the delivery to major Russian markets of local
agricultural and craft products and the output of the "downstream"

Ziablovskii, Zemleopisanie, Vol. 4, pp. 17, 25, 31. Peasants apparently
could earn substantial sums by hauling goods for merchants. In the early
nineteenth century Andrei Miagkov, a peasant izvozchik from Ugodichi
village (Rostov uezd), was able to lend 700 rubles to a Moscow merchant
of his acquaintance whose enterprises had been destroyed in the great fire
of 1812. /A. Ia. Artynov/, Vospominaniia krest'ianina sela Ugodich,
Iaroslavskoi gubernii Rostovskogo uezda, Aleksandra Artynova (Moscow,
1882), p. 85.

[115] Sb. IRIO, Vol. 107, pp. 133-34; TsGADA, f. 455 (Iaroslavskaia
provintsial'naia kantseliariia), op. 1, dd. 730, 886.

[116] GPB RO, F IV, No. 640, 1. 23; German, Statisticheskoe opisanie,
pp. 91-92. The peasant memoirist A. Ia. Artynov recounts that his
father, likewise a peasant of Ugodichi village, Rostov uezd, was about
the beginning of the nineteenth century a dealer in fish, which he
purchased in Saratov and Ural'sk and sold at the fair in the town of
Tikhvin (Novgorod guberniia). Artynov, Vospominaniia, pp. 13-14.

[117] Sb. IRIO, Vol. 93, pp. 298-99; E. N. Kusheva, "Torgovlia Moskvy
v 30-40-kh godakh XVIII v.," Istoricheskie zapiski, Vol. 23 (1947), p. 60.

provinces as well is also reflected in the complaints of the posad

population in Iaroslavl', Romanov, Borisoglebsk, Mologa and Liubim,

while several towns also pointed out that trading peasants returned

from these markets with consumer goods to be offered for sale in smaller

towns or rural markets.[118]   Peasants of the heavily forested Mologa

and Poshekhon'e districts dealt in lumber and firewood, which they

brought to various points on the Volga for disposal.[119]

The search for income frequently led migrants from Iaroslavl'

guberniia to settle in towns for greater or lesser intervals. Many

such migrants occupied themselves with retail trade in foodstuffs,

innkeeping and the sale of provisions to military units (markitantstvo).[120]

Another popular occupation was construction work, particularly among

peasants of Iaroslavl' uezd, who migrated to towns "predominantly" for

work as carpenters, stonemasons, bricklayers, plasterers and stove-

builders.[121]   Peasants of Rostov uezd, on the other hand, appeared in

towns chiefly to engage in "their favorite occupation," commercial

---

[118] Sb. IRIO, Vol. 93, pp. 215, 338-39, 398-99; Vol. 107, pp. 75-77, 133-34.

[119] Shchekatov, Geograficheskii slovar', Vol. 4, pp. 307, 1278-79; Ziablovskii, Zemleopisanie, Vol. 4, p. 29.

[120] GPB RO, F IV, No. 640, ll. 31, 36; Ziablovskii, Zemleopisanie, Vol. 4, pp. 7-8, 29, 34-35; German, Statisticheskoe opisanie, pp. 93-94; TsGADA, f. 1289 (M. M. Shcherbatov), op. 1, d. 595, ll. 1-45. The prominent role of immigrants from Iaroslavl' guberniia in trade in foodstuffs in Moscow was discussed in Chapter IV.

[121] Ziablovskii, Zemleopisanie, Vol. 4, p. 17; German, Statisticheskoe opisanie, pp. 90-91. Descriptions of individual villages of Iaroslavl' uezd in the ekonomicheskie primechaniia confirm the presence in these settlements of large numbers of such craftsmen, who presumably worked on otkhod. TsGIA, f. 1350, op. 312, d. 198, ll.7 ob.-11, 25 ob.-30, 93-94, 100-101 ob., etc.

vegetable gardening.[122] In addition to the above occupations, urban

immigrants from Iaroslavl' guberniia engaged in various craft professions

(working as tailors, cobblers, harness-makers, carriage-builders), were

employed by urban merchants and craftsmen and joined the factory labor

force.[123] Few towns in Russia, remarked a contemporary observer, were

without tradesmen from the peasantry of this province.[124] However,

according to contemporary accounts the most common destination of these

migrants was Moscow or Petersburg, while other Baltic ports (Riga,

Revel, Kronstadt), Orel and several of the rapidly expanding towns on

the eastern fringes of European Russia (Kazan', Astrakhan', Orenburg)

are also mentioned as frequent objectives of the migrating peasants.[125]

The towns of Iaroslavl' guberniia itself were not entirely neglected

by migrants from the local peasantry. It is true that most of the

complaints of these towns to the Legislative Commission of 1767 related

to competitive activities not involving immigration by peasants: to

the commercial and industrial pursuits of adjacent or nearby peasant

[122]GPB RO, F IV, No. 640, 1. 23; Ziablovskii, Zemleopisanie,
Vol. 4, p. 21; German, Statisticheskoe opisanie, pp. 91-92. The peasant
memoirist A. Ia. Artynov provides much detail on the activities of such
migrant gardeners from his village--both his contemporaries in the first
half of the nineteenth century and their ancestors--in Petersburg, Tikhvin
and other places. Artynov, Vospominaniia, esp. pp.7-8, 13-15, 34, 39,
44-48, 59, 77-83.

[123]GPB RO, F IV, No. 640, 11. 31, 36; German, Statisticheskoe
opisanie, pp. 90-92; Ziablovskii, Zemleopisanie, Vol. 4, pp. 7-8; TsGIA,
f. 1350, op. 312, d. 198, 11. 111-13.

[124]Ziablovskii, Zemleopisanie, Vol. 4, p. 9.

[125]Ibid., pp. 7-8, 17, 21, 29, 35; Topograficheskoe opisanie
Iaroslavskogo namestnichestva (1794), p. 44; GPB RO, F IV, No. 640, 1.
31; German, Statisticheskoe opisanie, pp. 90-92; Sretenskii, "Pomeshchich'ia
votchina," pp. 501-04; L.B. Genkin, "Nezemledel'cheskii otkhod krest'ian
Iaroslavskoi i Kostromskoi gubernii v pervoi polovine XIX v.," Uchenye
zapiski Iaroslavskogo gosudarstvennogo pedagogicheskogo instituta im.
K. D. Ushinskogo, Vol. 9/19 (1947), pp. 8-9.

communities, the development of rural markets and craft industries, the
dealings of peasant middlemen who brought rural products to the urban
market for sale but did not remain in the urban milieu for long periods
and the participation of peasants in long-distance transit trade.
However, many of the towns, including Iaroslavl', Rostov, Uglich,
Romanov, Liubim and Norskaia Sloboda, also called attention to various
forms of collusion with members of other categories which allowed
peasants to evade restrictive laws and set up enterprises within the
towns: the peasants rented stores from individual merchants and posed
as the agents or employees of merchants and nobles, with documents
(kreditnye or veriashchie pis'ma) from the latter authorizing the
recipients to conduct business "in their names."[126]

Uglich, Romanov and Mologa accused peasants of selling silks and
other valuable goods in the towns "secretly, from houses" and also
"carrying them through the streets and from door to door."[127] The
Rybinsk posad protested that peasants were active as grain dealers in
the town's busy grain market.[128] This important river port also
attracted many migrants for work as stevedores, while some peasants,

---

[126] Sb. IRIO, Vol. 93, pp. 215-16, 301, 339, 351, 399, 550. The
fact that the urban "instructions" of 1767 were not always wholly
individual documents but rather in many cases clearly the result of
collaboration among groups of nearby towns (see above, n. 25) makes it
difficult to determine the extent to which a given reference reflected
the specific experience of particular towns. There are strong similarities
between the "instructions" of Iaroslavl' and Norskaia Sloboda and
between those of Uglich and Romanov, with many points repeated verbatim.
The Liubim "instruction" is similar to that of Kostroma.

[127] Sb. IRIO, Vol. 93, pp. 398, 548; Vol. 107, p. 75. Once again the
complaints are phrased in identical terms in each "instruction".

[128] Ibid., Vol. 107, p. 133.

particularly from Mologa uezd, came to Rybinsk to work on the construction
of river boats.[129] Large numbers of peasants working on Volga shipping
also passed through this town, where the large vessels from "downstream"
normally ended their journey and the smaller ones proceeding toward
Petersburg began theirs. Many peasants of nearby villages were hired
by the blacksmiths of Norskaia Sloboda for work in the production of
nails. However, the town complained to the Commerce Commission in 1764
that many of these peasants, having learned the necessary skills,
returned to their villages and pursued this industry independently, in
competition with the posad population.[130]

Iaroslavl', with its large population, broad market and extensive
industries, attracted migrants seeking income through commercial
activities, craft industry and hired labor. In the mid-1770's Vasilii
Babaev, a peasant from the estates of Prince M. M. Shcherbatov in
Iaroslavl' uezd, operated inns in two houses he rented from Iaroslavl'
merchants and also sold candles, butter and other supplies from stores
in the courtyards of these buildings.[131] During the same period two
other peasants of the same estate requested and received permission to
erect structures on land owned by their master in Iaroslavl' and to use
this property for a period of thirty years.[132] In 1762 the Iaroslavl'
merchant Fedor D'iachkov informed the authorities that "unidentified
thieves" had broken into a store he owned and stolen assorted textile

---

[129]Shchekatov, Geograficheskii slovar', Vol. 4, p. 307; Klokman,
Sotsial'no-ekonomicheskaia istoriia, p. 227.

[130]TsGADA, f. 397, d. 441, 11. 117-117 ob.

[131]TsGADA, f. 1289, op. 1, d. 503, 11. 1-4. The document also
reveals that agents of Shcherbatov intervened on behalf of this serf
entrepreneur when he became involved in a violent conflict with a posad
official and was arrested by the posad authorities.

[132]TsGADA, f. 1289, op. 1, d. 425, 1. 54.

and metal goods worth seventeen rubles. These goods, however, belonged to the church peasant Petr Kobelev, who apparently had been using the facilities for his own commercial purposes.[133] Andrei Maksimov, a serf from Poshekhon'e uezd, was in 1747 employed by the widow of a Iaroslavl' merchant, for whom he "sat ...behind a counter and sold bread."[134] In the same year Ivan Bulashin, a church peasant of Iaroslavl' uezd, was employed as a "worker" by the Iaroslavl' merchant Ivan Moskatil'nikov, who sent him to sell goods at a fair in the town of Kashin.[135] Andrei Shliapnikov, a church peasant of Kostroma uezd (adjoining Iaroslavl' uezd to the east), worked for the Iaroslavl' merchant Vasilii Krasheninnikov, owner of a hat "factory," in the capacity of a steward (prikazchik). In 1759 he was sent to the Rostov fair with goods produced by his employer's enterprise.[136]

The available sources also document other cases in which peasants settled in Iaroslavl' (as well as in Rybinsk and Norskaia Sloboda) to work for local merchants.[137] However, descriptions of individual villages provided by the "economic notes" to the General Land Survey indicate that the main purpose of migration to Iaroslavl' was

---

[133]TsGADA, f. 807 (Iaroslavskii gorodovoi magistrat), op. 1, d. 546, l. 19.

[134]Ibid., l. 76.

[135]Ibid., l. 66.

[136]TsGADA, f. 807, op. 1, d. 471, ll. 1-2.

[137]TsGADA, f. 807, op. 1, d. 46, ll. 42-53; d. 513, ll. 1-2; f. 455, op. 1, dd. 883, 884, 886, 894. These cases, relating to peasants who subsequently enlisted in the urban classes, are discussed in detail below, in Chapter VI.

employment in the city's tanneries and textile manufactories.[138] This

conclusion is confirmed by the results of a census (podvornaia opis')

of Prince Shcherbatov's estates in the districts of Iaroslavl' and

Borisoglebsk, performed in 1793.[139] Of 51 households the members of

which were reported to be wholly or partially on otkhod, the migrants

were in Moscow in 30 cases, in Iaroslavl' in 11 cases, in Kazan' in 2

cases and "traveling the roads" (presumably as teamsters) in 8 cases.

All of those residing in Iaroslavl' worked in the factories.[140]

Further information on the migration of peasants to towns of

Iaroslavl' guberniia is provided by data on enlistment in the urban

classes of these towns. As in the case of Moscow guberniia, the

available sources provide data which although less than complete do

allow a reliable assessment of the magnitude of this influx from the

First Revision through the end of the century. According to the 1767

"Report on the Number of Souls," in the Second and Third Revisions only

Rostov and Romanov, among all the towns later included in Iaroslavl'

guberniia, reported any registrants enlisted in the posad according

to the provisions of the decree of April 13, 1722 ("mercantile peasants").[141]

---

[138]GPB RO, Sobranie A. Titova, No. 1716, ll. 1-12. etc.; TsGIA, f. 1350, op. 312, d. 198, ll. 80-82, 111-13. Much of the labor force in the Iaroslavl' textile manufactories was provided by "ascribed" workers bound to the factories. However, according to one source this industry also employed up to 1200 hired workers. (Topograficheskoe opisanie Iaroslavskogo namestnichestva /1794/, pp. 19-21.) The number employed by tanneries was apparently much lower.

[139]TsGADA, f. 1289, op. 1, d. 595, ll. 1-45.

[140]By contrast, peasants of these estates went to Moscow not for factory labor but primarily to operate inns or taverns (traktiry) and also to trade in foodstuffs.

[141]GPB RO, Ermitazhnoe sobranie, No. 242, ll. 3-11.

Moreover, the numbers involved were very small: each town had 4

registrants at the time of the Second Revision (1744-47), while by the

subsequent census (1762-65) the numbers had risen to 28 for Romanov and

16 for Rostov. Iaroslavl' itself was not credited with any "mercantile

peasants," but in 1744 the local authorities reported to the Chief

Magistracy that applications for membership in the Iaroslavl' <u>posad</u>

from three freed serfs and one "black" state peasant were pending.[142]

These data clearly represent a negligible level of peasant enlistment in

all the towns involved up the the time of the Third Revision.

In the period between the Third and Fourth Revisions, a much larger

influx into the urban classes of these towns took place. Partial data

for this period can be extracted from a series of tax registers (<u>okladnye</u>

<u>knigi</u>) for individual districts of Iaroslavl' <u>guberniia</u>, dating from the

year 1783.[143]   (See Table 24.) These documents give the number of

---

[142]TsGADA, f. 807, op. 1, d. 46, 11. 42-53. Individual case records
relating to six former serfs who entered the Iaroslavl' <u>posad</u> at the
time of the Third Revision also survive in the files of the Iaroslavl'
magistracy. However, it is not clear whether the surviving materials
identify all such freedmen absorbed into the <u>posad</u> at this time.

[143]TsGIA, f. 558, op. 2, d. 303, 11. 505 ob.-506 ob.; d. 304, 1.
661 ob.; d. 305, 1. 593 ob.; d. 306, 1. 927 ob.; d. 307, 1. 828 ob.;
d. 308, 1. 389 ob.; d. 309, 1. 689 ob.; d. 310, No. 4, 1. 1 ob.; d. 311,
1. 509 ob.; d. 312, No. 5; d. 313, No. 4, 1. 1 ob.; d. 314, 1. 422 ob.
The figures given by these tax registers represent the cumulative total
of peasant registrants in the <u>kupechestvo</u> of each town in 1783, since
the Fourth Revision had not released prior registrants from the
intermediate status requiring them to bear tax obligations as both
peasants and townsmen. (See above, Chapter II.) Theoretically, the
figures could include registrants who appeared before the Third Revision,
but as we have seen such registrants were very few in number and moreover
were confined to the towns of Rostov and Romanov. Therefore, almost all
the enlistment reported by the 1783 tax registers took place between the
Third and Fourth Revisions.

Table 24: Enlistment of Crown Peasants in Kupechestvo in Towns of
Iaroslavl' Guberniia, 1764-1782 (Number of Males)

Towns	Total kuptsy (1782)	Peasant registrants: econ.	court	unknown	total	% peasants
Iaroslavl'	1044	93	5	-	98	9
Uglich	739	-	-	106	106	14
Rostov	653	187	-	-	187	29
Rybinsk	173	33	-	-	33	19
Mologa	58	-	-	-	-	0
Romanov	197	12	-	-	12	6
Poshekhon'e	435	-	-	40	40	9
Borisoglebsk	210	-	-	18	18	9
Danilov	193	-	-	-	-	0
Liubim	213	1	-	-	1	0.5
Petrovsk	423	-	-	359	359	85
Myshkin	220	62	-	-	62	28
Norskaia Sloboda	55	-	-	-	-	0
Total[a]	4613	388	5	523	916	20

Sources: TsGIA, f. 558, op. 2, dd. 303-314 (see text, Chapter V, n. 143, for exact references).

[a]Another document (TsGIA, f. 558, op. 2, d. 315, ll. 125-6) states that the 4613 members of the kupechestvo included 1007 registrants from the crown peasantry, of whom 893 were economic peasants and 114 were court peasants.

crown peasants enlisted in the _kupechestvo_ of each town. Not reported
are registrants from the ranks of freed serfs and any crown peasants
enlisted in the _meshchanstvo_. According to the tax registers, the
kupechestvo of Iaroslavl' _guberniia_ totaled 4613 males, of whom 916
(20 percent) were registrants from the crown peasantry. The bulk of
these registrants were economic peasants, which is as expected, since
there were few court peasants in this province.[144] Surprisingly, the
largest amount of enlistment took place in the new town of Petrovsk,
where 85 percent of the _kupechestvo_ consisted of new registrants from
the crown peasantry. However, this total may represent in large
measure native inhabitants of the settlement who had not initially
joined the local _posad_ when it was created in 1777, since it would be
difficult to explain a large influx of outsiders into this weakly
developed town.[145] Otherwise, it was the three largest towns of the
province (Iaroslavl', Uglich, Rostov) which attracted the greatest
absolute numbers of registrants, each absorbing 98-187 peasants.[146]

---

[144] More than half the registrants reported by the 1783 tax registers
are not enumerated by peasant category. However, a concurrent fiscal
document relating to Iaroslavl' _guberniia_, citing a slightly higher total
of 1007 registrants from the crown peasantry, states that 893 (89 percent)
were economic peasants and 114 were court peasants. (TsGIA, f. 558, op.
2, d. 315, 11. 125-26.) According to the Fourth Revision, Iaroslavl'
guberniia contained only 5404 court peasants but 77,730 economic peasants
(male souls). (Kabuzan, _Izmeneniia v razmeshchenii naseleniia Rossii_
pp. 95-96.)

[145] The tax register for Petrovsk _uezd_, it is true, refers to
"registrants from the peasantry of various districts and settlements."
(TsGIA, f. 558, op. 2, d. 313, No. 4, 1. 1 ob.) However, it is not clear
how many of the registrants were actually outsiders or even whether this
statement was a description of the actual situation or merely a formula.

[146] The figure for Uglich includes "servitors /sluzhiteli/ of the
court and economic institutions." (TsGIA, f. 558, op. 2, d. 314, 1.
422 ob.)

As measured by the proportion occupied by peasant registrants in the total kupechestvo, however, the highest levels of enlistment (19-29 percent) occurred in Rostov, Myshkin and Rybinsk, while significant levels (9-14 percent) were also recorded in Iaroslavl', Uglich, Borisoglebsk and Poshekhon'e.[147] Only Mologa, Danilov and Norskaia Sloboda reported no enlistment at all from the crown peasantry.[148]

The available data thus indicate that between the Third and Fourth Revisions a substantial influx of peasants into the urban classes of Iaroslavl' guberniia took place and made a major contribution to the growth of the provincial kupechestvo. Many towns shared in this influx, with Rostov rather than Iaroslavl' apparently offering the strongest attraction for immigrants. Assuming, as is most likely to be the case, that the immigrants came predominantly from nearby districts, it appears that during the specified period peasants of Iaroslavl' guberniia were more likely to settle in the towns of their own province than in Moscow-- according to the Moscow census depositions of 1782 only 55 crown peasants from Iaroslavl' guberniia enlisted in the Moscow posad between the Third and Fourth Revisions.[149]

In the last two decades of the century the results of enlistment in these towns were less auspicious. Information on enlistment in the

---

[147] However, as in the case of Petrovsk, enlistment in the new towns of Myshkin and Poshekhon'e may to some extent represent the gradual absorption of native inhabitants into the newly established posad.

[148] Individual case records relating to several freed serfs who enlisted in the urban classes of Norskaia Sloboda in the early 1770's survive in the files of the Iaroslavl' provincial chancellery. TsGADA, f. 455, op. 1, dd. 884, 894, 987.

[149] See above, Chapter IV, Table 7.

Iaroslavl' _posad_ between the Fourth and Fifth Revisions (1782-1795) is
provided by reports of the Iaroslavl' magistracy for the years 1790,
1794 and 1795 on "the merchants declaring capital in the city of
Iaroslavl' and the inscription of various individuals in the _kupechestvo_."[150]
(See Table 25.) These reports indicate that a total of about 100
peasants of all categories (equally divided between economic peasants
and freed serfs) enlisted in the _kupechestvo_ and _meshchanstvo_ up to 1795.
Less than 2 percent of the Iaroslavl' _posad_ consisted of peasant
registrants absorbed since the Fourth Revision, although since three-
quarters of these registrants belonged to the _kupechestvo_ peasant
enlistment had a somewhat greater impact (8 percent) on this more
affluent segment of the _posad_ population. Nevertheless, the amount of
enlistment had clearly dropped since the preceding, albeit somewhat
longer, intercensus period--only about one-third as many crown peasants
inscribed in the Iaroslavl' _kupechestvo_ as had done so earlier. All
peasants enlisting in the _kupechestvo_ belonged to the third merchant
guild except for one family of former serfs (containing five male souls),
which declared a capital of more than 10,000 rubles and entered the
first guild in 1794.[151] Peasant registrants in Iaroslavl' thus were

---

[150] Gosudarstvennyi arkhiv Iaroslavskoi oblasti, Iaroslavl' (GAIaO),
f. 501 (Iaroslavskaia gorodskaia duma), op. 1, dd. 15, 28, 31. The data
offered by these documents are somewhat confused. Among other problems,
figures given for the _kupechestvo_ seem to take into account births and
deaths since the Fourth Revision, while those for the _meshchanstvo_ do
not. However, the discrepancies thus introduced may be regarded as
minor. The figures given for new registrants, although not clearly
labeled, obviously represent cumulative totals, presumably since the
previous census. In several categories of registrants the same figures
are cited in the 1790 and 1795 reports, and some individuals identified
as new registrants in the later document are shown by other sources to
have enlisted as early as 1787 or 1790.

[151] GAIaO, f. 501, op. 1, d. 31, ll. 6 ob.-7.

Table 25: Enlistment in Urban Classes of Iaroslavl', 1782-1795

(Number of Males)

Origin of registrants	Enlisted through 1790 in:			Enlisted through 1795 in:		
	k-stvo	m-stvo	total	k-stvo	m-stvo	total
Peasants						
economic	15	14	29	36	7	43
freed serfs	13	5	18	35	16	51
total	28	19	47	71	23	94
Other towns	1	49	50	20	35	55
Other categories						
clergy	–	44	44	–	44	44
non-Russians	–	28	28	–	28	28
other	1	6	7	4	9	13
total	1	78	79	4	81	85

Sources: GAIaO, f. 501, op. 1, dd. 15, 28, 31.

apparently concentrated in the middle levels of the urban community, as was the case in Moscow. In sharp contrast to the Moscow situation, however, peasant enlistment in Iaroslavl' did not rise markedly with the approach of the Fifth Revision but rather remained at about the same level it had been in the 1780's.[152] The Iaroslavl' posad also gained 55 new recruits from the urban classes of other towns and 85 from other population categories, chiefly "churchmen" and non-Russian elements ("from various nations"). These registrants appeared largely in the period before 1790 and belonged almost exclusively to the meshchanstvo.

For data on the remaining towns of Iaroslavl' guberniia during the period between the Fourth and Fifth Revisions, we turn to reports of the provincial treasury on the number of male souls in each tax category in the years 1794 and 1795.[153] These reports provide information on the numbers of new registrants from various categories who were added to the urban tax rolls in the indicated years but do not give any cumulative totals of such registrants since the previous census. The data provided by this source are summarized in Table 26. The largest numbers of registrants (70-72 souls apiece) were credited to Iaroslavl' and Rostov. However, the figures of the provincial treasury on enlistment in Iaroslavl' are not in agreement with those of the Iaroslavl' magistracy, which credit the city with only 20-30 peasant registrants during these

---

[152]This conclusion emerges from comparison of the cumulative figures given by the 1790 and 1795 reports. In several categories (e.g. economic peasants registered in the meshchanstvo) the 1795 document gives a lower total, possibly because some earlier registrants had dropped out of the posad or had transferred to a different urban category.

[153]TsGIA, f. 558, op. 2, d. 316, 11. 268 ob.-273, 308 ob.-316.

Table 26: Enlistment of Peasants in Towns of Iaroslavl' <u>Guberniia</u>,

1794-1795 (Number of Males)

Towns	Total in urban classes (1795)	Peasant registrants: econ. peasants	court peasants	freed serfs	total peasants
Iaroslavl'[a]					
kupechestvo	997	6	-	42	48
meshchanstvo	4237	7	=	17	24
total	5234	13	-	59	72
Uglich					
kupechestvo	986	8	-	3	11
meshchanstvo	1022	6	=	10	16
total	2008	14	-	13	27
Rostov					
kupechestvo	970	24	-	31	55
meshchanstvo	863	2	=	13	15
total	1833	26	-	44	70
Rybinsk					
kupechestvo	276	1	-	2	3
meshchanstvo	579	=	=	17	17
total	855	1	-	19	20
Mologa					
kupechestvo	59	-	-	-	-
meshchanstvo	921	=	=	1	1
total	980	-	-	1	1
Romanov					
kupechestvo	239	-	-	3	3
meshchanstvo	608	=	=	1	1
total	847	-	-	4	4
Poshekhon'e					
kupechestvo	229	-	3	4	7
meshchanstvo	576	=	=	9	9
total	805	-	3	13	16
Borisoglebsk					
kupechestvo	290	-	-	-	-
meshchanstvo	564	=	=	1	1
total	854	-	-	1	1

Table 26 (cont.)

Towns	Total in urban classes (1795)	Peasant registrants: econ. peasants	court peasants	freed serfs	total peasants
Danilov					
kupechestvo	172	-	3	-	3
meshchanstvo	349	=	1	5	6
total	521	-	4	5	9
Liubim					
kupechestvo	121	-	-	2	2
meshchanstvo	545	=	=	1	1
total	666	-	-	3	3
Petrovsk					
kupechestvo	370	-	-	-	-
meshchanstvo	88	=	=	3	3
total	458	-	-	3	3
Myshkin					
kupechestvo	163	1	-	-	1
meshchanstvo	118	=	=	1	1
total	281	1	-	1	2
Total for province					
kupechestvo	4872	40	6	87	133
meshchanstvo	10470	15	1	79	95
total	15342	55	7	166	228

Source: TsGIA, f. 558, op. 2, d. 316, ll. 268 ob.-273, 308 ob.-316.

[a]Figures for Iaroslavl' apparently include Norskaia Sloboda.

years.[154] A possible reason for the discrepancy is that the provincial treasury apparently included Norskaia Sloboda (the small "non-administrative" urban settlement in Iaroslavl' uezd) in its figures for the provincial capital. Uglich, Rybinsk and Poshekhon'e absorbed 16-27 registrants each, while at least one peasant joined the urban citizenry in all the remaining uezd towns.

According to the treasury reports a total of 228 peasants enlisted in the kupechestvo and meshchanstvo of all the towns during the two-year period covered. Nearly three-quarters of these registrants were freed serfs.[155] In a pattern which has already become familiar, crown peasants were drawn predominantly into the kupechestvo while former serfs were more evenly divided among the two main urban categories. The peasant registrants were apparently drawn predominantly from local sources. Of the 62 registrants from the crown peasantry reported by the provincial treasury, 42 originated in the district of the town where they settled, 5 came from other districts of Iaroslavl' guberniia and the rest were of unidentified origin.[156] Changes in population due to migration from

---

[154] For 1795 the provincial treasury reported an influx of 34 freed serfs into the Iaroslavl' kupechestvo and 17 into the meshchanstvo, which figures approximate the cumulative totals of such registrants given by the magistracy. Discrepancies in the figures for economic peasants are less pronounced. The reports of the provincial treasury presumably were prepared on the basis of information supplied by local magistracies. However, the magistracy reports cited above were intended not for the treasury but for the town duma, in the files of which they were found.

[155] It will be recalled from the preceding chapter that freed serfs predominated among peasants of Iaroslavl' guberniia enlisting in the Moscow posad.

[156] No information is provided about the geographical origin of former serfs.

one town to another were negligible according to the treasury's
information: the towns of Iaroslavl' guberniia gained six new citizens
from the urban classes of other towns while losing nine of their own
to emigration. The Rostov posad received a massive infusion of 385
souls from the ranks of former church personnel. These individuals
were remnants of the establishment of the local metropolitan, whose
headquarters had been transferred to Iaroslavl' during the 1780's, and
they comprised more than one-fifth of the Rostov urban classes in 1795.
In the remaining towns recruitment of "churchmen" and other raznochintsy
into the posad was negligible during the indicated years.

The 1794 and 1795 reports of the Iaroslavl' provincial treasury
confirm the supremacy of Rostov, at least among the uezd towns of the
province, as a pole of attraction for peasant immigrants. The town of
Petrovsk, which had received large numbers of registrants between its
creation in 1777 and the Fourth Revision in 1782, was credited with few
registrants in 1794 and 1795, which confirms the supposition that the
earlier enlistment represented a temporary phenomenon connected with
the establishment of a posad in this settlement. Otherwise, comparisons
with the preceding intercensus period are difficult because the 1794-95
documents cover only a short segment of the period between the Fourth
and Fifth Revisions. Assuming that enlistment took place at a fairly
steady rate throughout the period, as appears to have been the case in
Iaroslavl' according to the reports of the local magistracy, we would
expect the number of registrants for the entire period to be five or six
times the figures reported for 1794 and 1795 (1100 to 1300 peasants of
all categories, including 300-400 crown peasants). This estimate
suggests that peasant enlistment in the towns of Iaroslavl' guberniia,

taken as a whole, failed to grow in the period following the Fourth Revision and probably slackened somewhat.[157] On the other hand, these towns apparently continued to absorb more peasants of their province than did Moscow--from 1782 through 1795 250 households of peasants from Iaroslavl' guberniia (containing about 500 male souls) enlisted in the Moscow urban classes.[158] The gap was narrowing, however, reflecting the growing relative strength of Moscow's attraction for the peasantry of this province.

Data on enlistment in the urban classes of Iaroslavl' guberniia during the half-decade following the Fifth Revision are provided by another series of reports of the provincial treasury on the number of souls in each tax category.[159] (See Table 27.) These documents credit

---

[157]The 1783 tax registers reported the enlistment of 916 crown peasants in the kupechestvo alone during a period 50 percent longer than that under consideration. However, 359 of these registrants were attributed to Petrovsk and have been interpreted as representing principally the absorption of native inhabitants of the settlement into its newly established posad. If this special case were excluded, the per annum average levels of enlistment in the two period would be quite close.

[158]See above, Chapter IV, Table 12.

[159]TsGIA, f. 558, op. 2, d. 317, 11. 54-57, 61 ob.-65, 88 ob.-93, 106 ob.-110; d. 318, 11. 38 ob.-42, 80 ob.-84, 146 ob.-149, 206 ob.-212, 222 ob.-224. These semi-annual reports cover the years 1797-1801. For registrants from the crown peasantry the documents also provide a cumulative total of newcomers since the Fifth Revision (1795). This practice reflects the fact that crown peasants enlisting in the posad passed through an interim stage during which they were responsible for dual tax obligations. For this reason such registrants were listed as a separate group in the reports, while other registrants were identified only once, in the report covering the period of their enlistment, and afterwards absorbed into the overall totals for the kupechestvo and meshchanstvo. As a result, these reports provide data on enlistment from the crown peasantry from 1795 through 1801 but from other groups only from 1797 through 1801.

Table 27: Enlistment of Peasants in Towns of Iaroslavl' Guberniia,

1795-1801 (Number of Males)

Towns	Total in urban classes (1801)	Crown peasants:[a] econ.	court	other	Freed serfs[b]	Total peasants	%
Iaroslavl'[c]							
kupechestvo	653	4	-	3	13	20	3
meshchanstvo	4531	1	-	-	9	10	0.2
total	5184	5	-	3	22	30	0.6
Uglich							
kupechestvo	757	-	-	-	-	-	0
meshchanstvo	1323	-	-	-	9	9	0.7
total	2080	-	-	-	9	9	0.4
Rostov							
kupechestvo	650	38	58	-	10	106	16
meshchanstvo	1303	5	17	-	2	24	2
total	1953	43	75	-	12	130	7
Rybinsk							
kupechestvo	198	1	-	-	-	1	0.5
meshchanstvo	674	-	-	-	5	5	0.7
total	872	1	-	-	5	6	0.7
Mologa							
kupechestvo	67	6	1	-	-	7	10
meshchanstvo	1040	-	-	-	2	2	0.2
total	1107	6	1	-	2	9	0.8
Romanov							
kupechestvo	188	4	-	-	18	22	12
meshchanstvo	730	10	-	-	10	20	3
total	918	14	-	-	28	42	5
Poshekhon'e							
kupechestvo	156	-	-	-	-	-	0
meshchanstvo	648	1	-	-	12	13	2
total	804	1	-	-	12	13	2
Borisoglebsk							
kupechestvo	208	-	-	-	-	-	0
meshchanstvo	634	-	-	-	4	4	0.6
total	842	-	-	-	4	4	0.5

Table 27 (cont.)

Towns	Total in urban classes (1801)	Crown peasants:[a] econ.	court	other	Freed serfs[b]	Total peasants	%
Danilov							
kupechestvo	137	7	3	-	-	10	7
meshchanstvo	336	-	7	-	17	24	7
total	473	7	10	-	17	34	7
Liubim							
kupechestvo	90	-	-	5	-	5	6
meshchanstvo	470	-	-	-	2	2	0.4
total	560	-	-	5	2	7	1
Petrovsk							
kupechestvo	291	-	-	-	-	-	0
meshchanstvo	168	-	-	-	-	-	0
total	459	-	-	-	-	-	0
Myshkin							
kupechestvo	166	-	-	-	3	3	2
meshchanstvo	105	-	-	-	3	3	3
total	271	-	-	-	6	6	2
Total for province							
kupechestvo	3561	60	62	8	44	174	5
meshchanstvo	11962	17	24	-	75	116	1
total	15523	77	86	8	119	290	2

Source: TsGIA, f. 558, op. 2, d. 317, ll. 54-7, 61 ob.-65, 88 ob.-93, 106 ob.-110; d. 318, ll. 38 ob.-42, 80 ob.-84, 146 ob.-149, 206 ob.-212, 222 ob.-224.

[a]Enlisted from 1795 through 1801.

[b]Enlisted from 1797 through 1801.

[c]Figures for Iaroslavl' apparently include Norskaia Sloboda.

all towns of the province with 290 peasant registrants during the
indicated years, a total not far above that reported for 1794 and 1795.
It would therefore appear that in the aftermath of the Fifth Revision
peasant enlistment in these towns not only failed to grow but diminished
substantially. Enlistment in Rostov remained at a high level: one-third
of the indicated total of registrants was absorbed by this one town,
in which the new registrants constituted 16 percent of the kupechestvo
and 7 percent of the total posad. It should be pointed out, however,
that the Rostov contingent was swelled by registrants from the small
category of court peasants known as "falconers" (sokol'i pomytchiki),
which was in the process of liquidation, and that more than half the
Rostov total is thus attributable to accidental circumstances.[160] Of
the remaining towns Iaroslavl', Romanov and Danilov received the
largest numbers of registrants (30-42 each). Elsewhere scattered
enlistment was reported, with only Petrovsk receiving no registrants
at all. Several patterns previously observed are confirmed by the data
at hand. Crown peasants enlisted predominantly in the kupechestvo
while former serfs were more evenly divided between the kupechestvo
and meshchanstvo and in this case were more likely to be found in the
lesser category of urban citizens. Of the total number of crown peasants
enlisting in the towns of Iaroslavl' guberniia during this period, a
large proportion (45 percent) consisted of "falconer" peasants absorbed
by the Rostov posad. If this transitory phenomenon is disregarded, the
traditional predominance of freed serfs among peasants of this province
enlisting in the urban classes is once again in evidence.

---

[160] One of the major enclaves of these peasants was in the vicinity
of Rostov. See V. I. Semevskii, Krest'iane v tsarstvovanii imperatritsy
Ekateriny II, Vol. 2 (St. Petersburg, 1901), pp. 183-93.

Peasant immigration remained the chief form of population transfer affecting the urban classes of Iaroslavl' guberniia during the period following the Fifth Revision. (See Table 28.) These towns also gained 36 new citizens from the posad population of other towns (almost all of whom settled in Romanov) and 37 from various other categories of the population (principally "churchmen," returned runaways and persons of illegitimate birth). The overall effect of population transfer on the posad population of the province was positive, although modest--from the Fifth Revision through 1801 a gain of about 2 percent was recorded.

The incomplete data obtainable on enlistment of peasants in the posad population in towns of Iaroslavl' guberniia during the eighteenth century allow several conclusions. Enlistment was miniscule before the Third Revision but expanded rapidly in the period between the Third and Fourth Revisions (1764-1782) and made a significant contribution to the growth of the posad population. At the conclusion of the period new registrants from the crown peasantry alone accounted for 20 percent of the provincial kupechestvo. However, enlistment in these towns apparently peaked in this period and subsequently dropped back to lower levels, although the towns of Iaroslavl' guberniia continued to receive a steady if modest stream of peasant immigrants and remained noticeably more capable of attracting such immigrants than did the towns of Moscow guberniia (without Moscow). The towns of Iaroslavl' guberniia were able to compete successfully with Moscow itself for immigrants from the local peasantry--in the last third of the century peasants of this province were

Table 28: Net Effect of Population Transfers on Urban Classes of
Iaroslavl' Guberniia from Fifth Revision through 1801

| Towns | Enlisted from: | | | | Departed for: | | | | Net change |
	Peasantry	Other towns	Other groups	Total	Towns of Iaroslavl' gub.	Towns of other gub.	Other groups	Total	
Iaroslavl'	30	-	7	37	5	12	3	20	+17
Uglich	9	1	4	14	-	7	-	7	+7
Rostov	130	1	4	135	-	-	-	-	+135
Rybinsk	6	2	4	12	1	-	-	1	+11
Mologa	9	-	3	12	-	-	-	-	+12
Romanov	42	32	2	76	-	5	-	5	+71
Poshekhon'e	13	-	6	19	-	-	6	6	+13
Borisoglebsk	4	-	1	5	29	-	-	29	-24
Danilov	34	-	2	36	-	-	-	-	+36
Liubim	7	-	2	9	-	1	-	1	+8
Petrovsk	-	-	2	2	-	7	-	7	-5
Myshkin	6	-	-	6	-	-	-	-	+6
Total	290	36	37	363	35	32	9	76	+287

Sources: TsGIA, f. 558, op. 2, d. 317, ll. 54-110; d. 318, ll. 38 ob.-224.

[a]Data on enlistment by crown peasants covers 1795-1801; all other transfers reported for 1797-1801.

more likely to join the urban classes in nearby towns than in Moscow.[161]
The registrants, however, were distributed unevenly among these towns.
The one town consistently receiving large numbers of registrants was
not Iaroslavl', the provincial capital and largest urban settlement
of the province, but Rostov, which was only one-quarter its size.
Enlistment in Iaroslavl' and Uglich, which ranked second in size, peaked
between the Third and Fourth Revisions and subsequently diminished.
Most of the remaining towns shared to some extent in the steady trickle
of peasant immigration, although the numbers were not large enough to
have major effects on the posad population.

Data on the growth of the posad population in towns of Iaroslavl'
guberniia between the Second and Fifth Revisions are offered in Table 29.
As one of the largest concentrations of population in eighteenth-century
Russia exclusive of the capitals, Iaroslavl' presumably suffered to
some degree from the poor health conditions and negative natural
growth which were so blatantly evident in Moscow. The consequences of
this situation, combined with inadequate immigration, are visible in
the contraction of the Iaroslavl' posad population by 17 percent between
the Second and Fourth Revisions, after which it began to creep upward.
The reversal of the negative trend at this point, despite the fact that
the largest amount of immigration evidently took place between the
Third and Fourth Revisions, lends support to a theory suggested by the
data on Moscow: that significant improvements in urban health conditions
and consequently in the natural growth rate of the population in large
towns took place in the last few decades of the eighteenth century.

---

[161] The towns of Iaroslavl' guberniia also did not lose large
numbers of their own citizens to Moscow, as did the uezd towns of
Moscow guberniia, which is further evidence of the relative attenuation
of Moscow's powers of attraction in the more distant province.

Table 29: Growth of Urban Classes in Towns of Iaroslavl' Guberniia,
1744-1795 (Number of Males)

Towns	2nd Revision (1744)	4th Revision (1782)	5th Revision (1795)	% growth (1744-95)
Iaroslavl'[a]	5950	4950	5150	-13
Uglich	1700	1900	2050	21
Rostov	950	1350	1800	89
Rybinsk	600	750	850	42
Mologa	650	950	1100	69
Romanov	950	800	850	-11
Borisoglebsk	750	850	950	27
Liubim	650	600	550	-15
Total[b]	12200	12150	13300	9

Sources: GPB RO, Ermitazhnoe sobranie, No. 242 ("Vedomost' o chisle
dush po gorodam), ll. 2 ob.-11; TsGIA, f. 558, op. 2, d. 315, ll. 125-6;
d. 317, ll. 37 ob.-38; A. A. Kizevetter, Posadskaia obshchina v
Rossii XVIII stoletiia (Moscow, 1903), pp. 102-11.

[a]Figures for Iaroslavl' apparently indlude Norskaia Sloboda.

[b]Not including Poshekhon'e, Danilov, Petrovsk and Myshkin,
where posad was established only after 1775 reforms.

Among the uezd towns of Iaroslavl' guberniia, Rostov predictably recorded
the highest growth--the Rostov posad nearly doubled in size during the
half-century under review, largely, it would appear, because of peasant
enlistment and the absorption of remnants of the local archepiscopal
establishment. Of the remaining towns all except Romanov and Liubim
exhibited steady if less pronounced growth, and even in Romanov the
negative trend was reversed in the last two decades of the century.[162]
The growth was presumably the result, in varying degrees, of slow
immigration combined with modest natural increase.[163]

Nizhnii Novgorod Guberniia

Nizhnii Novgorod guberniia was on the borderline between the Central
Industrial and Middle Volga provinces and shared the characteristics
of both regions. Parts of the province, particularly its southeastern
districts, belonged to the fertile black-soil belt and supported a
relatively abundant agriculture. The infertile northern and western
districts along the Volga and Oka rivers exhibited the diversified
rural economy characteristic of the Central Industrial provinces.[164]

---

[162]The Romanov posad continued to grow after the Fifth Revision.
(See Table 28.)

[163]Exceptional events not illuminated by our sources may also have
contributed to growth of the posad population in some towns. These
events might include sudden infusions of registrants due to temporary
circumstances, such as occurred in Rostov, or administrative reclassification
of groups of persons residing in the town or in adjacent settlements.

[164]Ziablovskii, Zemleopisanie, Vol. 4, pp. 120-56; L. F. Zakharova,
Pomeshchich'i krest'iane Nizhegorodskoi gubernii i ikh klassovaia bor'ba
vo vtoroi polovine XVIII v. (dissertation, Gor'kii, Gor'kovskii
gosudarstvennyi universitet, 1954), pp. 43-44; N. A. Bogoroditskaia,
Pomeshchich'i krest'iane Nizhegorodskoi gubernii v pervoi polovine XIX v.
(po materialam Simbileiskogo imeniia grafov Orlovykh-Davydovykh) (kandidat
dissertation, Gor'kii, Gor'kovskii gosudarstvennyi universitet, 1966),
p. 21. According to data compiled by the Ministry of the Interior, at

The presence of these two major waterways--and their confluence at Nizhnii Novgorod--was a third major determinant shaping the economy of the province, drawing both urban and rural populations into participation in the water-borne commerce and transport and also attracting a large human traffic from outside the province for involvement in these pursuits.

As established in 1779, Nizhnii Novgorod guberniia consisted of thirteen districts. In the pre-reform era towns had been distributed sparsely in this territory, and thus only four of the districts were headed by previously existing towns. In addition to the provincial capital these included Balakhna (on the Volga about 30 kilometers above Nizhnii Novgorod), Arzamas (100 kilometers south of Nizhnii Novgorod on the non-navigable Tesha River) and Vasil', also known as Vasil'sursk (150 kilometers east of the provincial capital at the confluence of the Volga and Sura rivers). The remaining district towns (Makar'ev, Semenov, Gorbatov, Kniaginin, Perevoz, Sergach, Ardatov, Lukoianov, Pochinki) were settlements of court, economic and other crown peasants chosen by the government to serve as administrative centers.[165] Most of these new towns were economically negligible and

---

the beginning of the nineteenth century the province as a whole produced a considerable grain surplus (39-156 percent over local consumption needs from 1802 through 1804). (Ziablovskii, Zemleopisanie, Vol. 4, pp. 126-28).

[165]
PSZ, Vol. 20, No. 14908; Klokman, Sotsial'no-ekonomicheskaia istoriia, pp. 183-86, 280; Ziablovskii, Zemleopisanie, Vol. 41, pp.120-56; Den, Naselenie Rossii po piatoi revizii, Vol. 1, pp. 293-96. In 1796 the districts of Sergach, Pochinki and Kniaginin were abolished and their towns reduced to "non-administrative" status. These changes were accompanied by a general reshaping of district boundaries. The following year Kniaginin replaced Makar'ev and Perevoz among the district centers and the district boundaries were again redrawn. In 1798 further confusion was introduced into the territorial configuration of this province through

displayed few signs of potential urban development. They had not been selected from among the outstanding commercial and industrial villages in the province, which were mostly in the hands of private lords and thus unavailable for use as district centers, and at the time they acquired urban status all except Makar'ev and Semenov were predominantly or exclusively agricultural.[166] A survey of these towns conducted by the provincial administration (namestnicheskoe pravlenie) in 1796 found that in the interim they had developed only "the beginnings of trade and craft industry" and in some cases not even that. Peasants were still the predominant element in the population of Pochinki, Lukoianov, Perevoz, Sergach and Kniaginin, and the first three had hardly any posad population. Moreover, except for the presence of structures housing institutions of local administration the towns still resembled ordinary peasant villages in their physical appearance. For these reasons the survey concluded that none of these settlements could be considered "real" towns.[167]

As the site of one of the most important commercial fairs in Russia, Makar'ev perhaps deserves to be singled out from the remaining new towns. Founded two centuries earlier by the adjacent Makar'ev (St. Macarius)

---

the attachment of several districts of the adjacent Penza guberniia, which was abolished. However, this action was revoked in 1801, and the extra districts have been ignored in our discussion. See Den, pp. 294-96; Klokman, Sotsial'no-ekonomicheskaia istoriia, p. 280; V. I. Snezhnevskii, "Opis' delam Nizhegorodskogo namestnicheskogo pravleniia (za 1790-1799 gg.)," Deistviia NGUAK, Vol. 3 (Nizhnii Novgorod, 1898), pp. 251, 261-62.

[166]"Opisanie gorodov Nizhegorodskogo namestnichestva," in Sobranie sochinenii, vybrannykh iz mesiatseslovov, Vol. 6 (St. Petersburg, 1790), pp. 242-58; Klokman, Sotsial'no-ekonomicheskaia istoriia, p. 184.

[167]Snezhnevskii, "Opis' delam Nizhegorodskogo namestnicheskogo pravleniia," pp. 218-22. Some of these towns apparently did not even have their own institutions of urban government but instead were subject to the magistracies of the larger towns. See Snezhnevskii, "Opis' delam i dokumentam Nizhegorodskogo gorodovogo magistrata," pp. 35-37.

Monastery, the Makar'ev fair had grown to become one of the largest
entrepots for the industrial production of the entire empire as well as
for fish, furs and imported goods.[168] In the late eighteenth century
the fair occupied the entire month of July and was attended not only by
merchants and trading peasants from all parts of Russia but by Greeks,
Armenians, Germans, Englishmen and other foreigners for the purchase
and sale of goods.[169] However, the fair apparently provided little
stimulus for urban growth--the settlement remained small, populated,
according to the 1796 survey of the provincial administration, by only
600 male souls.[170] Little trade went on in the town except during the
fair, and the population made its living through rental of facilities
and provision of services to traders arriving for the fair, through
trade in wood and through craft industry (tailoring, carpentry, production
of linen cloth, bricks, chests).[171]

Also occupied at the end of the eighteenth century by a population
predominantly engaged in commercial and industrial pursuits were
Semenov and Gorbatov.[172] The inhabitants of Semenov, situated in a
particularly infertile area, no longer bothered with agriculture and
occupied themselves principally with craft industry, producing large

---

[168]See B. B. Kafengauz, Ocherki vnutrennego rynka Rossii pervoi
poloviny XVIII v. (Moscow, 1958), pp. 114-90.

[169]"Opisanie gorodov Nizhegorodskogo namestnichestva," p. 256;
Ziablovskii, Zemleopisanie, Vol. 4, p. 136.

[170]Snezhnevskii, "Opis' delam Nizhegorodskogo namestnicheskogo
pravleniia," p. 221.

[171]Ibid., pp. 221, 238; "Opisanie gorodov Nizhegorodskogo namestnichestva,"
p. 255; Ziablovskii, Zemleopisanie, Vol. 4, p. 137; Klokman, Sotsial'no-
ekonomicheskaia istoriia, pp. 184, 278.

[172]Snezhnevskii, "Opis' delam i dokumentam Nizhegorodskogo gorodovogo
magistrata," pp. 37-41, 63-64; Snezhnevskii, "Opis' delam Nizhegorodskogo
namestnicheskogo pravleniia," pp. 244, 249-50.

quantities of wooden articles as well as metal tools, linen cloth, leather, footwear and hats. The population of Gorbatov made its living from transit trade in fish and hemp, trade in textiles in the surrounding rural area, craft industry (production of metal goods, rope, fish nets), work on river transport, orchard-keeping and only to a limited extent from grain cultivation. In the remaining new towns agriculture remained the principal occupation, accompanied in most cases by minor craft industries but little in the way of trade, except at weekly markets and the small annual fairs in Ardatov and Pochinki.[173] In Gorbatov and Sergach markets were totally lacking, and goods produced in these towns had to be taken to nearby village markets for local sale.[174] Not much more promising was the older town of Vasil', where the posad consisted of no more than 450 males according to the Fifth Revision.[175] In addition to some agriculture the inhabitants were involved in the grain trade and in hauling goods on the Volga "in their own boats," but the town itself was virtually devoid of trade and industry.[176] So underdeveloped was the town market that the local population had to travel to nearby rural markets to purchase foodstuffs for consumption, since the peasants did not bother to bring their produce to the town itself.[177]

---

[173]Snezhnevskii, "Opis' delam Nizhegorodskogo namestnicheskogo pravleniia," pp. 218-22, 238-48, 251-54; "Opisanie gorodov Nizhegorodskogo namestnichestva," pp. 246-58; Ziablovskii, Zemleopisanie, Vol. 4, pp. 140-56.

[174]Snezhnevskii, "Opis' delam Nizhegorodskogo namestnicheskogo pravleniia," pp. 222, 253; Snezhnevskii, "Opis' delam i dokumentam Nizhegorodskogo gorodovogo magistrata," p. 63.

[175]TsGIA, f. 558, op. 2, d. 148, 11. 36-44.

[176]Snezhnevskii, "Opis' delam Nizhegorodskogo namestnicheskogo pravleniia," pp. 226-27, 239; "Opisanie gorodov Nizhegorodskogo namestnichestva," pp. 253-55; Ziablovskii, Zemleopisanie, Vol. 4, p. 139.

[177]Snezhnevskii, "Opis' delam Nizhegorodskogo namestnicheskogo pravleniia," p. 216. A similar situation prevailed in the new town of Gorbatov, which was totally without a market.

The province thus contained only three well developed urban
settlements, Nizhnii Novgorod, Arzamas and Balakhna. Nizhnii Novgorod,
recovering from an earlier period of decline, by the end of the
eighteenth century contained more than 2000 houses and a total population
of 10,000 to 15,000, of which 35-45 percent belonged to the urban
classes.[178] The city owed its economic importance to its position at
the confluence of the Volga and Oka and its consequent role as one of
the busiest Volga ports. At "Nizhegorod" cargoes of grain descending
the Oka and intended for distribution via the Volga crossed paths with
shipments of salt, iron, fish and other goods from the Urals and the
"downstream" provinces, headed toward Moscow via the Oka and Moskva or
toward Petersburg via the Upper Volga.[179] Since these cargoes frequently
had to be reloaded onto different vessels before continuing their
journey, Nizhnii Novgorod became a major center for the sale and
transshipment of these goods and for the hiring of labor to man the
boats. According to contemporary descriptions the harbor at Nizhnii
Novgorod was in the late eighteenth century visited annually by

---

[178]
    Snezhnevskii, "Opis' delam i dokumentam Nizhegorodskogo gorodovogo
magistrata," pp. 6-7; "Opisanie gorodov Nizhegorodskogo namestnichestva,"
pp. 244-45; Ziablovskii, Zemleopisanie, Vol. 4, p. 133; TsGIA, f. 558,
op. 2, d. 149, 11. 160 ob.-164. Other groups listed as contributing to
the population of Nizhnii Novgorod include nobles, officials, clergy,
military personnel, iamshchiki and peasants.

[179]In addition, shipments of wood, hemp and industrial goods
descended the Volga from Nizhnii Novgorod, although these were evidently
less voluminous than the upstream traffic.

between 2000 and 3000 vessels, employing up to 70,000 workers.[180]

The city was also on the important overland route connecting Moscow with Kazan', Orenburg and Siberia.[181]

The economic pursuits of the Nizhnii Novgorod population were naturally shaped by the proximity of the Volga and the heavy traffic passing through the town as a result. The wealthiest local merchants were those engaged in transit trade, dealing in grain, iron, fish, wood and tallow.[182] However, the role of Nizhnii Novgorod merchants in these lucrative pursuits was apparently not especially prominent. In 1799 the local magistracy reported that there were no "outstanding" (znatneishii) merchants in the town and no members of the first guild.[183] However, Nizhnii Novgorod merchants controlled a large domestic market, served as of 1787 by 468 stores, about one for every 20 inhabitants.[184]

---

[180]"Opisanie gorodov Nizhegorodskogo namestnichestva," pp. 242, 245-46; Ziablovskii, Zemleopisanie, Vol. 4, p. 134; Snezhnevskii, "Opis' delam i dokumentam Nizhegorodskogo gorodovogo magistrata," pp. 13-14; Klokman, Sotsial'no-ekonomicheskaia istoriia, p. 268.

[181]"Opisanie gorodov Nizhegorodskogo namestnichestva," pp. 242-43.

[182]Ibid., pp. 244-45; Snezhnevskii, "Opis' delam i dokumentam Nizhegorodskogo gorodovogo magistrata," pp. 41, 72-73. On the activities of Nizhnii Novgorod merchants in Saratov and other Lower Volga settlements and their participation in the fish trade, see also E.N. Kusheva, Saratov v tretei chetverti XVIII v. (Saratov, 1928), pp. 10-11.

[183]Snezhnevskii, "Opis' delam i dokumentam Nizhegorodskogo gorodovogo magistrata," p. 41. Observers in the late 1770's also commented negatively on the development of commerce among the population of Nizhnii Novgorod, finding that the town did not have such "extensive commercial enterprises" as would be expected from its location and significance. See "Primechaniia, sluzhashchie k poznaniiu domostroitel'stva i sostoianiia mest po reke Volge ot Nizhnego Novagoroda /sic/ do Syzrani lezhashchikh," Akademicheskie izvestiia na 1780 g., Vol. 5, pp. 506-07. These comments are repeated in Shchekatov's Geograficheskii slovar' (Vol. 4, p. 590).

[184]Snezhnevskii, "Opis' delam i dokumentam Nizhegorodskogo gorodovogo magistrata," p. 3.

Although they also dealt in textiles, iron goods, chandlery and "many other things," the principal business of these stores was the sale of foodstuffs, for which the heavy flow of itinerant merchants and laborers and other travelers provided a greatly expanded clientele.[185] Many townsmen profited from this traffic by operating inns.[186]

Large-scale industry in Nizhnii Novgorod was also responsive to the needs of the Volga traffic--it consisted mainly of a dozen enterprises producing various kinds of rope, with an output valued at nearly 100,000 rubles annually. These goods were sold locally for use by river vessels and also sent to other river ports both upstream and downstream.[187] Data collected by the Commerce Commission in the 1760's credit the town with 150-160 craftsmen, distributed among seventeen specialties and constituting about 10 percent of the male posad population of that time.[188] Many of these artisans were occupied in professions involving the production of finished goods from animal products (tanners, furriers, cobblers, glovers, hatters, candlemakers), industries which had a long

---

[185] Ibid., p. 41; "Opisanie gorodov Nizhegorodskogo namestnichestva," p. 245; Ziablovskii, Zemleopisanie, Vol. 4, p. 134.

[186] Snezhnevskii, "Opis' delam i dokumentam Nizhegorodskogo gorodovogo magistrata," p. 9.

[187] Ibid., pp. 21-23, 73; Snezhnevskii, "Opis' delam Nizhegorodskogo namestnicheskogo pravleniia," p. 236; Ziablovskii, Zemleopisanie, Vol. 4, p. 134. Also functioning in Nizhnii Novgorod were one fair-sized textile manufactory (producing linen sail-cloth), enterprises producing tallow candles, bricks and pottery, one foundry, one brewery, one malthouse and flour mills.

[188] TsGADA, f. 397, d. 441, ll. 55 ob., 218; Knabe, "Die Struktur der russischen Posadgemeinden," p. 320. According to the data of the Commerce Commission, the Nizhnii Novgorod posad included 59-69 craft-guild members and 92 craftsmen who were not members of guilds. Another source, however, refers to the presence of 216 craft-guild members at the time of the Third Revision (1762-65). GPB RO, Ermitazhnoe sobranie, No. 242, ll. 55 ob.-56.

history in this town.[189] The remaining artisans were mostly tailors,
carpenters, blacksmiths, silversmiths and other metal craftsmen. Later
sources also assign a prominent role in the town's craft industries to
tailors, cobblers, silversmiths and candlemakers, as well as to the
spinning of flax and the production of various linen and woolen articles.
In the 1790's each of these categories of artisans was reported to
produce goods worth thousands of rubles annually.[190]

Sources of the late eighteenth century credit Balakhna, the other
major Volga town of Nizhnii Novgorod guberniia, with a permanent
population of 3000-3500 persons of both sexes, of whom about 90 percent
belonged to the posad.[191] The economy of this town traditionally had
been based on the extraction of salt, but as this industry declined
rapidly in the second half of the eighteenth century the inhabitants
turned increasingly to various crafts, among which the most important
were boat-building and the production of ceramic tiles for use in building
stoves. Supplementing the output of local craftsmen were several "factory"
enterprises producing textiles, rope, leather, bricks and ceramics.
The wealthiest citizens of Balakhna were those involved in the Volga
transit trade, dealing in grain and contracting with the government salt

---

[189] See Klokman, Sotsial'no-ekonomicheskaia istoriia, pp. 267-68.

[190] Snezhnevskii, "Opis' delam i dokumentam Nizhegorodskogo gorodovogo
magistrata," pp. 23-25; see also "Opisanie gorodov Nizhegorodskogo
namestnichestva," p. 245; Ziablovskii, Zemleopisanie, Vol. 4, p. 134.

[191] "Opisanie gorodov Nizhegorodskogo namestnichestva," p. 257;
Klokman, Sotsial'no-ekonomicheskaia istoriia, p. 276. These estimates
are also supported by archival data from the Fifth Revision supplied by
Prof. Gilbert Rozman.

monopoly to transport salt shipments from the Lower Volga and the Kama

basin to various "upstream" points, while the lower strata of the town

population (as in most Volga towns) frequently turned to wage labor on

the river transport. The town itself was evidently of little importance

as a port or market.[192]

The town of Arzamas was in the late eighteenth century reported to

contain more than 1400 houses and a total permanent population approaching

6000, of which about 90 percent was included in the posad.[193] Unlike the

other large towns of the province Arzamas was not situated on a navigable

waterway but was on the important Moscow-Saratov overland route. This

town was primarily an industrial center, although its merchants also

did a large business in linen and hempen cloth (kholst)--in the 1790's

they reportedly purchased more than 1.5 million arshina annually for

resale in other markets.[194] Arzamas was particularly known for industries

involving the processing of animal products. The many tanneries and

soap factories of the town made a strong impression on contemporary

observers, both for their number and productivity and for the malodorous

---

[192] "Opisanie gorodov Nizhegorodskogo namestnichestva," pp. 257-58;
Ziablovskii, Zemleopisanie, Vol. 4, pp. 152-53; Snezhnevskii, "Opis' delam
Nizhegorodskogo namestnicheskogo pravleniia," p. 239; Klokman, Sotsial'no-
ekonomicheskaia istoriia, pp. 275-76; P. G. Ryndziunskii, Gorodskoe
grazhdanstvo doreformennoi Rossii (Moscow, 1958), p. 23.

[193] "Opisanie gorodov Nizhegorodskogo namestnichestva," p. 247; Klokman,
Sotsial'no-ekonomicheskaia istoriia, p. 272; also archival data from the
Fifth Revision supplied by Prof. Gilbert Rozman.

[194] Snezhnevskii, "Opis' delam Nizhegorodskogo namestnicheskogo
pravleniia," p. 246. (1 arshin=28 in.)

emissions they produced.[195] Craft industry also played a very large role in the town's economy. The data gathered by the Commerce Commission in the 1760's indicate the presence of 600-1000 craftsmen, constituting 27-45 percent of the total male posad population.[196] Another source maintains that the inhabitants were "almost all craftsmen" and were for the most part very prosperous.[197] Many of these artisans were engaged in converting leather produced by local tanneries into finished goods, particularly boots, and others in dyeing cloth for local merchants. Goods from Arzamas were sold in Petersburg, Astrakhan', Cherkassk, at the Makar'ev and other major fairs, and in other "faraway" places.[198]

Lacking in well developed towns among the settlements officially designated as such, Nizhnii Novgorod guberniia displayed an unusually high degree of "urbanization" in the countryside. According to a scholar who has studied the serf peasantry of this province, the descriptions of individual villages in the "economic notes" to the General Land Survey indicate that 70 percent of the serf population engaged to some degree in

[195]Ziablovskii, Zemleopisanie, Vol. 4, pp. 146-47; "Primechaniia, sluzhashchie k poznaniiu domostroitel'stva i sostoianiia mest okolo rek Sury i Sviagi lezhashchikh," Akademicheskie izvestiia na 1780 g., Vol. 5, pp. 55-62. According to data gathered by the provincial administration in 1797, these industries annually produced goods worth about 60,000 rubles. Snezhnevskii, "Opis' delam Nizhegorodskogo namestnicheskogo pravleniia," p. 246.

[196]TsGADA, f. 397, d. 441, l. 57; Knabe, p. 321. The materials of the Commerce Commission mention 616 non-guild artisans, while information on the number of guild members is ambiguous--it is given in various documents as 43, 421 and 438.

[197]Ziablovskii, Zemleopisanie, Vol. 4, p. 145. This comment was apparently drawn from the observations of P. S. Pallas, who visited the town in 1768. See Klokman, Sotsial'no-ekonomicheskaia istoriia, p. 272, n. 234.

[198]Snezhnevskii, "Opis' delam Nizhegorodskogo namestnicheskogo pravleniia," p. 246; "Opisanie gorodov Nizhegorodskogo namestnichestva," pp. 247-48; Ziablovskii, Zemleopisanie, Vol. 4, pp. 145-46.

non-agricultural occupations.[199] As in most provinces of the Central
Industrial Region, involvement in such occupations as a part-time
supplement to agriculture or by part of the population of an agricultural
village was widespread. However, Nizhnii Novgorod guberniia also
contained many villages where highly developed commercial and industrial
occupations employed virtually the entire population, and such settlements, by virtue of their size and economic development, were frequently
compared to towns by contemporary observers.

Perhaps the most widely known of these settlements was Pavlovo
village, a property of the Sheremetev family in Gorbatov uezd. By the
seventeenth century, the population of Pavlovo was already involved to
some extent in transit trade and craft industry.[200] In the late
eighteenth century the "village" reportedly had a population of about
6000 persons of both sexes, 6 stone churches, more than 200 stores and
26 inns, and was characterized by one description as "one of the most
important, wealthiest and most noteworthy settlements in this country."[201]
Its inhabitants were particularly famed as skilled metal craftsmen and
produced large quantities of locks, knives, scissors and even pistols,
which were marketed principally at the Makar'ev fair and from there

[199]Zakharova, Pomeshchich'i krest'iane Nizhegorodskoi gubernii, p. 96.

[200]K. N. Shchepetov, "Torgovo-promyshlennaia deiatel'nost' i
rassloenie krest'ianstva v votchinakh Cherkasskikh v XVII v.," in K
voprosu o pervonachal'nom nakoplenii v Rossii (XVII-XVIII vv.) (Moscow,
1958), pp. 55-63; V.S. Bakulin, "Orel kak khlebnyi rynok vo vtoroi
polovine XVII v.," in Goroda feodal'noi Rossii (Moscow, 1966), pp. 260-61.

[201]Ziablovskii, Zemleopisanie, Vol. 4, pp. 150-51; Zakharova, p.126;
Materialy po istorii krest'ianskoi promyshlennosti (MPIKP), Vol. 1
(Moscow-Leningrad, 1935), pp. 331-33. This population figure evidently
includes nearby hamlets (derevni) administratively subordinate to the
village.

distributed throughout Russia and exported to Persia as well.[202]

Industries involving the processing of animal products--tanneries and

soap factories--were also extensively developed in this settlement.

The industrial output of Pavlovo was valued at hundreds of thousands

of rubles and apparently surpassed that of Arzamas and Nizhnii Novgorod.[203]

Peasants of Pavlovo were active in transit trade, selling locally

produced goods in Moscow, Petersburg, Astrakhan', at the Makar'ev

fair and in other markets, purchasing raw materials for use by local

industries and dealing in foodstuffs. The village itself was a significant

market, where merchants came to buy finished goods and raw materials

and where rural industrial and agricultural producers of the surrounding

territory often shipped their own goods for sale. According to the

ekonomicheskie primechaniia, during weekly markets at Pavlovo 54 stores

selling metal goods were in operation, while other stores sold foodstuffs,

textiles, leather goods, chandlery, rope and assorted small household

---

[202] Ziablovskii, Zemleopisanie, Vol. 4, pp. 150-51; MPIKP, Vol. 1, pp. 331-35; Zakharova, p. 100. Not everyone shared a high opinion of arms made in Pavlovo, however. According to the deputy of the armorers (oruzheinaia sloboda) of Tula to the Legislative Commission of 1767, these guns were more dangerous to the user than to the intended victim, for which reason the Ukrainian Cossack regiments were prohibited from purchasing them. (Sb. IRIO, Vol. 8, pp. 260-61)

[203] The ekonomicheskie primechaniia for Gorbatov uezd, cited in several works, assign values to the major sectors of production in Pavlovo as follows: metal industries 240,000 rubles; soap factories 258,000 rubles; tanneries 110,000 rubles; total 608,000 rubles. (MPIKP, Vol. 1, p. 332; Zakharova, p. 100.) Data gathered by the provincial administration in 1797 give much lower values for the soap and leather industries (96,000 and 80,000 rubles respectively) while confirming the above valuation of the metal-goods sector. The same source credits Arzamas with an output of about 50,000 rubles from tanneries, 21,000 rubles from soap mills and 75,000 rubles from cloth-printing, while the output of Nizhnii Novgorod factories was placed at about 110,000 rubles. (Snezhnevskii, "Opis' delam Nizhegorodskogo namestnicheskogo pravleniia," pp. 236-37, 245-46.)

goods (shchepetil'nye tovary). One Pavlovo peasant, with a capital of 25,000 rubles, brought textiles from all parts of Russia for sale in the village.[204]

Another peasant settlement which "in view of its enormous size could be considered a town" was Murashkino (Kniaginin uezd). Tanneries were the chief industry in this village, but many inhabitants engaged in other industrial pursuits "suited only to towns," working as tin-smiths, coppersmiths, silversmiths, tailors, cobblers, glovers and soap-makers.[205] Lyskovo village (Makar'ev uezd) was already functioning as an important Volga port in the seventeenth century and in our period was a major entrepot of the Volga grain trade.[206] Its inhabitants participated in this trade, dealt in wood and sold various goods at the Makar'ev fair. The village also had much industry and produced dyed linen cloth, leather, rope and malt.[207] Gorodets (Balakhna uezd), another Volga settlement, somewhat resembled Lyskovo in that its inhabitants combined participation in the Volga grain trade with a variety of industries, producing textiles, dyes, leather goods and iron

---

[204] MPIKP, Vol. 1, pp. 332-34; Zakharova, p. 126.

[205] Ziablovskii, Zemleopisanie, Vol. 4, pp. 141-42; Snezhnevskii, "Opis' delam Nizhegorodskogo namestnicheskogo pravleniia," pp. 238-39; Zakharova, p. 98.

[206] TsGVIA, f. VUA, No. 18860, 1. 146; Snezhnevskii, "Opis' delam i dokumentam Nizhegorodskogo gorodovogo magistrata," pp. 13-14; Zhurnal, ili zapiska zhizni i prikliuchenii Ivana Alekseevicha Tolchenova, pp. 33-35, 50-51; F. N. Rodin, Burlachestvo v Rossii (Moscow, 1975), pp. 40-42.

[207] Snezhnevskii, "Opis' delam Nizhegorodskogo namestnicheskogo pravleniia," pp. 238-39; Ziablovskii, Zemleopisanie, Vol. 4, p. 137; "Primechaniia, sluzhashchie k poznaniiu domostroitel'stva i sostoianiia mest po reke Volge ot Nizhnego Novagoroda do Syzrani lezhashchikh," pp. 508-09.

wares (especially anchors). Among the larger industrial enterprises in the possession of these peasants were ten tanneries and a cloth-printing "factory". The weekly market in Gorodets did a large amount of business and attracted merchants and trading peasants from "various towns and districts."[208]

Rabotki village, on the Volga in Makar'ev uezd, was known for its blacksmiths, for boat-building and for the production of rope, and Vorsma (Gorbatov uezd) primarily for metallurgy.[209] Another center of metallurgical industry was Bezvodnoe village (Nizhnii Novgorod uezd), where the inhabitants specialized in the production of wire. The wealthiest peasants of Bezvodnoe occupied themselves with marketing the local product, principally in Moscow, in which activity they benefited from the assistance of Prince Iusupov, the owner of the settlement.[210] The tanneries and soap and tallow factories of Vyezdnaia Sloboda, a seigneurial village in Arzamas uezd, competed with those of Arzamas

---

[208] Snezhnevskii, "Opis' delam Nizhegorodskogo namestnicheskogo pravleniia," p. 242; Ziablovskii, Zemleopisanie, Vol. 4, p. 154; Shchekatov, Geograficheskii slovar', Vol. 1, p. 327; Sb. IRIO, Vol. 134 (St. Petersburg, 1911), p. 32. Gorodets, unlike most of the examples cited, was not a serf village but rather a court property.

[209] Snezhnevskii, "Opis' delam i dokumentam Nizhegorodskogo gorodovogo magistrata," p. 13; Snezhnevskii, "Opis' delam Nizhegorodskogo namestnicheskogo pravleniia," pp. 238-39; Ziablovskii, Zemleopisanie, Vol. 4, p. 138; MPIKP, Vol. 1, p. 335. Vorsma was another Sheremetev property.

[210] Snezhnevskii, "Opis' delam Nizhegorodskogo namestnicheskogo pravleniia," p. 238; Ziablovskii, Zemleopisanie, Vol. 4, p. 135; Zakharova, pp. 101-08. Iusupov established a "bank" in Moscow for these trading peasants, which accepted deposits repayable from estate funds in the village.

itself and drew the resentful attention of the Arzamas posad.[211]
Bogorodskoe (Gorbatov uezd) and Katunki (Balakhna uezd) specialized in
the production of leather and leather articles. In 1797 the Nizhnii
Novgorod provincial administration reported the presence of 46 tanneries
in the former and 25 in the latter.[212] The villages of Bor (Semenov
uezd) and Krasnoe (Arzamas uezd) and the settlements of Zauzol'skaia
volost' (Balakhna uezd) produced large quantities of felt articles
(hats, boots).[213] The rope production of Izbylets village (Gorbatov
uezd) was valued by the 1797 statistics of the provincial administration
at 40,000 rubles. This settlement also produced fish nets and footwear.[214]

The above listing covers only the most outstanding industrial
villages of Nizhnii Novgorod guberniia, settlements producing industrial
products worth tens or even hundreds of thousands of rubles annually.
Many of these villages also had significant commercial functions, serving
as major local markets and in at least one case as an important entrepot.
The most important branches of industry in such highly developed villages
were metallurgy, industries based on the processing of animal products
(production of leather and leather goods, felt articles, soap, tallow)
and the production of goods for use in various Volga industries (rope,
fish nets). Such industries and others as well were present, if less

---

[211]
Sb. IRIO, Vol. 134, pp. 24-25; Zakharova, pp. 112-13. In the
1760's the owner of Vyezdnaia Sloboda was Count S. V. Saltykov.

[212]
Snezhnevskii, "Opis' delam Nizhegorodskogo namestnicheskogo
pravleniia," pp. 241-42, 245-46; Ziablovskii, Zemleopisanie, Vol. 4,
pp. 151, 153; Zakharova, pp. 109-13.

[213]
Snezhnevskii, "Opis' delam Nizhegorodskogo namestnicheskogo
pravleniia," pp. 242-43, 248; Ziablovskii, Zemleopisanie, Vol. 4, p. 155.
The industries of Bor also produced metal goods, tallow and glue.

[214]
Snezhnevskii, "Opis' delam Nizhegorodskogo namestnicheskogo
pravleniia," pp. 245-46; Ziablovskii, Zemleopisanie, Vol. 4, pp. 151-52.

intensively developed, in many other villages. Rural metallurgical industries in the districts of Semenov and Arzamas produced a variety of tools (spades, axes, scythes, sickles, knives) as well as nails and bushings for wagon wheels. Makar'ev and Balakhna districts produced small decorative metal goods such as buttons, studs and rings, while Makar'ev and Semenov districts contributed articles made of iron leaf, including snuff-boxes and holders for tea glasses. Peasants in some villages of Balakhna, Gorbatov and Ardatov districts operated boatyards, while wheels, carts, sleighs and other land vehicles were constructed in the districts of Nizhnii Novgorod, Makar'ev, Gorbatov, Arzamas, Ardatov and Lukoianov. Linen textiles were produced and sold by peasants of Balakhna, Gorbatov, Semenov, Kniaginin, and Perevoz uezdy, while production of pottery is documented for Balakhna, Gorbatov and Arzamas uezdy. Production of various kinds of footwear and articles of clothing, of wooden vessels and utensils and of bast mats, sacks and cord was widespread in many districts.[215]

In general, rural industries were intensively developed in the northern and northwestern districts of the province, adjoining the Volga and Oka (the districts of Balakhna, Semenov, Gorbatov, Nizhnii Novgorod and Makar'ev), as well as in Arzamas uezd, but much less so on the eastern and southern fringes. In Vasil' uezd, at the easternmost edge of the province, the provincial administration found in 1797 that the peasants produced craft goods "only for their own use."[216] The same survey

---

[215] Ziablovskii, Zemleopisanie, Vol. 4, pp. 128-54; Snezhnevskii, "Opis' delam Nizhegorodskogo namestnicheskogo pravleniia," pp. 238-50.

[216] Snezhnevskii, "Opis' delam Nizhegorodskogo namestnicheskogo pravleniia," p. 239. Another source refers to the production of tallow and malt, some of which was sold in Petersburg, but no other industries. (Ziablovskii, Zemleopisanie, Vol. 4, p. 140.)

indicates that peasants in Perevoz uezd were involved only in household

textile industry and in the southerly Ardatov uezd engaged in a variety

of crafts but only on a part-time basis.[217]

Village industry and commerce, despite their high level of

development in this province, did not absorb all those peasants seeking

income through non-agricultural occupations and in fact coexisted with

a high level of temporary migration (otkhod). According to a scholar

who has studied data on passports issued by the government for this

purpose, 15 to 20 percent of the adult male peasant population was on

otkhod in 1765.[218] The largest numbers of migrants, particularly from

districts such as Balakhna, Semenov, Nizhnii Novgorod and Makar'ev, all

of which adjoined the Volga, found work on the river transport, which

had large manpower needs.[219] Departures for work on the Volga were

recorded even in villages with well developed industries. In 1765, 110

peasants of Bogorodskoe, mentioned above as a center of leather production,

left their village for this purpose.[220] In Vasil'evo village (Balakhna

---

[217] Snezhnevskii, "Opis' delam Nizhegorodskogo namestnicheskogo pravleniia," pp. 244, 249.

[218] Zakharova, p. 117. This level of migration, although impressive enough, appears to be substantially lower than that recorded by Iaroslval' guberniia.

[219] Ibid.; Ziablovskii, Zemleopisanie, Vol. 4, pp. 135, 140-41, 153; S. I. Arkhangel'skii, "Simbileiskaia votchina Vl. Gr. Orlova (1790-1800 gg.)," Trudy Nizhegorodskogo nauchnogo obshchestva po izucheniiu mestnogo kraia, Vol. 2 (Nizhnii Novgorod, 1929), pp. 176-78. One scholar has estimated that the river transport of the Volga basin, including the Volga itself from Astrakhan' to Rybinsk and the Kama, Oka and Moskva rivers, employed more than 200,000 workers in the late eighteenth century. (Rodin, Burlachestvo v Rossii, pp. 75-82.)

[220] Zakharova, p. 119.

uezd) the inhabitants reportedly worked on the Volga in the summer and in winter occupied themselves with production of pottery.[221] Peasant involvement in Volga shipping was not limited to service as hired laborers. Some peasants were the owners of river vessels, on which they transported their own cargoes or those of other traders. Of 84 vessels arriving in Iaroslavl' with shipments of grain, fish, caviar, salt and various other goods from June through November of 1765, 15 belonged to peasants of Lyskovo, Rabotki, Gorodets or other villages of Nizhnii Novgorod and Balakhna uezdy.[222] In some districts of Nizhnii Novgorod guberniia (Arzamas, Kniaginin, Vasil') overland transport (izvoz) was a major migratory occupation.[223]

In this province as elsewhere in the Central Industrial Region, peasants were also active in the transit trade served by this transport network, buying goods in the producing region or in entrepot markets and shipping them to distant points for resale. The involvement of peasants (and particularly those of such large Volga villages as Lyskovo, Rabotki and Gorodets) in the long-distance trade in grain has already been noted.[224] Peasants of Balakhna uezd and those of Lyskovo and Rabotki

---

[221] Ziablovskii, Zemleopisanie, Vol. 4, pp. 153-54.

[222] TsGADA, f. 455, op. 1, d. 409, ll. 1-14 ob. These data, of course, refer to the districts of Nizhnii Novgorod and Balakhna in their larger pre-reform configuration. Sixteen of the vessels belonged to peasants of ten other districts.

[223] Zakharova, p. 117.

[224] Ziablovskii, Zemleopisanie, Vol. 4, pp. 137, 154; Zakharova, p. 127; Snezhnevskii, "Opis' delam i dokumentam Nizhegorodskogo gorodovogo magistrata," p. 83.

also participated in the Volga trade in wood, which was shipped from
the forested "upstream" areas down river as far as Saratov and Astrakhan'.[225]
Many peasants, particularly those of Nizhnii Novgorod, Balakhna and
Makar'ev uezdy, were attracted to the fishing industries of the Lower
Volga and the Iaik (Ural) River and to trade in the resulting production,
some forming enterprises employing hired labor for the exploitation of
these fisheries. Various sources refer to the sale in Moscow by
peasants of Nizhnii Novgorod guberniia of fish either caught by their
own efforts or purchased in Saratov, Astrakhan', Samara, Syzran' and
other markets of the Lower Volga and Iaik territories.[226] Local trading
peasants, particularly those of such major industrial villages as
Pavlovo, Lyskovo and Bezvodnoe, sold the rural industrial production of
the province in Moscow, at the Makar'ev fair and in other markets and
also made purchases in these markets for resale elsewhere.[227] Peasants
of Ardatov uezd hauled locally produced vegetable oils to Moscow,
Petersburg and other towns for sale.[228]

Information on migration by peasants of this province to towns for
temporary or long-term settlement is limited, but it is evident that the

---

[225]
Snezhnevskii, "Opis' delam Nizhegorodskogo namestnicheskogo
pravleniia," p. 241; Ziablovskii, Zemleopisanie, Vol. 4, p. 137;
Zakharova, p. 127.

[226]
Zakharova, pp. 117, 121-24; Kusheva, "Torgovlia Moskvy," p. 54;
Kusheva, "Saratov v pervoi polovine XVIII v.," in Problemy sotsial'no-
ekonomicheskoi istorii Rossii (Moscow, 1971), pp. 44-49.

[227]
MPIKP, Vol. 1, pp. 331-35; Ziablovskii, Zemleopisanie, Vol. 4,
p. 137; Zakharova, pp. 101-08, 129; Kusheva, "Torgovlia Moskvy," pp. 56, 61.
[228]
Zakharova, p. 127.

towns of the Middle and Lower Volga were a major attraction. The

migrants were drawn to these towns by the fish trade, by work on Volga

transport and by employment in the extraction of salt, a major industry

of the region.[229] Some migrants, particularly those successful in

commercial activity and those no longer involved in the village economy

and therefore without incentive to return home, settled permanently

in these towns.[230] In 1745 and 1746 twelve houses in Saratov were

purchased by peasants from the estate of the Trinity-St. Sergei Monastery

in **Nizhnii** Novgorod uezd, several of whom later **enlisted in the Saratov**

kupechestvo.[231] **Some peasants of Semenov uezd reportedly worked in Moscow**

as carriage-builders.[232] However, the fact that Nizhnii Novgorod **guberniia**

contributed few of the peasant registrants absorbed into the Moscow

posad between the Third and Fifth Revisions, especially in comparison

with those Central Russian provinces which were closer to Moscow,

suggests that migration to the old capital was not particularly important

among the peasantry of this province.[233]

---

[229] Ibid., p. 117; Snezhnevskii, "Opis' delam Nizhegorodskogo namestnicheskogo pravleniia," p. 251; Bogoroditskaia, Pomeshchich'i krest'iane Nizhegorodskoi gubernii, pp. 74-75.

[230] As has been pointed out, peasants working on Volga transport were unable to participate significantly in agriculture, since the navigation and growing seasons were roughly the same. Agriculture might be continued by other members of the family, however, which would create an incentive for the migrant to return home during the off-season.

[231] Kusheva, "Saratov v pervoi polovine XVIII v.," p. 34.

[232] Zakharova, p. 117.

[233] See above, Chapter IV, Tables 7, 12.

The complaints of Nizhnii Novgorod, Arzamas and Balakhna to the
Legislative Commission of 1767 do not comment on immigration by peasants,
concentrating instead on competition from commercial and industrial
villages and peasant settlements adjacent to the towns themselves.[234]
However, it is clear that large numbers of migrants at least passed
through the provincial capital, which was one of the major hiring points
for work on the Volga transport network. There is also evidence of
long-term peasant settlement in the town. In 1783 the provincial
administration identified 283 court, economic and seigneurial peasants
residing in Nizhnii Novgorod "with and without passports, in their own
houses and in rented quarters in the houses of various kinds of people."[235]
In 1799 a report of the town _duma_ pointed out that peasants were settling
in Nizhnii Novgorod and "unlawfully engaging in urban commerce,"
principally by operating inns and taverns and producing and selling
various prepared foodstuffs. This activity was encouraged by the large
demand for these goods and services created by the heavy traffic of
merchants and laborers passing through the town, a demand which according
to the _duma_ the local population was not able to satisfy on its own.[236]

---

[234] Sb. IRIO, Vol. 134, pp. 4-10, 24-25, 32-33.

[235] Snezhnevskii, "Opis' zhurnalam Nizhegorodskogo namestnicheskogo
pravleniia za 1781-83 gg.," Deistviia NGUAK, Vol. 3, p. 177.

[236] Snezhnevskii, "Opis' delam i dokumentam Nizhegorodskogo gorodovogo
magistrata," pp. 30-32. The _duma_, representing all classes of the "urban
society" (_gradskoe obshchestvo_), proposed that the authorities recognize
the inevitability of this illicit trade and profit from it by legalizing
it and placing a tax on it. However, this proposal was resisted by the
magistracy, which spoke for the _posad_ alone.

Other documents of urban and provincial institutions refer to the fact
that local clergymen and other residents not belonging to the posad
sometimes constructed stores and warehouses on their property and rented
these to trading peasants.[237]

For further evidence of immigration by peasants into the towns of
Nizhnii Novgorod guberniia we may turn to data on enlistment of such
immigrants in the urban classes of these towns, although the available
data are more limited in this case than for the provinces discussed
earlier. As was mentioned in a previous chapter, the Second and Third
Revisions recorded a substantial number of "seigneurial peasants
registered in the mercantile oklad" in Nizhnii Novgorod uezd. These,
however, were apparently not registrants in the Nizhnii Novgorod posad
but rather residents of a suburban peasant settlement, Elagoveshchenskaia
Sloboda, who had been placed involuntarily in the urban tax category
because of their involvement in commercial and industrial pursuits.[238]
The Nizhnii Novgorod posad itself reported no registrants in the Second
Revision and 17 in the subsequent census.[239] The Second and Third
Revisions credited Balakhna with 16-21 registrants (1-2 percent of its
posad population), while Arzamas was reported in each census to have a
single peasant registrant.[240]

---

[237] Ibid., p. 9; Snezhnevskii, "Opis' delam Nizhegorodskogo
namestnicheskogo pravleniia," p. 259; TsGADA, f. 397, d. 441, l. 215.

[238] See above, Chapter III, p. 77, n. 7, 8.

[239] GPB RO, Ermitazhnoe sobranie, No. 242, ll. 55 ob. -57.

[240] GPB RO, Ermitazhnoe sobranie, No. 242, ll. 55 ob.-59.

Although we do not know the number of freed serfs who entered the posad population of these towns during the same period, it is safe to conclude that the overall level of enlistment was very limited. The only substantial contingent of peasants appearing on the urban tax rolls was an exceptional group whose presence was not related to rural-urban migration or voluntary enlistment. No data have been unearthed regarding enlistment in the towns of Nizhnii Novgorod guberniia between the Third and Fourth Revisions (1764-1782), but there is evidence that a major influx took place in the succeeding period. According to fiscal records of 1795 for this province, a total of 2310 male souls from the crown peasantry had enlisted in the urban classes of all towns since the Fourth Revision (1782), including 1442 in the kupechestvo and 868 in the meshchanstvo.[241] (see Table 30.) As of 1795 42 percent of the kupechestvo, 17 percent of the meshchanstvo and 27 percent of the total posad population in Nizhnii Novgorod guberniia consisted of crown peasants absorbed during the previous dozen years.[242] Court peasants predominated overwhelmingly among the registrants--91 percent of those who enlisted in the kupechestvo derived from this group.[243] Nizhnii Novgorod guberniia contained an unusually large concentration of court estates, although this alone is not enough to account for the preponderance

[241] TsGIA, f. 558, op. 2, d. 148, 11. 4 ob.-5, 27 ob.-28, 35-35 ob.

[242] The figures given are based on data of the Fourth Revision and do not take into account births and deaths subsequent to that census.

[243] Registrants in the meshchanstvo are not identified by peasant category in the document.

Table 30: Enlistment of Crown Peasants in Towns of Nizhnii
Novgorod Guberniia, 1782-1801 (Number of Males)

	Kupechestvo	Meshchanstvo	Total
1782-95			
Total membership (1795)[a]	3413	5080	8493
Enlisted from crown peasantry:			
economic	99		
court	1315		
other	28		
total	1442	868	2310
% peasants	42	17	27
1795-1801			
Total membership (1801)[b]	3098	6533	9631
Enlisted from crown peasantry:			
economic	115	119	234
court	184	356	540
other	37	19	56
total	336	494	830
% peasants	11	8	9

Sources: TsGIA, f. 558, op. 2, d. 148, ll. 4 ob.-154; d. 149, ll. 4-281.

[a]Based on data of Fourth Revision (1782), not including subsequent births and deaths.

[b]Based on data of Fifth Revision (1795), not including subsequent births and deaths.

of court peasants among the urban registrants.[244]

Unfortunately, the source gives no information as to which towns received registrants and in what numbers. More detailed data for the years following the Fifth Revision suggest that a substantial proportion of the total might be accounted for by the gradual absorption of native inhabitants of the new towns into their recently established urban classes. Ardatov and Kniaginin were both former court villages and continued to gain surprisingly large numbers of registrants in the period following the Fifth Revision. Most of the remaining enlistment probably occurred in the provincial capital. Another source indicates that from 1783 through 1787 166 court and economic peasants enlisted in the urban classes of Nizhnii Novgorod.[245] This influx may have grown rapidly with the approach of a new census in the 1790's, as was the case in Moscow.

Information on the years following the Fifth Revision can be obtained from reports of the provincial treasury on the number of "souls" in each tax category similar to those already cited regarding Moscow and Iaroslavl' gubernii.[246] In a pattern which has become familiar, these documents provide data on enlistment by crown peasants from the Fifth

---

[244]
According to the Fourth Revision court peasants made up 42 percent of the crown peasantry in the province, economic peasants 33 percent and other groups 25 percent. (Kabuzan, Izmeneniia v razmeshchenii naseleniia Rossii, pp. 95-97 .)

[245]
Klokman, Sotsial'no-ekonomicheskaia istoriia, p. 270.

[246]
TsGIA, f. 558, op. 2, d. 148, 11. 50 ob.-54, 61 ob.-65, 108 ob.-117 ob., 145 ob.-154; d. 149, 11. 4-24, 67 ob.-73, 160 ob.-167, 253 ob.-258 ob., 276 ob.-281.

Revision (1795) through 1801 but for all other categories of registrants cover only the years 1797-1801.[247] These reports indicate that a large number of registrants from the crown peasantry continued to swell the urban classes of the province: 830 male souls enlisted from 1795 through 1801. (See Table 30.) However, almost all the observed enlistment (92 percent) occurred not later than 1797, and this result confirms the conclusion indicated by the data on Moscow presented in the preceding chapter--that heavy enlistment by crown peasants tended to cluster about the time of the census. Once again court peasants predominated among the registrants, although not to the same degree as in the earlier period: 65 percent of the registrants from the crown peasantry were court peasants and 28 percent were economic peasants. The majority of these registrants (60 percent) belonged to the meshchanstvo, and nearly three-quarters of those deriving from the court peasantry were absorbed by this lower stratum of the urban citizenry. The reports of the provincial treasury indicate that freed serfs were much less important than crown peasants as a source of new members for the urban classes of this province. Between 1797 and 1801 70 crown peasants and 15 former serfs joined the posad population throughout the province.[248]

_____

[247]See above, n. 159.

[248]It is possible that larger numbers of freed serfs enlisted during the immediately preceding years, when enlistment by crown peasants was also much heavier. Other evidence has shown, however, that enlistment by freed serfs was not concentrated at the time of the census to the same degree as that of crown peasants. The Nizhnii Novgorod magistracy reported in 1796 that 47 former serfs had enlisted in the local meshchanstvo since the completion of the census. (Snezhnevskii, "Opis' delam i dokumentam Nizhegorodskogo gorodovogo magistrata," p. 19.)

The distribution of the peasant registrants from the years following the Fifth Revision among individual towns is shown in Table 31. The most striking feature of these data is the large number of registrants absorbed by several of the new towns, particularly Ardatov, where 58 percent of the posad population consisted of such registrants, but also Kniaginin, Semenov and Gorbatov, where newcomers from the peasantry contributed 11 to 30 percent of the posad population. These four towns received two-thirds of the total number of registrants reported by the provincial treasury. These results can be partially explained as the continuing absorption of native inhabitants of the new towns into their recently created urban classes, particularly as regards Ardatov and Kniaginin, former court villages which at the time of the Fifth Revision still contained large residual peasant populations.[249] The fact that most of the large Ardatov contingent entered the meshchanstvo and thus apparently consisted of persons of no great economic attainments also supports this explanation. In any case, it would be difficult to account for a large influx of outsiders into such weakly developed towns. With Semenov, economically the most developed of the new towns, the situation was otherwise. The Semenov posad affirmed in 1800 that "a large number of peasants from various settlements in this district...have enlisted in the kupechestvo and meshchanstvo here."[250] The reason for this immigration remains obscure.

---

[249] See Klokman, Sotsial'no-ekonomicheskaia istoriia, p. 277.

[250] Snezhnevskii, "Opis' delam i dokumentam Nizhegorodskogo gorodovogo magistrata," p. 64.

Table 31: Enlistment of Peasants in Towns of Nizhnii Novgorod
Guberniia, 1795-1801 (Number of Males)

Towns	Total in urban classes (1801)	Peasant registrants:			
		crown peasants[a]	freed serfs[b]	total peasants	% peasants
Nizhnii Novgorod					
kupechestvo	669	106	6	112	17
meshchanstvo	2046	77	2	79	4
total	2715	183	8	191	7
Arzamas					
kupechestvo	407	14	-	14	3
meshchanstvo	2190	11	=	11	0.5
total	2597	25	-	25	1
Balakhna					
kupechestvo	262	-	-	-	0
meshchanstvo	1149	9	=	9	0.8
total	1411	9	-	9	0.6
Vasil'					
kupechestvo	147	9	-	9	6
meshchanstvo	291	-	=	-	0
total	438	9	-	9	2
Semenov					
kupechestvo	278	83	-	83	30
meshchanstvo	102	11	=	11	11
total	380	94	-	94	25
Gorbatov					
kupechestvo	455	5	-	5	1
meshchanstvo	52	51	=	51	98
total	507	56	-	56	11
Ardatov					
kupechestvo	308	59	4	63	20
meshchanstvo	292	287	=	287	98
total	600	346	4	350	58
Kniaginin					
kupechestvo	150	34	-	34	23
meshchanstvo	92	39	=	39	42
total	242	73	-	73	30

Table 31 (cont.)

Towns	Total in urban classes (1801)	Peasant registrants: crown peasants[a]	freed serfs[b]	total peasants	% peasants
Makar'ev					
kupechestvo	290	–	2	2	0.7
meshchanstvo	202	=	1	1	0.5
total	492	–	3	3	0.6
Others[c]					
kupechestvo	132	26	–	26	–
meshchanstvo	117	9	=	9	=
total	249	35	–	35	–
Total for province					
kupechestvo	3098	336	12	348	11
meshchanstvo	6533	494	3	497	8
total	9631	830	15	845	9

Sources: TsGIA, f. 558, op. 2, d. 148, 11. 50 ob.-154; d. 149, 11. 4-281.

[a]Enlisted 1795-1801.

[b]Enlisted 1797-1801.

[c]No registrants reported for remaining towns (Pochinki, Sergach, Lukoianov, Perevoz); 35 registrants reported without identification of towns involved.

Most of the remaining registrants were absorbed by the provincial capital, which continued to receive a major influx. According to the reports of the provincial treasury 183 crown peasants enlisted in the urban classes of Nizhnii Novgorod from 1795 through 1801 and 8 freed serfs enlisted from 1797 through 1801. Thus, about one-quarter of the registrants reported for the whole province were absorbed by the provincial capital. To these figures can be added 47 former serfs enlisted in the meshchanstvo since the Fifth Revision, as reported by the local magistracy in 1796.[251] According to the combined figures, 17 percent of the kupechestvo, 6 percent of the meshchanstvo and 9 percent of the posad as a whole consisted in 1801 of peasants enlisted since the Fifth Revision. In contrast to the situation in Moscow and the towns of Moscow and Iaroslavl' gubernii, where crown peasants enlisted predominantly in the kupechestvo, the kupechestvo and meshchanstvo in Nizhnii Novgorod attracted roughly equal numbers of registrants from the crown peasantry.[252]

The Nizhnii Novgorod "register of inhabitants" (obyvatel'skaia kniga) of 1800, studied by S. I. Arkhangel'skii, provides some information on the occupational characteristics of peasant registrants.[253] Arkhangel'skii analyzed only those sections of the register dealing with

---

251
 Ibid., p. 19.
252
 However, as was observed earlier (Chapter III), Nizhnii Novgorod guberniia shared this characteristic with the provinces of the Middle and Lower Volga.
253
 S. I. Arkhangel'skii, Ocherki po istorii promyshlennogo proletariata Nizhnego Novgoroda i Nizhegorodskoi oblasti XVII-XVIII vv. (Gor'kii, 1950), pp. 63-71.

the meshchanstvo and with members of craft builds. The former segment
lists 743 households, of which 445 are identified as "long-time residents"
(starozhily) and 298 (40 percent) as "newcomers" (vnov' prishedshie)--
since what date is not clear. Unfortunately, the obyvatel'skaia kniga
rarely indicates the origin of the newcomers and in fact does so only
in 25 cases. In 21 of these the registrants derived from the peasantry,
and in view of the large amount of peasant enlistment in Nizhnii
Novgorod shown by other data it is likely that peasants predominated
overwhelmingly among the unidentified newcomers as well.[254] The most
common occupation among the immigrants was small-scale trade, which
absorbed 52 percent of the group as well as 43 percent of the long-time
residents. Eleven percent of the newcomers were tailors, blacksmiths
or craftsmen of various other specialties, while 8 percent made their
living from "hand-work" (rukodelie), a term frequently denoting the
spinning of yarns and the sewing or knitting of various articles of
clothing. Ten percent were involved in rope-making (priadil'noe delo),
in most cases apparently as hired labor--it will be recalled that this
was the principal form of "factory" industry in Nizhnii Novgorod--while
16 percent supported themselves through "miscellaneous labor." Of 161
members of craft guilds, 80 were identified as newcomers. These craftsmen included 30 cobblers, 12 tailors, 11 carpenters (stoliary), 4
blacksmiths, 11 silversmiths and 12 bakers.

The data on peasant enlistment in the towns of Nizhnii Novgorod
guberniia, although much more limited than those available for the other
provinces, allow several conclusions. Between the First and Third

---

[254] The data of the Nizhnii Novgorod provincial treasury show little
enlistment by members of non-peasant categories in the city's posad
population during the years 1797-1801.

Revisions very few peasants enlisted in these towns as "mercantile peasants," according to the procedures established by the decree of April 13, 1722, and there is no reason to believe that a substantial influx of freed serfs occurred during this period. In the last two decades of the century, however, peasants enlisted in massive numbers relative to the size of the residual posad population. According to the incomplete data available more than 3100 male souls joined the urban classes of the province from 1782 through 1801.[255] Assuming no major changes due to natural growth or to attrition among the registrants, these newcomers would account for nearly one-third of the provincial posad population at the beginning of the nineteenth century. The evidence suggests that of the major towns in the province (Nizhnii Novgorod, Arzamas, Balakhna) only the provincial capital shared significantly in this influx. Some of the new district towns created as a result of the 1775 reforms received large numbers of registrants, partly because they were gradually absorbing their native populations into the urban classes and partly for other reasons which cannot be determined

---

[255]However, for reasons previously explained, there is some possibility of duplication in the data on enlistment from before and after the Fifth Revision. The government decided that only those who had enlisted before the decree announcing the new census (June 23, 1794) were entitled to release from peasant status, while those who had enlisted later would continue in their interim status until the next revision, owing both peasant and urban obligations, and would therefore be classified in fiscal documents as new registrants "since the Fifth Revision." The central fiscal authorities raised the question of whether all the registrants reported by the Nizhnii Novgorod provincial treasury as having enlisted "before the Fifth Revision" had actually done so before the required date, but the outcome of this inquiry is not recorded. (TsGIA, f. 558, op. 2, d. 148.)

from the available information. The crown peasantry was the chief source
of recruits for the urban classes of this province, with court peasants
playing the largest role.

The effects of peasant enlistment are plainly reflected in the
dynamics of the posad population in the major towns of the province
during the eighteenth century. (See Table 32.) Between the First and
Third Revisions, during which time little enlistment took place, the
posad population did not grow substantially in any of these towns and
underwent a noticeable contraction in Nizhnii Novgorod and Balakhna.
In the three decades between the Third and Fifth Revisions the Nizhnii
Novgorod posad grew by more than 50 percent, while Arzamas and Balakhna,
which apparently enjoyed much less peasant immigration, experienced
less favorable results. The posad population in the small town of
Vasil' also grew markedly, for unknown reasons.

Patterns of Urban Immigration

The three provinces surveyed in this chapter each displayed to a
marked degree the diversified peasant economy characteristic of the
Central Industrial Region. The non-agricultural pursuits of the
peasantry in these provinces took on a variety of forms and included
in each case rural trade and industry, itinerant occupations such as
transit trade and work on overland and water-borne transport, and
migration to towns for greater or lesser periods for work and trade.
The emphases, however, varied from province to province. Iaroslavl'
guberniia was notable for the exceptionally large number of peasants
who departed from their villages for work in towns and other migratory

Table 32: Growth of Urban Classes in Towns of Nizhnii Novgorod

Guberniia (Number of Males)

Towns	1st Revision (c.1725)	2nd Revision (c.1744)	3rd Revision (c.1762)	5th Revision (1795)	% growth: 1744-95	1762-95
Nizhnii Novgorod	2150	1950	1700	2550	31	50
Arzamas	2100	2250	2200	2550	13	16
Balakhna	1800	1550	1400	1400	-10	0
Vasil'	250	250	?	450	80	?

Sources: GPB RO, Ermitazhnoe sobranie, No. 242 ("Vedomost' o chisle dush po gorodam"), ll. 55 ob.-59; TsGIA, f. 558, op. 2, d. 148, ll. 36-51; A. A. Kizevetter, Posadskaia obshchina v Rossii XVIII stoletiia (Moscow, 1903), pp. 88-111.

pursuits. Otkhod was common in Nizhnii Novgorod guberniia as well, but
here the most striking characteristic of the peasant economy was the
emergence of many commercial and industrial centers in the countryside,
settlements which matched and surpassed many significant towns in
population and economic development. In Moscow guberniia, of course,
the proximity of the old capital, with its great opportunities for
trade and employment, exerted an especially strong influence on the
peasant economy.

The available quantitative information on rural-urban migration in
these provinces comes principally from data on enlistment of peasants
in the urban classes, and the broader implications of these data need
to be assessed with some caution. Peasants who acquired formal urban
citizenship may be assumed fairly representative of long-term settlers
as a whole and consisted of that portion of the total influx which was
most advanced in its social and economic assimilation into the urban
milieu and most successful in negotiating the legal obstacles to
enlistment. Where sufficient data can be accumulated, the level of
enlistment should thus reflect with approximate accuracy the differential
attraction of particular towns for long-term migrants at a given time.
Less congruence can be assumed between seasonal or other temporary
migration and enlistment, although temporary residence unquestionably
could lead to permanent settlement, and the available evidence suggests
that a heavy influx of seasonal migrants often coincided with high levels
of enlistment in the urban classes (for example, in Moscow and Nizhnii
Novgorod).

Enlistment was also affected by other factors as well as the level
of migration, particularly by the prevailing legal requirements and

procedures, and such factors need to be taken into account in interpreting the data. The available evidence indicates that little enlistment took place in any towns of the Central Industrial Region (except Moscow) before the Third Revision. These results do not necessarily mean that the towns attracted no settlers or migrants during this period but rather were probably due in large measure to the retarding effect of unattractive provisions requiring the registrants to bear both peasant and urban obligations in perpetuity. Substantial numbers of registrants first appear in the data for the period between the Third and Fourth Revisions (1764-1782). We do not have information on when during the two intervening decades most of the recorded enlistment took place and therefore cannot determine the extent to which it was a response to the 1775 reforms, which appeared to promise and finally did lead to more favorable terms for peasant registrants, but the legal changes are certainly likely to have been a significant factor. In the last two decades of the century, under largely constant legal conditions, we do not find evidence of a steep rise in enlistment in the urban classes of provincial and district towns of the Central Industrial Region comparable to that which occurred in Moscow during the same period. In the towns of Moscow guberniia (without Moscow) and Iaroslavl' guberniia, enlistment appears to have leveled off or dropped following the Fourth Revision. (For Nizhnii Novgorod guberniia the data are not sufficient to define the situation.) These results suggest the possibility that enlistment was stimulated by the 1775 reforms, which resulted in the absorption of a backlog of earlier immigrants into the posad population under the newer and more attractive conditions, but that the growth of enlistment was not sustained by a steep and continuous rise in peasant immigration, as was evidently the case in Moscow.

We have observed significant differences in the geographical
patterns of migration exhibited by the peasantry in each of the provinces
investigated and in the ability of towns in these provinces to attract
peasant immigrants. Most immigrants from the peasantry of Moscow
guberniia were absorbed by Moscow itself, and few were attracted to
the uezd towns of this province, even several which were quite large
and had well developed and prosperous economies. Iaroslavl' guberniia
was also a major source for immigration to Moscow, but more of its
peasants apparently settled in the towns of their own province. The
balance was evidently changing in favor of the former, however, as
local enlistment leveled off in the closing decades of the century
while settlement in Moscow continued to grow rapidly. Other information
suggests that Petersburg and some of the rapidly developing towns on
the eastern and southeastern fringes of European Russia were also
significant poles of attraction for the peasantry of this province,
but quantitative assessment of the resulting enlistment must await
further research. In Nizhnii Novgorod guberniia migration to the
capital cities did not play a major role. Migrants from the peasantry
of this province were absorbed locally or were attracted to the towns
of the "downstream" provinces by involvement in the fish trade, work on
river transport and other "Volga enterprises."

Notwithstanding the attenuation of its powers of attraction with
increasing distance and the intervention of competing economic influences,
Moscow claimed by far the largest numbers of immigrants of any town in
the Central Industrial Region. Except for several of the new towns,
which in most cases probably drew registrants in the urban classes

chiefly from their own residual peasant populations, only two towns in the provinces surveyed (Rostov and Nizhnii Novgorod) were able consistently to attract large numbers of registrants relative to their size. The reasons for the primacy of Moscow as a destination for peasant immigrants have already been explored: the vast economy of the old capital provided by far the greatest and most diverse opportunities to newcomers in search of income through commercial activity and hired labor, while lesser towns could offer only much more limited possibilities. As a result, Moscow was able not only to monopolize rural-urban migration in its own province but to draw large numbers of migrants from the neighboring provinces and some from yet more distant areas. In contrast, immigrants in the smaller towns of the Central Industrial Region were usually drawn from strictly local sources--in most cases from the surrounding district, sometimes from a nearby district and very rarely from more remote areas.

Less apparent are the attractions exerted on peasant immigrants by Rostov, despite the fact that this town was the site of one of the most important commercial fairs in Russia and also had a well developed permanent market. The inducements for permanent settlement created by periodic trade functions, if any, remain obscure, and otherwise it is difficult to see what distinguished Rostov radically from many other towns, including the nearby and much larger Iaroslavl'. The case of Rostov must await illumination from further research, particularly into individual case histories and census depositions relating to peasants who enlisted in the Rostov posad.

The case of Nizhnii Novgorod is more explicable on the basis of the available sources. Nizhnii Novgorod guberniia was largely beyond

the orbit of Moscow, and the provincial capital apparently did not
have to compete with Moscow or Petersburg for migrants from local
sources. In this area peasants in need of work characteristically
turned to the Volga rather than the capital cities, and as one of the
most important Volga ports Nizhnii Novgorod was a major center for the
hiring of labor to serve on Volga shipping. This role assured the
city of a massive influx of temporary migrants, and such migration
could contribute to permanent settlement where attractive opportunities
for work and trade existed within the town itself. In Nizhnii Novgorod
the heavy traffic passing through the town stimulated local trade in
food products and other provisions, pursuits in which trading peasants
were characteristically involved. Further insight into the factors
drawing permanent peasant settlers to Nizhnii Novgorod could be gained
from a study of documents relating to individual immigrants and also
from an investigation of the concurrent peasant immigration into the
towns of the Middle Volga, with which Nizhnii Novgorod shared many
characteristics.

CHAPTER VI: INDIVIDUAL PATHS TO URBAN CITIZENSHIP

The preceding chapters have been concerned mainly with analyzing
quantitative data on the numbers, origins and economic attainments of
peasant registrants in the urban classes and with relating the observed
patterns to the economic characteristics of regions and localities.
Additional insight into the factors encouraging and facilitating the
urbanization of peasants, and especially the varying ways in which
these factors could combine and interact in particular instances, can
be gained by exploring enlistment from the perspective of individual
experience. The present chapter is based to a large extent on individual case records found in the files of local and provincial
institutions of Iaroslavl', specifically the magistracy (magistrat),
provincial chancellery (provintsial'naia kantseliariia) and provincial
treasury (kazennaia palata).[1] It also makes considerable use of the
previously discussed Moscow census depositions and some use of random
cases culled from various published documents and secondary sources.

The cases recovered from files of the Iaroslavl' institutions
deal chiefly with freed serfs and to a lesser extent with crown
peasants who enlisted under the provisions introduced by Catherine II.
These cases span the period between the Second Revision (1744) and the

---

[1] Tsentral'nyi gosudarstvennyi arkhiv drevnikh aktov, Moscow
(TsGADA), f. 455 (Iaroslavskaia provintsial'naia kantseliariia); f. 807
(Iaroslavskii gorodovoi magistrat); Gosudarstvennyi arkhiv Iaroslavskoi
oblasti, Iaroslavl' (GAIaO), f. 55 (Iaroslavskii gorodovoi magistrat);
f. 100 (Iaroslavskaia kazennaia palata).

end of the century and concern peasants who enlisted in the urban classes
of Iaroslavl' itself and of "non-administrative" (zashtatnyi) urban
settlements in Iaroslavl' uezd, as well as peasants originating in
Iaroslavl' provintsiia or guberniia who registered in towns elsewhere
in the country. The typical case file consists of the following
elements: (1)a copy or paraphrase of the applicant's petition for
posad membership; (2)additional documents submitted by the petitioner
in support of his case, including deeds of manumission, passports and
affidavits from posad members backing his entry into their community;
(3)notations on the procedure to be followed in acting on the petition
and communications with other institutions regarding the matter;
(4)citations from relevant decrees; and (5)a record of the final dis-
position of the case and the steps taken to implement this decision.

The petitions submitted by applicants for urban citizenship were
normally written by clerks of the institutions receiving these petitions,
by other government clerks or by free-lance scriveners, and they
consequently exhibit a certain standardization of form and content.
Moreover, this content reflected the concerns of the authorities, who
in such cases wished to be assured mainly that the applicant was not
a runaway, had not evaded or defaulted on prior state obligations,
and was capable of earning a living in the world of urban commerce, by
virtue of his experience, possession of capital or knowledge of a craft
profession. Despite these limitations, the petition is normally the
most informative segment of a case file, at least as regards the
immigrant's background and the forces which propelled him into the
urban world. The usual petition states the identity and origin of
the applicant, his reasons and justification for residing in the town,

the circumstances of his release from his former status and his qualifications for membership in the posad, concluding with a promise to
pay all taxes and perform all other posad obligations in full and to
obey the urban authorities. The petition is sometimes supplemented
by the record of a personal interrogation of the applicant, which
provides additional information on his background.

The career of the ex-serf Andrei Esipov, which is documented with
an unusual degree of thoroughness, provides a suitable illustration of
the process by which peasants were drawn into the urban community and
of the factors which could encourage and assist such an outcome.
Esipov was born in 1728, on the estate of the widow M. B. Mikhneva in
Iaroslavl' uezd. Stepan Esipov, father of Andrei, was one of the
elected officials (vybornye) of the village and was apparently a
trusted agent of the landowner. In 1736 he was appointed steward of
her newly purchased estate in Kostroma uezd and moved there with his
family. In 1738, during a visit by Mikhneva to this new estate, Stepan
Esipov took the opportunity to request manumission for his ten-year-old
son so that the latter might enlist in the posad. In return for what
Andrei Esipov, in his petition for posad membership, later described as
"suitable compensation," the serfowner agreed, granting full manumission
and promising not to require further payment of dues from Andrei or
claim him as a serf in the next revision, on condition that the remainder
of the family continue to perform obligations according to the usual
manpower assessments (tiaglo).[2] Andrei Esipov then settled in Iaroslavl'

---

[2] Neither party apparently wished to make use of the provisions of
the decree of April 13, 1722, allowing enlistment in the posad without
manumission.

to "learn commerce" and lived in the house of his brother-in-law, the
Iaroslavl' merchant Ivan D'iakonov. By the onset of the Second Revision
(1744), the sixteen-year-old Esipov was already an applicant for urban
citizenship. He claimed a capital of 1000 rubles and trade in "various
ports" and was added to the Iaroslavl' kupechestvo by the new census
as requested.[3]

Esipov's problems did not end with his successful application for
posad membership, since the heirs of Mikhneva refused to recognize his
manumission and attempted to reclaim him as a serf during the 1750's and
again at the time of the Third Revision, a decade later. Although these
efforts were unsuccessful, they caused considerable trouble for Esipov,
whose arrest was ordered by the Chief Magistracy at one point and who
was temporarily deprived of the right to travel on passports for business
purposes.[4] In the meantime, Andrei Esipov became one of the more prominent
merchants of Iaroslavl'. From 1748 through 1751, in partnership with
several other Iaroslavl' merchants, he held a contract for the farming
of customs and liquor revenues in Liubim uezd, and about the same time
he managed a distillery in his former village on behalf of the landlord.
In the 1750's and 1760's Esipov was involved in the long-distance grain
trade, shipping grain from Orel via the Oka and Volga in his own vessels.[5]
Esipov figured prominently among the important Iaroslavl' merchants who
signed the "instruction" (nakaz) prepared for the city's deputy to the
Legislative Commission of 1767.[6] In the same year Esipov built a new

---

[3] TsGADA, f. 807, op. 1, d. 46, ll. 33-39.

[4] Ibid., ll. 1-18 ob., 61-62.

[5] TsGADA, f. 807, op. 1, d. 44, ll. 5-6; d. 46, ll. 1-2, 14 ob.-15 ob.

[6] Sbornik Imperatorskogo russkogo istoricheskogo obshchestva (Sb. IRIO),
Vol. 93 (St. Petersburg, 1894), p. 345.

stone trading "row" in the center of Iaroslavl'.[7]

Unfortunately, Esipov's enterprises, like most commercial activity of this era, were prone to disasters against which there could be little protection, and these misfortunes eventually led to his ruin. Esipov suffered his first major setback in 1758, when his cargo vessel foundered on the Oka during a storm and he lost "all his capital" as a result. To keep his business going under these circumstances, Esipov had to resort heavily to credit in securing the necessary money and goods. The merchant experienced further losses in 1768, when his boat was rammed by another vessel on the Oka, and more of his assets were destroyed by fires in Iaroslavl' in 1768 and 1770. Esipov's business affairs increasingly became a struggle to keep ahead of his accumulating debts. In 1774 Esipov mortgaged all his remaining property to the Iaroslavl' merchant Ivan Kochurov for 2000 rubles. The last reference to Andrei Esipov in the documents dates from the later 1770's: he was living in a house belonging to his wife and was being pursued by numerous creditors for nonpayment of promissory notes totaling at least 2500 rubles. However, posad officials were unable to find any movable or immovable property to confiscate for payment of these debts. Despite his ruined condition, Esipov's absorption into the urban community was irreversible, and the notion of ejecting him from the posad did not arise.[8]

---

[7]L. V. Sretenskii, Pomeshchich'ia votchina nechernozemnoi polosy Rossii vo vtoroi polovine XVIII v. (dissertation, Iaroslavl', Gosudarstvennyi pedagogicheskii institut im. K. D. Ushinskogo, 1959), p. 80. In Russian towns of the eighteenth century, the construction of new buildings of masonry, rather than wood, was considered a major event.

[8]TsGADA, f. 807, op. 1, d. 44, ll. 1-31.

The record of Andrei Esipov's progress from serf status to membership in the Iaroslavl' kupechestvo suggests that the process by which peasants were drawn into and absorbed by the urban commune can be broken down into a number of distinct events or developments. These include the original decision or compulsion to leave the village and take up residence elsewhere, the initiation and expansion of urban-based economic activity, the establishment of personal ties within the urban milieu, the loosening of legal bonds to the rural population, and lastly the formal process of enlistment. Further exploration of individual case histories discloses that these constituent events of the urbanization process could be brought about in many different ways, followed no fixed sequence and also overlapped and interacted with one another in ways which varied from case to case, so that the general framework described encompasses a multiplicity of possible pathways from peasant origins to urban citizenship.

Departure from the Village

The original impetus for the emergence of Andrei Esipov in the urban milieu evidently derived from the ambition of his father, a relatively prosperous rural peasant, to extend the social and economic ties of their family beyond the limited world of an ordinary serf village. This ambition is further reflected in the fact that the elder Esipov apparently had already established kinship ties to the urban kupechestvo by marrying his daughter to a Iaroslavl' merchant.[9]

---

[9] The daughter is not mentioned in the documents, but the merchant Ivan D'iakonov, with whom Andrei Esipov lived in Iaroslavl', is identified as his ziat', which term means the husband of a daughter or sister.

Such relationships, as will be evident from many cases to be discussed

below, were quite common and could in themselves provide a strong

motivation for resettlement, since they promised potential immigrants

assistance from within urban society for their attempts to penetrate

its barriers.

Not all immigrants, of course, enjoyed such positive inducements.

Many came from the opposite end of the village economic scale and left

their original environment in pursuit of mere survival rather than

advancement, without benefit of personal connections in the urban

population. The monastery peasant Semen Golovanov, from an estate in

Iaroslavl' uezd, testified in his petition for posad membership that

he had abandoned his native village and come to Iaroslavl' as a child,

because of "utter poverty."[10] Similarly, Filka Popov, a state "black-

plowing" peasant from Dvina uezd in the far north, settled in Iaroslavl'

during adolescence, following the death of his father and because of the

"propertylessness" of his family.[11] Golovanov and Popov, unlike Andrei

Esipov, came from the ranks of those who had no viable place in the

village economy and were perhaps unable even to participate in it, due

to the breakdown of the family unit or a lack of the necessary economic

resources. Since they made no economic or fiscal contribution to the

village, such individuals were readily dispensed with by the estate

authorities and the peasant community and were allowed to settle

wherever they wished in the hope that they might earn enough to pay

---

[10]TsGADA, f. 807, op. 1, d. 46, ll. 50-50 ob.

[11]Ibid., ll. 52-53. Like Andrei Esipov, Golovanov and Popov
enlisted in the Iaroslavl' posad at the time of the Second Revision.

their share of taxes and dues. Forced to go elsewhere in search of subsistence, these migrants had little incentive to return to the village even on a seasonal basis, as did many peasants for whom temporary work in towns was a supplementary form of income, and they instead tended to become permanent urban residents. Both Golovanov and Popov lived in Iaroslavl' for several decades prior to their admission to the posad and paid rural obligations annually from their earnings.

We may suspect that in addition to those who arrived in towns with a definite intention of taking up permanent residence, some peasant registrants began as seasonal or other temporary migrants and were gradually drawn into the permanent urban population as a result of desirable economic opportunities, widening ambitions or growing personal ties. Some registrants, it must be added, owed their presence in the urban environment not to voluntary migration but to the fact that they had been brought there by their lords or were the offspring of urban house serfs or of peasants who had previously settled in the town. The former serf Maksim Andreev, who applied for admission to the Iaroslavl' posad in the early 1760's, had earlier been purchased from a rural landowner by a minor government official and taken to Iaroslavl' for use as a house serf.[12] In an earlier chapter we referred to the activities of Petr Linev, a peasant from the estates of Count M. M. Saltykov who settled in Moscow with a passport in the early 1730's and became a cloth-dyer.[13] Petr Linev apparently never gained urban

---

[12] TsGADA, f. 807, op. 1, d. 515, 11. 1-11.

[13] Materialy po istorii krest'ianskoi promyshlennosti (MPIKP), Vol. 1 (Moscow-Leningrad, 1935), pp. 229-42.

citizenship, but his son Ivan (born about 1748) enlisted in the Moscow kupechestvo in 1774 and in 1795 was reported to be trading in one of the textile "rows" in Moscow.[14]

Role of Family and Personal Relationships

The growth of kinship and other personal ties to members of the urban population was a necessary concomitant of the peasant immigrant's assimilation into the urban milieu and could assist the process greatly, aiding him in his economic pursuits, protecting this activity from possible suppression by the urban authorities and providing the required backing for his eventual entry into the urban classes. As in the case of Andrei Esipov, however, personal ties frequently preceded the immigrant's arrival and provided a strong inducement to migrate, since they assured the newcomer's immediate survival and offered a protective and supportive environment for his apprenticeship in urban commerce, as well as valuable assistance in the later stages of his assimilation. Among other possibilities, family ties between urban and rural elements were an inevitable by-product of the continuing absorption of peasants into the posad, since peasants who attained urban citizenship usually left behind them in the villages an array of close and distant relatives who could now look to the registrant for assistance in their own entry into the urban milieu.

The available evidence records numerous instances in which peasant registrants had been preceded into the posad by a brother, uncle, cousin

[14] Materialy dlia istorii moskovskogo kupechestva (MDIMK), Vol. 3 (Moscow, 1885), p. 31 (No. 206); Vol. 4 (Moscow, 1886), p. 25 (No. 203).

or other relative who could then be called upon to provide shelter, training, employment and other aid to the newcomer.[15] The appearance of the economic peasant Mikhaila Loskutov in the Moscow kupechestvo in 1782, for example, was followed in 1791 by the enlistment of two of his male relatives, who lived in his house and were employed by or associated with him in business.[16] Prior enlistment of unrelated individuals from the same village or estate could offer the potential immigrant similar inducements and benefits. A. A. Kizevetter records a case in which three thoroughly penniless serfs belonging to Prince M. M. Golitsyn were able to enlist in the St. Petersburg kupechestvo in the 1740's because a former fellow-villager who had enlisted earlier lent them the required capital and arranged for the necessary affidavits and guarantees.[17] Surviving ties among persons originating in the same peasant community could induce a steady stream of immigration from a particular village or estate or lead to the simultaneous appearance of large numbers of fellow-villagers in a town already colonized by them.[18]

Kinship ties between peasant and urban families were frequently established by marriage. The enlistment of peasants in the urban classes was often accompanied or preceded by marriage of the registrant to the daughter or widow of an urban merchant. The peasants Semen

---

[15] For example, MDIMK, Vol. 4, pp. 39 (No. 379), 310 (No. 413), 481 (No. 89), 634 (No. 860). See also A. A. Kizevetter, Posadskaia obshchina v Rossii XVIII stoletiia (Moscow, 1903), pp. 40-41.

[16] MDIMK, Vol. 3, p. 384 (No. 106); Vol. 4, pp. 747 (No. 87), 751 (Nos. 138-39).

[17] Kizevetter, Posadskaia obshchina, pp. 41-42.

[18] Ibid., p. 41; MDIMK, Vol. 4, pp. 233-34, 296-98.

Golovanov, Filka Popov and Il'ia Krasil'nikov, who applied for admission to the Iaroslavl' posad at the time of the Second Revision (1744), were all married to "native Iaroslavl' women."[19] Andrei Mazaev, a state peasant (odnodvorets) of Tambov guberniia, married the sister of a Moscow merchant in 1776 and in the same year enlisted in the Moscow kupechestvo.[20] Mikhaila Chirkov, an economic peasant from Bogorodsk uezd who enlisted in the Moscow third merchant guild in 1795, had married the daughter of a Moscow merchant about five years earlier.[21] Another economic peasant, from Rogachevo village in Dmitrov uezd, married the daughter of a Moscow meshchanin no later than 1788 and joined the Moscow kupechestvo in 1792.[22] Nikita Mikhailov, of serf origin, married the daughter of Moscow merchant Petr Alekseev no later than 1787 and became a member of the kupechestvo in 1793.[23] Older immigrants, already married and with grown children, might marry their offspring into urban families. The former serf Aleksei Semenov married his son to the daughter of a Moscow merchant not later than 1789 and in 1790 enlisted with his family in the Moscow kupechestvo.[24] Afanasii Shebanov, a court peasant of Vladimir guberniia, married his son to the

[19]TsGADA, f. 807, op. 1, d. 46, 11. 42-43 ob., 50-50 ob., 52-53.

[20]MDIMK, Vol. 3, p. 400 (No. 158).

[21]Ibid., Vol. 4, p. 534 (No. 411).

[22]Ibid., p. 661 (No. 141).

[23]Ibid., p. 701 (No. 98). Many similar instances are recorded in the census depositions of the Moscow posad. See, for example, Ibid., pp. 534 (Nos. 403-04), 620 (No. 703), 621 (No. 713), 623 (No. 729), 626 (No. 770).

[24]Ibid., p. 836 (No. 532).

daughter of a Moscow meshchanin not later than 1792, and the family joined the Moscow kupechestvo that same year.[25]

If peasant immigrants frequently sought and obtained urban brides, it was apparently just as common for male members of the urban classes to marry peasant women. Of 456 wives belonging to households registered in two large Moscow slobody according to the Fourth Revision (1782), 201 derived from the Moscow posad, 51 from the urban classes of other towns, 131 from the peasantry and 73 from various other categories of the population.[26] In other words, 29 percent of the wives of these townsmen were peasant women. Some of the above households, of course, consisted of recent registrants from the peasantry, and some of the marriages recorded had taken place before enlistment, but even if we consider only those families which had belonged to the Moscow posad at least since the Second Revision, we find that 20 percent of the wives were of peasant birth. Peasant brides of urban merchants were most likely to derive from the court or economic peasantry, although a substantial number came from the ranks of seigneurial peasants and house serfs as well.

Some urban families turned habitually to the peasantry for marriage partners. The brothers Ivan and Andrei Kuznetsov, for example, came from a family which had belonged to the Moscow posad at least since the First Revision. In the materials of the Fourth Revision they are identified as being married to women from the economic peasantry and

---

[25] Ibid., p. 773 (No. 268). Similar cases: Ibid., pp. 774 (No. 286), 832 (No. 488).

[26] Ibid., Vol. 3, pp. 8-37, 230-256. A small number of wives whose origin cannot be determined, usually because they are identified as the widow rather than the daughter of a particular individual, have been dropped from the sample.

the court peasantry respectively, while one of their sisters was married
to a court peasant of Pokrovskoe village. Three remaining siblings were
unmarried.[27] Similarly, Grigorii and Koz'ma Tarygin, whose family also
had been in the Moscow posad since before the First Revision, each
married the daughter of an economic peasant during the 1770's.[28] The
Tarygin brothers came from one of the less fortunate families of the
Moscow urban classes--their father had been conscripted into the army
during their infancy, and they apparently had grown up in the home of
in-laws. At the time of the Fourth Revision the family was only of
meshchanstvo status. In contrast, the first-guild merchants Grigorii
Zaplatin and his son Larion were at the upper end of the economic
spectrum. The father, a merchant from the town of Iur'ev-Pol'skoi
who transferred to the Moscow posad in 1754, was married to the daughter
of a court peasant, while his son married a serf woman about 1771.[29]

On the circumstances surrounding marriages between persons of
peasant and urban status, the available sources provide only scattered
clues. In many cases, no doubt, the peasant families involved in these
arrangements were already established as urban residents, but brides
were brought from the villages as well. Wealthy peasants desiring to
form kinship ties to the urban classes may sometimes have offered
large dowries or otherwise made marriage to their offspring financially

[27] Ibid., Vol. 1 (Moscow, 1883), "Perepisnaia kniga 1747 g.," p. 93
(No. 7379); Vol. 3, p. 236 (No. 31).

[28] Ibid., Vol. 1, "Perepisnaia kniga 1747 g.," p. 95 (No. 7609);
Vol. 2 (Moscow, 1885), "Skazki otdel'nykh lits," p. 72 (No. 108); Vol. 3,
p. 240 (No. 67).

[29] Ibid., Vol. 2, "Okladnye skazki 1766 i 67 gg.," p. 141; Vol. 3,
p. 431 (Nos. 163-64).

advantageous, and such incentives would have been particularly attractive to urban families threatened by financial difficulties or otherwise ailing fortunes, as frequently occurred. Some marriages apparently grew out of regular business dealings or some other kind of economic relationship between merchants and peasants. The demographic structure of urban populations, usually characterized by a surplus of males, probably forced some posad families to search for brides among the peasantry. However they came about, such marriages created a network of in-law relationships linking peasant and urban families, and these relationships undoubtedly played a role in encouraging and facilitating rural-urban migration.

The case of Andrei Esipov, the ten-year-old ex-serf who went to live with his brother-in-law in Iaroslavl' and soon turned up in the Iaroslavl' kupechestvo, is an excellent illustration of this point. Similarly, the economic peasant Efrem Ivanov, who enlisted in the Moscow meshchanstvo in 1794, at the age of fifteen, lived with his brother-in-law, the Moscow meshchanin Petr Vasil'ev.[30] The brothers Anton and Ivan Koz'min, economic peasants from Pereslavl'-Zalesskii uezd, enlisted in the Moscow kupechestvo in 1785 at the ages of twelve and eleven respectively. In 1795 these registrants were living with an in-law, the Moscow merchant Danila Semenov, who presumably bore a major share of the responsibility for their quick absorption into the urban classes.[31] It was not only such underage immigrants who might depend on their urban in-laws in this manner. As was noted in a

---

[30] Ibid., Vol. 4, p. 482 (No. 99).

[31] Ibid., p. 561 (No. 195).

previous chapter, unattached females and other adult peasants entering

the Moscow urban classes apparently without resources of their own

were frequently found to be living with in-laws.[32]   The economically

more capable and ambitious immigrants, of course, could benefit just

as much from the assistance of such relations. The economic peasant

Mikhaila Loskutov enlisted in the Moscow kupechestvo in 1782 and at

that time was living with an in-law, the Moscow merchant M. A. Medovshchikov.

By 1795 Loskutov had acquired his own house and had assisted two of his

rural relatives and two other peasants of his native district in

entering the urban classes, providing them with lodging and employment.[33]

Some peasant immigrants derived similar benefits from urban in-laws

who were not members of the posad. Most frequently these relations

were peasants living in the town without enlistment in the urban classes

or in suburban villages, but members of other population categories

were also involved.[34]

In contrast to in-law relationships, which could readily precede

and influence migration, marriages between peasant immigrants and urban

women generally arose at a more advanced stage of the newcomers'

assimilation into the urban environment. Most such marriages apparently

took place about the time of enlistment or a few years earlier, at which

juncture many of the peasants involved were perhaps already prepared for

enlistment but were awaiting the approach of a new census or other

---

[32]Examples: Ibid., Vol. 4, pp. 481 (No. 84), 483 (No. 116), 487
(No. 163), 531 (No. 374), 631 (No. 830), 636 (No. 884), 838 (Nos. 554,
556). See also above, Chapter IV.

[33]Ibid., Vol. 3, p. 384 (No. 106); Vol. 4, pp. 747 (No. 87), 750
(No. 128), 751 (Nos. 138-40).

[34]Examples: Ibid., Vol. 3, p. 444 (No. 321); Vol. 4, pp. 244 (No.
718), 262 (No. 921), 480 (Nos. 77-78), 668 (No. 221).

favorable circumstances.[35] Longer intervals, however, are sometimes
to be noted. The court peasant A. A. Emel'ianov married the daughter
of a Moscow merchant of the second guild no later than 1766. Ten
years afterward Emel'ianov enlisted in the Moscow kupechestvo and
himself became a second-guild merchant.[36] The economic peasants Petr
Fedorov and Miron Lukin married into the families of Moscow merchants
in the 1770's but did not enter the Moscow posad until 1795.[37] Dmitrii
Grachev, son of E. I. Grachev, the well known serf industrialist of
Ivanovo village, married the daughter of the Moscow first-guild merchant
T. D. Shevaldyshev no later than 1786 but appeared in the Moscow
kupechestvo, together with his father, only in 1795.[38] In some cases
lengthy intervals between marriage and enlistment were apparently the
result of difficulties in obtaining manumission. The house serf
Dmitrii Fedorov, for example, married the daughter of a Moscow merchant
about 1771. The son resulting from this union was legally also a serf
but was freed by the serfowner and was inscribed in the Moscow kupechestvo
in 1782, at the age of ten. It was not until 1788, however, that
Dmitrii Fedorov himself was able to obtain manumission and register as
a merchant.[39]

---

[35] The revizskie skazki usually do not give the date of marriage,
which must therefore be estimated from the ages of children. This
method, although not completely reliable for individual cases, is
approximate enough to allow a general conclusion.

[36] MDIMK, Vol. 3, p. 459 (No. 129).

[37] Ibid., Vol. 4, pp. 622 (No. 726), 734 (No. 157).

[38] Ibid., pp. 377 (No. 69), 411 (No. 536). E. I. Grachev himself
was married to the daughter of a merchant of the town of Suzdal', one
of several urban settlements in the vicinity of Ivanovo.

[39] Ibid., p. 464 (No. 428).

The sources are largely mute regarding the motivations of parties entering into such marriages, although the purposes of the peasant suitors are fairly obvious: in addition to the material advantages already described, marriage into an urban family could give the immigrant a desirable sense of community with his new environment and its inhabitants, legitimizing his physical presence in the town and his aspirations for urban citizenship. For urban families, marriage alliances with promising peasant entrepreneurs who appeared to have a good future in the world of urban commerce may have seemed economically advantageous or at least a suitable way to dispose of unmarried daughters. Many marriages, one would suppose, grew out of some sort of business association. Such was evidently the case with Iakov Vasil'ev, a court peasant who married the daughter of a Moscow craft-guild member and weaver of silk ribbons about 1790 and enlisted in the kupechestvo in 1795. The registrant himself was a weaver of ribbons and was much older than his bride, belonging apparently to her father's generation.[40]

Peasants not firmly ensconced on the urban scene but backed by material assets or commercial attainments gained elsewhere may also have been favorably received as suitors. Even less well endowed peasants could probably find brides among the many urban families afflicted by declining fortunes, chronically low economic status or outright ruin. The daughters of such households obviously had limited prospects, and peasant immigrants, who regardless of the financial condition of the bride's family could make good use of the rights of

---

[40] Ibid., p. 615 (No. 642).

urban citizenship it possessed, are likely to have been less choosy
regarding dowries and other matters affecting the selection of a mate.
The skazki from the Fourth Revision reveal, for example, that Avdot'ia
Prianishnikova and Avdot'ia Altukhova, both daughters of Moscow merchants,
had married house serfs, while Kseniia Ogorodnikova had married a
peasant from the estates of the important government official P. D.
Eropkin. All three women came from families which had been decimated
and virtually destroyed by the Moscow plague of 1771.[41] Even very
wealthy peasant immigrants sometimes took their wives from such ruined
urban families. Fedot Novikov, an economic peasant who enlisted in
the Moscow kupechestvo in 1778, was so successful that as of 1782 he
was a member of the first guild. Novikov's wife, whom he married about
1774, was the daughter of a Moscow merchant who had died in the 1771
plague. All other male members of the family had died earlier, and the
only other survivor was the bride's mother, who lived with her son-in-law.[42]

Peasant immigrants sometimes married into the families of urban
dwellers not belonging to the posad, merchants from other towns or
peasants of villages adjacent to or near the town, and these unions
presumably carried at least some of the same advantages as did marriage
into the local urban classes. Andrei Loginov, a state peasant of
Kaliazin uezd (Tver' guberniia), married the daughter of a Moscow factory

---

[41] Ibid., Vol. 3, pp. 20 (No. 86), 21 (Nos. 88-89). A similar case: Ibid., Vol. 4, p. 379 (No. 105).

[42] Ibid., Vol. 3, pp. 23 (No. 105), 35 (No. 244). The fortunes of Fedot Novikov subsequently declined. By the time of the Fifth Revision (1795) he had dropped to meshchanstvo status and was no longer living "in his own house" but rather in rented quarters. Ibid., Vol. 4, p. 28 (No. 239).

artisan not later than 1775 and enlisted in the Moscow kupechestvo two decades later.[43] The state peasant Egor Belkin, from Egor'evsk uezd (Riazan' guberniia), married the daughter of a Moscow iamshchik (postman) about 1791, while his older brother had married into the family of a Moscow merchant several years earlier. Both brothers entered the Moscow kupechestvo in 1795.[44] The economic peasant Makar Varfolomeev married the daughter of a Moscow guild artisan, while his brother Egor married the daughter of a merchant of the town of Serpukhov. Both brothers enlisted in the Moscow kupechestvo in 1795 and at that time were making their living as glovers.[45] Since the slaughterhouses and tanneries of Serpukhov were among the suppliers of hides and other animal products for the industries of Moscow, it is possible that the marriage of Egor Varfolomeev grew out of and perhaps further cemented a business collaboration.[46]

Other peasants who enlisted in the Moscow posad were married to daughters of merchants from the towns of Iaroslavl', Suzdal', Shuia and Maloiaroslavets.[47] Fedor Baluev, a former serf from Bogorodsk

[43] Ibid., Vol. 4, p. 560 (No. 183).

[44] Ibid., p. 485 (Nos. 143-44).

[45] Ibid., p. 623 (No. 727).

[46] On the economy of Serpukhov, see Sostoianie stolichnogo goroda Moskvy, 1785 g. (Moscow, 1879), pp. 19-20; E. Ziablovskii, Zemleopisanie Rossiiskoi Imperii dlia vsekh sostoianii, Vol. 3 (St. Petersburg, 1810), pp. 253-54; E. N. Kusheva, "Torgovlia Moskvy v 30-40-kh godakh XVIII v.," Istoricheskie zapiski, Vol. 23 (1947), p. 56.

[47] MDIMK, Vol. 4, pp. 411 (No. 536), 621 (No. 709), 622 (No. 725), 627 (No. 780), 830 (No. 462), 857 (No. 184). Since no attempt was made at a systematic search for similar cases, the above undoubtedly do not exhaust the list of towns involved.

uezd, married into the family of a Moscow merchant about 1787, but his
two older brothers had earlier married peasant women from the court
estates in the vicinity of Moscow, the importance of which as a way
station for peasants and other outsiders seeking access to the Moscow
economy has already been discussed. All three brothers entered the
Moscow kupechestvo in 1790.[48] Grigorii Potapov, an economic peasant
from Voskresensk uezd, married the daughter of a court peasant of
Khoroshevo volost' (which is within the boundaries of present-day Moscow)
and about seven years later enlisted in the Moscow kupechestvo, while
another registrant from the economic peasantry married a woman of
Kolomenskoe village, the old suburban seat of the Muscovite tsars.[49]
In some cases seigneurial peasants from relatively remote districts
who enrolled in the Moscow urban classes were married to women from
their masters' suburban estates.[50] Similarly, one registrant from the
economic peasantry of Kargopol' uezd, in the remote northwestern corner
of the country, was married to a serf woman from one of Count N. P.
Sheremetev's estates in the vicinity of Moscow.[51] Such marriages could
give peasants from distant areas a secure base of operation comfortably
near the town where they hoped to settle, if not inside it.

The personal ties developed by peasant immigrants in the course of
their assimilation into the urban population were not limited to those
of marriage, although it is the bonds of matrimony which are most

---

[48] Ibid., p. 835 (No. 515).

[49] Ibid., pp. 534 (No. 415), 751 (No. 133).

[50] Ibid., p. 543 (Nos. 509, 510, 513).

[51] Ibid., p. 623 (No. 734).

readily traceable in the available documents. We have suggested that
many marriages grew out of business ties or other economic relationships
between the immigrant and the bride's family. Undoubtedly, such
relationships could also give rise to personal ties which did not
culminate in marriage but still assisted the immigrant in overcoming
the obstacles on his path to urban citizenship. Even long-term employment
of peasants by urban merchants could lead to supportive personal ties.
The monastery peasant Petr Poliakov, for example, was sponsored for
admission to the Iaroslavl' kupechestvo in the early 1760's by the
wealthy Iaroslavl' merchant P. D. Kropin, for whom he had worked since
his arrival in the city.[52]

Initiation and Development of Economic Activity

Evidence already cited suggests that family and other personal ties
to posad members and other urban dwellers sometimes made a major contribution to the peasant immigrant's efforts to infiltrate the urban
economy. The immigrant enjoying such ties could count on his relatives
or other contacts in the urban population to provide him with training
and employment, to include him in an established business, or to aid
him in initiating and expanding his own, by giving him access to capital,
useful business connections, commercial experience and knowledge of the
urban market. Such assistance could enable even adolescent immigrants
to acquire (at least nominally) substantial capital and enterprises
within a short period of time. We have seen that by the age of sixteen,
six years after his arrival in Iaroslavl', the ex-serf Andrei Esipov

---

[52]TsGADA, f. 807, op. 1, d. 513, ll. 1-4.

was able to claim 1000 rubles in capital and trade in "various ports,"
largely, it must be suspected, because of the generous aid of his
brother-in-law, the Iaroslavl' merchant Ivan D'iakonov.[53]   The cooperation
of friendly posad members was also valuable in protecting enterprises
belonging to peasant immigrants from interference by the urban authorities.
By allowing peasants to acquire stores and other property and conduct
business under their names, sympathetic merchants enabled the immigrants
to operate freely in the urban market, in contravention of the law.
Even such a fabulously successful peasant entrepreneur as E. I. Grachev,
the textile manufacturer of Ivanovo village, relied on "merchants of
his acquaintance" in conducting commercial activity in Moscow prior to
his enlistment in the kupechestvo.[54]

Immigrants who did not benefit from close personal relationships
with members of the urban population in the earlier stages of their
assimilation could often find a place for themselves in the urban
economy as employees of merchants. Russian merchants of the eighteenth
century, particularly those involved in long-distance trade, of
necessity relied on trusted subordinates in conducting their operations.
These subordinates were delegated to buy and sell goods in widely
scattered markets, to supervise the transport of merchandise along land
and water routes, to tend stores, to deliver and receive payments and
generally to oversee their masters' interests at all the far-flung
points at which they were engaged. It is apparent that peasants were

---

[53]TsGADA, f. 807, op. 1, d. 46, ll. 33-39.

[54]Istoriia Moskvy, Vol. 2 (Moscow, 1953), p. 301.

very frequently hired for such duties.[55] We learn, for example, that

in the 1760's the Nizhnii Novgorod first-guild merchant Mikhail Kokorev,

himself by origin a peasant of a local monastery, conducted his business

through a large staff of agents, many of whom were peasants of the same

monastery. These subordinates attended to their master's interests

and enterprises in Astrakhan', Dmitrievsk, Moscow, Petersburg and

various Upper Volga towns, dealing in a variety of domestic and imported

goods and in sums as high as 15,000 rubles.[56] Many peasants who later

enlisted in the posad served their apprenticeship in commerce as such

employees, and many continued to work in this capacity even after

enlistment.[57] Semen Golovanov and Filka Popov, both of whom arrived

in Iaroslavl' as boys, penniless and apparently without connections,

went to work for various local merchants and in the process "learned

the art of commerce" and accumulated 300 rubles apiece in capital.[58]

The monastery peasant Petr Poliakov (from Belozersk uezd) lived with

and worked for the wealthy Iaroslavl' merchant P. D. Kropin. While

doing so he was able to acquire a capital of 500 rubles, and he was

---

[55] Many urban communes complained to the Legislative Commission of 1767 about the widespread practice of hiring peasants for work as stewards, storekeepers and commercial agents, asserting that these jobs should be reserved for the poorer members of the posad. See Sb. IRIO, Vol. 93, pp. 164-66 (Kostroma), 350-51 (Rostov), 376-79 (Ruza), 398-400 (Romanov), 517-19 (Nerekhta); Vol. 107 (St. Petersburg, 1900), pp. 42-43 (Sol' Bol'shaia), 149-50 (Pereslavl'-Zalesskii), 426 (Tver'), etc.

[56] E. N. Kusheva, Saratov v tret'ei chetverti XVIII v. (Saratov, 1928), p. 10.

[57] In the Moscow census depositions from the Fifth Revision, more than 100 households of recent registrants from the peasantry are identified as employees of merchants or other members of the urban classes. See above, Chapter IV, Table 17.

[58] TsGADA, f. 807, op. 1, d. 46, ll. 50-53.

admitted to the Iaroslavl' kupechestvo at the time of the Third

Revision.[59] Ivan Naumov, a native of a serf village in Iaroslavl'

uezd, was allowed by his lord to settle in Norskaia Sloboda (a small

urban settlement located on the Volga a few miles above Iaroslavl'),

where he "resided" with merchants and was sent by them to various

"downstream" towns on business. Ivan Naumov enlisted in the kupechestvo

in 1773.[60] The court peasant Afanasii Ivanov settled in Moscow in

1756 and lived with various merchants to "learn the art of commerce."

By 1761 he was operating his own store and was a candidate for membership

in the Moscow kupechestvo.[61] Mikhaila Sidorov, a former house serf

who enrolled in the Moscow kupechestvo in 1795, at the age of fifteen,

was at the time of his enlistment selling goods for the Moscow merchant

Ivan Gordeev and was living in his house.[62]

The sources give only a vague indication of how such immigrants

were able to rise in the world of urban commerce through their

employment. In applying for posad membership these immigrants frequently

referred to the training they had received, claiming that working for

merchants had enabled them to "learn the art of commerce." Some

applicants mentioned the "adequate payment" they had received for their

---

[59]TsGADA, f. 807, op. 1, d. 513, ll. 1-2.

[60]TsGADA, f. 455, op. 1, d. 884, ll. 1-3.

[61]S. I. Volkov, Krest'iane dvortsovykh vladenii Podmoskov'ia v seredine XVIII v. (Moscow, 1959), p. 65.

[62]MDIMK, Vol. 4, p. 636 (No. 880).

services and implied that they had acquired their capital by saving
from these earnings.[63] It is also to be suspected that hired agents
were often able to use their position to pursue profit-making activities
of their own while furthering the interests of their employers.

The above possibilities do not exhaust the list of avenues by
which peasant immigrants could gain entry to the urban economy.
Additional alternatives have been illustrated elsewhere in this dissertation.[64] In large population centers and major markets experiencing
a heavy flow of traffic, opportunities for participation in small-scale
retail trade were extensive and readily available to the enterprising
newcomer. Some immigrants brought with them industrial skills acquired
elsewhere and were able to function as independent craftsmen as soon
as they arrived in the town, while unskilled newcomers could acquire a
craft profession through apprenticeship or employment under urban
craftsmen and manufactories.

Dissolution of Legal Ties to the Peasantry

Immigrants who had attained a sufficient level of social and
economic assimilation into the urban milieu and could contemplate
enlistment in the posad confronted the problem of severing or loosening
their legal ties to the rural population, if they had not already
done so. Under the legislation of Peter I, of course, this question

---

[63] TsGADA, f. 455, op. 1, d. 884, ll. 1-3; d. 894, ll. 1-2 ob.;
d. 987, ll. 1-3. In the available materials, such references appear
only in interrogations of applicants conducted by the Iaroslavl'
provincial chancellery. They may therefore represent a standard formula
used by officials of this institution.

[64] See above, particularly Chapter IV.

did not necessarily arise, since both crown peasants and serfs could enlist as "mercantile peasants" without losing their original status. Moreover, until 1762 the law did not even require that such peasants obtain permission from the lords or institutions controlling them for enlistment.[65] Evidence cited in a previous chapter shows that in Moscow at least most peasant registrants in the pre-1762 period enlisted as mercantile peasants and retained peasant status and obligations along with their membership in the urban commune. On the other hand, serf registrants undoubtedly found it preferable to obtain full manumission if possible, and some of them, such as Andrei Esipov, succeeded in this end.

From 1762 onwards most peasants could enlist in the posad only with the authorization of their lords or controlling institutions ("commands").[66] Not required by the 1762 decree was the consent of

---

[65] The decree of April 13, 1722, which instituted these procedures of enlistment, stipulated that qualified peasants were "free" to register in the posad "no matter whom they belong to" (Polnoe sobranie zakonov Rossiiskoi imperii s 1649 g. /hereafter PSZ/, Vol. 7, No. 4312), and subsequent legislation before 1762 does not mention the need for permission from lords or estate authorities. According to E. I. Indova, however, the court estate administration did maintain tight control over enlistment by court peasants, requiring oaths and guarantees for proper payment of dues and often advance payment of these obligations. (See E. I. Indova, "Rol' dvortsovoi derevni pervoi poloviny XVIII v. v formirovanii russkogo kupechestva," Istoricheskie zapiski, Vol. 68, 1961, p.194.) The court administration, it will be recalled, was also unique in its ability to reclaim from the posad mercantile peasants who defaulted on their rural obligations. (See above, Chapter II.)

[66] PSZ, Vol. 15, No. 11426. The decree refers specifically to court peasants, seigneurial peasants and church peasants (soon to become state "economic" peasants). Not mentioned are "black-plowing" peasants and various other categories of the state peasantry. However, subsequent decrees established clearly that all crown peasants had to have the authorization of their "commands" for enlistment. (PSZ, Vol. 20, No. 14632; Vol. 24, No. 18213.)

the village commune (mir) to entry of its members into the urban classes,
and the case of Fedor Maksimov, an economic peasant of Iaroslavl'
uezd who applied for membership in the Moscow kupechestvo in 1767,
indicates that the mir did not possess any authority over the process
at this time. After obtaining permission from the Economic College
and fulfilling various other requirements, Maksimov was able to complete
his enlistment despite the claims of village officials that he owed
more than 30 rubles in tax arrears, which had been paid on his behalf
by the commune, and there is no evidence that this circumstance impeded
or even delayed his entry into the urban classes.[67] A 1777 decree,
however, added the mir to the list of authorities which had to agree
to the enlistment of crown peasants in the posad, allegedly in order
to make sure that such registrants were not evading rural taxation,
military conscription or other outstanding obligations.[68] In consequence of this new requirement, crown peasants applying for urban
citizenship in the late eighteenth century had to present a decree
(prigovor) of the village commune releasing the petitioner for transfer
to the urban classes, certifying that he was not subject to any tax
arrears, unpaid debts or military obligations, and specifying what
arrangements had been made for payment of his rural taxes until the
next revision. The taxes were usually assumed by members of the
registrant's family or by other individual peasants of the village.[69]

---

[67]TsGADA, f. 455, op. 2, d. 34, 11. 1-6 ob.

[68]Cited in PSZ, Vol. 24, No. 18213.

[69]GAIaO, f. 100, op. 7, d. 54, 11. 2-41.

The need to negotiate with the mir as well as with higher instances

of the estate administration complicated the task of crown peasants

attempting to enlist in the urban classes. No doubt the consent of

the village commune sometimes had to be purchased, and the reluctance

of the village to part with its more capable taxpayers might also

contribute to the difficulty of securing the desired agreement. Such

situations could lead to serious conflict. When Osip Fedorov, a

peasant from Makar'ev uezd (Nizhnii Novgorod guberniia), attempted in

1793 to enlist in the kupechestvo without the agreement of his village,

the community responded by beating and imprisoning his wife and

expressed the intention of releasing him for enlistment only after

"stripping him of all his property."[70] For registrants who did not

leave family members behind in the village, the necessary arrangements

for payment of peasant taxes until the next revision could be expensive,

since persons who agreed to assume these obligations would usually

expect reimbursement for several years in advance, possibly with an

additional fee for their services. Further expenses and delays,

resulting from corruption and administrative inertia, could confront

the registrant in his dealings with higher levels of the estate

administration. The court peasant Fedor Stepanov complained in 1781

that he had been forced to pay a bribe to officials of the court estate

administration in seeking permission to register in the Kostroma

kupechestvo, and such cases were probably frequent.[71]

---

[70] Iu. R. Klokman, Sotsial'no-ekonomicheskaia istoriia russkogo
goroda (vtoraia polovina XVIII v.) (Moscow, 1966), p. 94.

[71] Ibid., p. 95.

Notwithstanding these obstacles, the circumstances under which crown peasants could be released from their original status for enlistment in the urban classes were at least defined by established norms. The available evidence suggests that permission was likely to be granted if the applicant met the relevant property requirements, was living in a town on a regular basis, was "accustomed" to gaining his living from participation in the urban economy rather than from peasant agriculture, was acceptable to the urban commune he wished to join and was not responsible for any tax arrears or other unfulfilled rural obligations.[72] For serfs, on the other hand, everything depended on the arbitrary will of the lord, without whose consent enlistment in the posad was not possible after 1762. Nonetheless, we have seen that in the late eighteenth century a surprisingly large number of serfs did succeed in obtaining manumission and gaining entry to the urban classes: during the last two decades of the century nearly 5000 male ex-serfs were absorbed by the Moscow posad.[73] The ways in which such serfs were able to gain emancipation and the motivations which induced serfowners to part with some of their human property are only partially illuminated by the available materials, but these sources do indicate a variety of circumstances which could lead to the freeing of serfs.

Among the lords who emancipated some of their peasants for enlistment in the urban classes, the names of the old noble families and great landed proprietors of Catherinian Russia--Sheremetev, Golitsyn,

---

[72]PSZ, Vol. 22, No. 16188 (Art. 92); Vol. 24, No. 18213; Vol. 28, No. 21484; GAIaO, f. 100, op. 7, d. 54, ll. 2-41.

[73]See above, Chapter IV.

Dolgorukii, Lopukhin, Razumovskii, Orlov, Rumiantsev, Naryshkin, Golovkin, Saltykov, Musin-Pushkin, Shcherbatov, Odoevskii and others-- appear frequently, but so also do those of more obscure and less wealthy landowners. It has been widely assumed that serfs who obtained manumission for enlistment in the urban classes normally bought their way to freedom with large payments and therefore that only very wealthy serfs could hope to accomplish this change of status.[74] Such cases unquestionably did occur: for example, the textile entrepreneur E. I. Grachev paid 130,000 rubles for his freedom to his master, Count Sheremetev, in 1795.[75] However, the modest economic attainments of most freedmen absorbed by the Moscow posad, many of whom were of meshchanstvo status and house-serf origin, indicate that the capacity to pay a large indemnity was not necessarily or even usually a prerequisite for emancipation. Even where a monetary transaction was involved, the payment is not sufficient to explain the motivation of the serfowner, who after all was the legal owner of all the property of his serfs and in freeing a successful trading peasant was dispensing with a potentially lucrative investment.[76] Human feelings and personal

---

[74]
Cf. Istoriia Moskvy, Vol. 2, p. 318; G. L. Vartanov, "Kupechestvo i torguiushchee krest'ianstvo tsentral'noi chasti Evropeiskoi Rossii vo vtoroi polovine XVIII v.," Uchenye zapiski Leningradskogo gosudarstvennogo pedagogicheskogo instituta im. A. I. Gertsena, Vol. 229 (1962), p. 187.

[75]I. V. Meshalin, Tekstil'naia promyshlennost' krest'ian Moskovskoi gubernii v XVIII i pervoi polovine XIX v. (Moscow-Leningrad, 1950), p. 106, n. 2.

[76]
There were, of course, practical difficulties in exploiting such "investments". Wealthy serfs might conceal their property or place it under the names of outsiders, and some serfowners did not even bother to exploit systematically the wealth of serf entrepreneurs belonging to them, apparently remaining satisfied to regard the entrepreneur and his possessions as part of the seigneurial domain.

generosity--as in the desire to reward a trusted servant--should not be
dismissed as a possible motivation. Several former house serfs claimed
in their applications for admission to the Iaroslavl' posad that they
had been freed as a reward for "flawless" or "honest" service.[77]
Similar motives were surely involved in cases where freed serfs continued
to live with and work for their erstwhile lords after manumission and
enlistment, since no separation from the seigneurial household was
intended by either party.[78]

In other cases serfowners could sometimes be induced to free one
member of a peasant family as a favor, particularly if the remaining
members cushioned the loss by agreeing to bear obligations on behalf
of the freedman, at least until the next revision.[79] Losses to a
serfowner's interest in the emancipation of a child or a woman were
minimal, and it was thus easier for peasant families to secure freedom
for such peripheral members of the household than for adult males.
In the case already described above, the father of Andrei Esipov was
able to induce a serfowner who valued his services to free his ten-year-
old son, while he and another son remained serfs and also made a
"substantial payment" to their benefactor.[80] The house serf Dmitrii
Fedorov, who married the daughter of a Moscow merchant about 1771,

---

[77] TsGADA, f. 807, op. 1, d. 515, 1. 3 ob.; op. 2, d. 17, 11. 1-1 ob.

[78] Examples: MDIMK, Vol. 4, pp. 66 (No. 650), 67 (No. 664), 244
(Nos. 719, 721), 247 (No. 747), 429 (No. 735), 628 (No. 792), 857 (No.
182), etc. See also above, Chapter IV.

[79] TsGADA, f. 807, op. 1, d. 46, 11. 42-43 ob.; d. 513, 11. 1-3.

[80] TsGADA, f. 807, op. 1, d. 46, 11. 8-9 ob.

secured manumission for his young son and registered the boy in the

Moscow kupechestvo in 1782, but he was unable to gain his own freedom

and enlist as a merchant until 1788.[81] If senior members of the family

aspired to join the urban population, the emancipation of a minor or

a woman could give them a legal foothold in the urban community: the

freed member could be enlisted in the posad and used as a front for

the family's commercial activity while the remaining members continued

their efforts to secure manumission. The former serf Aleksei Avramov,

for example, enlisted in the Moscow kupechestvo in 1793, at the age of

twelve, and in the Fifth Revision was reported to be living in his own

house and trading in "Russian broadcloth." Also residing in young

Avramov's house were his grandfather, mother, uncle, aunt, brother and

three sisters. These latter family members evidently received manu-

mission later than the boy Aleksei and appeared in the Moscow kupechestvo

only in 1795.[82] Agaf'ia Prokhorova, a fifteen-year-old serf girl who

enlisted in the Moscow meshchanstvo in 1795, lived in Moscow in the

house of her father, who apparently remained a serf.[83] The materials

of the Fifth Revision also identify many cases in which children or

women emancipated from serfdom appeared in the Moscow urban classes

without apparent means of support.[84] In at least some of these cases

the registrants were probably surrogates for senior members of their

families who could not gain manumission.

---

[81] MDIMK, Vol. 4, p. 464 (No. 428).

[82] Ibid., p. 772 (Nos. 259, 262).

[83] Ibid., p. 336 (No. 195).

[84] Examples: Ibid., pp. 71 (No. 718), 179 (No. 243), 336 (No. 195), 363 (No. 227), 416 (No. 579).

Some serfs wishing to enter the urban classes thus attained freedom only with considerable difficulty and delay and often had to settle for the emancipation of a single and peripheral member of the family. In other cases serfowners were less grudging in their willingness to release applicants for urban citizenship, emancipating large families in one stroke and even dozens of households within a short period of time. The ex-serf Evgraf Nikiforov enlisted in the Moscow kupechestvo in 1790 with a large household including three generations and twelve male souls. All of these serfs had been freed by their master, Major-General N. I. Shemiakin.[85] Similarly, two large families bearing the surname Kolobov, formerly house serfs of Count A. G. Golovkin, enlisted in the Moscow kupechestvo in 1792 with a total of fourteen male souls.[86] The Elmenov family, peasants freed by Count A. S. Musin-Pushkin, appeared in the Moscow kupechestvo in 1793 with ten male souls.[87] In the early 1790's Count Musin-Pushkin also emancipated at least eight other families from his estate in Borisoglebsk uezd for enlistment in the urban classes of Moscow.[88] Musin-Pushkin was not unique in his generosity--in the early 1780's the landowner P. F. Berkh freed at least 17 households of serfs from his estate in Bronnitsy uezd, while

---

[85] Ibid., p. 639 (No. 918). Two daughters of E. Nikiforov, it is true, joined the rest of the family in the Moscow posad only in 1795, evidently having been freed somewhat later.

[86] Ibid., p. 57 (Nos. 561, 563).

[87] Ibid., p. 638 (No. 910).

[88] Ibid., pp. 230-32 (Nos. 889, 891, 898, 900, 905, 930), 640 (Nos. 925, 927).

V. A. Vsevolozhskii freed no less than 22 households.[89] In 1785 23
families of "house serfs" formerly attached to the factories of Ia. B.
Tverdyshev in Ufa guberniia were added to the Moscow kupechestvo and
meshchanstvo.[90]

The available sources cast little light on the reasons for such
wholesale emancipation of village peasants. Many house serfs, however,
were probably freed because their services were not needed by the
seigneurial household and because of the considerable expenses involved
in their upkeep. Such costs could be a serious burden on the revenue
of even a large and wealthy landowner. For example, in 1831 the estates
of the Iusupov family possessed 551 house serfs and incurred expenses
of 60,000 rubles in providing them with food, clothing, other necessities
and "salary".[91] Unneeded house serfs could be converted to agricultural
peasants and settled on vacant land, but even if such were available
this choice would probably not be practicable if the individuals
involved were hereditary household servants and had no agricultural

[89] Freed by P. F. Berkh: Ibid., pp. 401 (No. 424), 537-39 (Nos. 443, 447-49, 454, 456, 458-60, 463-65, 467), 636 (No. 891), 639 (No. 917), 838 (No. 549); freed by V. A. Vsevolozhskii: Ibid., pp. 401-02 (Nos. 418-23, 425-29, 431-34), 405 (No. 480), 430 (No. 754), 432 (Nos. 787-88), 558 (No. 160), 641 (No. 935), 701 (No. 104), 834 (No. 514).

[90] Ibid., pp. 64-66 (Nos. 625-47). Additional if less spectacular examples of the emancipation of many serfs at once for enlistment in the Moscow urban classes include the following: Ibid., p. 156, Nos. 190-94 (serfs of P. I. Semenov); pp. 257-58, Nos. 870-74 (serfs of G. A. Khomutov); pp. 537-39, Nos. 442, 444-46, 455, 468 (serfs of S. S. Lopukhin); p. 777, Nos. 318-25 (serfs of P. I. Matiushkina).

[91] K. V. Sivkov, "O sud'be krepostnykh khudozhnikov sela Arkhangel'-skogo," Istoricheskie zapiski, Vol. 38 (1951), p. 270. Similarly, N. I. Turgenev observed that "often,...far from deriving any benefit from the possession of large numbers of house serfs, proprietors must spend considerable sums to maintain them even miserably." N. I. Tourgenieff (Turgenev), La Russie et les russes, Vol. 2 (Brussels, 1847), p. 85.

experience. Instead, superfluous house serfs were frequently allowed
to settle in urban areas and find ways to support themselves. Serfowners
had the option of retaining their hold on such immigrants and collecting
dues from those who proved able to make money, but they sometimes chose
to emancipate these serfs and allow them to enter the urban classes.[92]
Manumission by widows was very common, which suggests that a contraction
of the seigneurial household following the death of its head often led
to the freeing of unneeded serfs.[93] Similarly, surviving husbands,
unmarried daughters and other heirs might emancipate the personal
servants of the deceased as well as other unnecessary household
personnel.[94]

The evidence cited above indicates that serfs might obtain manumission for enlistment in the urban classes as a result of money
payments to the serfowner, generous or beneficent sentiments on his
part, his willingness to release an occasional individual where no
great losses to his interests were involved, or his need to rid himself
of excessive numbers of house serfs. Much about the complex of
motivations which led Russian nobles in the late eighteenth century to
emancipate such a considerable number of serfs undoubtedly remains in
the dark, however, hopefully to be illuminated by further research.

---

[92]TsGADA, f. 455, op. 1, d. 883, ll. 1-3; d. 886, ll. 1-2 ob.;
d. 987, ll. 1-3.

[93]TsGADA, f. 807, op. 1, d. 518, ll. 1-24; d. 520, ll. 1-3 ob.;
op. 2, d. 17, ll. 1-2; MDIMK, Vol. 4, pp. 246 (No. 734), 247 (No. 752),
257 (No. 860), etc. In the Moscow census depositions, women in fact
make up a large proportion of those identified as having emancipated
serfs for enlistment in the urban classes. However, their marital
status usually cannot be determined from the information given.

[94]MDIMK, Vol. 4, pp. 244 (No. 711), 245 (No. 725), 246 (No. 735),
248 (No. 760), 255 (No. 842), etc.

Once the agreement of the serfowner had been secured, it remained to draw up a formal deed of manumission.[95] These documents, sometimes written by the serfowner himself and sometimes by clerks of government institutions, merchants or other persons possessing the necessary knowledge and skills, were usually simple and straightforward. The lord stated his intention to emancipate the specified serfs and renounced all obligations, claims and responsibilities connected with them on behalf of himself and his descendants. The document sometimes indicated that the subject was being released "at his own request" or "according to his wishes" for enlistment in the posad but otherwise gave little information on the causes and circumstances of manumission. Also mentioned in some cases were the provisions which had been made for payment of the rural soul tax until the next revision--sometimes the obligation fell on the family of the freedman and sometimes the latter gave his former lord a sum of money to cover the tax, but more often the serfowner agreed that the tax would be paid by himself or "from his votchina" (i.e. by the other peasants of his estate).[96]

---

[95] The document was usually known as an uvol'nitel'noe pis'mo or otpusknoe pis'mo but in at least one case was referred to as an apshit (evidently from the German Abschied). TsGADA, f. 807, op. 1, d. 46, ll. 34 ob.-35, 50-50 ob.; d. 513, l. 3; d. 515, ll. 3-3 ob.; d. 518, ll. 3-3 ob., 18-18 ob.; d. 520, ll. 3-3 ob.; op. 2, d. 17, l. 2; f, 455, op. 1, d. 883, ll. 2-2 ob.; d. 884, l. 2; d. 886, ll. 2-2 ob.; d. 987, l. 2; GAIaO, f. 55, op. 1, d. 82, ll. 2-4.

[96] A 1775 decree made the former lord responsible for payment of the soul tax of a freed serf until the next revision. PSZ, Vol. 20, No. 14294 (Art. 11).

The deed concluded with the signature of the serfowner and usually of several witnesses.[97] The completed document was then registered and validated at local government chancelleries.[98]

Formal Process of Enlistment

The final stage in a peasant immigrant's absorption into the posad was his formal enrollment as an urban citizen. Several historians have alluded, usually on the basis of slender evidence, to the prolonged, tortuous and burdensome character of this process.[99] While the Russian state administration of the eighteenth century is justifiably not credited with efficiency, speed or honesty, it should be recognized that the difficulties and delays of the enlistment process varied markedly with the status of the applicant, the requirements and procedures which were in effect at the given moment, and other circumstances. During most of the eighteenth century petitions for membership in the urban classes were most commonly received and acted upon by the urban authorities (magistrat or ratusha).[100] Such petitions might also be

[97]In several cases where the serfowner was a woman and apparently illiterate, her husband or father signed in her place.

[98]As with most government services, such registration entailed the payment of fees. In Iaroslavl' province in the early 1770's these fees totaled 39 kopecks. TsGADA, f. 455, op. 1, d. 883, 11. 2-2 ob.; d. 886, 11. 2-2 ob.

[99]Of. Klokman, Sotsial'no-ekonomicheskaia istoriia, pp. 93-100; Vartanov, "Kupechestvo i torguiushchee krest'ianstvo," pp. 187-93; P. G. Ryndziunskii, Gorodskoe grazhdanstvo doreformennoi Rossii (Moscow, 1958), pp. 52-61.

[100]The role of the Chief Magistracy in the proceedings is not entirely clear. In 1744, at the outset of the Second Revision, this newly resurrected central institution of urban government ordered that no applicants be enrolled without its approval. (TsGADA, f. 807, op. 1, d. 46, 1. 41; Kizevetter, Posadskaia obshchina, pp. 35-36.) Two years

addressed to provincial administrative institutions, particularly if
the applicant had originated in a different province or was seeking
citizenship in a small "non-administrative" urban settlement--one
which was not the seat of institutions of territorial administration.
The provincial institutions then considered these applications in
consultation with the urban authorities.[101] These procedures were
drastically changed, however, by the 1797 decree on enlistment of
crown peasants in the urban classes.[102] Henceforth these peasants

---

later, however, this order was withdrawn, and local magistracies were
apparently given full authority to deal with applications for membership
in the urban classes, at least those submitted by freed serfs. (TsGADA,
f. 807, op. 2, d. 17, ll. 9-9 ob.; Sb. IRIO, Vol. 8 /St. Petersburg,
1871/, p. 15.) In the available records of individual cases, applications
submitted to local magistracies after the Second Revision were in fact
acted upon without reference to the Chief Magistracy or any other central
institution. Nonetheless, the Chief Magistracy continued to participate
in the enlistment process in some cases. Materials of the Third Revision
indicate that some new peasant registrants in the Moscow urban classes
had been enrolled "by order of the Chief Magistracy" and others "by
order of the Moscow magistracy," (MDIMK, Vol. 2, "Svodnye vedomosti
po III revizii," pp. 61-62; "Skazki otdel'nykh lits," pp. 25, 31-32,
51, 78-80, etc.) Registrants accepted between the Third and Fourth
Revisions, on the other hand, are almost invariably listed as enrolled
by order of the Moscow magistracy. (MDIMK, Vol. 3, pp. 31-37, etc.)
The Chief Magistracy was abolished as a result of the 1775 reform of
administrative institutions. Further research is necessary to clarify
the above issue.

[101] TsGADA, f. 807, op. 1, d. 46, ll. 42-42 ob.; GAIaO, f. 55, op.
1, d. 82, ll. 1-17. In the early 1770's, applications for citizenship
in the Upper Volga settlement of Rybnaia Sloboda (later Rybinsk) were
received by the Iaroslavl' provincial chancellery, while those for
citizenship in Norskaia Sloboda, another "non-administrative" town in
Iaroslavl' uezd, were received by the local ratusha. In the latter
cases the petitions were referred to the provincial chancellery for
action, and in all these cases the chancellery had the primary role in
investigating and acting on the petitions. The role of the ratusha was
confined to determining whether the applicant was acceptable to the
community. (TsGADA, f. 455, op. 1, dd. 883, 884, 886, 894, 987.) It
is possible, although legislation to this effect has not been discovered,
that urban institutions in such minor towns did not have the right to
act independently on applications for citizenship, while those of larger
and more important towns did have this right.

[102] PSZ, Vol. 24, No. 18213.

were to apply not to urban or territorial administrations but to their
"commands"--the institutions supervising their villages--and these
bodies were to investigate the applicants' qualifications and forward
their petitions to the Senate for action. Urban institutions, apparently
because of their earlier laxity in screening applicants, no longer
had an active role in the process and merely received decrees from the
Senate ordering the incorporation of approved candidates into the urban
classes.[103]

In considering petitions for admission to the posad, the magistracy
or provincial administration sought to establish that the applicant's
departure from the rural milieu was lawful and was not subject to
any "suspicion"--specifically, that he was legally absent from his
village and not a runaway, that he was not responsible for any tax
arrears or other unfulfilled rural obligations, and (after 1762) that
he had the consent of his lord or "command" to enlistment in the urban
classes. Sometimes documents presented by the petitioners, such as deeds
of manumission or passports, were deemed sufficient proof, and no
further investigation of his identity, origin and status was conducted.[104]
In other cases the institution involved sought to verify the applicant's
claims by checking local census and tax records, communicating with
other institutions (usually provincial and district administrations) or

---

[103] GAIaO, f. 100, op. 7, d. 754, ll. 2-41. However, the Senate
refused an application for admission to the Riga kupechestvo because of
the special laws and privileges affecting that city and because it had
not determined whether the applicant was acceptable to the urban
community. (Ibid., ll. 12-14 ob.)

[104] TsGADA, f. 807, op. 1, d. 46, ll. 50-53; d. 515, ll. 1-11;
d. 518, ll. 1-24; d. 520, ll. 1-10.

contacting his former lord.

The available evidence does not allow firm conclusions as to why additional inquiry was initiated in some cases and not in others. Persons who originated outside the uezd were usually investigated, and it also might arouse suspicion if the applicant presented a deed of manumission which had not been registered and validated by an appropriate government institution.[105] However, in the early 1770's the Iaroslavl' provincial chancellery routinely checked all candidates for identity and tax arrears, consulting local records for those originating in Iaroslavl' uezd and communicating with other institutions regarding those from elsewhere.[106] Other kinds of confirmation besides official documentation were sometimes accepted. When Sergei Chekulaev, a house serf freed by Baroness M. A. Stroganova, applied for admission to the Iaroslavl' kupechestvo in 1765, he invoked the testimony of local merchants who had business dealings with the Stroganovs and were familiar with the signature and seal of "Her Highness" to prove that his deed of manumission was genuine.[107] If the applicant was a crown peasant needing the authorization of his "command" for enlistment, a decree from the appropriate institution had to be requested and awaited.[108]

The other main concern of the urban or provincial authorities was to determine whether the applicant met the requirements for admission to

---

[105]TsGADA, f. 807, op. 1, d. 46, 11. 42-43 ob.; d. 513, 11. 1-6 ob.; GAIaO, f. 55, op. 1, d. 82, 11. 1-17.

[106]TsGADA, f. 455, op. 1, dd. 883, 884, 886, 894, 987.

[107]TsGADA, f. 807, op. 2, d. 17, 11. 1-4.

[108]TsGADA, f. 455, op. 2, d. 34, 11. 1-6 ob.

the urban classes. The specifics of these requirements varied during
the course of the century, but in general they included possession of
capital, active participation in the urban economy and a demonstrable
ability to meet the obligations of urban citizenship. The latter
requirement was normally satisfied through the provision of guarantors
(poruchiteli) from the posad population, who assumed responsibility for
fulfilment of the registrant's tax and service obligations. For this
purpose it was once again useful to have relatives, in-laws or other
close associates who already belonged to the posad, since only those
with a considerable knowledge of and confidence in the applicant's
affairs, as well as the motivation to assist him, would be inclined
to assume such extensive and potentially burdensome commitments. Andrei
Esipov, enlisting in the Iaroslavl' posad in 1744, offered as guarantors
his brother-in-law, the Iaroslavl' merchant Ivan D'iakonov, and another
member of the D'iakonov family, while two decades later the former serf
Petr Poliakov was backed by his long-time employer, the wealthy
Iaroslavl' merchant Petr Kropin, as well as another citizen of Iaroslavl'.[109]
It is also possible that guarantors sometimes served for payment, presumably a large one in view of the hazards involved. The number of
guarantors varied--from two to six in cases considered by the Iaroslavl'
magistracy in the 1740's and 1760's.[110]

The Petrine legislation governing enlistment of peasants in the
urban classes required that registrants possess a capital of at least

[109]TsGADA, f. 807, op. 1, d. 46, 1. 39; d. 513, 11. 1-4.

[110]TsGADA, f. 807, op. 1, d. 46, 11. 39, 42-43 ob.; d. 513, 1. 4;
d. 515, 1. 4; d. 518, 11. 5-5 ob., 17-17 ob.; d. 520, 11. 4-4 ob.; op. 2,
d. 17, 11. 4 ob.-5.

300 rubles, although it is not clear how stringently this stipulation
was applied to freed serfs. In cases dealt with by the Iaroslavl'
magistracy at the time of the Second Revision (1744), all registrants,
including former serfs, claimed at least the above amount and provided
witnesses to prove their contentions.[111] Frequently these witnesses
were the same local merchants who served as guarantors for the fulfilment of the registrant's obligations. In the 1760's, however, freed
serfs did not have to prove that they controlled a specific amount of
capital, although this was still required of crown peasants enlisting
under the decree of April 13, 1722.[112] Registrants wishing to enter
the posad as guild artisans were tested by the relevant guild, but an
unfavorable evaluation did not necessarily doom the applicant's chances.
In 1762 the ex-serf Fedot Sokol'nitskii was rated "highly qualified" as a
maker of both "German" and "Russian" clothing by the tailors' guild in
Iaroslavl', while another freed serf, Gerasim Ivanov, was declared to
be "still at the average apprentice level" by the cobblers' guild. Both
applicants, however, were admitted to the posad and the desired guild.[113]

According to the legislation of Catherine II, membership in merchant
guilds was determined by the ability and willingness to "declare"
specified amounts of capital and pay a tax of 1 percent on the stated
sum, but since such declarations were to be "on their honor" no proof

---

[111] TsGADA, f. 807, op. 1, d. 46, 11. 39, 42-43 ob., 50-50 ob., 52-53.

[112] TsGADA, f. 807, op. 1, d. 513, 11. 1-10; op. 2, d. 17, 11. 1-15;
f. 455, op. 2, d. 34, 11. 4-6 ob.

[113] TsGADA, f. 807, op. 1, d. 518, 11. 6, 13; d. 520, 11. 5, 9 ob.-10.

of possession was required.[114] There is some evidence that this
permissive attitude extended to enlistment by peasants as well, at
least for a time. When the brothers Ivan and Fedor Prautin, formerly
house serfs of the Moscow official M. A. Eropkin, applied for membership
in the Iaroslavl' kupechestvo in 1786 with a declared capital of 1010
rubles, they were required to present a written statement that they
possessed the indicated sum but no witnesses or other corroborative
evidence.[115] The possible results of such laxity came to the government's attention in 1797, when the Senate discovered that "a great
many" peasants were entering the urban classes "without possessing
either capital or enterprises" and consequently instituted the new
procedures for enlistment by crown peasants under which the applicants
were to be screened by their "commands" and approved by the Senate.[116]
In cases reviewed by the Iaroslavl' provincial treasury (which had
authority over all economic and other state peasants of Iaroslavl'
guberniia) in 1798 and 1799, the successful applicants convinced the
treasury that they were "more suited by habit and ability to commercial
activity than to peasant labor" and that they possessed at least 2000
rubles in capital "gained through work and trade," usually in the town
where they aspired to citizenship.[117] However, the documents do not

---

[114]PSZ, Vol. 20, Nos. 14275, 14327; Vol. 22, No. 16188 (Art. 92,
93, 97).

[115]GAIaO, f. 55, op. 1, d. 82, 1. 5.

[116]PSZ, Vol. 24, No. 18213.

[117]GAIaO, f. 100, op. 7, d. 754, 11. 2-41. In the indicated years
2000 rubles was the required minimum for membership in the third merchant
guild.

indicate what proof, if any, was required in substantiation of these claims. Nor does the available evidence reveal what screening was applied to crown peasants who wished to enter the meshchanstvo.

The many variables involved in the enlistment process led to pronounced differences in its duration in individual cases. Notwithstanding the legendary inertia of Russia's administrative institutions, the formalities could sometimes be negotiated very swiftly, at least in cases involving freed serfs. Such applicants usually appeared with their deeds of manumission in hand, and once it was determined that they were not runaways and were qualified for posad membership there were no further obstacles to approval. After the Second Revision urban magistracies or provincial administrations could decide these cases unilaterally, without reference to higher authorities and without involving other institutions, except to request information. Moreover, the urban and provincial authorities were naturally interested in seeing the applicants inscribed on the local tax rolls as soon as possible. In 1765 the Iaroslavl' magistracy took only two weeks to approve Sergei Chekulaev, an ex-serf formerly belonging to the Stroganov family, and order him enrolled as an urban taxpayer.[118] Similar cases examined by the magistracy in 1762 were resolved in about one month.[119] In the early 1770's former serfs applying for membership in the kupechestvo of Norskaia Sloboda were processed by the Iaroslavl' provincial chancellery in one to three months.[120] Less expeditious

---

[118] TsGADA, f. 807, op. 2, d. 17, ll. 1-15.

[119] TsGADA, f. 807, op. 1, d. 515, ll. 1-11; d. 518, ll. 1-24.

[120] TsGADA, f. 455, op. 1, d. 884, ll. 1-7; d. 894, ll. 1-7; d. 987, ll. 1-10.

was the treatment of the Prautin brothers, who were kept waiting for
more than eight months in 1786-87 for reasons not readily apparent in
the documents.[121]

Freed serfs had a strong advantage in that their applications for
urban citizenship did not engage the interests of other state institutions,
since the participation of such institutions inevitably slowed down
the process of enlistment. Crown peasants, from 1762 onwards, had to
await the action of their "commands" and later of the Senate, which
did not share the priorities of urban magistracies and were in no hurry
to get the business done. The economic peasant Fedor Maksimov applied
for admission to the Moscow kupechestvo in 1767 but was left dangling
for two years while the Moscow magistracy awaited the necessary decree
from the Economic College authorizing his enlistment.[122] The Senate,
which according to the procedures introduced in 1797 had final authority
over enlistment by crown peasants, also failed to act expeditiously in
such matters, as is shown by its response to cases referred by the
Iaroslavl' provincial treasury in 1798 and 1799. Rather than considering
these cases promptly, the Senate allowed them to accumulate for sixteen
months and decided them all at once at the end of 1799.[123]

The insights emerging from this exploration of documents relating
to individual registrants in the urban classes are best summarized in
the course of an overall review of the evidence on rural-urban migration
and peasant enlistment in the posad introduced in the course of this
dissertation.

---

[121] GAIaO, f. 55, op. 1, d. 82.

[122] TsGADA, f. 455, op. 2, d. 34, ll. 1-6 ob.

[123] GAIaO, f. 100, op. 7, d. 754, ll. 2-41.

CONCLUSION

Discussion of rural-urban migration and its contribution to the
development of the urban sector in eighteenth-century Russia has been
impeded by the discrepancy between official classification of population
groups and actual patterns of residence and economic activity, and by
the resultant confusion over what constituted the urban population during
this period. Under the prevailing conditions of enserfment and rigid
legal stratification of the population, such migration was possible but
did not usually relieve the migrant of his original legal status as a
serf or crown peasant. With permission of the lords or institutions
controlling them, peasants could obtain documents authorizing departure
from the village for periods of up to three years, and with repeated
renewal of these "passports" the departure could become essentially
permanent. Among the beneficiaries of the passport system were masses
of seasonal migrants, who took advantage of slack periods in the village
economy to seek supplementary income elsewhere, but many migrants spent
all or most of the year in towns. Peasants "temporarily" absent from
their villages played a major role in the urban economy. They performed skilled and unskilled labor in manufactories, dominated the
construction industry, serviced the local transportation system and
worked in various capacities for merchants and craftsmen. Many peasants
operated commercial or industrial enterprises of their own, ignoring
restrictive laws or circumventing them with the help of collaborators
from the nobility, merchantry, clergy and other groups possessing the
needed prerogatives.

Notwithstanding continued legal ties to their original environment
and responsibility for rural taxes and dues, such "temporary" settlers
(excepting seasonal migrants) clearly belonged to the urban population.
Unfortunately, they have until recently received little attention in
this context, as study of Russia's urban history has focused chiefly on
the groups possessing legal status as urban taxpayers (the posad population). Because of such conceptual obstacles and the difficulty of
assembling an adequate concentration of source material, rural-urban
migration during this period has not been extensively studied. The
absence of a thorough and systematic investigation has produced a tendency,
evident in much Soviet as well as "bourgeois" literature, to exaggerate
the extent to which serfdom and other legal obstacles impeded migration
and has also precluded a satisfactory assessment of urbanization in
early modern Russia, since no such assessment is possible without taking
into account the impact of peasant immigration on the development of the
urban sector and the shaping of urban society.

The present study has involved an effort to make use of the relatively accessible and systematic documentation on peasant immigrants who
enlisted in the officially established urban population groups to shed
light on the broader phenomenon of rural-urban migration. In view of
the limits of this preliminary investigation, which has been devoted
primarily to the Central Industrial Region and to selected towns and
provinces within it, much further research is required to bring this
approach to full fruition. Yet it is clear from the materials presented
that these documents, used in conjunction with other relevant evidence
and carefully interpreted, can indeed be used to identify geographical
patterns of migration, economic and occupational characteristics of the

migrants, the forces drawing them into the urban environment, the ways
in which they interacted with other elements of the urban population
and the factors encouraging or impeding their assimilation.

The data presented in this study demonstrate that a great increase
in peasant enlistment in the urban classes took place in the later
decades of the century, an increase which has been completely overlooked
in earlier literature. It is probable that there was a concurrent rise
in rural-urban migration as a result of the ongoing development of
commerce and industry, the growing need of peasants for non-agricultural
income and a lessening of restrictions on peasant involvement in the
urban economy. An overall increase in migration cannot be inferred
directly from the data on enlistment, since major but heretofore un-
noticed changes in the relevant legal provisions during the reign of
Catherine II made such enlistment easier and more desirable and undoubtedly
contributed to its growth. Legal factors, however, do not explain the
geographical distribution of enlistment or the marked changes in this
distribution which occurred during Catherine's reign, and we can thus
posit a much closer relationship between these results and the trend of
migration. The towns which recorded particularly rapid growth in enlistment in the urban classes are likely to have experienced a comparable
increase in peasant immigration. A case in point is Moscow, where
enlistment grew much more steeply and continuously than in most other
towns of the Central Industrial Region. These results suggest not only
that Moscow was the main destination of migrating peasants in this region,
which had been the case earlier in the century as well, but also that
the city was attracting a greatly expanded influx of immigrants as the
century drew to a close. The enlistment data also suggest a pronounced

upswing in migration to towns of the Volga, Ural and Central Agricultural regions and indicate the need for more detailed investigation of these areas.

This study began with the assumption that peasants who enlisted in the urban classes were to some extent representative of the larger pool of immigrants from which they were drawn and consisted primarily of those who were most advanced in their assimilation and most successful in overcoming the obstacles to a change of legal status. Although the process of selection which brought some immigrants into the posad has not been clarified in all its aspects, the evidence presented here does illuminate some of the factors which determined whether or not immigrants attained urban citizenship and thus allows us to refine our conception of what differentiated registered from unregistered immigrants.

In the first place, the data surveyed in the course of this study contradict the impression prevailing in earlier literature that only a few and for the most part very wealthy peasants were able to gain release from their original status and become members of the urban classes. Tens of thousands actually enlisted in the posad during the course of the century, and in Moscow at least few of these registrants were wealthy entrepreneurs. The majority of the newcomers were to be found among the small merchants and craftsmen who populated the third merchant guild, while many subsisted at the lower economic levels of urban society, lacking any capital and living by some form of wage labor. It is true that stiff property requirements existed for entry into the kupechestvo, but this obstacle was mitigated in the closing decades of the century by the fact that the applicant's claims to meeting this qualification were apparently not carefully verified and by the possibility of enlistment in the meshchanstvo, which did not require possession of capital.

It is also worth noting that claims to possession of the required
capital could readily be fabricated with the help of relatives or other
collaborators within the posad. Registrants other than freed serfs did
need sufficient resources to bear the prescribed period of dual taxation,
although here too support from others could substitute for actual
possession of means by the registrant. In other words, the evidence
indicates that entry into the posad was not limited to immigrants who
had achieved even a modest economic success, although those who possessed
some wealth certainly had advantages in seeking urban citizenship and
were more likely to attain it. In terms of economic status, therefore,
the registrants are not clearly demarcated from other immigrants, although
it is very likely that they were more prosperous on the average. There
is also no clear demarcation in terms of occupational characteristics:
the occupations popular among peasants enlisted in the Moscow posad
are known to have been equally widespread among other peasant immigrants
residing in Moscow.

Peasants wishing to transfer to the urban classes had to secure the
consent of various authorities, including the urban commune and (after
1762) their lords or "commands". Crown peasants also needed the authorization of their village communes (after 1777) and after 1797 of the
Senate. Agreement of the urban commune was apparently not difficult to
obtain, and there is no reference in the materials examined to its being
refused. The posad was always eager to recruit new taxpayers and
normally accepted applicants who demonstrated an ability to meet the
fiscal obligations of urban citizenship. Such an ability was usually
established by offering guarantors from within the commune who agreed
to assume responsibility for fulfilment of tax and service obligations
by the registrant, and for this purpose it was once again useful to have

relatives, in-laws or other close associates who already belonged to the posad and could be called upon to undertake this burden.

Prior to 1762 serfs could enlist in the posad as "mercantile peasants" without the consent of their masters but also without losing serf status and responsibility for rural taxes and dues. At least in Moscow, few serfs took advantage of this opportunity, even in comparison to the modest numbers of court and church peasants enrolled under this burdensome system. It was later in the century, when manumission was a prerequisite for enlistment, that the influx of serfs into the Moscow posad increased spectacularly and overtook that of crown peasants. These results indicate that the need to obtain manumission was not the virtually insuperable obstacle it has sometimes been thought and also suggest growing involvement by the serf population in migration to Moscow. We have discussed various circumstances which could lead to the freeing of serfs, but here the outcome was largely arbitrary, depending on the will of the individual serfowner. It is evident, however, that serfs living among the town population were more likely to be freed if they were house serfs who had been dismissed from the seigneurial establishment for one reason or another than if they were village peasants. In contrast, the release of crown peasants for enlistment in the urban classes was regulated by established norms. The available evidence suggests that applicants who were well entrenched in the urban population, divorced from village life and the agricultural economy, acceptable to the urban commune they wished to join and not delinquent on their tax or other obligations were considered entitled to approval. On the other hand, crown peasants too could encounter arbitrary obstacles in the form of administrative inertia, conflict with officials or the village commune, and corruption. In this situation possession of wealth was once again an advantage, if only for the purpose of paying bribes to those who stood in the way.

Much remains to be learned about the complex of causes which led to the exodus of peasants from village to town in eighteenth-century Russia, although the evidence presented in this study reveals several factors which contributed to this migration. Socio-economic differentiation in the village, resulting in the pauperization of part of the rural population and its effective expulsion from the agricultural economy, was responsible for the appearance of some immigrants in the urban population. Such refugees from rural destitution were readily integrated into the urban world through wage labor in urban commerce and industry and sometimes were eventually able to enter the urban classes. The need of many agricultural peasants for supplementary income and the resulting seasonal migration likewise brought large numbers of peasants into contact with urban life and resulted in the permanent absorption of some of these peasants into the urban population. However, in the Central Industrial Region the factor of economic need was weakened as an urbanizing force by the availability of extensive non-urban alternatives for peasants seeking employment outside the agricultural economy. This effect is clearly reflected in the low levels of enlistment in the urban classes encountered in most towns of the region. Still unanswered is the question of why in particular cases peasants turned to urban or rural activity in the search for non-agricultural income. Since data on enlistment in the urban classes can often serve to identify the geographical origins of immigrants arriving in the towns and thus to pinpoint areas in which to search for the causes of the observed migration, further research along these lines can help resolve the above question.

Less predictable than the factor of economic need is the observed role of kinship and other personal ties to members of the urban population in encouraging immigration and facilitating the assimilation of newcomers. It is likely that personal connections in the urban commune were more typical of those immigrants who joined the posad themselves than of others, since these connections, as has been pointed out repeatedly, were most useful in overcoming the obstacles to enlistment. However, there is some evidence that ties to urban dwellers other than posad members (usually urbanized peasants but sometimes members of other groups) could also play a role in encouraging peasant immigration, but without offering any special advantages in the process of enlistment. To some extent, rural-urban migration can be seen as a self-sustaining process, since the arrival and assimilation of immigrants tended to induce a further influx of relatives, in-laws, fellow villagers and other peasants enjoying personal connections with the original newcomers.

It would be premature to attempt an overall portrayal of urban society in eighteenth-century Russia on the basis of the research on peasant immigration completed thus far, but the evidence presented in this study does suggest that substantial revisions of the traditional and still widely accepted viewpoint on this question are in order. In the first place, it is clear that the population actually residing in towns was far larger than has been granted by traditional estimates encompassing the posad alone and also larger than recent and more generous estimates, which do not take into account most peasant immigrants. Nor does the urban society glimpsed in the preceding pages resemble the closed, ingrown world depicted in much of the literature, particularly that emanating from non-Soviet sources. Instead of a

stagnant and exclusive environment where life was dominated by the
burdens of state service and a narrow-minded citizenry jealously guarded
its prerogatives and resisted influences from without, we find a dy-
namic social organism teeming with newcomers who successfully overcame
the barriers to urban settlement and involvement in the urban economy.
Moreover, although urban communes repeatedly appealed to the authorities
for exclusion of these outsiders and reinforcement of posad privileges,
it would be unwise to conclude from these collective petitions that
individual members of the posad behaved accordingly and displayed what
some scholars have characterized as a "closed estate mentality."[1] The
evidence surveyed in this dissertation shows that outsiders seeking entry
into the urban population were frequently welcomed and assisted by posad
members, who became their employers, employees, business associates,
customers, friends and in-laws. Admittedly, much of the evidence on which
this perception is based relates to Moscow, which because of its huge
peasant population and the largely non-native origins of its posad was
an exceptional case, but there is some evidence that the same phenomena
occurred at least to some extent elsewhere. The ways in which posad
members interacted with newcomers on a personal level, and particularly
the frequency of intermarriage, suggest that the role of "estate con-
sciousness" in the outlook of the posad population should perhaps not be
overstressed. As with many other questions raised by this exploration of
materials relating to rural-urban migration in eighteenth-century Russia,
this issue must be clarified by further research.

---

[1]See J. Michael Hittle, The Service City: State and Townsmen in
Russia, 1600-1800 (Cambridge, Mass., 1979), p. 62; Wallace Daniel, "The
Merchants' View of the Social Order As Revealed in the Town Nakazy from
Moskovskaia Guberniia to Catherine's Legislative Commission," Canadian-
American Slavic Studies, Vol. 11, No. 4 (Winter 1977), pp. 503-22;
David H. Miller, City and State in Muscovite Society: Iaroslavl', 1649-
1699 (Ph.D. dissertation, Princeton University, 1974), p. 366.

LIST OF ABBREVIATIONS USED IN SOURCE REFERENCES

GAIaO: Gosudarstvennyi arkhiv Iaroslavskoi oblasti, Iaroslavl'

GPB RO: Gosudarstvennaia publichnaia biblioteka im. Saltykova-Shchedrina, Leningrad, Rukopisnyi otdel

MDIMK: Materialy dlia istorii moskovskogo kupechestva, 9 vols. (Moscow, 1883-89)

MPIKP: Materialy po istorii krest'ianskoi promyshlennosti, 2 vols. (Moscow-Leningrad, 1935-50)

NGUAK: Nizhegorodskaia gubernskaia uchenaia arkhivnaia komissiia

PSZ: Polnoe sobranie zakonov Rossiiskoi imperii s 1649 goda, 45 vols. (St. Petersburg, 1839-43)

Sb. IRIO: Sbornik Imperatorskogo russkogo istoricheskogo obshchestva, 148 vols. (St. Petersburg, 1867-1916)

TsGADA: Tsentral'nyi gosudarstvennyi arkhiv drevnikh aktov, Moscow

TsGIA: Tsentral'nyi gosudarstvennyi istoricheskii arkhiv, Leningrad

TsGVIA, f. VUA: Tsentral'nyi gosudarstvennyi voenno-istoricheskii arkhiv, Moscow, fond Voenno-uchenogo arkhiva

VEO: Vol'noe ekonomicheskoe obshchestvo

LIST OF SOURCES

I. Archival sources

Gosudarstvennaia publichnaia biblioteka im. Saltykova-Shchedrina, Leningrad, Rukopisnyi otdel (GPB RO)

Ermitazhnoe sobranie

No. 242: "Vedomost' o chisle dush po gorodam" (1767)

No. 288: "Topograficheskoe opisanie Iaroslavskoi gubernii, sochinennoe v Iaroslavle v 1798 g."

F IV

No. 640: "Topograficheskoe opisanie Iaroslavskoi gubernii" (1803)

Sobranie A. Titova

No. 1716: "Ekonomicheskoe opisanie Zakotorostnogo stana Iaroslavskogo uezda" (ekonomicheskie primechaniia)

Gosudarstvennyi arkhiv Iaroslavskoi oblasti, Iaroslavl' (GAIaO)

f. 55 (Iaroslavskii gorodovoi magistrat)

op. 1, d. 82: "Delo o zapisi v iaroslavskoe kupechestvo byvshikh dvorovykh liudei pomeshchika Eropkina" (1786-87)

f. 100 (Iaroslavskaia kazennaia palata)

op. 7, d. 754: "Raporty kazennoi palaty v Pravitel'stvuiushchii senat o prichislenii krest'ian v kupechestvo" (1798-1800)

f. 501 (Iaroslavskaia gorodskaia duma)

op. 1, d. 13: "Vedomost' o kuptsakh, ob"iavivshikh kapitaly po gorodu Iaroslavliu na 1789 g. i o prichislenii raznykh lits v kupechestvo"

op. 1, dd. 15, 18, 28, 31: the same, 1790, 1791, 1794, 1795

Tsentral'nyi gosudarstvennyi arkhiv drevnikh aktov, Moscow (TsGADA)

f. 248 (Senat, 1 departament)

kn. 3676, ll. 769-791 ob.: "Vedomost' o chisle dush po nyneshnei revizii..." (1765-67)

kn. 4109, ll. 209-25: report of Moscow kazennaia palata on crown peasants of Moscow guberniia enlisted in urban classes through 1782 (1787)

f. 397 (Komissiia o kommertsii)

    d. 441: inquiry of Commerce Commission on "burdens and needs" of kupechestvo (1764)

    d. 483: debate on issue of peasant commerce (1765)

f. 455 (Iaroslavskaia provintsial'naia kantseliariia)

    op. 1, d. 409: register of cargo vessels arriving at Iaroslavl' (1765)

    op. 1, d. 730: the same, 1772

    op. 1, d. 760: enlistment of freed serf Ivan Demidov in Iaroslavl' kupechestvo (1772)

    op. 1, d. 836: register of cargo vessels arriving at Iaroslavl' (1773)

    op. 1, dd. 883, 884, 886, 894, 987: enlistment of various peasants in urban classes of Rybnaia Sloboda (Rybinsk) and Norskaia Sloboda (1773-74)

    op. 2, d. 34: enlistment of economic peasant Fedor Maksimov in Moscow kupechestvo (1767-69)

f. 807 (Iaroslavskii gorodovoi magistrat)

    op. 1, d. 44: suit against Iaroslavl' merchant Andrei Esipov for non-payment of promissory notes (1776)

    op. 1, d. 46: enlistment of Andrei Esipov and other peasants in Iaroslavl' posad (1744-65)

    op. 1, d. 471: "Delo po chelobit'iu derevni Volkova krest'-ianina Andreia Shliapnikova na iaroslavtsa Balandina v zakhvatnom im tovaru" (1760)

    op. 1, dd. 513, 515, 518, 520: enlistment of various peasants in Iaroslavl' posad (1762)

    op. 1, d. 546: files of petitions submitted in 1747 and 1762

    op. 2, d. 17: enlistment of freed house serf Sergei Chekulaev in Iaroslavl' kupechestvo (1765)

f. 1289 (M. M. Shcherbatov)

op. 1, d. 425: "journals" of reports from stewards and petitions from peasants of estates in Iaroslavl', Romanov and Rostov uezdy (1765-78)

op. 1, d. 503: affair of peasant Vasilii Babaev, innkeeper in Iaroslavl' (1774)

op. 1, d. 595: podvornaia opis' of Shcherbatov's estates in Iaroslavl' and Borisoglebsk uezdy (1793)

Gosarkhiv, r. XVI

d. 1012, ch. 1: "Doneseniia general-gubernatora Alekseia Mel'gunova o Iaroslavskoi, Vologodskoi i Kostromskoi guberniiakh" (1777-84)

Tsentral'nyi gosudarstvennyi istoricheskii arkhiv, Leningrad (TsGIA)

f. 558 (Senat, Ekspeditsiia dlia revizii /svidetel'stvovaniia/ gosudarstvennykh schetov)

op. 2, d. 126: "Po IV revizii Moskovskoi gubernii o chisle dush, ob obrochnykh stat'iakh i o dokhode po nim" (1794-95)

op. 2, d. 127: "Delo po Moskovkoi gubernii o chisle liudei po IV revizii..."

op. 2, d. 128: "Delo o chisle dush i s nikh ob okladakh s nachala V revizii po 1 sentiabria 1799 g. i o dokhode s obrochnykh statei po Moskovskoi gubernii"

op. 2, d. 129: the same, Sept. 1, 1799-Jan. 1, 1803

op. 2, d. 148: "Delo po Nizhegorodskoi gubernii o chisle dush i s nikh ob okladakh s nachala V revizii po 1 sentiabria 1799 g...."

op. 2, d. 149: the same, Sept. 1, 1799-Jan. 1, 1802

op. 2, dd. 303-314: tax registers (okladnye knigi) for individual districts of Iaroslavl' guberniia (1783)

op. 2, d. 315: "Delo po Iaroslavskoi gubernii o chisle liudei po IV revizii i s nikh o dokhode ravno i ob obrochnykh stat'-iakh..."

op. 2, d. 316: the same, 1794-95

op. 2, d. 317: "Delo o chisle dush i s nikh ob okladakh s nachala V revizii po 1 sentiabria 1799 g. i o dokhode s obrochnykh statei po Iaroslavskoi gubernii" op. 2, d. 318: the same, Sept. 1, 1799-Jan. 1, 1802

f. 571 (Ministerstvo finansov, Departament raznykh podatei i sborov)

op. 9, d. 1: "Okladnaia kniga po vsemu gosudarstvu o chisle
dush po V revizii po 1 genvariia 1800 g."

f. 1350 (Mezhevoi departament)

op. 312, dd. 198-199: "Ekonomicheskoe primechanie Iaroslavskogo
uezda"

Tsentral'nyi gosudarstvennyi voenno-istoricheskii arkhiv, Moscow (TsGVIA)

f. Voenno-uchenogo arkhiva (VUA)

No. 18859, ch. 1: "Ekonomicheskie primechaniia po Dmitrovskomu
uezdu" (1773)

No. 18860: "Opisanie Moskovskoi gubernii gorodov, 1776 g."

No. 19176: "Topograficheskoe opisanie Iaroslavskoi gubernii"
(1783)

II. Published documents

Akty istoricheskie, sobrannye i izdannye Arkheograficheskoiu komissieiu
(AI), Vols. 4-5 (St. Petersburg, 1842).

Materialy dlia istorii moskovskogo kupechestva (MDIMK), Vols. 1-4
(Moscow, 1883-86).

Materialy po istorii krest'ianskoi promyshlennosti (MPIKP), 2 vols.
(Moscow-Leningrad, 1935-50).

Polnoe sobranie zakonov Rossiiskoi imperii s 1649 goda (PSZ), 45 vols.
(St. Petersburg, 1839-43).

Sbornik Imperatorskogo russkogo istoricheskogo obshchestva (Sb. IRIO),
148 vols. (St. Petersburg, 1867-1916).

Snezhnevskii, V. I., "Opis' delam i dokumentam Nizhegorodskogo gorodovogo
magistrata (1787-1861)," Deistviia Nizhegorodskoi gubernskoi uchenoi
arkhivnoi komissii, Vol. 2, No. 15 (Nizhnii Novgorod, 1895), Part 3,
pp. 3-120.

_____, "Opis' delam Nizhegorodskogo namestnicheskogo pravleniia (za
1790-1799 gg.)," Deistviia Nizhegorodskoi gubernskoi uchenoi arkhivnoi
komissii, Vol. 3 (Nizhnii Novgorod, 1898), pp. 193-269.

_____, "Opis' zhurnalam Nizhegorodskogo namestnicheskogo pravleniia za 1781-83 gg.," Deistviia Nizhegorodskoi gubernskoi uchenoi arkhivnoi komissii, Vol. 3 (Nizhnii Novgorod, 1898), pp. 89-192.

Zabelin, I. E., Materialy po istorii, arkheologii i statistike goroda Moskvy, Vol. 2 (Moscow, 1891).

III. Contemporary descriptive surveys, travel accounts, memoirs

/Artynov, A. Ia./, Vospominaniia krest'ianina sela Ugodich, Iaroslavskoi gubernii Rostovskogo uezda, Aleksandra Artynova (Moscow, 1882).

Chernov, S., Statisticheskoe opisanie Moskovskoi gubernii 1811 g. (Moscow, 1812).

/Chulkov, M./, "Slovar' uchrezhdennykh v Rossii iarmarok i torgov," in Novyi i polnyi geograficheskii slovar' Rossiiskogo gosudarstva, Vols. 4, 6 (Moscow, 1788-89).

/Georgi, I. G./, "O pobochnykh krest'ianskikh rabotakh (otvet na zadannuiu Vol'nym rossiiskim ekonomicheskim obshchestvom v Sankt-Peterburge na 1782 g. zadachu)," Trudy Vol'nogo ekonomicheskogo obshchestva, Vol. 33 (1783), pp. 100-72.

German, K., Statisticheskoe opisanie Iaroslavskoi gubernii (St. Petersburg, 1808).

Istoricheskoe i topograficheskoe opisanie pervoprestol'nogo grada Moskvy (Moscow, 1796).

Opisanie goroda Rybinska (Rybinsk, 1910).

"Opisanie gorodov Nizhegorodskogo namestnichestva," in Sobranie sochinenii, vybrannykh iz mesiatseslovov, Vol. 6 (St. Petersburg, 1790), pp. 242-58.

"Otvety na ekonomicheskie voprosy po Galitskoi provintsii," Trudy Vol'-nogo ekonomicheskogo obshchestva, Vol. 10 (1768), pp. 79-96.

"Otvety na ekonomicheskie voprosy po Kashinskomu uezdu," Trudy Vol'nogo ekonomicheskogo obshchestva, Vol. 26 (1774), pp. 3-91.

"Primechaniia, sluzhashchie k poznaniiu domostroitel'stva i sostoianiia mest, okolo rek Sury i Sviagi lezhashchikh," Akademicheskie izvestiia na 1780 g., Vol. 5, pp. 53-76.

"Primechaniia, sluzhashchie k poznaniiu domostroitel'stva i sostoianiia mest, po rekam Kliaz'me, Moskve i Oke lezhashchikh," Akademicheskie izvestiia na 1780 g., Vol. 4, pp. 472-95.

"Primechaniia, sluzhashchie k poznaniiu domostroitel'stva i sostoianiia
mest, po reke Volge ot Nizhnego Novagoroda /sic/ do Syzrani lezhashchikh," Akademicheskie izvestiia na 1780 g., Vol. 5, pp. 506-32.

"Primechaniia, sluzhashchie k poznaniiu domostroitel'stva i sostoianiia
mest v verkh po reke Volge, ot eia vershiny do Nizhnego Novagoroda
/sic/ lezhashchikh," Akademicheskie izvestiia na 1780 g., Vol. 5,
pp. 284-311.

Ruban, V. G., Opisanie imperatorskogo stolichnogo goroda Moskvy
(St. Petersburg, 1782).

Shchekatov, A., Geograficheskii slovar' Rossiiskogo gosudarstva, 7 vols.,
(Moscow, 1801-09).

Sostoianie stolichnogo goroda Moskvy, 1785 g. (Moscow, 1879).

"Svedeniia o Iaroslavskom namestnichestve," Uedinennyi poshekhonets
(ezhemesiachnyi zhurnal) (Iaroslavl', 1786).

Tokmakov, I., Istoriko-statisticheskoe i arkheologicheskoe opisanie
goroda Dmitrova (Moskovskoi gubernii) s uezdom i sviatyniami
(Moscow, 1893).

Topograficheskie izvestiia, sluzhashchie dlia polnogo geograficheskogo
opisaniia Rossiiskoi imperii, Vol. 1, Part 4 (St. Petersburg, 1774).

Topograficheskoe opisanie Iaroslavskogo namestnichestva, sochinennoe v
Iaroslavle v 1794 g. (Iaroslavl', 1794).

Zhurnal ili zapiska zhizni i prikliuchenii Ivana Alekseevicha Tolchenova
(Moscow, 1974).

Ziablovskii, E., Zemleopisanie Rossiiskoi Imperii dlia vsekh sostoianii,
Vols. 3-4 (St. Petersburg, 1810).

IV. Secondary sources

A. N. Radishchev: materialy i issledovaniia (Moscow, 1936).

Aksenov, A. I., Moskovskoe kupechestvo v XVIII v.(opyt genealogicheskogo
issledovaniia) (dissertation, Moscow, Institut istorii SSSR Akademii
nauk SSSR, 1974).

_____, "Polozhenie i sud'by gostei v kontse XVII-XVIII v.," in
Problemy otechestvennoi istorii (Moscow, 1973), pp. 66-87.

Alefirenko, P. K. Krest'ianskoe dvizhenie i krest'ianskii vopros v Rossii
v 30-50-kh gg. XVIII v. (Moscow, 1958).

Alexander, John T., Bubonic Plague in Early Modern Russia: Public Health and Urban Disaster (Baltimore, 1980).

Arkhangel'skii, S. I., Ocherki po istorii promyshlennogo proletariata Nizhnego Novgoroda i Nizhegorodskoi oblasti XVII-XIX vv. (Gor'kii, 1950).

_____, "Simbileiskaia votchina Vl. Gr. Orlova (1790-1800 gg.),"
Trudy Nizhegorodskogo nauchnogo obshchestva po izucheniiu mestnogo kraia, Vol. 2 (Nizhnii Novgorod, 1929), pp. 166-92.

Artemenkov, M. N., "Naemnye rabochie moskovskikh manufaktur v 40-70-kh gg. XVIII v.," Istoriia SSSR, 1964, No. 2, pp. 133-43.

Bakhrushin, S. V., "Torgovye krest'iane v XVII v.," in Bakhrushin, Nauchnye trudy, Vol. 2 (Moscow, 1954), pp. 118-33.

Bakulin, V. S., "Orel kak khlebnyi rynok vo vtoroi polovine XVII v.," in Goroda feodal'noi Rossii (Moscow, 1966), pp. 256-63.

Baron, Samuel H., "The Town in 'Feudal' Russia," Slavic Review, Vol. 28, No. 1 (March 1969), pp. 116-22.

Bernadskii, V. N., "Ocherki po istorii klassovoi bor'by i obshchestvenno-politicheskoi mysli Rossii v tretei chetverti XVIII v.," Uchenye zapiski Leningradskogo gosudarstvennogo pedagogicheskogo instituta im. A. I. Gertsena, Vol. 229 (1962).

Blum, Jerome, Lord and Peasant in Russia (New York, 1964).

Bochkarev, V. N., "Ekonomicheskii stroi i sotsial'naia struktura nizhegorodskogo kraia serediny XVIII v.," Trudy Nizhegorodskogo nauchnogo obshchestva po izucheniiu mestnogo kraia, Vol. 1 (Nizhnii Novgorod, 1926).

Bogoroditskaia, N. A., Pomeshchich'i krest'iane Nizhegorodskoi gubernii v pervoi polovine XIX v. (po materialam Simbileiskogo imeniia grafov Orlovykh-Davydovykh) (kandidat dissertation, Gor'kii, Gor'kovskii Gosudarstvennyi universitet, 1966).

_____, "Promyslovaia deiatel'nost' krest'ian v krupnoi obrochnoi zemledel'cheskoi votchine v pervoi polovine XIX v.," Uchenye zapiski Gor'kovskogo gosudarstvennogo universiteta, Vol. 135 (1971), pp. 22-29.

_____, "Rassloenie krest'ian v Simbileiskom imenii Nizhegorodskogo uezda v pervoi polovine XIX v.," Ezhegodnik po agrarnoi istorii vostochnoi Evropy, 1967 g. (Moscow, 1970), pp. 265-79.

Bulygin, I. A., "Ob osobennostiakh gorodov Srednego Povolzh'ia vo vtoroi polovine XVIII v.," in Goroda feodal'noi Rossii (Moscow, 1966), pp. 486-97.

_____, "Rassloenie krepostnogo krest'ianstva vo vladeniiakh Polianskikh v poslednei treti XVIII v.," in K voprosu o pervonachal'-nom nakoplenii v Rossii (XVII-XVIII vv.) (Moscow, 1958), pp. 324-41.

Cherkasova, A. S., "Nekotorye voprosy istoriografii russkogo goroda XVIII stoletiia," Uchenye zapiski Permskogo gosudarstvennogo universiteta im. A. M. Gor'kogo, Vol. 227 (1970), pp. 50-61.

Chulkov, N. P., "Moskovskoe kupechestvo XVIII i XIX vv. (genealogicheskie zametki)," Russkii arkhiv, 1907, No. 3, pp. 489-502.

Daniel, Wallace, "The Merchantry and the Problem of Social Order in the Russian State: Catherine II's Commission on Commerce," Slavonic and East European Review, Vol. 55, No. 2 (Apr. 1977), pp. 185-203.

_____, "The Merchants' View of the Social Order As Revealed in the Town Nakazy from Moskovskaia Guberniia to Catherine's Legislative Commission," Canadian-American Slavic Studies, Vol. 11, No. 4 (Winter 1977), pp. 503-22.

Danilova, L. V., "Torgovye riady Iaroslavlia v kontse XVII v.," in Voprosy sotsial'no-ekonomicheskoi istorii i istochnikovedeniia perioda feodalizma v Rossii (Moscow, 1961), pp. 83-90.

Den, V. E., Naselenie Rossii po piatoi revizii, Vol. 1 (Moscow, 1902).

Ditiatin, I. I. Ustroistvo i upravlenie gorodov Rossii v XVIII stoletii, 2 vols. (Vol. 1: St. Petersburg, 1875; Vol. 2: Iaroslavl', 1877).

Doroshenko, A. P., "Rabochaia sila v ukaznoi legkoi promyshlennosti Rossii v 1730-1760 gg.," Istoriia SSSR, 1958, No. 5, pp. 144-67.

_____, "Rabota na domu v tekstil'noi promyshlennosti Moskvy v seredine XVIII v.," Istoricheskie zapiski, Vol. 72 (1962), pp. 259-75.

Drakokhrust, E. I., "Rassloenie krepostnogo krest'ianstva v obrochnoi votchine XVIII v.," Istoricheskie zapiski, Vol. 4 (1938), pp. 113-40.

Eaton, Henry L.,"The Decline and Recovery of Russia's Cities from 1500 to 1700," Canadian-American Slavic Studies, Vol. 11, No. 2 (Summer 1977), pp. 220-52.

Fedorov, V. A., Pomeshchich'i krest'iane Tsentral'no-promyshlennogo raiona Rossii kontsa XVIII-pervoi poloviny XIX v. (Moscow, 1974).

Genkin, L. B., "Nezemledel'cheskii otkhod krest'ian Iaroslavskoi i Kostromskoi gubernii v pervoi polovine XIX v.," Uchenye zapiski Iaroslavskogo gosudarstvennogo pedagogicheskogo instituta im. K. D. Ushinskogo, Vol. 9/19 (1947), pp. 3-42.

Golikova, N. B., Naemnyi trud v gorodakh Povolzh'ia v pervoi chetverti XVIII v. (Moscow, 1965).

Grekov, B. D., "Opyt obsledovaniia khoziaistvennykh anket XVIII v.,"
Letopis' zaniatiia Arkheograficheskoi komissii, Vol. 35 (1929),
pp. 39-105.

Hellie, Richard, "The Stratification of Muscovite Society: The Townsmen,"
Russian History, Vol. 5, Part 2 (1978), pp. 119-75.

Hittle, J. Michael, The Service City: State and Townsmen in Russia,
1600-1800 (Cambridge, Mass., 1979).

Iakovtsevskii, V. N., Kupecheskii kapital v feodal'no-krepostnicheskoi
Rossii (Moscow, 1953).

Iatsunskii, V. K., "Nekotorye voprosy metodiki izucheniia istorii
feodal'nogo goroda v Rossii," in Goroda feodal'noi Rossii (Moscow,
1966), pp. 83-89.

Indova, E. I., "Les activités commerciales de la paysannerie dans les
villages du tsar de la région de Moscou (première moitié du XVIIIe
siècle)," Cahiers du monde russe et soviétique, Vol. 5, No. 2
(Apr.-June 1964), pp. 206-28.

_____, "Moskovskii posad i podmoskovnye dvortsovye krest'iane v
pervoi polovine XVIII v.," in Goroda feodal'noi Rossii (Moscow,
1966), pp. 479-85.

_____, "Rol' dvortsovoi derevni pervoi poloviny XVIII v. v formirovanii
russkogo kupechestva," Istoricheskie zapiski, Vol. 68 (1961),
pp. 189-210.

Indova, E. I., Preobrazhenskii, A. A., and Tikhonov, Iu. A., "Klassovaia
bor'ba krest'ianstva i stanovlenie burzhuaznykh otnoshenii v Rossii
(vtoraia polovina XVII-XVIII v.)," Voprosy istorii, 1964, No. 12,
pp. 27-53.

Istoriia Moskvy, Vol. 2 (Moscow, 1953).

Jones, Robert E., "Urban Planning and the Development of Provincial
Towns in Russia during the Reign of Catherine II," in J. G.
Garrard, ed. The Eighteenth Century in Russia (Oxford, 1973),
pp. 321-44.

Kabuzan, V. M., Izmeneniia v razmeshchenii naseleniia Rossii v XVIII-
pervoi polovine XIX v. (po materialam revizii) (Moscow, 1971).

_____, Narodonaselenie Rossii v XVIII-pervoi polovine XIX v. (Moscow,
1963).

Kafengauz, B. B., "Klebnyi rynok v 30-40-kh gg. XVIII v.," Materialy po
istorii zemledeliia SSSR, Vol. 1 (Moscow, 1952), pp. 459-510.

_____, Ocherki vnutrennego rynka Rossii pervoi poloviny XVIII v.
(Moscow, 1958).

Kapustina, G. D., "K istorii khlebnogo rynka Moskvy v nachale XVIII v.," in Goroda feodal'noi Rossii (Moscow, 1966), pp. 375-85.

Kashtanov, S. M., "The Centralized State and Feudal Immunities in Russia," Slavonic and East European Review, Vol. 49, No. 115 (Apr. 1971).

Kazantsev, B. N., "Zakonodatel'stvo russkogo tsarizma po regulirovaniiu krest'ianskogo otkhoda v XVII-XVIII vv.," Voprosy istorii, 1970, No. 6, pp. 20-31.

Kizevetter, A. A., Posadskaia obshchina v Rossii XVIII stoletiia (Moscow, 1903).

_____, "Posadskaia obshchina v Rossii XVIII stoletiia," in Kizevetter, Istoricheskie ocherki (Moscow, 1912), pp. 242-63.

_____, "Proiskhozhdenie gorodskikh deputatskikh nakazov v Ekaterininskuiu komissiiu 1767 g.," in Kizevetter, Istoricheskie ocherki (Moscow, 1912), pp. 209-41.

Klokman, Iu. R., "Gorod v zakonodatel'stve russkogo absoliutizma vo vtoroi polovine XVII i XVIII vv.," in Absoliutizm v Rossii (Moscow, 1964), pp. 320-54.

_____, Ocherki sotsial'no-ekonomicheskoi istorii gorodov severo-zapada Rossii v seredine XVIII v. (Moscow, 1960).

_____, Sotsial'no-ekonomicheskaia istoriia russkogo goroda, vtoraia polovina XVIII v. (Moscow, 1967).

Knabe, Bernd, "Die Struktur der russischen Posadgemeinden und der Katalog der Beschwerden und Forderungen der Kaufmannschaft (1762-1767)," Forschungen zur osteuropäischen Geschichte, Band 22 (1975).

Kogan, E. S., "Rassloenie krest'ianstva v arkhangel'skoi votchine Kurakinykh v kontse XVIII v.," in K voprosu o pervonachal'nom nakoplenii v Rossii (XVII-XVIII vv.) (Moscow, 1958), pp. 296-323.

Kopanev, A. I., Naselenie Peterburga v pervoi polovine XVIII v. (Moscow-Leningrad, 1957).

Kulisher, I. M., Ocherk istorii russkoi torgovli (Petrograd, 1923).

Kusheva, E. N., "Saratov v pervoi polovine XVIII v.," in Problemy sotsial'no-ekonomicheskoi istorii Rossii (Moscow, 1971), pp. 26-51.

_____, Saratov v tret'ei chetverti XVIII v. (Saratov, 1928).

_____, "Torgovlia Moskvy v 30-40-kh gg. XVIII v.," Istoricheskie zapiski, Vol. 23 (1947), pp. 44-104.

Liashchenko, P. I., History of the National Economy of Russia to the 1917 Revolution, trans. L. M. Herman (New York, 1949).

Man'kov, A. G., Razvitie krepostnogo prava v Rossii vo vtoroi polovine XVII v. (Moscow-Leningrad, 1962).

Meshalin, I. V., Tekstil'naia promyshlennost' krest'ian Moskovskoi gubernii v XVIII i pervoi polovine XIX v. (Moscow-Leningrad, 1950).

Miliukov, P. N., Ocherki po istorii russkoi kul'tury, Vol. 1 (St. Petersburg, 1909).

Miller, David H., City and State in Muscovite Society: Iaroslavl', 1649-1699 (Ph.D. dissertation, Princeton University, 1974).

Milov, L. V., Issledovaniia ob "Ekonomicheskikh primechaniiakh" k general'nomu mezhevaniiu (k istorii russkogo krest'ianstva i sel'-skogo khoziaistva vtoroi poloviny XVIII v.) (Moscow, 1965).

_____, "K istorii sozdaniia 'Geograficheskogo slovaria' Afanasiia Shchekatova," Arkheograficheskii ezhegodnik za 1968 g. (Moscow, 1970), pp. 166-83.

_____, "O tak nazyvaemykh agrarnykh gorodakh Rossii XVIII v.," Voprosy istorii, 1968, No. 6, pp. 54-64.

Mironov, B. N., "Traditsionnoe demograficheskoe povedenie krest'ian v XIX-nachale XX vv.," in Brachnost', rozhdaemost' i smertnost' v Rossii i SSSR (Moscow, 1977).

Munro, George E., The Development of St. Petersburg as an Urban Center during the Reign of Catherine II (1762-1796) (Ph.D. dissertation, University of North Carolina, 1974).

Murav'eva, L. L., Derevenskaia promyshlennost' tsentral'noi Rossii vo vtoroi polovine XVII v. (Moscow, 1971).

_____, "O razvitii krest'ianskogo podriada vo vtoroi polovine XVII v," in Novoe o proshlom nashei strany (Moscow, 1967), pp. 281-90.

Ocherki istorii Leningrada, Vol. 1 (Leningrad, 1955).

Ocherki istorii SSSR, period feodalizma: Rossiia v pervoi chetverti XVIII v. (Moscow, 1954).

Orekhov, A. M., "Iz istorii bor'by Nizhegorodskogo posada protiv belomesttsev," in Goroda feodal'noi Rossii (Moscow, 1966), pp. 247-55.

Pavlov-Sil'vanskii, N. P., Proekty reform v zapiskakh sovremennikov Petra Velikogo (St. Petersburg, 1897).

Pazhitnov, K. A., Problema remeslennykh tsekhov v zakonodatel'stve russkogo absoliutizma (Moscow, 1952).

Polianskii, F. Ia., Gorodskoe remeslo i manufaktura v Rossii XVIII v. (Moscow, 1960).

Portal, Roger, "Aux origines d'une bourgeoisie industrielle en Russie," Revue d'histoire moderne et contemporaine, Vol. 8 (1961), pp. 35-60.

_____, "Du servage à la bourgeoisie: la famille Konovalov," Revue des études slaves, Vol. 38 (1961), pp. 143-50.

Pullat, R. N., "Istoricheskaia demografiia v SSSR (znachenie, mesto, itogi i perspektivy razvitiia)," in Problemy istoricheskoi demografii SSSR (Tallinn, 1977).

Rashin, A. G., "Dinamika chislennosti i protsessy formirovaniia gorodskogo naseleniia Rossii v XIX-nachale XX vv.," Istoricheskie zapiski, Vol. 34 (1950), pp. 32-81.

_____, Formirovanie promyshlennogo proletariata v Rossii (Moscow, 1940).

Razgon, A. M., "Promyshlennye i torgovye slobody i sela Vladimirskoi gubernii vo vtoroi polovine XVIII v.," Istoricheskie zapiski, Vol. 32 (1950), pp. 133-72.

Rodin, F. N., Burlachestvo v Rossii (Moscow, 1975).

Rosovsky, Henry, "The Serf Entrepreneur in Russia," Explorations in Entrepreneurial History, Vol. 6 (1953), pp. 207-29.

Rozman, Gilbert, "Comparative Approaches to Urbanization: Russia, 1750-1800," in Michael F. Hamm, ed., The City in Russian History (Lexington, Ky., 1976), pp.69-85.

_____, Urban Networks in Russia, 1750-1800, and Premodern Periodization (Princeton, 1976).

Rubinshtein, N. L., "Topograficheskie opisaniia namestnichestv i gubernii XVIII v.--pamiatniki geograficheskogo i ekonomicheskogo izucheniia Rossii," Voprosy geografii, Vol. 31 (1953), pp. 39-89.

Ryndziunskii, P. G., Gorodskoe grazhdanstvo doreformennoi Rossii (Moscow, 1958).

_____, "Krest'iane i gorod doreformennoi Rossii," Voprosy istorii, 1955, No. 9, pp. 26-40.

_____, "Osnovnye faktory gorodoobrazovaniia v Rossii vtoroi poloviny XVIII v.," in Russkii gorod (Moscow, 1976), pp. 105-27.

_____, Soslovno-podatnaia reforma 1775 g. i gorodskoe naselenie," in Obshchestvo i gosudarstvo feodal'noi Rossii (Moscow, 1975), pp. 86-95.

Sakovich, S. I., "Sotsial'nyi sostav moskovskikh tsekhovykh remeslennikov 1720-kh gg.," Istoricheskie zapiski, Vol. 42 (1953), pp. 238-61.

_____, "Torgovlia melochnymi tovarami v Moskve v kontse XVII v.," Istoricheskie zapiski, Vol. 20 (1946), pp. 130-49.

413

Semevskii, V. I., *Krest'iane v tsarstvovanii imperatritsy Ekateriny II*, 2 vols. (St. Petersburg, 1881-1901).

Serbina, K. N., *Krest'ianskaia zhelezodelatel'naia promyshlennost' Severo-zapadnoi Rossii XVI-pervoi poloviny XIX v.* (Leningrad, 1971).

Shapiro, A. L., "K istorii krest'ianskikh promyslov i krest'ianskoi manufaktury v Rossii XVIII v.," *Istoricheskie zapiski*, Vol. 31 (1950), pp. 153-64.

_____, "Krest'ianskaia torgovlia i krest'ianskie podriady v petrovskoe vremia," *Istoricheskie zapiski*, Vol. 27 (1948), pp. 202-39.

_____, "Krest'ianskie otkhody i krest'ianskii naem v petrovskoe vremia," *Uchenye zapiski Leningradskogo pedagogicheskogo instituta im. M. N. Pokrovskogo*, Vol. 5, No. 1 (1940), pp. 23-44.

Shchepetov, K. N., *Krepostnoe pravo v votchinakh Sheremetevykh* (Moscow, 1947).

_____, "Torgovo-promyshlennaia deiatel'nost' i rassloenie krest'-ianstva v votchinakh Cherkasskikh v XVII v.," in *K voprosu o pervonachal'nom nakoplenii v Rossii (XVII-XVIII vv.)* (Moscow, 1958), pp. 53-72.

Sivkov, K. V., "O sud'be krepostnykh khudozhnikov sela Arkhangel'skogo," *Istoricheskie zapiski*, Vol. 38 (1951), pp. 270-73.

_____, "Podmoskovnaia votchina serediny XVIII v.," *Moskovskii krai v ego proshlom*, Vol. 1 (Moscow, 1928), pp. 75-96.

Smirnov, P. P., *Posadskie liudi i ikh klassovaia bor'ba do serediny XVII v.*, Vol. 1 (Moscow-Leningrad, 1947).

Sorina, Kh. D., "K voprosu o protsesse sotsial'nogo rassloeniia goroda v sviazi s formirovaniem kapitalisticheskikh otnoshenii v Rossii v XVIII-nachale XIX v. (gorod Tver')," *Uchenye zapiski Kalininskogo gosudarstvennogo pedagogicheskogo instituta im. M. I. Kalinina*, Vol. 38 (1964), pp. 281-301.

Sretenskii, L. V., "Ekonomika Iaroslavskoi gubernii vo vtoroi polovine XVIII v.," *Uchenye zapiski Iaroslavskogo gosudarstvennogo pedagog-icheskogo instituta im. K. D. Ushinskogo*, Vol. 33/43 (1958), pp. 99-102.

_____, "Pomeshchich'ia votchina Iaroslavskoi gubernii vo vtoroi polovine XVIII v.," *Uchenye zapiski Iaroslavskogo gosudarstvennogo pedagogicheskogo instituta im. K. D. Ushinskogo*, Vol. 25/35 (1958), pp. 475-530.

_____, *Pomeshchich'ia votchina nechernozemnoi polosy Rossii vo vtoroi polovine XVIII v.* (kandidat dissertation, Iaroslavl' Gosudarstvennyi pedagogicheskii institut im. K. D. Ushinskogo, 1959).

Sviridov, N. S., "Torguiushchie krest'iane kontsa krepostnoi epokhi," Istoriia SSSR, 1969, No. 5, pp. 48-67.

Sytin, P. V., Iz istorii moskovskikh ulits, (3rd ed., Moscow, 1958).

Tikhomirov, M. N., "Gorod Dmitrov, ot osnovaniia goroda do poloviny XIX v." Trudy Muzeia dmitrovskogo kraia, Vol. 2 (Dmitrov, 1925).

Tourgenieff (Turgenev), N. I., La Russie et les russes, Vol. 2 (Brussels, 1847).

Troitskii, S. M., "Obsuzhdenie voprosa o krest'ianskoi torgovle v Komissii o kommertsii v seredine 60-kh gg. XVIII v.," in Dvorianstvo i krepostnoi stroi Rossii XVI-XVIII vv. (Moscow, 1975), pp. 227-39.

Tugan-Baranovskii, M., Russkaia fabrika v proshlom i nastoiashchem, Vol. 1 (7th ed., Moscow, 1938).

Ustiugov, N. V., "Ekonomicheskoe razvitie russkogo gosudarstva v XVII v. i problema skladyvaniia vserossiiskogo rynka," in Ustiugov, Nauchnoe nasledie (Moscow, 1974), pp. 18-74.

Vartanov, G. L., "Gorodskie iarmarki tsentral'noi chasti Evropeiskoi Rossii vo vtoroi polovine XVIII v.," Uchenye zapiski Leningradskogo gosudarstvennogo pedagogicheskogo instituta im. A. I. Gertsena, Vol. 194 (1958), pp. 137-68.

_____, Kupechestvo gorodov Moskovskoi gubernii vo vtoroi polovine XVIII v. (kandidat dissertation, Leningrad, Gosudarstvennyi pedagogicheskii institut im. A. I. Gertsena, 1966).

_____, "Kupechestvo i torguiushchee krest'ianstvo tsentral'noi chasti Evropeiskoi Rossii vo vtoroi polovine XVIII v.," Uchenye zapiski Leningradskogo gosudarstvennogo pedagogicheskogo instituta im. A. I. Gertsena, Vol. 229 (1962), pp. 161-96.

_____, "Moskovskoe i inogorodnee kupechestvo vo vtoroi polovine XVIII v.," Uchenye zapiski Leningradskogo gosudarstvennogo pedagogicheskogo instituta im. A. I. Gertsena, Vol. 278 (1965), pp. 272-90.

Vodarskii, Ia. E., "Chislennost' i razmeshchenie posadskogo naseleniia v Rossii vo vtoroi polovine XVII v.," in Goroda feodal'noi Rossii (Moscow, 1966), pp. 271-97.

_____, "Iz istorii sozdaniia Glavnogo magistrata," in Voprosy sotsial'no-ekonomicheskoi istorii i istochnikovedeniia perioda feodalizma v Rossii (Moscow, 1961), pp. 108-12.

_____, Naselenie Rossii v kontse XVII-nachale XVIII v. (chislennost', soslovno-klassovoi sostav, razmeshchenie) (Moscow, 1977).

Volkov, M. Ia., "Formirovanie gorodskoi burzhuazii v Rossii XVII-XVIII vv.," in Goroda feodal'noi Rossii (Moscow, 1966), pp. 178-206.

_____, "Iz istorii sela Ivanova nachala XVIII v.," in Novoe o proshlom nashei strany (Moscow, 1967), pp. 337-42.

_____, "Materialy pervoi revizii kak istochnik po istorii torgovli i promyshlennosti Rossii pervoi chetverti XVIII v.," Problemy istochnikovedeniia, Vol. 11 (1963), pp. 266-306.

_____, "Otmena vnutrennikh tamozhen v Rossii," Istoriia SSSR, 1957, No. 2, pp. 78-95.

_____, "Puti formirovaniia gorodskikh poselenii Rossii v XVIII v.," in 250 let Permi: Materialy nauchnoi konferentsii "Proshloe, nastoiashchee i budushchee Permi" (15-17 noiabria 1972 g.) (Perm', 1973), pp. 14-21.

Volkov, S. I., Krest'iane dvortsovykh vladenii Podmoskov'ia v seredine XVIII v. (Moscow, 1959).

Voronov, N. V., "Stachka moskovskikh kirpichedel'tsev letom 1779 g.," Istoricheskie zapiski, Vol. 37 (1951), pp. 290-303.

Vvedenskii, R. M., "Razvitie nezemledel'cheskogo otkhoda v obrochnoi derevne promyshlennogo tsentra Rossii v pervoi polovine XIX v. (k voprosu o formirovanii postoiannykh kadrov vol'nonaemnykh rabochikh v doreformennoi Rossii--po votchinnym arkhivam Golitsynykh)," Uchenye zapiski Moskovskogo gosudarstvennogo pedagogicheskogo instituta im. V. I. Lenina, Vol. 187 (1962), pp. 27-60.

Zaborovskii, L. V., "Bor'ba posadov Vladimira i Suzdalia s belomesttsami v XVII v.," in Goroda feodal'noi Rossii (Moscow, 1966), pp. 239-46.

Zakharova, L. F., Pomeshchich'i krest'iane Nizhegorodskoi gubernii i ikh klassovaia bor'ba vo vtoroi polovine XVIII v. (dissertation, Gor'kii, Gor'kovskii gosudarstvennyi universitet, 1954).

Zaozerskaia, E. I., "Moskovskii posad pri Petre I," Voprosy istorii, 1947, No. 9, pp. 19-35.

_____, "Pomeshchik Zhukov i ego khoziaistvo," in Dvorianstvo i krepostnoi stroi Rossii XVI-XVIII vv. (Moscow, 1975), pp. 213-26.

_____, Rabochaia sila i klassovaia bor'ba na tekstil'nykh manufakturakh Rossii v 20-60-kh gg. XVIII v. (Moscow, 1960).

Zviagintsev, E. A., "Rost naseleniia v moskovskikh slobodakh XVIII v.," Moskovskii krai v ego proshlom, Vol. 2 (Moscow, 1930), pp. 135-48.